Pius Engelbert, OSB

Sant'Anselmo in Rome

Sant'Anselmo in Rome

College and University

From the Beginnings to the Present Day

Pius Engelbert, OSB

Translated by Henry O'Shea, OSB

LITURGICAL PRESS
Collegeville, Minnesota

www.litpress.org

Cover design by Jodi Hendrickson.

Cover images: Top: Sant'Anselmo from the North; image from the Archives of the Archabbey of Beuron. Bottom: Sant'Anselmo from the South; image from the Archives of St. Ottilien.

This work was first published as *Sant'Anselmo in Rom: Kolleg und Hochschule*

1st German edition, Rome, 1988

2nd German edition, Sankt Ottilien, 2012

1 2 3 4 5 6 7 8 9

Library of Congress Cataloging-in-Publication Data

Engelbert, Pius.
[Geschichte des Benediktinerkollegs St. Anselm in Rom. English]
Sant'Anselmo in Rome : College and University : From the Beginnings to the Present Day / Pius Engelbert, OSB ; translated by Henry O'Shea, OSB.
pages cm
"1st German edition, Rome, 1988. 2nd German edition, Sankt Ottilien, 2012."
Includes bibliographical references.
ISBN 978-0-8146-3713-5 — ISBN 978-0-8146-3738-8 (ebook)
1. Pontificio Ateneo S. Anselmo. I. Title.

BX920.I8E5413 2015
271'.1045632—dc23 2014038326

Laudemus viros gloriosos et parentes nostros in generatione sua.
[Let us sing the praises of famous men, our ancestors in their generation.]
—Sirach 44

Eine Chronik schriebt nur derjenige,
dem die Gegenwart wichtig ist.
Über Geschichte kann niemand urteilen,
als wer an sich selbst Geschichte erlebt hat.
[Only he can write a chronicle
to whom the present is important.
No one can make a judgment on history
except one who himself has experienced history.]
—Goethe, *Maximen und Reflexionen*

Contents

Foreword

The first edition of this book was titled *History of the Benedictine College of St. Anselm in Rome*. Although this was an accurate title when applied to the first decades of Sant'Anselmo, given that the college and university were a single entity, it cannot now be considered appropriate in light of the actual situation of both institutions. In addition, the original title would be misunderstood were the study to be seen as dealing only with the college.

The new edition is the response to a suggestion from the EOS-Verlag at the Archabbey of Sankt Ottilien and its energetic director, Fr. Dr. Cyrill Schäfer, OSB. From the beginning, it was clear to me that there could be no question of a simple reprint of the 1988 book. It is true that, apart from some small corrections, the main part of the book remains unaltered. (I simply did not have the energy to do more.) But it was absolutely necessary to bridge the gap between 1988 and the present day. This section appears under the title "Epilogue." The resulting history, "from the beginnings (1888) to the present time," is not an official history approved by the authorities of Sant'Anselmo but my personal view of events that occurred and persons active on the Aventine. Clearly, the historian not only has to base his writings on his sources and interpret these correctly but also must strive to formulate a just assessment of a past whose way of thinking is very difficult for us to understand today. I was always conscious of both of these demands.

Before my study appeared, historians had already concerned themselves with the beginnings of the college. Suffice it to mention here the history of the foundation of Sant'Anselmo in the third volume of the monumental *Aus der Rechtsgeschichte benediktinischer Verbände* by the first abbot of Gerleve, Raphael Molitor OSB, a pioneering work firmly based on multiple sources. The extent to which the picture I presented can become even clearer by the consideration of new sources is demonstrated by Fr. Ádám Somorjai's article, "Leone XIII e la fondazione di S.Anselmo nell'Urbe," in *Archivium Historiae Pontificiae* 47 (2009): 41–61.

Other periods of Sant'Anselmo's history can and ought to be brought into higher relief by further research.

Special thanks are due to Fr. Cyrill Schäfer for the provision of illustrations for this book.

Pius Engelbert, OSB
Abbot Emeritus of Gerleve
Rome
November 20, 2011

From the Foreword to the First Edition (1988)

This book is a commissioned work. It had been planned to produce a historical overview of the last hundred years for the *festschrift* on the occasion of the centenary of the International Benedictine College of Sant'Anselmo. During the writing of this projected article, the material available to the author grew and grew. If unpublished documents that would be of use to future historians were to be included, the framework of an article would not have been adequate. Colleagues encouraged me not to shorten the work but to tell the history of the unique Benedictine institution which is Sant'Anselmo in all the detail that would help the many former alumni of the college to understand that institution. Further, I was encouraged to provide illustrative examples and, if possible, to be entertaining. In keeping with this, the book does not provide a list of all the professors who taught at Sant'Anselmo for longer or shorter periods, nor of the cellarers and lay brothers without whose work the house could not have survived. There is no analysis of administrative procedures, but, rather, an attempt to present burning issues and events in the history of Sant'Anselmo and to describe trends. What was the guiding spirit among professors and students in the different periods of Sant'Anselmo's existence? To what ideal did one feel oneself committed? How did one live in the college? But also: what influence did the Benedictine Confederation, represented by the Congress of Abbots and Synods of Abbots President have in promoting, helping, correcting, or in some cases, disturbing the life of the college itself.

Again, Sant'Anselmo's own tradition is expressed most clearly in the work, example, and limitations of its most important professors. For this reason, biographical sketches of these professors are included. An exception, however, has been made in the case of professors who are still alive. The personality and influence of persons who are still alive are not material for historical research.

The last two decades of Sant'Anselmo's history have only been summarized briefly and the last few years completely omitted. The reasons for this omission are easily surmised. In addition, the separation of college and university that has taken place since the late 1960s—despite the fact that both institutions have to cope with sharing the same buildings—requires a different style of presentation than the one chosen for this study which attempts to do justice to the original unity of a monastic college and an academic institute.

Fr. Pius Engelbert, OSB
Rome
January 4, 1988

Chapter 1

From the Foundation of the College to the Transfer to the Aventine

1. The Foundation and Its Prehistory

The International Benedictine College of Sant'Anselmo was established on January 4, 1888.[1] The institute was a new foundation but juridically was considered the successor of the homonymous college of the Cassinese Congregation, which had ceased to exist only a few decades before.[2] On February 20, 1887, Pope Leo XIII, under whose

[1] The work of Raphael Molitor is essential for the history of the establishment of the new Sant'Anselmo. Molitor (1873–1948) was the first abbot of the Abbey of St. Joseph at Gerleve in Westphalia. An expert in canon law, his most important work is: *Aus der Rechtsgeschichte benediktinischer Verbände—Untersuchungen und Skizzen*, vol. 1: *Verbände von Kloster zu Kloster* (Münster, 1929); vol. 2: *Verband und Exemption* (Münster, 1931); vol. 3, *Unionsversuche im 19. Jahrhundert. Die Leonische Konföderation aller Kongregationen der Benediktiner* (Münster, 1933). All further references to Molitor will provide the author's last name and page number. For a one-sided account, see T. Leccisotti, *Il Cardinale Dusmet* (Catania, 1962), 125–63. Further, see G. Locher, "Eröffnung und Konstituierung von Neu-St. Anselm," *BenM* 20 (1938): 216–23; Philibert Schmitz, *Histoire de l'Ordre se Saint-Benoît* (Belgium, 1942–1956). All further references to Schmitz will provide the author's last name and page number; T. Leccisotti, "Gli inizi del rinnovato Collegia di S.Anselmo e della Confederazione benedettina," *Ben.* 23 (1976): 65–88; Renner 232–50. A useful—but incomplete—collection of sources is: L. T. Della Marra, *Il Collegio S. Anselmo in Roma e il Cardinale Dusmet* (Catania, 1901). A study containing no new source material: G. Oesterle, "*70 Jahre Kolleg St. Anselm in Rom*," *BenM* vol. 34 (1958): 43–56; see also Oesterle, "Beuron und die Anfänge des Studienkollegs St. Anselm in Rom," in *Bueron 1863–1963. Festschrift zum Hundertjährigen Bestehen der Erzabtei St. Martin* (Beuron, 1963), 268–80.

[2] Founded in 1687 and housed in the Abbey of St. Paul's Outside the Walls, the college was abolished by the French in 1810 and, following a brief restoration, finally came to an end in the 1840s. An attempt to reopen the college in St. Paul's city monastery of St. Callisto in Rome on the orders of Pope Pius IX ended with the

dogged insistence the college was reestablished in a new form, had announced to the Roman prelates who had come to congratulate him on the ninth anniversary of his election to the papacy that he did not wish to delay the establishment of the college until new buildings could be provided, but that he had arranged for temporary accommodation in a part of the Palazzo dei Convertendi. This stately building was located on the Piazza Scossa Cavalli between the two streets of Borgo Nuovo and Borgo Vecchio which led to St. Peter's. In the summer of 1937, when the Via della Conciliazione was being laid out, the building was demolished and rebuilt on the right-hand side of the new boulevard. Today it houses the offices of the Congregation for Oriental Churches. The old building was called "Dei Convertendi" (House of the Converts) because in earlier times converts from Protestantism were housed here in a kind of spiritual quarantine before being released into the Catholic population of Italy. In his *Les Confessions*, Jean Jacques Rousseau painted a grim picture of a similar institute in Turin.[3]

Leo XIII had ordered the preparation of temporary accommodation for the new Sant'Anselmo on the third floor of this building. The only access was via a not very convenient stairs of over one hundred steps. With a keen instinct for publicity, the archbishop of Catania, Msgr. Giuseppe Benedetto Dusmet, OSB, to whom Leo XIII had entrusted the refoundation of Sant'Anselmo[4], invited cardinals, archbishops, bishops, and abbots. "The modest rooms of the Scossa Cavali presented the picture of a Benedictine council in miniature."[5] Archbishop Dusmet gave the formal address and with Sicilian verve encouraged all the Benedictine Congregations, and in particular the Cassinese, actively to respond to the expectations and generosity of the pope. He concluded with the words, *Nihil arduum est humilibus, nihil asperum mitibus* (Nothing is too hard for the humble nor too difficult for the gentle). At the conclusion of the celebration, all repaired to the house chapel situated

---

occupation of Rome in 1870. S. Bäumer, "*Das Collegium des hl. Anselm vor 200 Jahren*," *StudMitt* 8 (1887): 239–45. T. Leccisotti, "*Il collegio di S. Anselmo dalla fondazione alla prima interruzione*," *Ben*. 3 (1949): 1–53.

[3] J.-J. Rousseau, *Les Confessions* (Paris, 1964), 65–75.

[4] On Dusmet, see the biography written with a view to the prelate's beatification by Leccisotti, *Il Cardinale Dusmet*. See also R. Rios, *Menschen, die Gott gefunden. Benediktiner von heute*, ed. P. Böllmann (Salzburg, 1945), 90–109; A. Schmitt, "Kardinal Joseph Benedikt-Melchior Dusmet, OSB. Erzbischof von Catania 1818–1867–1894," *BenM* 33 (1957): 179–207, 279–91; R. Baurreis, [2]*LThK* 3 (1959): 616.

[5] Locher, *Eröffnung und Konstituierung von Neu-St. Anselm*, 216–23; cf. p. 216. M. K(inter), "Das neueröffnete Benedictiner-Collegium S. Anselmi in Rom," *StudMitt* 9 (1888): 159–63.

Pope Leo XIII (1810–1903) founder of the Benedictine College of Sant'Anselmo

on the ground floor, some distance from the actual rooms of the college, where a thanksgiving *Te Deum* was sung.

The words of Leo the Great with which Dusmet concluded his address were also intended to encourage the small community of the new college. In fact, the beginnings were modest enough, the furnishings of the rooms shabby, and, above all, the lack of books the most serious deficiency. Most of the students had arrived only after Christmas. When lectures began on January 5, there was a total of fourteen students. A further two arrived in February. They were young men from all over the world, the youngest being nineteen years old (Joseph Wenninger from the Beuronese Abbey at Prague, later prior of the monastery on Mount Sion in Jerusalem), the eldest were twenty-six years old or a little older. St. Vincent in Pennsylvania alone had sent three students, two came from Monte Cassino, two from S. Giuliano in Genoa (Subiaco Congregation), two belonged to Emmaus/Prague, one to Maredsous in Belgium (the later canonist Pierre Bastien), and one each from Seitenstetten and Göttweig in Austria. The remainder came from Belloc (France), Monterserrat (Catalonia), Fort Augustus (Scotland), and Douai (a monastery of the English Congregation in France).[6]

The rector of the tiny community was titular Abbot Gaetano Bernardi from Monte Cassino, his representative and prior being Fr. Adalbert Miller from St. Vincent. Dusmet had been able to obtain the services of seven Benedictine professors. In addition to Bernardi and Miller, already mentioned, these were Wilfrid Wallace from the Beuronese monastery of Erdington in England, who taught church history, scriptural exegesis, and Greek; Fr. Chrysostomus Stelzer from Emmaus/Prague—soon to become one of the pillars of Sant'Anselmo—taught dogma and moral theology;[7] Fr. Robert Monroe from St. Vincent taught philosophy and mathematics; and Fr. Gerard van Caloen (Maredsous) taught liturgy and was prefect of clerics. Fr. Wilfred Corney of Downside taught Gregorian chant and acted as cellarer. The abbot-rector himself taught Italian

[6] AAt, Matricola 1888/1937, nos. 1–29.

[7] In Bernardi's letters, Fr. Chrysostomus Stelzer always receives high and unconditional praise. Stelzer, born on February 7, 1855, in Sigmaringen, pursued his theological studies in Innsbruck, where he was ordained priest in 1878 and obtained a doctorate in theology *cum acclamatione*. After several years of pastoral work in the diocese of Würzburg, in 1883 he entered the monastery of Emmaus/Prague. From 1888 to 1892 he was a professor and for a time master of clerics at Sant'Anselmo. In 1892 he became prior of Beuron. In 1904 Archabbot Placidus Wolter sent him as first prior to the newly founded monastery of Gerleve. He died unexpectedly in Bonn on February 2, 1905, following an operation. ArchGerleve, "Totenchronik Chr. Stelzer," *AOSB* (1893–1908): 201.

language and literature; his prior, natural sciences and Hebrew.

Abbot Gaetano Bernardi (1827–1895)

In addition, there were five lay brothers all aged about forty and all belonging to the Beuronese Congregation. These were: Brothers Alexius Keller, Engelbert Kniedler, Johann Baptist Nutz, Columban Abt, and Paulin Beil. The latter was the shortest of the brothers and served Sant'Anselmo faithfully for twenty-five years—he died in 1931—and remained in the memory of hundreds and thousands of Old Anselmians as a model of the saintly religious.[8]

Before considering life in the first year of the new college and recounting the efforts of the rector in this and subsequent years to find suitable accommodation, we should like first to take a look backward and ask what the factors were that led to the refoundation of Sant'Anselmo.

From the beginning of his pontificate, Leo XIII showed a lively interest in the renewal of the old orders and in particular the Benedictines. In July 1878, he said,

> It happens to me often that I seem to hear the voice of God in me saying: remember the Orders! They have taken the life of the Church to themselves, the Church must give it to them again. The worse the times, all the more must one reach out to the Orders, the old as well as the new, because they are all necessary, in the North and in the South, in East and West. I must even remember the old Basilians. With regard to the Order of St. Benedict: the sap of this old tree has not dried up. We shall experience proofs of this.

Again, in November 1883:

> I often think of the Benedictine Order. Having given the Church so much, may it still do great things for her. It is the Order that enjoys great trust everywhere. I have been able to establish that this reaches even to the East . . . I need the Order particularly in Greece. Black Monks of the old Order, learned monks, would overcome all obstacles there; everything seems to point toward a preparation of this movement.[9]

[8] Locher, *Eröffnung und Konstituierung von Neu-St. Anselm*, 219.
[9] F. Cabrol, *Histoire du Cardinal Pitra* (Paris, 1893), 330f. Molitor, 81f.

Fr. Adalbert Miller (1832–1906)

The pope was already thinking of the training of co-workers for the great goal of which he dreamed: the reunification of the Church of the East with Rome.[10] At the end of 1886, Leo XIII said at an audience for French abbots: "The East will be brought back to the unity of the Church only through the Black Benedictines. Up to now, no Order has been able to acquire such an influence in the East as the Benedictines. Eastern bishops whom I have asked about this, confirm that it is so."[11] The pope's plan was that, starting from Rome, the influence of the Benedictines should radiate once more to East and West, for the good of the Church. In the pope's mind, Sant'Anselmo should be more than only a reestablishment of the defunct Cassinese college, more than an international house of studies for Benedictines from all over the world; it should resurrect the ecclesiastical-cultural role of the Benedictines of the Middle Ages. Without a doubt this goal was not only conceived in a spirit of restoration but also was too ambitious. Disappointments were inevitable. The pope became aware of this already in the first years of Sant'Anselmo even though to the end of his life he took a lively interest in the development of the college.

Fr. Chrysostomos Stelzer (1855–1905)

As early as 1885, the pope took the first concrete steps toward the realization of his plan when he summoned a council of Cassinese abbots in Rome to discuss three issues: regular observance, monastic studies, and the reopening of the Collegium S. Anselmi, the latter of which should be open to young monks of other Congregations. At the request of Abbot President Morcaldi, Leo XIII nominated the Benedictine bishop Dusmet as chairman of the conference. Since the immediate issues concerned only the Cassinese Congregation, it is easy to understand why Leo XIII did not entrust the task to the Benedictine Cardinal Pitra, who was living in Rome, but to the archbishop of Catania.

[10] R. F. Esposito, *Leone XIII e l'oriente cristiano* (Rome, 1961), 606ff. Also, W. De Vries, "Leo XIII und die Orientalen," *Stimmen der Zeit* 169 (1961–1962): 375–79.

[11] A. Houtin, *Dom Couturier, abbé de Solesmes* (Angers, 1899), 236L.

Giuseppe Cardinal Dusmet (1818–1894)

Dusmet, himself a Cassinese, lived as a monk surrounded by monks in his modest house. As archbishop he had participated in 1882 in the conference of abbots that prepared an edition of the constitutions of his Congregation.[12]

On December 4, the gathering of abbots that had been meeting since the end of November 1886 in the Palazzo San Callisto in Trastevere issued a report on the reopening of Sant'Anselmo, which already went into great detail and in particular outlined precise disciplinary regulations for the projected house of studies.[13] Clearly the Cassinese abbots had not grasped that the pope was interested in more than a new version of the old Sant'Anselmo. This became clear to all, however, by January 4, 1887, when Leo XIII responded to the work of the Cassinese conference in a solemn papal brief addressed to Archbishop Dusmet.[14]

> The brief is not simply an approval of the preceding congress. It summons Archbishop Dusmet to oversee the beginnings of the college. More: it outlines a program through the realization of which Leo XIII wishes to restore the Benedictine Order to its former greatness. . . . For this reason it is one of the most important documents in the recent history of the Order. It is an act the consequences of which . . . are, directly, the international college on the Aventine and, indirectly, the connection between all Benedictine Congregations.[15]

The brief *Quae diligenter* in the Italian version "Abbiamo appreso" of January 4, 1887, is, in fact, the foundation charter of Sant'Anselmo.

The pope first recalls the glorious past of the Benedictine Order, particularly in Italy (Monte Cassino is mentioned), and adds the wish that the Cassinese, despite the unfavorable circumstances of the times, would maintain the seriousness of their monastic discipline and their tradition of scholarship. The pope's view, however, reaches further: Since strength comes from a shared purpose, more can be hoped for the future only if

[12] Molitor, 84; Leccisotti, *Il Cardinale Dusmet* (appendix 5), 133–37.

[13] Molitor, 230–32. Still earlier, *StudMitt* 8 (1887): 100ff.

[14] Ed.: Leonis XIII P.M. Acta, vol. 7 (Rome, 1888), 1–6; Molitor, 232–37.

[15] Molitor, 89.

the members of the Order, spread throughout the world, grow together to form one *body* with uniform laws and a uniform leadership (*quasi in corpus unum coalescerent, unis iisdemque legibus, una eademque rectione*).

The pope does not, however, dwell further on this topic but turns immediately to what had been the main topic of the Cassinese Congress in Rome: studies. He expresses his wish that the College of Sant'Anselmo, founded two hundred years before by Innocent XI, would be reopened. He praises the suggestions of the abbots that in addition to canon law and a full course in theology (with Church history, biblical exegesis, patristics, Christian archaeology, Greek, and Hebrew) the students should study Thomistic philosophy as well as physics and mathematics. He states that today philosophy is indispensable for the defense of the light of reason and of belief: knowledge of the natural sciences should not be left to the "enemies" alone.

The new college, continues the pope, should, like the old college, be open to all Cassinese students, but not only to them: to achieve the goal of a greater unity of the Order, the other Benedictine monasteries should be invited to send their younger monks to Sant'Anselmo. These include the American-Cassinese Benedictines, the monasteries in France, Belgium, Switzerland, Austria, Hungary, Germany, England, Bavaria, and other countries.

Thus the pope concludes his letter, "You know how close this matter is to our heart. At the same time it helps to achieve other goals, in particular the well-being of the Church of the East [*praesertim ecclesiae orientali profutura*]." He will do all in his power to help financially and otherwise trusts that Dusmet will establish the college in accordance with the pope's wishes and vision.

The surprise among Benedictines was great. Pleasure at the honor shown to the Benedictine family by the words and deeds of the pope was mixed with the worry that the latter's objective might be the centralization and uniformity of Black Monks which, in fact, a short time later, Leo XIII demanded of the Franciscans and the Trappists.

Despite such suspicions, however, the short-term goal, i.e., the opening of the college, was less problematic. Without delay, Dusmet sent the papal brief and the recommendations of the Cassinese abbots of 1886, along with an accompanying letter, to all the Benedictine abbots of the world. The aim was to waken interest and participation within the whole Order to realize the pope's farsighted plans. Replies, however, were slow in coming, and while most of these accepted the basic idea, practical reservations predominated. Many monasteries were, in fact, not in a position to provide funding, professors, or students for the proposed college. Most monasteries were poor, others had insufficient vocations and were overburdened by excessive work. In some countries, particularly in Austria-Hungary, the monasteries were under strict state supervision. Solesmes was suffering the effects of the anticlerical legislation of the 1880s.[16] Again, the Beuronese, following the end of the *Kulturkampf*, were going through a phase of hectic development that required the deployment of all available personnel.

Worried by the lack of effective response from the abbots, Archbishop Dusmet, having consulted the pope, decided to immediately send Anselm O'Gorman, abbot president of the English Congregation and well-known in Rome and among the Cassinese and Subiaco Congregations, on a visit to the non-Italian Benedictine monasteries in Europe in order to explain the papal brief and rally support for the planned college.[17] Archabbot Boniface Wimmer of St. Vincent received a similar letter of recommendation from the secretary of state, Cardinal Jacobini, asking him to make the pope's plans known to the American abbots.[18]

Abbot Benedikt Braunmüller (1825–1898)

On February 3, 1887, in the middle of an unusually long and harsh winter, Abbot O'Gorman set out on his way north.[19] A thirty-four-hour journey brought him to Vienna on the night of February 4. From the Alps to the imperial city there was snow, snow everywhere, deep snow. In Vienna he met the Benedictine cardinal prince-bishop Ganglbauer and the abbot of the Schottenkloster, as well as the abbot of Melk in the latter's townhouse in Vienna. Signs were already evident of the many difficulties that stood in the way of the realization of the pope's plans. "All help willingly when they can," reported O'Gorman, "the problem is, however, how much they are able to help." The journey continued to Pannonhalma and from there to Admont. Continuing to Graz, the traveler arrived there in the dark and surrounded by mountains of snow. A thermometer at the railway station

[16] V. Kessler, "French Benedictines Under Stress," *AbenR* 17 (1966): 314–33.

[17] Edward Anselm O'Gorman (1833–1901) was Irish by birth. He was one of the first foreigners to make profession under Abbot P. Casaretto in Subiaco (1850). Later, he was part of the founding group in Ramsgate but in 1858 transferred to the English Congregation, of which he became president from 1883 to 1888. See Molitor, xvi.

[18] ASV, Segr. Di Stato 1901, Rubr. 9, fasc. 2, ff. 30–31 (O'Gorman's commission dated January 27, 1887), ff. 38–39 (Wimmer's commission for the United States).

[19] Regarding what follows, see Molitor, 99–104.

showed twenty one degrees below zero on the Réaumur temperature scale. The journey to St. Lambrecht in an open carriage lasted one-and-a-half hours. "I had to cover my face and ears with my traveling rug, otherwise I would have become a second version of Lot's wife." At ten o'clock on the following morning, O'Gorman had a meeting with the abbot of St. Lambrecht. "He is eighty-six years old, does not need spectacles, has a beard, and takes cares of all of the abbey's correspondence on his own. Nevertheless, he is too old and showed at once the reticence, mistrust, and fear of having to give something, typical of someone of his age." On February 26, O'Gorman was in Gries; on March 4, in Einsiedeln, where on the following day he explained the project to the abbot. On March 6, O'Gorman reported to Dusmet[20] that the prince-abbot of Einsiedeln praised the pope's idea and thanked him for his benevolence toward Benedictines. "But we do not need such an institute, because we are concerned only with Switzerland (I allowed myself to remark that the matter under discussion was not just a question of what Switzerland needed but concerned the College of Sant'Anselmo)." In the opinion of the prince-abbot, such a college should be established at Monte Cassino. The necessary accommodation was in place and the new activities would also result in attracting vocations to Monte Cassino itself. Furthermore, it was the practice in Einsiedeln to train all of its monks in the monastery itself. "I permitted myself the observation that this was the case almost everywhere." The Einsiedeln abbot continued, "It is true that our numbers are large, but we also need many monks." In the matter of money, he complained that they had the reputation of being rich, but it was just that, a reputation! "I could send one or two students for a year or two but never for six years! We have good professors and, naturally, we want to keep them." I said to him that if all monasteries were to think in this way, then nobody would go to Rome. "So, Most Reverend Lord," O'Gorman concluded, "where I had expected much, I received only promises."

Abbot Basil Oberholzer once more emphasized his position and that of the Swiss monasteries in a letter to Archbishop Dusmet on December 20, 1887.[21] The letter did little more than bemoan the difficult situation of the monasteries and the impossibility of doing anything for Sant'Anselmo. He agreed that it was true that Engelberg sent its students to Salzburg for theology, but they did this only because they could live

[20] APr, Arch. Dusmet I ɪ C/3.
[21] APr, Arch. Dusmet I ɪ E/3.

virtually for nothing in Sankt Peter in return for participating in the Divine Office in choir.

O'Gorman went from Einsiedeln to St. Stephan in Augsburg, a monastery with a large secondary school, and from there to Metten, where he arrived on March 17 in the middle of a violent snowstorm. On April 4, traveling via Salzburg, Lambach, and Kremsmünster, he reached Vienna. Cardinal Ganglbauer had summoned the Austrian abbots by telegraph, despite the fact that Holy Week was fast approaching. "The planned visits to Maredsous or to other Beuronese monasteries did not take place, partly because of the distances involved and partly the expense that such visits would entail was too great and again, partly because the congregation had already promised to help."[22] On April 6, O'Gorman was once more in Rome.

Prince-Abbot Basilius Oberholzer (1821–1895)

Although the abbot could not hide his disappointment over the meager results of his journey, it had, in fact, not been for nothing. It showed the Benedictine monasteries how serious the pope was about the college. Again, the journey made the Roman authorities aware that many obstacles were not to be overcome by mere ordinances, but only by enthusiasm for the project. In a long letter in Latin dated December 15, 1887, Benedckt Braunmüller, abbot of Metten and president of the Bavarian Congregation, made this unequivocally clear to Archbishop Dusmet.[23] The abbot explained that in Bavaria, state legislation required that those who were to teach in the monastery's secondary school must have completed a full university course in the subjects to be taught and this in a local university. Indeed, at this time, Metten had to employ—and pay—four laypersons in the secondary school because there were not sufficient monks who could be employed as teachers. In a school of 350 pupils, three of the monks who taught were already over eighty

[22] Molitor, 102.

[23] APr, Arch. Dusmet I ɪ D/4: "Curet quaeso Sanctitas Sua atque id agat, ut in patria nostra nos monachi ad maiorem libertatem pertingamus, us scilicet post studia etiam Romae persoluta facultatem docendi grammaticam saltem accipiamus. Sed ne Doctoribus Theologiae quidem haec facultas datur remisso examine philologico, et si quis ex nostris Romae per sexennium summis studiis se dederit, reversus in patriam aliquot denuo annos in aliqua universitate debet incumbere ad studia philologica. Credere non possum, Sanctiatem Suam rite de his causis nostris informatam jubere velle quae jussi exequi nequeamus."

years of age; another two were already seventy. The Holy Father, wrote the abbot, not without a certain acidity, should concern himself with obtaining more freedom for the Bavarian monasteries. Then they too could send students to Rome!

The rather sobering, if not disillusioning, impression made on O'Gorman during his two-month journey in Austria, Bavaria, and Switzerland, along with the evasive replies or outright rejections received from other abbots in the course of 1887, ought surely to have disheartened the pope and Dusmet.[24]

It seems, however, that the mounting difficulties had the effect of strengthening the pope in his purpose. On July 10, 1887, Leo XIII sent a new brief to Dusmet ("Già altra volta"), in which he pushed for the immediate opening of the college and offered temporary accommodation in the Palazzo dei Convertendi close to the Vatican.[25] The brief

[24] On July 27, 1887, the abbot general of the Subiaco Congregation, Nicola M. Canevello, and the procurator general, Romarico Flugi, wrote directly to Pope Leo XIII: "Noi Cassinesi P.O., non ostante il desiderio che nutriamo vivissimo di secondare le sapientissime mire della Santità Vostra, sentiamo di non potere prendere parte, a cagione delle circostanze a quest'opera benche se in medesima così bella, utile e grandiose." The reasons they give are (1) the poverty of the monasteries; (2) dangers to monastic observance; (3) fears regarding the preponderance of the Cassinese and the *Anglo-Benedictines*, i.e., two Congregations "that have always been our enemies." ASV, Segr. Di Stato 1901, Rubr. 9, fasc. 2, ff. 40–41. Also, f. 42, a reply of July 14, 1887: the pope does not agree with the reservations expressed; in matters of discipline Sant'Anselmo will be immediately subject to the Holy See. Similar rejection of the pope's plans are to be found in "Notes sur le Collège de S. Anselme" (by Dom Couturier?): ASV, Segr. Di Stato 1901, Rubr. 9, fasc. 2, ff.10–16. The author argues (1) Sant'Anselmo as planned is not consonant with the Rule of St. Benedict nor with monastic tradition; (2) there will be no choral office at Sant'Anselmo; (3) the college would be completely dependent on support from other monasteries, hence its existence would not be guaranteed; (4) "il n'est généralement pas populaire dans l'Ordre, et cela pour plusieurs motifs: a) in ne répond pas à un vrai besoin, au point de vue des études, cells-ci se faisant actuellement mieux et à moins de frais dans les monastères ou dans les Congrégations respective; b) la partie observante et monastique de l'Ordre craint de voir ses jeunes moines perdre l'esprit monastique, étant privés de ce qui fait l'essence de la vie du moine, à savoir, la vie de famille et la liturgie; c) la partie non-monastique de l'Ordre craint, au contraire, que ses jeunes religeux ne soient gagnés aux idées monastiques par le contact des autres." Thus the author, following an attack on the Cassinese, proposes a meeting of abbots in Rome to consider the matter of reform of the Order. He has no desire to have a central college but a real abbey in Rome with a scholasticate attached, to which other monasteries and Congregations could send young monks for the purpose of studies.

[25] Printed in Molitor, 237. Dusmet's circular letter dated June 12, 1887, announcing the opening of the college: *StudMitt* 8 (1887): 435–37.

appointed Archbishop Dusmet, up to then responsible only for the preparatory work, superior of the new college. At the same time, he was given the right to appoint a monk of his choice as his plenipotentiary and representative, particularly for the periods during which he, Dusmet, would be absent from Rome because of the demands of his own diocese in Sicily.

Dusmet chose Getano Bernardi, an already elderly monk of Monte Cassino and respected for his abilities as a teacher. In December 1887, the pope, following Dusmet's suggestion, appointed Bernardi abbot and rector of Sant'Anselmo.[26]

2. The First Years in the New College

Already on January 18, 1881, a few days after the opening of the college, Dusmet compiled a comprehensive report on what had been achieved to date. This report was addressed to Msgr. Gabriele Boccali, *Uditore di Sua Santità,* a true friend of the new college, who in the years ahead became the intermediary between Sant'Anselmo and the pope. Dusmet's report was, of course, intended for the pope himself.[27]

Abbot Boniface Wimmer (1809–1887)

Dusmet begins with a list of financial help actually received or definitely promised by the monasteries. In the first place he praises the swift response from the geographically most distant Benedictine Congregation, the American-Cassinese, whose founder, Boniface Wimmer had, sadly, died on December 8, 1887. Dusmet refers to Wimmer as a "passionate protagonist" (*appassionato fautore*) of the college. As early as the 1860s, Wimmer had established a college in Rome for American Benedictine students, the College of St. Elizabeth, close to the church of S. Andrea della Valle. From there, the students attended lectures at the Gregoriana. The college had to be closed following the occupation of Rome by Italian troops.[28] As a consequence, Wimmer reacted

[26] ASV, Cong. Ep. Er Reg., Posizioni Regolari, Agosto-Dicembre 1887: Nomination decree of Abbot G. Bernardi (ex Audientia SSmi on December 21, 1887) dated December 26, 1887 (Prot. 8207/13).

[27] APr, Arch. Dusmet I I D/6. Partly printed by Della Mara (appendix 1) 43–47.

[28] The Collegium S. Elisabethae in the via dei Chiaveri, founded in 1865, closed in 1870, reopened in October 1880, but had to be definitively closed in August

enthusiastically to the notion of a Benedictine college in Rome. Not only did he immediately send two professors to Rome along with three students, but he also made a donation of 40,000 lire, the real value of which can be gauged from the fact that the cost per year of keeping a student in the college was 1,000 lire. The Cassinese Congregation gave 40,000 lire; the Beuronese, 20,000 lire. The Congregation of Solemes, represented by Cardinal Pitra, approached the pope with a request—which was granted—to be dispensed from sending money or students to Sant'Anselmo for the duration of their exile. Clearly displeased, Dusmet reported that he had replied to the cardinal that he expected to hear from him as soon as the situation of the Congregation of Solesmes improved. In fact, Dom Couturier, the abbot of Solesmes, had no intention of sending monks from his Congregation to Sant'Anselmo. In his view, one does not leave the world in order subsequently to acquire the intellectual means of conquering that world. Above all, he was worried about monastic observance. Would monks not return to their home monasteries with liberal and worldly attitudes and habits? Training for the priesthood could, he argued, be provided at home by the monks of the Solesmes Congregation themselves. They had no need of Sant'Anselmo for this. Without a doubt, Dom Couturier would have immediately obeyed a direct papal order to send the young French monks to the new college. In the absence of such a command, however, the Congregation of Solesmes kept its distance from Sant'Anselmo.[29]

The Swiss abbots had informed the archbishop that *hoc saltem tempore nec aptis personis nec pecuniis Collegium adiuvare posse* (that at least for the time being they could not support the college either by sending suitable monks or with money). Following a decision by his chapter, Archabbot Claudius Vaszary of Pannonhalma promised 1,000 Austrian gulden per annum, "for as long as the College of Sant'Anselmo exists and as long our circumstances permit us to do so." He regretted, however, that for the time being, because of the pressure of state-school regulations, he was not in a position to send any students.[30] The Austrian monasteries contributed 8,270 Austrian gulden.

1883, a victim of a road building program. J. Oetgen, *An American Abbot, Boniface Wimmer, OSB, 1809–1887* (Latrobe, PA, 1976), 222, 283. The house and the church of S. Elisabetta dei Fornari—which remained until 1886—was the property of the German bankers' guild in Rome. For the documents concerning the letting of this property to Wimmer, see A. Schmidt, "DasArchiv des Campo Santo Teutonico, nebst geschichtlicher Einleitung," in *RQ. Suppl. Bd.* 31 (Freiburg, 1967), 54, 209f.

[29] A. Houtin, *Dom Couturier, abbé de Solesmes* (Angers, 1899), 237ff.

[30] APr, Arch. Dusmet I I E/2: "quoadusque Collegium S. Anselmi florebit nobisque per adiuncta licebit."

Archabbot Claudius Vaszary (1832–1915)

Understandably, in the matter of the internal organization of the only recently established college, Dusmet confines himself to a few remarks. Thanks to the help of the Beuronese Congregation, it has been possible from the very first day to entrust all domestic services in the house to lay brothers. Dusmet states, "You, Monsignore, will easily understand what a great help this is toward the maintenance of discipline, silence, and order in the house and providing the best care for professors and students." It was too early to make a judgement on how studies were progressing but: *Le scuole vanno bene* (teaching is going well), "The professors are happy with the students and vice versa."

For the most part, the regime of the house and the study plan were in accordance with the recommendations of the Cassinese Abbots' Conference of 1886. In a letter dated February 26, 1888, Fr. Chrysostomus Stelzer describes the timetable as it applied then to lecturers:

> We rise at five o'clock; there follows a long pause after which at 5:30 there is common meditation in the chapel. Prime follows meditation (to which the *Capitulum culpae* is added twice a month). Then I have to wait for half-an-hour before I can say Mass. After breakfast I prepare the morning's lecture which takes place at 9:30. Then I recite the remaining Small Hours, which is usually followed by further study until 11:15. After recreation I recite Vespers, and follow this with the preparation of the afternoon lecture, which at present takes place at 3:30, but, depending on the time of the Ave Maria, can be postponed until later toward evening. This is usually followed by a *disputatio* or a kind of *colloquium*, for purposes of revision. This is followed every day by a walk—this being Lent, we usually visit the stational churches if they are not too far away. Following the walk I say the Rosary; then there is Compline in common, followed by a visit to the Blessed Sacrament; after that a half-an-hour of study before supper which takes place at 7:30. On three days of the week I also have (at present) a kind of *privatissimum* for two clerics who are more advanced in dogmatics and are not following the general course. Following recreation we have common *recollectio* and evening prayer, after which one can do some more work or anticipate [Matins?] or go straight to bed.[31]

[31] Quoted from Molitor, vol. 3.

Dom Charles Couturier (1817–1890)

It is clear from the letter that in the beginning only a small part of the Liturgy of the Hours was prayed in common, namely, Prime and Compline. The full Office was prayed in choir only on Sundays and feast days, on which, if possible, Vespers was sung. The daily meditation, however, was held in the chapel, a practice which may reflect an old Cassinese tradition. Twice a week there was a spiritual conference, one on Sunday from the abbot-rector for the whole community and another during the week from the Master of Clerics for those entrusted to his care. In accordance with Church practice at the time, all nonpriests attended the daily Conventual Mass but received Communion only on Sundays and feast days. Special permission was needed in order to receive Communion more frequently. Students were permitted to leave the house only in groups and no one could leave the house in the evening. The porter was required to give the keys to the superior after supper.[32]

The course of studies in the first statutes of the college takes up no more than half-a-page in the printed text and appears as *Declaratio II* to the Rule of Benedict chapter 48.1 (*certis horis in lectione*). According to this *Declaratio*, the six-year course was to include two years of scholastic philosophy as well as mathematics and natural sciences. In the subsequent four years the following subjects were taught: dogmatic-scholastic theology, Hebrew and Greek, interpretation of the Bible, patristics, moral theology, church history, canon law, liturgy, Christian archaeology, and Gregorian chant. The students had four hours of instruction every day. Professors had to recite the creed of the Council of Trent "according to the formula of Pius IV with the additions of Pius IX of blessed memory."

More can be learned about studies from a report from Abbot Francesco Leopoldo Zelli, abbot of St. Paul Outside the Walls, to Archbishop Dusmet, dated April 2, 1888.[33] Zelli had been appointed *Ispettore e Visitatore delle Scuole del Collegio di S. Anselmo*. In this capacity he participated on Monday of Holy Week 1888 in the *disputationes* which were usual at that period and for a long time after. In the *disputationes*, the students were expected to expound independently on the material that had been presented in the lectures. At a time when seminars did not yet exist,

[32] Cf. appendix 4 of this work.

[33] APr, Arch. Dusmet I 2 A/b. Zelli's next report is dated December 15, 1888: APr, Arch. Dusmet I 2 A/a.

this was certainly a useful instrument for deepening and enlivening the topics studied.

In the theological-dogmatic *disputationes* in which Zelli took part, the subject was the possibility and provability of Christ's miracles, the resurrection as a proof of Christ's divine mission, and the power of the witness of the martyrs to and for the faith: all theses with an apologetic thrust which was commonplace following the First Vatican Council. The visitator intervened personally in the philosophical *disputatione* held in the afternoon which dealt with the divisions of the powers of the soul on the basis of action and according to the object toward which they were essentially ordered. In his intervention, the visitator emphasized the significance of this thesis for the refutation of the "false teachings" of Rosmini. As one can see, from the beginning Sant'Anselmo was firmly neoscholastic.

Despite all of his praise, the visitator nevertheless stressed to Dusmet the need to increase the number of professors in order to leave teachers more time to perfect their skills and knowledge in their areas of specialization. This exhortation was as justified as it was difficult to implement, a fact which was soon to become evident.

Disputationes and visitations were a kind of supplement to the examinations that were held all together at the end of the academic year. The "students of the theological classes" had a further opportunity to demonstrate their learning in the sermons they had to preach twice a year in the refectory in the presence of the professors and fellow students.[34]

The private audience granted to the college by Leo XIII on July 1, 1888, was a particular mark of esteem and the crowning of the first year of the new Sant'Anselmo. Abbot Bernardi speaks about this in his first annual report to the abbots of the Order on July 24, 1888. His letter to Dusmet, however, written on the evening of the audience itself—which took place at 4:30 in the afternoon—is much livelier and informative.[35]

[34] Regarding the sermons Bernardi writes in a circular letter dated July 20, 1892: "Quoad disputationes, visitationes, examina, eadem servata est methodus, quam plurium annorum experimentia jam comprobarat. Solummodo studiis hucusque usitatis addebantur publica artis oratoriae exercitia. Festis nempis principalioribus Alumni Theologi sermones in refectorio habebant de materia sive dogmatica sive ascetica libere selects." In the first years the (oral) examinations were held before the whole teaching body. Each professor had a certain number of white and black balls. A student's final mark was determined by the number of white balls received. Cfr. AAt, Annuale scolastico 1888–1928/1929, f. 4.

[35] Bernardi, circular letter dated July 24, 1888. Letter to Dusmet, in APr, Arch. Dusmet I I F.

The pope made a brief speech in Latin, addressed primarily to the students: "Read the history, the glorious history of your Order! It has given the Church many popes and a great number of cardinals, bishops, saints, and scholars. Take these as your example and say to your superiors, abbots, priors, and rectors that the pope desires this of the Order of St. Benedict, that monks be strong defenders of truth and goodness." His one regret is that Sant'Anselmo still has no fixed and worthy accommodation, but he would like to help in this matter. He had done what he could, and this willingly, but he expects that on their side the Benedictines would gladly do what remains to be done, *ne vana evadant desideria nostra, et ne opus quod aggressi sumus pereat* (so that our desires might not remain unfulfilled and the work we have begun not perish).

Fr. Paul Schindler (1838–1908)

The audience ended with an episode which today, several decades after the Second Vatican Council, is difficult to understand, but which is easily reconcilable with the ecclesiastical and social ambience of the late nineteenth century.

Gaetano Bernardi was indeed the abbot of Sant'Anselmo, but had not, however, received the abbatial blessing, which was not usual among the Cassinese. Furthermore, the Cassinese abbots, with the exception of the ordinaries, wore the pectoral cross only on certain Church occasions. At the audience Bernardi asked the pope for permission to wear the pectoral cross always, both inside and outside the college. In addition, he asked to receive the abbatial blessing. The pope granted both requests immediately. He conferred the abbatial blessing, however, simply by using the usual formula of blessing, *Benedictio Dei omnipotentis,* etc. This was, perhaps, somewhat of a disappointment for Bernardi. What at first sight may appear as ridiculous vanity on the part of the first rector of Sant'Anselmo was in fact symptomatic of a desire to raise the prestige of the college by means of the usages common in the society of the time: Bernardi immediately approached the Curia to have this privilege confirmed for future superiors of Sant'Anselmo.[36]

The "Studien und Mitteilungen aus dem Benedictiner- und dem Cistercienser-Orden," which in the years before the First World War saw itself not only as an academic journal but also as a newsletter, commu-

[36] Indult dated July 12, 1888: cf. appendix 3.

nicated already some minor changes in the teaching body in the second academic year: "Fr. Wilfrid Wallace from the Beuronese congregation was replaced in the subjects of ecclesiastical history and introduction to the Bible by Fr. Augustin Haudeck from St. Martinsberg (Pannonhalma). Fr. Paul Schindler from Einsiedeln became responsible for moral theology. The role of spiritual director of the students was assumed by Fr. Chrysostomus Stelzer who at the same time became professor of dogmatics in place of Fr. Gerard [van Caloen] from the Beuronese congregation."[37] The correspondent noted regarding the content of the studies, "This year, too, a theological and philosophical course was begun. Dogmatics started with Tractatus V. de Deo Uno with diligent use of the Summa of St. Thomas (every student had received a copy of the latest edition of this, Romae, ex Typographia Senatus, volumina VI); lectures in ecclesiastical history began with Constantine; in moral theology the course started with Praeceptum III; the introduction to the Bible began with the Tractatus de SS. Scripturae Textibus."

Fr. Robert Monroe (1850–1889)

From outside everything seemed to have gotten off to a good start. Bernardi's letters, however, reveal the worries that had quickly begun to trouble the rector. On May 3, 1888, Bernardi complained to Abbot Hildebrand de Hemptinne of Maredsous about Fr. Gerard van Caloen, who by the back door and without informing any of his superiors in the Order, asked permission from the Curia to found a Congregation for the missions or an Oriental college.[38] Bernardi stated that the archabbot of Beuron should immediately forbid this. Further, he, the archabbot, should order that Fr. Gerard "should never again set foot on Roman soil." Rather, he should be summoned to Beuron "where his frivolous and erratic character" (*suo carattere leggiero e incostante*) can be remedied. In fact, Archabbot Maurus Wolter immediately removed van Caloen from Rome, putting him in charge of the Maredsous house of studies at Louvain—but here, too, things did not go well for long.

More serious was the loss of the young professor of philosophy, Fr. Robert Monroe from St. Vincent, who died of smallpox on January 26, 1889, after a few days' illness. He was buried in the cemetery of Campo

[37] *StudMitt* 9 (1888): 674f.

[38] APr, Arch. Dusmet I I G/6. On Gerard van Caloen: cf. N. N. Huyghebaert, *Bibliographie nationale . . . de Belgique*, Supplément III (Brussels, 1961), 151–61.

Verano.[39] This death not only immediately caused near panic among the residents but also forced the rector to find a new professor. For the time being, a secular priest from the "Appollinare" (today's Lateran University) was engaged to help with moral theology.

At the end of May the number of students sank to thirteen. By the end of the academic year the whole community consisted of twenty-five persons. In the following year, 1889–1890, there were only twenty, a frighteningly small number, even if "St. Joseph, St. Benedict, and St. Anselm hurried to fill the gaps."[40] One can understand that under such circumstances, Bernardi had more than once during his period as rector to battle with discouragement and bitterness. There is no clearer expression of the cares that plagued him than his letter of December 2, 1889, to Hildebrand de Hemptinne. Given the gravity of the opinions expressed concerning Sant'Anselmo in this letter, it is here quoted at length:

> Having been constrained to accept the nomination as abbot of this college, I had a long confidential conversation with Msgr. Boccali. This was eighteen months ago. I used this opportunity to express to him my little faith in the future of the college, because of a grave mistake made right at the beginning. The mistake was the following: When the Holy Father wished not only to reestablish the college founded by Innocent XI for the Cassinese Congregation but also to open it to the other Benedictine Congregations, *nigris coloris*, all the Italian and foreign abbots should have been summoned and given the opportunity to discuss the basis of the renewed institution and principles on which agreement could be reached. Thus, all would have had an interest in the life and future of the college and we should never have lacked either professors or students to fill that college every year. The good prelate agreed with my opinion and asked how this mistake could be rectified. Understandably, I replied: by doing what had not yet been done. I added, however, that one should also consider how one might achieve the other goal of the Holy Father, namely, to gather the scattered forces of the Order into a powerful unity.
>
> Nor did I forgo the opportunity to point out the need for an adequate financial endowment for the Abbey of Sant'Anselmo, so that this abbey would be in a position, apart from covering extraordinary expenses, to acquire the books which are needed by

[39] Molitor, 111.

[40] "Ma S. Giuseppe, S. Benedetto e Sant'Anselmo si sono affrettati a far riempiere le lacune." Letter from Bernardi to Dusmet dated November 5, 1889, APr, Arch. Dusmet I 2 A/a.

a house which promotes the wide-ranging and important study which is theology.

The prelate replied that he would submit my suggestions to the judgment of the Holy Father, so that he could take care of the issues. I said at once that I did not think that this was the right time to act, so soon after the opening of the college. One should wait for a favorable opportunity. This opportunity, I suggested, could present itself when a start had been made on building the college, at the laying of the foundation stone and not before. Otherwise it might appear that one was trying to correct the work that had been done by the Congress of the Cassinese Abbots under the chairmanship of H. E. Dusmet. Good, the prelate replied, remind me of these things when you think the time is right and I will present them to the Holy Father who will certainly agree.[41]

[41] "Costretto di accettare la nomina di Abate in questo Collegio mi accadde, diciotto mesi fa, di avere un lungo colloquio confidenziale con Monsignor Boccali e fu in questa occasione che io gli espressi francamente la mia poca fiducia nell'avvenire del Collegio, perche era stato commesso un grave errore sin da principio; e l'errore era questo, che, avendo voluto il Santo Padre non soltanto risuscitare il Collegio fondato da Innocenzo XI per la Congregazione Cassinese, ma ampliarne il benefizio a tutte le altre Congregazioni Benedettine, *nigri coloris*, sarebbe stato conveniente radunare tutti gli Abati italiani e forestieri. E lasciar discutere da essi le basi da dare alla rinnovata Istituzione, e i capitoli di un accordo. Per tal modo tutti si sarebbero interessati alla vita e all'avvenire del Collegio, e non sarebbero mai mancati Professori ed Alunni da riempierlo ogni anno felicemente. Il degno Prelato si mostrò persuaso di questa mia osservazione, e mi chiese in che modo si sarebbe potuto riparare a questa omissione. Gli risposi, naturalmente, che bisognava ripararvi col fare appunto quello che non era stato fatto. Ma soggiunsi, che conveniva altresì di studiare il modo come si sarebbe potuto raggiungere l'alto fine vagheggiato dal Santo Padre, di raccogliere cioè in una poderosa unità le sparse forze dell'Ordine. Gli feci anche notare l'anormalità di un Abate, *paterfamilias*, senza una sua propria figliolanza, tanto più necessaria in una Istituzione come il nostro Collegio Sant'Anselmo, nel quale bisognava creare una buona e sicura tradizione della disciplina e delle costumanze della Casa; il che non potrebbe ottenere, senza il benefizio di una famiglia stabile e veramente conservatrice. Né trascurai di accenargli anche la necessità di una discreta dotazione alla Badia Anselmiana, affinché si fosse in grado di provvedere, oltre che ai bisogni straordinari, anche all'acquisto dei libri indispensabili a una casa di studi tanto larghi e importanti, quali sono appunto gli studi sacri! Gli disse anche parecchie altre cose importanti, che qui è inutile di riferire. Mi rispose allora Monsignore, che ben volentieri avrebbe sottomesse al giudizio del Santo Padre queste mie considerazioni, affinché si fosse potuto provvedere. Ma io gli raggiunsi, che non era il momento di agire dopo così breve tempo trascorso dall'apertura del Collegio, e che bisognava cogliere un'occasione opportuna. Questa occasione, conclusi, poteva offrircela l'edificazione del Collegio, quando sarebbe stato scelto e fissato il luogo dove porre la prima pietra, ma non prima, per non

3. The Search for a New Home

The pope had foreseen the rooms in the Palazzo dei Convertendi only as a temporary solution to the question of accommodation. Thus, from the beginning Abbot Bernardi was on the search for a new and suitable site for the college. In addition, the small community had to leave the Palazzo dei Convertendi sooner than expected. The above-mentioned death from smallpox of Fr. Robert Monroe raised the fear of infection. For this reason, on the very evening of Fr. Monroe's death, the community fled in great haste to the completely empty hospital of S. Marta situated behind the Vatican Sacristy. Some years before, the hospital had been prepared by the pope in preparation for any eventual outbreak of cholera in Rome. The proximity of the Campo Santo Teutonico had the effect that eight students of the College of St. Boniface, established in the Campo Santo for German student priests, attended lectures at Sant'Anselmo. In return, Msgr. De Waal, rector of Campo Santo, gave lectures to the Benedictines on Christian archaeology.[42]

Although the community was able to return to the Palazzo dei Convertendi after a few months, the incident demonstrated the urgency of finding healthier and more spacious premises.

There was no lack of plans and ideas. The short list included a delightfully situated villa on the Via Nomentana between the Porta Pia and the church of S. Agnese, which belonged to an elegant widowed German duchess known personally to the pope. In fact, the pope himself took the matter in hand and spoke with the lady. To Bernardi, who had expressed certain doubts, the pope said, "Relax, your college is a duty to which I am in honor bound. Just leave the care of this matter to me and tell all the middle-men that the pope himself is behind this matter and so they should keep out of it." The project to buy the villa came to nothing, however, because of the unacceptable demands of the pious lady to sell only part of the land attached to it.[43]

There were already concrete proposals to make S. Saba on the Aventine the seat of the college. The idea recommended itself immediately

---

dare a vedere che si voleva emendare l'opera già compiuta dagli Abati Cassinesi nella Dieta presieduta dall'Emo Dusmet. Ebbene, ripigliò Monsignore, quando a Lei piacerà, mi ricordi queste cose, e io le riferirò al Sante Padre, al quale riusciranno certamente assai gradite." Letter from Bernardi dated December 2, 1889: APr, Arch. Dusmet I I G/6.

[42] APr, Arch. Dusmet I I F: Letter from Bernardi to Dusmet dated January 28, 1891. On A. de Waal, cf. E. Gatz, "Anton de Waal (1837–1917) und der Campo Santo Teutonico," in *RQ Suppl. Bd.* 38 (Rome, 1980).

[43] APr, Arch. Dusmet I I F: Letter from Bernardi to Dusmet dated June 24, 1889.

because of its apparent persuasiveness. S. Saba was an ancient Roman church, an ancient Greek monastery—which had been dissolved for a long time and the buildings assigned to the Collegium Germanicum as a summer residence (*villegiatura*)—and in a picture-book location. All this seemed to recommend S. Saba. At relatively little cost, so it appeared, Sant'Anselmo could find a new home here. At Bernardi's request, P. Gislain de Béthune came from Maredsous to draw up plans for the conversion of the house. He was the first to have an unfavorable impression of the chosen site and he made no secret of this. In his opinion, S. Saba, at that time an isolated spot, would soon be surrounded by busy streets. He learned this from the city's plans for the laying out of streets. In addition, a conversion of the house presented difficulties, and neighbors had little good to say about the terrain.[44] Finally, S. Saba was classified as a *Monumento nazionale* and as such was under state supervision. Nevertheless, Cardinal Rampolla was enthusiastic about the idea and the architect's plans, as was Dusmet. Thus Béthune, despite being increasingly plagued by doubts, continued his work. The sale of the site required not only the agreement of the Collegium Germanicum but also of the Italian authorities. The necessary steps were taken and success seemed assured but finally everything collapsed. This was a bitter experience which later superiors of Sant'Anselmo were also to have with Italian bureaucracy.

The basilica of St. Saba

Thus Bernardi continued his search. The fact that after several vain attempts, a site on the side of the Aventine finally became a possibility is attributable to Abbot Zelli of St. Paul's. He was the "happy Columbus who discovered this site that, as it were, had been staring all in the face" (R. Molitor). Already once before, Zelli had brought Bernardi's attention to the site, but the latter had demurred because of the high cost of laying foundations. In December 1889 the matter suddenly reached a new juncture. Count Alessandro Barbiellini Amidei—whom Zelli did not know—visited the abbot and presented himself as the owner of the site and of the house contained in the fortifications of Paul III on the Aventine. He, the count, had heard that the College of Sant'Anselmo was

[44] Molitor, 115.

searching for a site on which to build and that, being a great friend of the Benedictines and their history, he was prepared to sell the property.[45]

The wedge-shaped site on the western peak of the Aventine was separated from the property of the Knights of Malta by a steep path that ran from the Tiber, past the church of the Maltese priory, and on to the Piazza dei Cavalieri di Malta. The boundaries on the two other sides were the Via della Marmorata, directly under the sharp drop of the hill, and the Via di S. Maria del Priorato, today's Via di Porta Lavernale. The site of 43,000 square meters was a vineyard. At the level of the present Aula III stood the house of the tenant who worked the vineyard. Indeed, following the purchase, it was only with difficulty that it was possible to remove the man and his family from the site.

Bernardi was correct in describing the site as "one of the most beautiful situations in Rome from which one has a marvelous view" of the city, the Tuscan hills, and as far as Ostia. The apartment blocks of Testaccio did not yet exist.[46]

In fact, Bernardi could not have found a more suitable site in Rome. Only half-an-hour on foot from the busy Piazza Venezia, even today the property is a relatively silent oasis in the middle of the deafening Roman traffic. Again, despite the polluted air of the city, what Jotsald, a monk of Cluny, wrote in the eleventh century is still true, "This hill has finer houses than the rest of the city, overlooks them from the summit, makes the summer heat more bearable because of the constant breeze, thus creating a pleasant environment for its residents."[47]

Negotiations with Count Barbiellini were concluded quickly. A first audience of the count with Leo XIII lasted a full hour-and-a-half. On April 21 Bernardi was already able to report that all aspects were covered, even if investigations regarding the foundations still had to be undertaken.[48] On July 14, Bernardi reported that at the wish of His Holiness, it was planned that the sale be made in the name of the son of the Marquess Sachetti.[49] In a circular letter a few days later, on July

[45] APr, Arch. Dusmet I 2 A/b: Letter from Zelli to Bernardi dated December 16, 1889.

[46] Apr, Arch. Dusmet I I F: Letter to Dusmet dated April 21, 1890.

[47] "In monte Aventino, qui prae ceteris illius urbis montibus aedes decoras habens, et suae positionis culmen in altum tollens, aestivus fervores aurarum algore tolerabiles reddit, et habilem in se habitationen facit." Jotsaldus, Vita S. Odilonis II, 9: PL 142, 923 C.

[48] ASV, Segr. di Stato 1901, Rubr. 9, fasc. 2, ff. 45–60. Correspondence on the survey of the ground under Sant'Anselmo, in particular the Tiber aquifer.

[49] APr, Arch. Dusmet I I F.

26, he was able to inform all Benedictine abbots that the long-desired site for the college had at last been found. "It is on the Aventine Hill on which our St. Odo [of Cluny], thanks to the generosity of Alberich from the family of the Counts of Tusculum, built a monastery and church in honor of Mary; the hill on which the Abbey of Saints Augustine and Alexius flourished." He then mentioned Gregory VII, who had spent his youth in a monastery here and closed with the words, "Of all the places in Rome what better place could we have wished for!"[50]

Bernardi had no part in the negotiation of the sale. Nor was he told how much had been paid. A commission under the chairmanship of the cardinal secretary of state, Rampolla, decided in February 1892, that the property should not be registered in the name of a private person but under the title of the *Sacri Palazzi*, i.e., the Vatican.[51] This remains the situation to this day.

Originally, Bernardi had thought of P. Ghislain de Béthune of Maredsous as architect. For personal reasons, however, the latter was no longer a candidate. He was replaced by the artistically gifted Hildebrand de Hemptinne, who had only recently in Monte Cassino received the abbatial blessing as abbot of Maredsous.[52] Bernardi had known Dom Hildebrand since 1888 when he had visited Maredsous for the consecration of the abbey church. Already in May 1890, without having seen the site, Hemptinne made a first sketch for a college on the Aventine. Clearly, the pope knew of this when on October 11 he granted an audience to Archabbot Maurus Wolter and the newly blessed abbot of

[50] Bernardi's circular letter dated July 26, 1890. Instead of "ubi Abbatia Sanctorum Augustini et Alexii floruit," the writer should have said, "Sanctorum Bonifatii et Alexii floruit."

[51] ASV, Segr. di Stato 1901, Rubr. 9, fasc. 2, ff. 5–7. Legal opinion by Giordani on the legal representatives in the sale of Sant'Anselmo (April 28, 1892). In the matter of the sale price, cf. ASV, Segr. Di Stato 1901, rubr. 9, fasc. 2, f. 61. Note dated July 12, 1890. The total cost of the *orto Barbiellini all'Aventino* was 270,000 lire. Of this sum, 120,000 lire came directly from the pope himself and he had advanced 150,000 lire. On July 18, 1890, a telegram of thanks was sent by Dusmet to Rampolla. Cf., however, 54 below.

[52] Regarding the origins of the former officer of the papal zouaves, Félix-Pierre-François-Joseph de Hemptinne, see A. de Riemaecker, *Histoire et généalogie de la Famille de Hemptinne* (Ghent, 1894), 14f. Also, biography by H. de Moreau, *Dom Hildebrand de Hemptinne, abbé de Maredsous, premier primat de l'ordre bénédictin (1849–1913)* (Paris, 1930). German edition, *Hildebrand de Hemptinne, Mönch von Beuron, Abt von Maredsous, erster Primas des Benediktinerordens 1849–1913*, trans. H. Kiene (Beuron, 1938); Ph. Schmitz, *Biographie nationale . . . de Belgique*, Supplément III (Brussels, 1961–1962), 445–51.

Maredsous.[53] Leo XIII raised the matter of the purchase of the expensive site and underlined his willingness, despite his straitened financial circumstances, to finance the building. He had commissioned Cardinal Rampolla, the architect Sig. Vespignani, and a Franciscan architect to survey and assess the site. Archabbot Maurus Wolter drew attention to Hemptinne's capabilities and remarked that a Franciscan would have difficulty grasping what was fitting for our Order. Leo XIII reacted immediately to this hint and commissioned Hemptinne to join Rampolla and the two architects in the assessment of the site.

As soon became clear, this audience was decisive for the choice of Hemptinne as architect of the new college. Vespignani, a well-known and self-confident architect, declared himself willing to cooperate with Hemptinne and only with Hemptinne for the technical execution of the plans. The pope asked for a building for eighty students and twenty professors. The church should serve only the needs of the college, though be open to visitors who, it was envisaged, would be few.

Hemptinne set to work with great enthusiasm.[54] At the same time and with astonishing energy, he prepared the plans for the women's Abbey of St. Scholastica at Maredret, close to Maredsous in Belgium. As early as January 1891, he was able to send his drawings for the future college to Rome. Bernardi presented these immediately to the cardinal secretary of state. On the morning of June 6, 1891, Hemptinne had the opportunity of presenting and explaining the plans to the pope himself in the presence of Cardinal Rampolla and Bernardi. We know how the audience went from a letter of Hemptinne to his prior and also, in greater detail, from a report of Bernardi to Cardinal Dusmet.[55] The pope had the plans spread out on the large table in his private library and examined every detail. "Bene, bravo, ottimamente," was his comment. When he saw the drawing of the grandiose facade on the Via Marmorata side he exclaimed, "Magnifico, bellissimo, monumentale! Ma Lei è

[53] G. Ghysens, "Dom Hildebrand de Hemptinne, architecte de Saint-Anselme, premier Abbé-Primat de l'ordre bénédictin," *Lettre de Maredsous* 1 (1979): 4–8; 2 (1979): 5–15; 3 (1979): 10–12.

[54] ASV, Segr. di Stato 1901, Rubr. 9, fasc. 2, ff. 18–20. Hemptinne's letter to Bernardi dated December 26, 1890, "Ho fatto tutto per esprimere coi mattoni le intenzioni del Sommo Pontefice che mira a fare di Sant'Anselmo un centro intellettuale potente nel nostro Santo Ordine non meno che un incentivo di vita monastica e di santità nello medesimo." Because the choral office does not have the importance it should have in every abbey of the Order, the college church must be so constructed that the liturgy can be celebrated there in an exemplary manner.

[55] ArchMaredsous, Hemptinne's letter to Prior Basilisu de Meester dated June 9, 1891. APr, Arch. Dusmet I I F, Letter from Bernardi to Dusmet dated June 10, 1891.

architetto vero!" (Magnificent, beautiful, a real monument! But you are a true architect!). Hemptinne replied modestly, "I am a mere dilettante, but the thought that I was serving the Holy Father strengthened my abilities." The pope wanted at once to keep the Belgian abbot in Rome but Hemptinne pointed out that he had duties in Maredsous and also that is was not necessary that he be constantly present during building operations on the Aventine.

Once again, Leo XIII availed himself of the opportunity to present his vision of the renewal of the Benedictine Order. Referring to the name of the college, he recalled St. Anselm's life as a monk at Bec under Abbot Herluin and in Lanfranc's school, saying, "When the college is filled with young students and has an abbot such as Herluin and professors such as the Blessed Lanfranc, the Benedictine Order will once more give the Church great and holy monks such as these who spread Christian teaching and culture all over the world. I bless your task and work already begun. May God make it to prosper!"

In spite of the pope's enthusiasm, the execution of the plans began slowly. Indeed, Bernardi, who tended toward pessimism, feared for a while that the building would never materialize. The pope had appointed Cardinal de Ruggiero as chairman of the building committee. Supervision of building operations and technical management were entrusted to the architect Sig. Vespignani.[56] The original estimate amounted to 1,750,000 lire. The pope impressed on the cardinal that he could not give more than 1,200,000 lire. The project must be tailored to take this into account. In fact, the result was not only a reduction in the size of the building but also—as became painfully clear later—in the inadequate finishings of the interior. In addition, Cardinal de Ruggiero was anxious to have the whole sum promised by the pope at once. He was afraid—and not without reason—that were the pope, who was nearly ninety years old, to die suddenly, both the funds and the enthusiasm to finish the project would evaporate. He had, however, to be satisfied with 300,000 lire for the first year.[57]

Everything seemed to have been agreed upon, but still nothing happened on the actual building site because the Vatican had not yet given the go-ahead. Bernardi was justifiably uneasy. At the beginning of January 1892, he pressed Cardinal Dusmet urgently to come to Rome. The college had many enemies in the Curia who appeared even to have the ear of the

[56] ASV, Segr. di Stato 1901, Rubr. 9, fasc. 2, ff. 69–71. Letters from Vespignani to Cardinal Rampolla regarding the building site at Sant'Anselmo.

[57] APr, Arch. Dusmet I I F: Letter from Bernardi to Dusmet dated July 18, 1891.

Hemptinne's building plans (1891/1892)

pope.[58] When Bernardi visited the pope on the day before Christmas Eve 1891, for the usual expression of Christmas good wishes, he found him changed. Instead of the usual questions to the abbot about the college, he simply gave him his blessing and dismissed him. Rumors were rife in the city that the pope wanted to give the college another, less costly, premises.

> But that is not all. The Holy Father has not only noticed with disapproval that the Cassinese Congregation has only one student at the college. He is also aware of the tensions in Monte Cassino between the monks and their superiors and between the monks

[58] APr, Arch. Dusmet I 2 A/a. Letter from Bernardi to Dusmet dated January 6, 1892.

> themselves. In addition, he knows about the appeal by five monks of Cava to the Congregation for Bishops and Religious against their Abbot. . . . Presumably he also knows that fifteen or sixteen Benedictines, mostly Austrians, some from Bavaria, are studying at the University of Innsbruck. For these reasons, it would be no cause for wonder, if in justifiable anger he were to consider—if he has not already done so—not throwing away so much money, a gift that is apparently so unwelcome to so many abbeys (*buttar via tano danaro per un beneficio assai sgradito a molte Badie*), and which we Benedictines so little deserve![59]

It had been possible for him, Bernardi, to gloss over matters with the pope and the Curia, but he wanted to say openly to Dusmet that he had received hardly any replies to the circular letters that he had sent personally to every abbot. In addition, there was the precarious financial position of the college. The fees paid by the students did not cover expenses. It was true that, at the opening of the college, abbots had promised to help, but one could not place any faith in such promises, "because those who were supposed to give make the excuse that they are not able." In the meantime he was forced in June of the previous year to obtain a loan of 6,500 lire from the Schmidt Bank—of which to date only half had been repaid. The cellarer was shortly going to need more money, "and I do not know where I am going to find it. One must also concern oneself with these financial problems which give me shivers down the spine!"

Did there really exist in the papal entourage, as Bernardi suspected, powerful people who were trying to persuade Leo XIII not to build a new college and instead give Sant'Anselmo an existing building in the city? By way of ascertaining whether or not the pope still supported the plan to build, Bernardi asked for permission to hold an official *Benedictio loci* (blessing of the site). This permission was granted.

[59] Ibid. The Italian original reads: "E non è tutto. Il Santo Padre, oltre che non vede di buon occhio che la Congr. Cassinese abbia nel Collegio un solo alunno, conosce i malumori che ripassano in Montecassino tra i Monaci e i Superiori, e tra gli stessi monaci tra loro. Conosce anch il ricorso di cinque Monaci di Cava presentato alla S.ª Congr. De'VV. e RR. Contro il loro Abate . . . Credo finalmente che il Santo Padre non ignori che quindici o sedici Benedettini, di Austria i più, e qualcuno di Baviera, siano alunni dell'Università di Innsbruck. Per tutte queste ragioni non sarebbe da meravigliare punto ch'Egli, giustamente disgustato, pensasse di smetttere, o avesse già smesso il pensiero di buttar via tanto danaro per un beneficio assai sgradito a molte Badie, e così poco meritato da noi Benedettini!"

On the morning of April 21, 1892, the feast of St. Anselm, professors, students, and some guests arrived in brilliant sunshine at the future building site, drew up in two lines as for the choral office, and sang the psalms foreseen by the *Rituale* as well as the Te Deum. This was followed by a modest reception in the three rooms of the Casino in the sixteenth-century fortifications on the edge of the property.[60]

Actual building work did not, however, begin until July 1.[61] But then things went quickly. At any one time there were five hundred workers on site. When the foundation stone was laid nearly a year later, the walls of the college already reached beyond the first floor.

It will be remembered that already on December 2, 1889, Bernardi had spoken about the need to summon the Benedictine abbots to Rome to make clear to them their common responsibility for Sant'Anselmo. It was thanks to Bernardi's zeal and the preparatory work he had done that led to the brief of Leo XIII, dated December 9, 1892, addressed to Cardinal Dusmet in which the latter was empowered to invite the abbots to Rome for the laying of the foundation stone of Sant'Anselmo. This gathering would also present an excellent opportunity for the participants to discuss matters of common concern and of benefit to the whole Order.[62] The cardinal fulfilled this commission in a circular letter addressed to the abbots dated February 19, 1893, and sent to all on that same day.[63]

"Livy once said, 'Trust awakens further trust.' The letter of convocation was so formulated that it did not constitute a strict command but, rather, a pressing invitation. One was in suspense to see what effect the expression of a mere wish would have."[64] The subject matter of the discussions was not announced. While the occasion of the invitation was the laying of the foundation stone on the Aventine, the establishment of a Benedictine Confederation quickly became the primary task of the congress.

[60] APr, Arch. Dusmet. I 1 F; Letter from Bernardi to Dusmet dated May 1, 1892.

[61] APr, Arch. Dusmet. I 1 G/6; Letter from Bernardi to Hemptinne dated July 2, 1892.

[62] Brief "Quae Nobis cura" dated December 9, 1892; APr, Arch. Dusmet I 2 B. Printed in Leonis XIII P.M. Acta 12 (Rome, 1893), 349f. Cf. Molitor, 239f.

[63] APr, Arch. Dusmet I 2 B, 2. Printed in *StudMitt* 14 (1893): 282.

[64] B. Adlhoch and M. Kinter, "Die Plenar-Versammlung der Benediktiner-Aebte zu Rom vom 16. April bis zum 2. Mai 1893," *StudMitt* 14 (1893): 279–301; here, 282.

4. Laying the Foundation Stone of the College and the Nomination of the First Abbot Primate

As the appointed day approached, about half of those invited by Dusmet came personally to Rome.[65] Most of the others sent representatives. Apart from the abbot of Atchison, who was ill, all the North American abbots came as did all the English. "Similarly, all the Belgian, French, Swiss, Italian, and Prussian [abbots] came. Of the Spanish abbots, only one was missing and from Bavaria, if one wishes so to name it, the youngest of the abbeys was not represented, i.e., Sankt Ottilien." At that time, however, Sankt Ottilien was not recognized as a Benedictine monastery and was not an abbey. Apart from the cardinal, there were sixty participants with the right to vote. Most of the abbots were lodged in the Palazzo S. Callisto in Trastevere, where the meetings also took place. The remainder of the abbots, mostly in Congregational groups, were accommodated in various houses in the city. There was no printed program, but this did not dampen the generally upbeat feeling of the participants.

Tuesday, April 19, 1893, was the day chosen for the laying of the foundation stone. One participant at the ceremony reported that the abbots, dressed in mozzetta and manteletta, along with the delegates and other monks, altogether one hundred persons, gathered in the church of the Order of Malta where they received Cardinal Dusmet. Then, "at about 9:30, all moved in procession to the building site. Just inside the entrance to the site, a richly decorated covered tribune had been erected for the guests and a second tribune for His Eminence, and the participants had been placed near the planned site of the church which had been outlined in yellow sand." Fr. Augustin Haudeck from Pannonhalma, professor of canon law at the college and representative of the Hungarian Congregation, who had been appointed chancellor of the gathering of abbots, read the foundation charter. Following the usual prayers from the ritual and the Te Deum sung on the site, the procession returned to the Order of Malta church, where the prior of Solesmes celebrated Mass "to implore the blessings of heaven on the building just begun."

[65] Cf. previous footnote for the following quotations. Further, "Nouvelles bénédictines, Rome," *RBén* 10 (1893): 279–84 (with list of participants). ASV, Segr. di Stato 1901, Rubr. 9, ff. 97–104: Report by A. Haudek on the Congress of Abbots and the laying of the foundation stone, with the text of the charter of the latter signed by the presidents of the Benedictine Congregations. Charter printed in *StudMitt* 15 (1894): Supplement S. 3f.

The following days of the congress were devoted to the establishment of the union of the old Benedictine Congregations, suggested for so long and urgently desired by the pope. An important result for Sant'Anselmo was the decision that the *Repraesentans* of the Order who was about to be elected for twelve years (any title such as Primate was consciously avoided) should at the same time be abbot of Sant'Anselmo. He was to nominate a rector to be responsible for studies and for the discipline of the house but who could not act without the consent of the abbot-representative. In the event of the sudden death of the abbot, it would be the function of the rector to invite the abbots for a new election.[66]

On May 2 the abbots had an audience with Leo XIII, during which the pope once more underlined the significance of the college for the Order and the Church:

Participants at the laying of the foundation stone on April 18, 1893, and at the following Congress of Abbots. Cardinal Dusmet in the middle.

[66] *Deliberationes Praesidum et Abbatum Benedictinorum Atratorum Actae in Conventu habito Romae dieb. 20, 22, 24 April. 1893*. Printed in Molitor, 243f.

> When you send young people there, they will be raised in the strictest monastic discipline and learning, as was the case under Lanfranc and Herluin, the holy abbots of Bec, who raised St. Anselm. The Order must supply outstanding professors of theology, philosophy, and the other disciplines. Thus, the young clerics, when they return to their monasteries, will bring with them the true monastic spirit and a deep learning. They will be a blessing for their homelands and guarantors of the full resurrection of the Order which is a cause so close to Our heart.[67]

Within a few weeks, with the brief *Summum Semper*, dated July 12, 1893, the pope took the final step in the unification of the Benedictine Congregations.[68] The suggestions made by the Congress of Abbots were essentially confirmed but, instead of the consciously understated title of *Repraesentans* for the symbolic head of the Confederation, the pope wished that the clearer title of *Primas* be used. Instead of nominating Bernardi as first Primate, which many had expected, the pope nominated the abbot of Maredsous, Hildebrand de Hemptinne.[69] Bernardi himself, in view of his age and state of exhaustion, had asked not to be considered a candidate.[70] His time at Sant'Anselmo was coming to an end. His last circular letter, dated July 20, 1892, is signed as always, *Abbas et rector Collegii*. At that time the number of students was fourteen.[71] In contrast, the next circular letter, dated July 10, 1893, was written by Adalbert Miller of St. Vincent, hitherto prior of Sant'Anselmo, and signed *O.S.B. studiorum Praefectus*.

[67] Cf. *StudMitt* 14 (1893): 300.

[68] For the text of the brief, cf. *ASS* 26 (1893–1894): 371–74. Also in Molitor, 245–48. For the decree "Inaestimabilis" of the Congregation for Bishops and Religious dated September 16, 1893, with additional provisions, see *ASS* 26 (1893–1894): 743–46, and Molitor, 248–50. On the legal aspects, cf. Molitor, 122–96, and Renner, 247–58.

[69] ASV, Segr. di Stato 1901, Rubr. 9, fasc. 2. f. 131. The cardinals entrusted with the assessment of the suggestions made by the Congress of Abbots recommended the nomination of Hemptinne as Primate and abbot of Sant'Anselmo; cf. ibid., f. 170–71 for the decree "Inaestimabilis" with Hemptinne's nomination. Some Austrian abbots seem to have thought of Fr. Augustin Haudek as a possible Primate, cf. Arch. Pannonhalma 64, no. 3 and 67, no. 2.

[70] Letter from Bernardi to Abbot d'Orgemont of Monte Cassino dated May 18, 1893, printed in Leccisotti, *Ben.* 23 (1976): 77. Letter from Bernardi to Abbot Krug of Cesena dated May 18, 1893, printed in Leccisotti, *Ben.* 23 (1976): 78f.

[71] On December 6, 1892, Bernardi sent his last reports on studies at Sant'Anselmo to the Curia. At that time there were eight professors, seventeen students, and three lay brothers. ASV, Segr. di Stato 1901, Rubr. 9, fasc. 2, ff. 89–90. See also B. Adlhoch, "Jahresbericht über die Schuljahr 1891/92 und 1892/93," *StudMitt* 14 (1893): 472–79.

Because the number of students began to increase following the Congress of Abbots, while the accommodation in the Palazzo dei Convertendi was extremely restricted, the new Primate decided to move the seat of the college elsewhere before the completion of building operations on the Aventine. He chose a house belonging to the Order of Malta in the Via della Bocca di Leone 68, close to the Piazza di Spagna. This was the former Hotel New York. On the instructions of the Primate, Fr. Gerard van Caloen of Maredsous, once more in Rome, this time as procurator-general of the Beuronese Congregation, rented the property from the Order of Malta for 14,000 lire per annum. The building had first to be adapted for Benedictine use.[72] From autumn 1893 until the move to the Aventine in autumn 1896, this spacious house was the seat of the college and of the first Abbot Primate.[73]

Abbot Primate Hildebrand de Hemptinne

Under new leadership, and indeed as a result of the Congress of Abbots, the number of students increased rapidly.[74] In the academic year 1893–1894 there were twenty-eight, of whom six came from Maredsous alone. The following year the number grew to thirty-five. Following the departure of Bernardi, the new Primate appointed Laurentius Janssens of Maredsous—not yet forty years old—first as pro-rector and then as rector. Up to then, Janssens had taught at the school in Maredsous and had already been considered by Bernardi as a possible successor. Janssens, enormously talented with great artistic gifts, a linguistic genius, and a brilliant Latinist—the Primate's first letter to the abbots was in fact drafted by him[75]—was a happy choice as rector of Sant'Anselmo. According to the brief *Summum Semper*, the Primate was also

[72] Contract between G. van Caloen and Bailli Alessandro Capranica, *Ricevitore del Gran Priorato di Roma del Sovrano Ordine di Malta*, dated September 18, 1893, in APr, Collegio II II. Cf. also a letter from Bernardi to Abbot D. Krug dated September 2, 1893, printed by Leccisotti in *Ben.* 23 (1976): 84.

[73] "Nouvelles bénédictines, Collège St-Anselme" in *RBen* 11 (1894): 38–43.

[74] The following statistics are taken from Hemptinne's circular letters dated September 8, 1894, and August 15, 1895.

[75] "Litterae caritative Abbatis Primatis" dated November 9, 1893, printed in *StudMitt* 15, Supplement (1894): 11–20. Cf. also, with a French translation, *RBen* 11 (1894): 145–68.

abbot of Sant'Anselmo with ordinary jurisdiction over the college. The rector, who was answerable to the Primate, was intended to support him in the running of the house and its discipline. It was also his function, with the consent of the Primate, to choose professors and "carefully to construct a suitable plan for studies appropriate to the needs of every Congregation."

As early as 1889, in a letter to Dusmet, Bernardi had touched on the problem of academic degrees in Sant'Anselmo. Prior Adalbert Miller and the canonist of the young college, Fr. Augustin Haudek, had doubts about whether the privileges granted by Pius IX in this matter to the Cassinese college, then housed in S. Callisto, were valid for Sant'-Anselmo without a specific confirmation.[76] Two years later Bernardi was able to report that Leo XIII had commissioned Cardinal Zigliara to draw up a brief to address the matter of the conferring of degrees.[77] And indeed, on August 20, 1891, a rescript signed by Cardinal Zigliara was issued granting the college authority to confer academic degrees in theology. Regarding philosophy, power to grant doctoral degrees was to be

[76] APr, Arch. Dusmet I ı F, Bernardi's letter to Dusmet dated July 24, 1889, "Aspetto una risposta su questo argomento [the finances of Sant'Anselmo] e sul conferimenti dei gradi, intorno ai quali me é parso conveniente sentire il parere di Lui [Msgr. Boccali], perché l'approvazione di Pio IX, se era validissima pel Collegio conceduta a san Callisto, non lo era per questo rinnovato Sant'Anselmo, tanto più, che nel Breve di Leone XIII non c'è nessuna explicita dichiarazione sul proposito; e il Priore e D. Agostine, canonista, sostenevano che non si possono conferire gradi, senza esplicita facoltà del S.to Padre."

[77] APr, Arch. Dusmet I ı F, letter from Bernardi to Dusmet dated July 18, 1891, "Il Santo Padre accolse benevolmente l'istanza mia presentatagli da Mgr. Boccali per i gradi dottorali. Commise di redigere al Card. Zigliara il Breve di concessione, dicendogli di mettersi di accordo con me. Mi fece perciò chiamare l'Emo, e fu tutto concertato tra noi, ponendo un terzo anno al corso di Filosofia, come usa nell'Apollinare, nel Gregoriano e nel Domenicano, essendo questa una condizione *necessaria*. Redatto che avrà in Breve, me lo manderà, affinché lo discuta col Rmo. Ab. Zelli e poi lo presenterà al Papa, ridotto in quella forma che meglio piacerà a noi. Fu pieno di amorevolezza verso di me." [The Holy Father has graciously acceded to my request presented to him by Msgr. Boccali regarding doctoral degrees. He commissioned Cardinal Zigliara to draw up a brief conceding this right, instructing him to reach agreement with me. Thus, His Eminence summoned me and between us we agreed on everything, adding a third year to the course in philosophy as is the case in the Apollinare, in the Gregorian, and with the Dominicans, this being a *necessary* requirement. As soon as the brief is drawn up, the cardinal will send it to me so that I can discuss it with the Most Revd. Abbot Zelli. Following this the cardinal will present the brief to the pope, formulated in the form which is most acceptable to us. The cardinal was full of affection toward me.]

Support from Maredsous, the Abbot Primate's home abbey—left, Dom Gerard van Caloen 1853–1932); right, Dom Laurentius Janssens (1855–1925)

requested for each individual case.[78] On January 15, 1892, the first doctoral degree in theology, an honorary degree, was conferred on Fr. Augustin Haudek, former professor of canon law at the Anselmianum.[79]

Fr. Augustin Haudek, born on November 24, 1852, in Apatin in the Bácska, entered Pannonhalma in 1871, from which he was sent for further studies to the University of Innsbruck. With a rare gift for language, "seemingly without effort, he learned English, French, and Italian, acquiring such a perfect command of these languages, both in speech and writing, as he had of his mother tongue." He pursued additional studies at Lille where he learned Hebrew, Aramaic, and Syriac. As secretary to Archabbot Claudius Vaszary, the young monk had an important influence on the administration of the Hungarian monasteries. In 1888

[78] APr, Collegio II 12 C, published with an accompanying letter from Cardinal Zigliara in appendix 5 below.

[79] The following is taken from the obituary in *StudMitt* 27 (1905): 397f. Haudek's personal remarks are to be found in *ArchPannonhalma* 64, no. 3 and 67, no. 2.

Fr. Augustin Haudek (1852–1904)

he went to Sant'Anselmo as professor of canon law and ecclesiastical history. Soon, however, he gained influence and respect in the Roman Curia where he worked to the advantage of the Hungarian Church. "His views were influential in the provision for several Hungarian bishoprics," a fact that won him enemies as well as friends in his home country. A Roman plan to raise Haudek to the archbishopric of Agram foundered on the objections expressed by Bishop Strossmayer and others. In 1891 he returned to Hungary where he became financial administrator of the Abbey of Zalavár. To the astonishment of all, he was an outstanding success in this role. When he was in Rome briefly in the winter of 1893, Abbot Bernardi and the professorial body of Sant'Anselmo thought that there could be no better way of honoring his extraordinary theological learning and his services to the college than conferring on him the title of doctor of theology. "The solemn academic act at which the certificate and doctoral hat were presented was presided over by the rector and Abbot Bernardi in the presence of all members of the college."[80] Haudek, whose whole personality seemed to have destined him to fulfill a greater role than that permitted him by contrary circumstances, died on September 1, 1904, in his fifty-second year.

This first honorary doctorate from Sant'Anselmo was followed by a second in 1901, this time in philosophy. The recipient was Fr. Maurus Kinter of Raigern, the intrepid editor of Studien und Mitteilungen.[81] A third honorary degree—in theology—was conferred on Fr. Athanasius Staub of Einsiedeln in 1902.[82] There followed a gap of fifty years until another honorary doctorate was conferred![83]

The first four ordinary doctorates in theology were conferred in 1893. One of those who received a degree on that day was Gregorio Grasso

[80] Chr. St[elzer], *StudMitt* 13 (1892): 136. The conferral was justified in the following words, "pro eximia in S. Theologiae disciplinis doctrina atque eruditione, quam et dissertationibus publicis juris factis et disputationibus, necnon tentaminibus sat superque manifestavit: pro egregia S. Theologiam tradendi ratione, quam quum in ipso nostro Collegio per tres annos magisterii munere fungeretur singuli magnopere probabunt: pro studio et amore denique qua tum Romanae Ecclesiae ejusque juribus tuendis, tum Sacro Ordini Benedictino et novis incrementis promovendis semper excellebat." Circular letter from Bernardi dated July 20, 1892.

[81] The certificate was backdated to November 10, 1900. Cf. *StudMitt* 22 (1902): 499f.

[82] AAt, Matricola 1888/1937 notes with regard to no. 104 (D. Atanasio Staub), "Professore di teologia dogmatica, Maestro degli'Alunni da 1894 à 1902. Creato Dottore in teologia da S. Santità, ritornò nel proprio monastero in Luglio 1902."

[83] On Fr. Matthäeus Rothenhäusler, see pp. 202–05 below, AAt, Acta Conc. Fac. Theol. 1933–1934/1957–1958, 94–94 verso.

from the Subiaco Congregation, later abbot of Praglia, subsequently of Montevergine, who died in 1929 as archbishop of Salerno.[84]

5. Gaetano Bernardi, Abbot-Rector of Sant'Anselmo[85]

Following the appointment of the first Abbot Primate, Bernardi had left Sant'Anselmo and Rome and had returned to Monte Cassino.[86] On the death in 1894 of Abbot Michele Morcaldi, president of the Cassinese Congregation, Bernardi succeeded him but after only a few months in office died on February 7, 1895, at Monte Cassino as a result of a stroke. He was sixty-nine years old. As first rector of Sant'Anselmo, Bernardi had not only wisely run the college and untiringly engaged himself on its behalf at the Roman Curia, and even with Leo XIII himself, but also made it possible to build on the Aventine, even though he was not to see its completion.

Bernardi came from the small town of Caramanico Terme in the Abruzzi, where he was born on October 29, 1827. Even when rector of Sant'Anselmo, he enjoyed returning to Caramanico regularly in the summer to take the waters. He pursued his studies at the seminary in Chieti, where from early on he distinguished himself through his talent for the humanities. The annalist notes that "already in his early years he achieved a rare perfection in his native language, so that he was one of the few who had the privilege of being able to boast of never having dishonored the beautiful, melodious Italian language either in speech or in writing." Later, in the early years of Sant'Anselmo, he taught Italian language and literature. His many letters to Dusmet witness to his stylistic capabilities and acute powers of observation.

[84] A. Schmitt, "Carlo Gregorio M. Grasso, Erzbischof von Salerno," *BenM* 3 (1955): 298–314.

[85] Obituary in *StudMitt* 16 (1895): 178–80 and 359–63; A. Capecelatro, "Commemorazione di Don Gaetano Bernardi abate presidente della Congregazione Casinese," in *Nuovi Discorsi, Omelie, Lettere, Pastorali e Prose varie* 1 (Rome, 1901), 13–65 (here, I quote the details given by Capecelatro); A. Jodice, "L'amicizia del cardinale Alfonso Capecelatro con i benedettini di Montcassino," *Ben.* 21 (1974): 259–89; on Bernardi, ibid., 272–77. T. Leccisotti, "Gli inizi del rinnovato Collegio di S. Anselmo e della Confederazione benedettina," *Ben.* vol. 23 (1976): 65–88.

[86] ASV, Segr. di Stato 1901, Rubr. 9, fasc. 2, ff. 132–33; Nomination of Bernardi as titular abbot of S. Matteo *servorum Dei* and visitator of the Cassinese Congregation. Cf. also Dusmet's letter to Rampolla dated September 29, 1893 (ASV, Segr. di Stato 1901, Rubr. 9, fasc. 2, infra f. 179).

In 1848 Bernardi left the seminary. It would appear that he had abandoned the idea of becoming a priest. For a time he was a teacher at Sulmona but soon he returned, unemployed, to Caramanico. There in 1854, a Neapolitan nobleman, Alfonso della Valle, Marquess di Casanova, who was traveling through the Abruzzi, met Bernardi by chance. Casanova invited him to act as tutor to his young nephew and thus Bernardi came to Naples. In the houses of the Neapolitan nobility, he soon learned how to behave with tact and discretion while at the same time deepening his own literary education. From this time, and thanks to the influence of his friend Alfonso Casanova, his model both in speech and writing was Alessandro Manzoni. Bernardi was not a scholar in the nineteenth-century sense of the term, nor did he later become a great theologian. He could, rather, be considered one of the last literary figures in the style of the eighteenth century. It was not by chance that his main literary work, which he was only able to put on paper once he had returned to Monte Cassino, was titled *Avviamento all'Arte del dire* (Introduction to the Art of Speaking).[87]

It was not, however, only his love of the Italian language and national literature that won friends in Naples for the rather brittle Bernardi. He soon proved his talents as an educator so that in 1866 he became a teacher at the Collegio Vittorio Emanuele. One of his pupils wrote later, "His classes were relaxed and even amusing. This led to an open and trusting thinking about, discussion of, and an examination of things not usually dealt with in school."

With his competent performance and his acute, practical understanding, along with his wide network of contacts, the way was clearly open for Bernardi to pursue a brilliant career. To the surprise of his friends, however, Bernardi asked for admission to Monte Cassino. He was able to be persuaded to remain for a further year in Naples as tutor to the young nobleman Francesco Antonacci, but at the beginning of October 1868 he finally moved for good to Monte Cassino. On October 4, in the chapel of the abbot's townhouse in the city of Monte Cassino, still known at that time as San Germano, he received the habit from Abbot Carlo de Vera.

De Vera decided wisely and deliberately that the forty-one-year-old should remain a postulant for a full year before accepting him into the canonical novitiate in September 1869. One year later, Don Gaetano made simple profession. He was already ordained a priest by September 5, 1872, while solemn profession did not take place until May 2, 1874. A second candidate for profession on that day was Fr. Anselm Caplet,

[87] G. Bernardi, *Avviamento all'Arte del dire. Lezioni. Ad uso delle Classi Superiori del Ginnasio*, 5th ed. (Naples, 1882).

Abbot Gaetano Bernardi (1827–1895), portrait in oils in Sant'Anselmo

French by birth, who was to work in Sant'Anselmo from 1897 to 1907, first as professor of moral theology and then for many years as professor of ecclesiastical history.[88]

At that time there were few monks at Monte Cassino and Don Gaetano's workload was not inconsiderable. He was put in charge of the monastery school and for many years he combined this charge with that of cellarer of the monastery. He worked for fifteen years at Monte Cassino until, on the advice of Archbishop Dusmet, Pope Leo XIII appointed him to lead the new Sant'Anselmo. In this position Bernardi was a brilliant success. Who could have foreseen that following his work in Rome he had less than three years to live?

The portrait of Bernardi in Sant'Anselmo shows him as an abbot wearing the *mozzetta*. He is short, strongly built but not obese. The face is benevolent, but the eyes behind the rimless spectacles are cool, indeed skeptical. Bernardi's natural friendliness won over those with whom he spoke, but he also knew how to behave at the same time with dignity and firmness. His letters reveal a sober, acute observer who tended toward pessimism rather than enthusiasm. The first letters from his Sant'Anselmo period contain mocking judgments on his collaborators, all of whom, to his sorrow, were non-Italians. Thus Prior Adalbert Miller is described as *stranissimo su tutti gli strani di là dell'Oceano* (the strangest of the strange from over the ocean). Bernardi wrote in July 1888 that the prior went almost daily to Tivoli to take the waters, *E mangia e beve, e beve e dorme, e si bagna e beve* (and eats and drinks, and drinks and sleeps, and bathes and drinks). Again and again he complains about the German cuisine of the good brothers from Beuron and longs for an Italian cook: "Your Excellency is furthermore aware of my views on *all* of our dear confreres from beyond the Alps and from overseas" (*la mia opinione circa i nostri cari Confratelli oltramontani e oltramarini.*)[89] Such outbursts are, however, rare in Bernardi's letters. The longer he spent in Sant'Anselmo, the more he grew into his task. He overcame all obstacles with toughness and determination. In fact, Dusmet could not have found a more suitable candidate to fill the post of first rector of Sant'Anselmo than Gaetano Bernardi. With great self-denial he prepared the house for those from abroad who were to rule Sant'Anselmo after him. Reading his surviving letters to Dusmet, with their characteristic unchanging slanted handwriting, one's respect for the achievement and personality of the first and only abbot-rector of Sant'Anselmo grows and grows.

[88] Anselm Caplet, born April 30, 1836; professed April 21, 1871; died June 8, 1916. Cf. T. Leccisotti, *Montecassino,* 10th printing (Badia di Montecassino, 1983), 254.

[89] APr, Arch. Dusmet I I F, Letter from Bernardi to Dusmet dated July 19, 1888.

Postcard of Sant'Anselmo

Chapter 2

The First Years on the Aventine up to the Outbreak of the First World War

1. The Consecration of the Church at Sant'Anselmo

Papal Commemoration coin for 1895
with the College of Sant'Anselmo on the reverse

In a circular letter dated August 15, 1896, the last such letter before the transfer to the Aventine, Abbot Primate de Hemptinne outlined his ideas about future studies at the college. Following the request of several abbots (probably mostly from Austria), in addition to the "long course" which consisted of three years of philosophy followed by four years of theology leading to the doctorate, a *cursus brevior* was to be established. This course would make it possible for students to study both philosophy and theology over four years, without, however, obtaining an academic degree. This *cursus brevior*, which in different forms was to survive until the reorganization of studies in the late 1960s, was intended, in the words of the Abbot Primate, for those Benedictines who, following their ordination to the priesthood, were to pursue further studies in state universities with a view to qualifying as teachers in secondary schools.

The Primate's vision reached even further. He wanted to give Sant'Anselmo the possibility, in the course of time, of offering, after the basic course in theology, specializations in the disciplines *sive biblicis, sive juridicis, sive historicis, sive demum physicis* (biblical, juridical, historical, or natural-scientific). Of all of this, only the special course in canon law leading to the doctorate actually became a reality, and this only for a time. In another way, however, the reform of studies following the Second Vatican Council took up this idea of the first Abbot Primate, particularly in the form of the liturgical institute, but probably without being aware of the original plans.

In the meantime, the building operations on the Aventine were rapidly coming to an end. The level of papal interest and participation is illustrated by the amusing report that Leo XIII, who could not leave the Vatican, followed the progress of the building through a telescope in the papal observatory.[1] In 1895, at the wish of the pope, the commemorative medal struck every year on the feast of St. Peter had the College of Sant'Anselmo as its motif. One side of the medal contains the profile of Leo XIII, the other, against the backdrop of the new college, St. Anselm with two young Benedictine monks. The inscription runs, *Alumnis magni Benedicti in spem veteris gloriae instituendis* (For the training of the disciples of the great Benedict in the hope of former glory).[2]

The college transferred to the Aventine in October 1896. The number of students had risen to fifty-five and for these there were seven professors.[3] The rector, Fr. Laurentius Janssens, and Fr. Athanasius Staub of Einsiedeln taught dogmatic theology. Moral theology was taught by Fr. Anselm Caplet of Monte Cassino, while Fr. Franz Sales Tiefenthal from Einsiedeln taught exegesis and ecclesiastical history. Fr. Odo Haug from Beuron taught canon law and Fr. Beda Adlhoch of Mettem gave the main course in philosophy. *Philosophia minor* was entrusted to the then-thirty-three-year-old Fr. Josef Gredt of the Beuronese Congregation—the first time Gredt is mentioned in the annals of Sant'Anselmo. Among the students of this first year were Fidelis von Stotzingen, later Abbot Primate; Placidus de Meester from Maredsous, destined to

[1] G. Ghysens, "Dom Hildebrand de Hemptinne, architecte de Saint-Anselme, premier Abbé-Primat de l'ordre bénédictin," *Lettre de Maredsous* 2 (1979): 15.

[2] *StudMitt* 16 (1895): 719f.

[3] The following data are taken from Hemptinne's circular letter dated August 15, 1897.

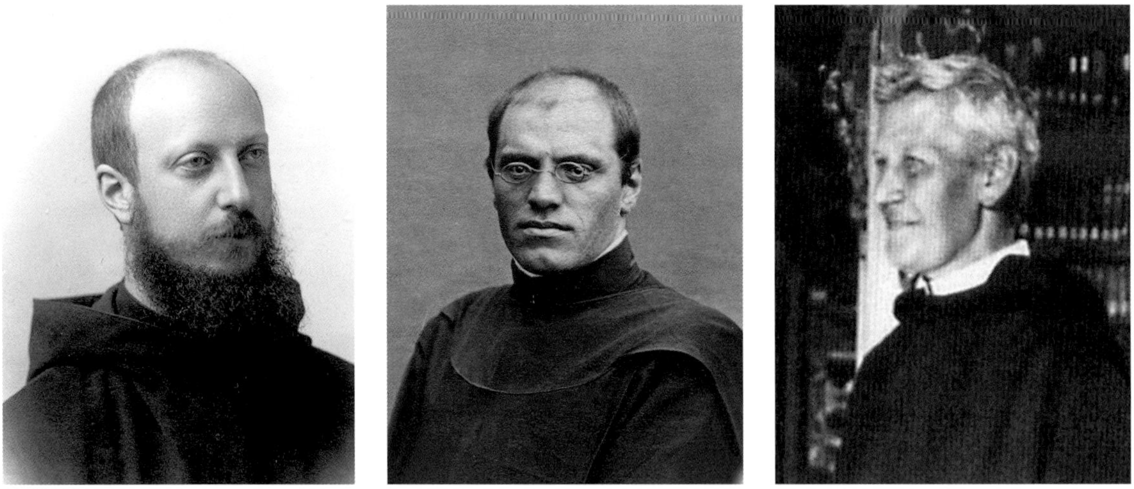

From left to right: Fr. Placide de Meester (1873–1950), Fr. Franz Sales Tiefenthal (1840–1917), Fr. Beda Adlhoch (1854–1910)

become a prominent expert on the Church of the East; Raphael Molitor, afterward the first abbot of Gerleve; Hildebrand Höpfl from Emmaus/Prague, later Sant'Anselmo's biblicist; Laurentius Zeller for Seckau who died in 1945 as abbot president of the Brazilian Congregation and titular bishop of Dorylaeum; Placido Nicolini of Praglia, who died at the age of ninety-seven in 1973, having been bishop of Assisi for forty-five years.

One of those who experienced the beginnings at Sant'Anselmo wrote later, "There was much lacking in the large house. For years a large hall was used as an oratory. The crypt and church were empty, without al-

Hemptinne's design for the painting of the interior of the College church in the Beuronese style

tars, without choir stalls."[4] It had been Hemptinne's intention to paint the interior of the church he had designed—with a nave, two aisles, and six bays—in the Beuronese style. But this came to nothing. For the time being, one had to be satisfied with less. Cardinal de Ruggiero, the general supervisor of building operations, died in 1896. With his death the college lost a good friend in the Vatican, a loss that soon became painfully noticeable with regard to the equipping of Sant'Anselmo. Abbot Primate Hemptinne's first concern was for the needs of the students. For the time being, everything else had to be postponed and "left to divine providence and the generosity" of the abbots.[5] Indeed, central heating was not installed until 1928.[6] Happily, the number of young clerics was constantly growing and by 1900 had reached sixty-seven.

The solemn consecration of the abbey church on November 11, 1900, was intended to be the crowning event in the reestablishment of the College of Sant'Anselmo. It is difficult today to imagine both the interest this consecration aroused in the Catholic world and beyond as well as the solemnity with which it was celebrated in accordance with the wishes of the pope. Already on March 21, the Abbot Primate sent a circular letter to all the abbots of the Order, inviting them to the celebrations which were deliberately planned so that the students could also be present.[7]

We know a great deal about the conduct of the ceremonies and the effect they had on the participants from the reports in the many Italian and foreign newspapers, some by special correspondents. Pope Leo XIII would have preferred to perform the consecration in person, but this was not possible because of the still unresolved "Roman Question." Thus he chose the most solemn form of representation possible by nominating no less a personage than the cardinal secretary of state, Mariano Rampolla del Tindaro, a particular friend of the college, as consecrating bishop and furthermore by appointing him *Legatus a latere* so that the consecration

[4] Cf. Molitor, 142.

[5] "Emmo enim Cardinali de Ruggiero e vivis erepto, Anselmiani aedificii administrator Supremi Pontificis voluntate creatus, quum plurima nondum esse soluta comperissem, huic mihi curae prius incumbendum duxi, ut, confectorum operum pretio dato, necessaria alumnis nostris procurarem, reliquia vero cum a Providentia divina, tum a vestra liberalitate in futurum expectarem." In Hemptinne, circular letter dated August 15, 1897. On the appearance of Sant'Anselmo at the time, cf. R.C.A., "Saint-Anselme sur l'Aventin," *RBén* 14 (1897): 32–38.

[6] Stotzingen, circular letter dated July 11, 1928, *AOSB* (1928): 65f.

[7] APr, II I C. Among other things this document says, "Licet enim basilica nostra aedesque, Ordinis universi plausa, inaudita Christi vicarii munificentia, septimo abhinc anno incoepta, penitus nondum absoluta sint, instante Anno dupliciter Sacro, solemnitas ista longius protrahenda nullatenus videbatur."

1
2
3
4
5
6
7
8
9
10
11
12
13
14
15
16
17
18
19
20
21
22
23
24
25
26
27
28
29
30
31
32
33
34
35
36
37
38
39
40
41
42
43
44
45
46
47
48
49
50
51
52
53
54
55
56
57
58
59
60
61
62
63
64
65

1. Abbot Aidan Gasquet, Downside, England, President of the English Benedictine Congregation
2. Archabbot Leander Schnorr, St. Vincent, United States
3. Abbot Victor Corvaja, Montevergine, Italy
4. Abbot-Bishop Rosendo Salvado, New Norcia, Australia
5. Abbot Primate Hildebrand de Hemptinne
6. Abbot Bonifacio Oslaender, St. Paul's Outside the Walls, Rome, Italy
7. Abbot Benedetto Bonazzi, Cava, Italy
8. Abbot Eugen Gebele, St. Stephan, Augsburg, Germany
9. Abbot Kolumban Brugger, Einsiedeln, Switzerland
10. Abbot Joseph Smith, Ampleforth, England
11. Abbot Ildefons Schober, Seckau, Austria
12. Abbot Silvano de Stefano, S. Pietro, Assisi, Italy
13. Abbot Anton Ruera, Cassinese of the Primitive Observance, Spanish Province
14. Abbot Gotthard Heigl, Afflighem, Belgium
15. Abbot Joseph Bourigaud, Ligugé, France
16. Abbot Cölestin Baumgartner, Lambach, Austria
17. Abbot Frowin Conrad, Conception Abbey, United States
18. Abbot Leo Maria Treuinfels, Marienberg, Austria
19. Employee
20. Abbot Christophe Gauthey, Marseilles, France
21. Abbot Pedro Rueda, Samos, Spain
22. Abbot Thomas Bergh, Ramsgate, England
23. Abbot Felice Vaggioli, S. Giorgio, Venice, Italy
24. Abbot Amandus Mertens, Steenbrugge, Belgium
25. Abbot Joseph Pothier, Saint-Wandrille, France
26. Prior Wilfrid Raynal, Belmont, England
27. Abbot Ansgar Höckelmann, Erdington, England
28. Abbot Domenico Serafini, Subiaco, Italy
29. ?
30. Abbot Rupert Metzenleitner, Scheyern, Germany
31. Abbot Leo Mergel, Metten, Germany
32. ?
33. ?
34. ?
35. Abbot Laurence Larkin, Douai, England
36. ?
37. Abbot Athanasius Schmitt, St. Meinrad, United States
38. Abbot Willibrord Benzler, Maria Laach, Germany
39. Abbot Robert de Kerchove, Louvain, Belgium
40. Abbot Albert Wildauer, Fiecht, Austria
41. ?
42. Abbot Vinzenz Motschi, Mariastein . A Swiss community in exile in Delle, France.
43. Abbot Augustin Bastres, Belloc, France
44. Abbot Leander Lemoine, La-Pierre-qui-Vire, France
45. ?
46. Fr. Conrad Banckaert, Downside, England
47. ?
48. ?
49. Abbot Edmund Ford, Downside, England
50. Prior Ambrosio Maria Amelli, Montecassino, Italy
51. ?
52. ?
53. ?
54. Fr. Adalbert Miller, Atchison, United States, prior of Sant'Anselmo
55. Fr. Benedict Mackey, Douai, England
56. ?
57. Fr. Odilo Wolff, Emmaus, Prague
58. Fr. Wilfrid Corney, Cellerar of Sant'Anselmo
59. Representative of the Greek college
60. ?
61. ?
62. ?
63. ?
64. Fr. Martin Aignherr, Scheyern-Ettal, Germany
65. ?

Participants at the Congress of Abbots 1900 in front of Sant'Anselmo

The photograph commemorating the dedication of Sant'Anselmo on November 11, 1900, was not taken until November 15, by which time several abbots had left Rome.

Gaetano Cardinal de Ruggiero (1816–1896). Portrait in oils in Sant'Anselmo

Mariano Cardinal Rampolla del Tindaro (1843–1913). Portrait in oils in Sant'Anselmo

would be celebrated in the name of and in place of the pope.[8] In addition to Rampolla, twelve other cardinals participated, as did sixteen archbishops and bishops, fifty-two abbots, the superiors general of almost all the major orders, and the rectors of the Roman seminaries and colleges. Further, all the ambassadors accredited to the Holy See were present, among them the ambassadors of Austria-Hungary, France, Spain, Portugal, and Brazil, as well as the Prussian and Bavarian ministers. Also among the participants were numerous representatives of the European nobility.[9]

In accordance with the then-lengthy and tedious rite of the consecration of a church, the celebration already started on the previous day, on the afternoon of Saturday, November 10. The cardinal legate verified the relics which were to be inserted in the altars on the following day. The most important of these relics were the bones of an alleged Roman martyr named Alexander that had been deposited since the eighteenth century in the monastery of the Benedictine nuns at S. Maria in Campo Marzio.[10] These latter relics were placed in a costly shrine of cedarwood, while the smaller relics intended for the side altars and the sixteen altars in the crypt were placed in silver boxes made specially for this purpose. The chapter room had been transformed into a chapel for the purpose of the authentication of the relics, and there the residents of Sant'Anselmo alternated in groups throughout the night to recite Matins and Lauds "of the Holy Martyrs."

[8] APr, IT I A, 4, brief of Leo XIII, dated November 6, 1900, addressed to Cardinal Rampolla containing his nomination as cardinal legate.

[9] Collected material, cf. *Calendarium Collegii S. Anselmi de Urbe pro anno scholastico 1900–1901* (Rome, 1902), 5–19. Also, C. W. Corney, "The College of St. Anselm, Rome," *Downside Review* 20 (1901): 31–46. Further reports in *StudMitt* 21 (1900): 676ff., and *Messager de S. Benoir* 2 (1900): 165–68, 181–90.

[10] APr, II I A, Letter dated October 11, 1900, from the Abbess M. Scolastica Peccia of S. Maria in Campo Marzio to Abbot Primate Hemptinne and including two certificates of authenticity.

Memorial to Pope Leo XIII in the sacristy at Sant'Anselmo as "Founder of the Anselmian Benedictine College"

LEO XIII P M

It was raining, though not heavily, when in the early morning of November 11, the cardinal legate and the many guests arrived on the Aventine. The celebrations lasted from eight o'clock in the morning until half-past two in the afternoon, no fewer than six-and-a-half hours. Three papal masters of ceremonies, Riggi, Ciocci, and Marzolini, were responsible for conducting the ceremonies. While the cardinal legate consecrated the high altar, two Benedictine bishops simultaneously consecrated the two side altars, while sixteen abbots consecrated the altars in the crypt.[11] They were assisted by 120 clerics from various Roman colleges.

It was already 11:30 a.m. when the first pontifical Mass began in the newly consecrated church. The guests of honor had taken their places in two tribunes draped in red which had been erected in the transepts, cardinals on the left and on the right (the "Epistle" side) the diplomats and members of the nobility. Bishops and abbots had to be content with places in the nave. Because the High Mass had the same status as a papal Mass, students from the Greek college acted as deacon and subdeacon as they would have in St. Peter's. The Greek chant and liturgy were represented by the singing of the Epistle and Gospel in Greek as well as Latin. The rector of Sant'Anselmo, Fr. Laurentius Janssens himself directed the Gregorian chant in a masterly fashion according to the restored version of Solesmes—a novelty in the Rome of the time.

Following the lengthy ceremonies, those with special invitations—about four hundred persons—gathered for lunch, which was served in the refectory and in the second largest lecture hall. The students did not join the guests for lunch but served instead. Those who reported on the meal not only praised the perfect organization but also emphasized the quality of the food.[12] During the festive meal, the choir of Sant'Anselmo, under the direction of the rector, sang the *Laudes Hincmari* with verses honoring Leo XIII, the cardinal legate, and other personages. Every

[11] APr, II I A, charter certifying the consecration of the altars signed by the consecrating prelates.

[12] For readers interested in such details, we include the menu as printed in the "Messagero" of November 12, 1900, "La minuta componevasi di consomme, antipasti, galatina, vitella, roastbeef, insalta maltese, gelati, pasticcini, frutta, dessert, caffè, cognac e anisetta; il tutto innaffiato abbondantemente da vini dei castelli, di Capri e fi Falerno." The Austrian reporter in *StudMitt* 21 (1900): 677, speaks, however, of "a modest breakfast." The lunch was not prepared by the lay brothers of Sant'Anselmo but by Signor Pio Antonini of the Caffè di Roma as reported in *L'Osservatore Romano* of November 13, 1900.

The majestic complex overlooking Testaccio

guest had a copy of the printed text.[13] When the guests left in the late afternoon, the rain was pouring in torrents. "The fourteen flags flying in front of the building—that of the pope, the legate, as well as those of the countries in which the Order was represented—were dripping wet. It was the first birthday of the third king of a 'united,' Italy, which was celebrated in his 'liberated' capital, the most 'untouchable' of all cities."[14] Among the guests, there were no representatives either of the kingdom of Italy or of the city of Rome. They had not been invited.

With astonishing skill and military precision, Abbot Primate Hemptinne had personally worked out in detail matters such as precedence among the guests. One who was present at the time wrote many years later about Hemptinne, "One noticed the former officer and—not without reason—a confrere once remarked that one could hear the sound

[13] APr. II I D, "Laudes post dedicationem ecclesiae primatialis nomine SS.D. Leonis XIII ab Eminentissimo Legato a latere D. Mariano Tit. S. Caeciliae Card. Rampolla Tyndride supremo ritu peractam in triclinio Collegii S. Anselmi decantatae."

[14] Cf. *Kathol. Kirchenzeitung*, Salzburg, November 16, 1900, p. 739.

Lay brothers working the garden at Sant'Anselmo

of the spurs under the habit when he strode at a brisk pace along the corridors."[15]

The consecration itself, however, did not mean the end of the celebrations. Festivities lasted a full eight days with pontifical Masses (including a Mass at the Greek college), a special papal audience, and a meeting of all abbots and representatives of the Order on November 13 at which the Abbot Primate, in a long Latin address, reported on Sant'Anselmo and the affairs of the Order.[16] The Abbot Primate availed himself of this opportunity to reveal what the building and fitting out of the college had cost to date. The abbots learned that Leo XIII had bought the site for 250,000 lire and for the building itself had donated 1,700,000 lire. But this latter sum was not enough, and so the Benedictine Congregations had to help, along with generous benefactors of the college who were not lacking. Altogether the building of Sant'Anselmo on the Aventine cost 2,500,000 lire. The Primate was worried about the costs of running the college, for which the pope did not provide. The yearly

[15] Pl. Glogger, "Monastischer Lenz, Monastischer Sommer," *BenM* 16 (1934): 138.

[16] *Oratio quam in Congressu Ordinis ad consecrationem Ecclesiae S. Anselmi anno iubilari MCM Romae adunati habebat illustrissimus ac Reverendissimus Dominus D. Hildebrandus de Hemptinne, Primas Odinis S. Benedicti, Abbas S. Anselmi de Urbe necnon S. Benedicti de Maredsous, die Festo Omnium Sanctorum O.S.B.,* Romae Typis Vaticanis, MCM.

fee of 1,000 lire hitherto charged for each student was not sufficient.[17] Hence, Hemptinne hoped not only for supplementary gifts (*subsidia*) from the monasteries but also for the establishment of an endowment for Sant'Anselmo, an idea frequently discussed in subsequent decades without ever leading to a satisfactory outcome.

The Primate did not only speak about finances but also emphatically and at length about studies and their improvement. The usual course in philosophy included not only strictly philosophical topics but also topics leading to theological study, such as ecclesiastical history and Oriental languages. The Primate defended this modification of the course in philosophy, asserting that students would be fatigued by a surfeit of purely speculative material.[18] After three years, the student could obtain a doctorate in philosophy and after a further four years a doctorate in theology. Hemptinne once more outlined his dream of providing specialized studies at Sant'Anselmo in canon law, Scripture, history or archaeology and even—*si tamen fieri possit*—the natural sciences.[19] Hemptinne's greatest worry, however, was the provision of suitable

[17] The above-mentioned sums must be seen in the context of current prices in Italy at the time as presented, for example in, K. Baedeker, Italien, Handbuch für Reisende, 1. Teil, Oberitalien, Leipzig, 1^3, 1891, "On average, the traveler must think in terms of twenty to twenty-five fr. [= lire] per person. In the case of a longer stay at the same place, ten fr. should be sufficient. Gentlemen who can find and adapt to local practices and customs can travel more cheaply in twos or threes. Generally, when traveling with ladies the costs are higher." (p. xi). Lunch à la carte in a trattoria cost between one-and-a-half and three lire.

[18] "Philosophiae cursus, praeter ipsius philosophiae argumenta atque historiam, comprehendit et disciplinas sive ad Sacram Scripturam, sive ad theologiam praeparatorias: historiam scilicet ecclesiasticam, linguarum orientalium saltem rudimenta, atque rerum naturalium scientias. Quae quidem disciplinae iuvenibus maxime videntur utiles, utpote quorum non solum mentes variis nobilibusque cognitionibus adornant, verum etiam animi facilitates multifariam explicant. Intellectus enim abstractis studiis defessum iucunde reficiunt historia, scientiae physicae, ipsaque linguarum orientalium elementa, in quibus practicus sensus, memoria atque imaginatio suas vicissim partes vindicant, ita ut, ab istis exercitationibus sese mens iterum as ardua philosophiae cum instaurato ardore convertat." Hemptinne, *Oratio* (cf. n105 infra.), 11f.

[19] "Nec isto duplici cursu tota quam molimur institutionem continetur. In votis quippe est, ut quatuor alios doctoratus apud nos assequi possint, qui iam una alterave laurea sint insigniti, aut, solidis praemissis studiis, in speciali disciplina excellere cupiant. Primus complectitur ius canonicum, de quo doctoralis cathedra iam est erecta; secundus Sacras Scripturas atque linguas orientales; tertius historiam tum sacram tum profanam, necnon disciplinam archaeologiae nomine decoratam; quartus demum, si tamen fieri possit, res ipsas naturales sive physicas." Hemptinne, *Oratio,* 14.

professors from within the Order. The bitter experience acquired during his short time in office, that abbots summoned the best teachers back to their home monasteries, very often after a short period in Sant'Anselmo, lent an unexpected asperity to his words. He concluded this section of his address with praise for the lay brothers and their evident value in giving the house a monastic stamp. He hoped to establish a novitiate for lay brothers who would be prepared to make profession for Sant'Anselmo.

2. Life in the College and the Development of Studies

Following the festivities in November, life in Sant'Anselmo returned to the daily round of studies and the monastic life. The *Calendarium Collegii S. Anselmi de Urbe* for the years 1900–1901, alas, not continued

View from the College over Trastevere and, in the middle ground, the Magistral Villa of the Order of Malta.

Abbot Primate Hildebrand de Hemptinne, builder of the college of Sant'Anselmo. The inscription in the document he is holding reads "The College of Sant'Anselmo planned in 1891–1892."

in later years, recounts with colorful detail in the manner of early medieval annals, the day-to-day events, great and small, of the life of the college and school in the course of the year. The content of doctoral dissertations is reported as are excursions to the Alban Hills, the lake at Bracciano, to Casamari and Trisulti, to Fiumicino and Ostia. The more serious aspects of Sant'Anselmo are written in Latin, the more amusing in English, German, French or Italian. The reader feels the inseparable unity of college and school at Sant'Anselmo where, as in many medieval universities, professors and students lived and worked together, but also the obvious formative influence of the liturgy in the complex as a whole.

When Hildebrand de Hemptinne became Primate, he immediately introduced the daily common recitation of the monastic office. Since at that time, however, almost every day was a saint's day with three nocturns, Hemptinne asked Leo XIII for the privilege that Sant'Anselmo could replace such lengthy Matins with the shorter ferial office. In a private audience in November 1891, the pope agreed to this.[20] This emergency solution became superfluous in 1912, however, when with his reform of the liturgical calendar and breviary, Pius X once more gave the Church's year, and with it the ferial office, its proper place.

The following timetable for weekdays in winter gives a rough idea of an ordinary day in the life of the college:[21]

5:00 a.m.	Rise;
5:30 a.m.	Lauds, Prime, Terce, conventual Mass followed by breakfast and private study;
8:30-11:30 a.m.	lectures;
11:40 a.m.	Sext, None, examination of conscience;
12:00 p.m.	lunch, recreation;
1:15 p.m.	Vespers followed by exeat until 3:00;
3:15 p.m.	lectures, private study;
7:00 p.m.	supper, recreation;
8:00 p.m.	Compline (on Saturdays before supper), Matins, night blessing, examination of conscience.

On Sundays and feast days, Terce, High Mass, and Sext were at 9:00 a.m. None, with sung Vespers and Benediction, at 2:00 p.m. was followed by exeat until 7:00 p.m. At 8:30 p.m. every Sunday, the Abbot Primate or

[20] APr, Collegio II 1893–1913, II 12 G. For the text, see appendix 7 below.

[21] *Liber Usuum et Manuale Chori Abbatiae primatialis et Collegii S. Anselmi de Urbe* (Subiaco, 1909), 9f.; cf., with slight variations, *Calendarium Collegii S. Anselmi de Urbe pro anno scholastico 1899–1900*, 5.

The Abbot's chapel in former times and today

the rector gave a spiritual conference in the chapter room for professors and students together. Every Thursday at 7:30 in the morning, alternatively for senior and junior students, there was a chapter of faults. At least once a month either the Abbot Primate or the rector held a similar chapter for professors and officials.

The degree to which the monastic character of Sant'Anselmo was close to the hearts of the abbots becomes clear from the minutes of the Synod of Abbots President of 1907.[22] The abbots expressed themselves satisfied with monastic life in the college, but they criticized the lack

[22] *Protocollum seu Relatio des sessionibus a Reverendissimis et illustrissimis Praesidibus Congregationum O.S.B. in aedibus S. Anselmi de Urbe mense maio 1907 ab Illustrissimo et Reverendissimo D. Hildebrando de Hemptinne Primate O.S.B. ad synodum convocatis habitis* (Rome: Typis Vaticanis, 1907) 9f. At the synod the question of whether the Primate (abbot of Sant'Anselmo) should always, in addition, be abbot of another monastery: "unanimi consensus respondetur, minime hoc esse necessarium, immo optandum esse, ut haec coniunctio Abbatiarum in Primate non fieret." Similarly, the suggestion was expressly rejected that a "permanens familia monastica" should be established at Sant'Anselmo. "Abbatiam S. Anselmi non convenire ut pertineat ad unam familiam, sed pertineat necesse esse, sicut nunc, ad totum Ordinem ita ut omnes ex dissitis nationibus Romam confluentes monachi Benedictini ibi inveniant quasi domum paternam, et hanc ab illo Primate modo prudentissimo viam stratam minime esse dereliquendam, et Abbatia S. Anselmi remaneat qualis sit." *Protocollum* 10f. Cf. *Quaestiones et Desiderata* (1907): 9–11.

of observation of silence among the students and expressly wished that they should be required to attend daily meditation. They were particularly worried about clerics from far-distant monasteries (here, they were thinking mostly of those from America) who were unable to return to their home monasteries during the holidays. The presidents recommended that the abbots of such monks should require them to stay in another abbey of the Confederation, *ne ullo modo imitentur, quod SS. Pater Benedictus maxime detestaretur, girovagos* (so that they would not become gyrovages, a thing of which our Holy Father St. Benedict would strongly disapprove).

Sant'Anselmo, however, had not been founded as a monastery but as an institute for higher studies. This was quite clear to the intellectually versatile first Primate. He was certainly not short of ideas, but most of them could not be realized because of lack of personnel and money. One example was his idea of an "Academy of St. Gregory." This was a plan completely in keeping with the thinking of Leo XIII who was always open to historical studies. In the circular letter for 1902, Hemptinne mentioned for the first time his idea of founding at Sant'Anselmo a center for the study and editing of liturgical, patristic, Benedictine, and if possible, even secular historical sources. Seven Benedictine experts would form this *Academia Sancti Gregorii*, one of whom to be appointed by the Primate to be its head.[23] Lack of funds meant that this institute, imitating the various "historical institutes" of various countries being established in Rome at that time, came to nothing. An even greater reason for the failure was the reluctance of abbots to free suitable monks for such research along the lines of the famous Congregation of St. Maur. By 1905, the academy had been able to attract only two members, the procurator general of the English Congregation, Dom Benedict Mackey, and Dom René Ancel from Ligugé. The first was a scholar well-known for his edition of the works of St. Francis de Sales—but he died in 1906. The second, Dom Ancel, was—surprisingly for a Benedictine—interested in the pontificate of Pope Paul IV, Carafa, about whom he published several studies.[24] After working for seven years in Rome, he returned, for reasons of health, to his home monastery where he died in 1932. With Ancel's departure, the academy ceased to exist.[25]

More important than the academy, the main purpose of Sant'Anselmo was and remained the training of young Benedictines in philoso-

[23] Circular letter dated September 29, 1902. This is treated in detail by M. K[inter] in *StudMitt* 24 (1903): 233–39.

[24] For a list of Ancel's studies on Pope Paul IV, cf. DThC vol. 12, pt. 1, 1933, col. 23.

[25] *AOSB* (1909): 38f.

phy and theology. The Primate worked quietly for the improvement of these studies, just as, since 1900, he quietly and from modest beginnings built up a *cursus maior* leading to a doctorate in canon law. From 1901 this course bore the rather grand title of *Facultas Juris*. The single chair was held by Fr. Odo Haug from Beuron.[26]

We know almost nothing about the philosophical-theological studies themselves, about the professors' areas of interest, or what the students' favorite subjects were. Nor do we know whether, following the death of Leo XIII,[27] Sant'Anselmo welcomed or felt oppressed by the sharp antimodernist

Fr. Benedict Mackey (1846–1906)

Dom René Ancel (1860–1932)

[26] Cf. Hemptinne, circular letters dated September 9, 1900, and September 30, 1901. Fr. Odo Haug (born on November 27, 1843), following studies at Freiburg and Würzburg was ordained priest at the archdiocesan seminary of St. Peter in Freiburg. Following a period as curate in various parishes he became a teacher at the secondary school in Breisach. In 1872 he entered Beuron where he was simply professed on May 25, 1874. Shortly afterward he went with the community [expelled from Germany in the course of the *Kulturkampf*] to Volders in the Tyrol and then to Emmaus in Prague. Later, he spent some time in the Beuronese foundation at Erdington in England. From 1885, he was reader in moral theology and prefect of clerics at the Beuronese Congregation's house of studies, first at Seckau in Austria and, from 1887, in the reopened abbey at Beuron. In 1892 he went to Sant'Anselmo where he was professor of canon law and instructor of the lay brothers until 1909. He died at Beuron on June 23, 1919. Cf. Arch-Beuron, obituary of Fr. Odo Haug. In 1910 he was created "Dottore in diritto canonico . . . da S. Santità," cf. AAt, Matricola 1888/1937, No. 554.

[27] Among the last Latin poems of Leo XIII are his verses on St. Anselm of Canterbury:

Puber Beccensi cupide se condere claustro
Patricia Anselmus nobilitate parat.
Sub duce *Lanfranco* Studiosus et acer alumnus,
Sub patre *Herluino* crescit et usque pius.
Florentem ingenio iuvenem, ad caelestia natum
Quem non perficiat tale magisterium? . . .
Hinc Pastor; Fidei divino hinc munere Doctor
Sublimi in Superis vertice conspicuus.

Fr. Odo Haug (1843–1919)

Fr. Thomas Aquinas Weikert (1863–1906)

wind blowing from the Vatican. Again, we know little that can help us to recapture the spirit that animated the college as a *studiuim generale*.[28] Minutes of the meetings of the professorial body were not kept, and the Primate's yearly reports are short and seldom go beyond a list of statistics. Very seldom is the curtain lifted to give us a glimpse of the life of individuals.

One such glimpse is of the sudden death of Fr. Thomas Aquinas Weikert from the American Abbey of St. Meinrad.[29] He was professor of Oriental languages at Sant'Anselmo.

Born in 1863 in Obereisbach in Bavaria, like many Germans at the time he emigrated when very young to North America, where at the age of twenty he entered the Abbey of St. Meinrad. Following his ordination to the priesthood, he stud-

Cf. Leonis XIII, *Carmina novissima* (Typis Vaticanis, 1903). See also *Messager de S. Benoît* 6 (1904): 142–46 (with French translation). Also, Hemptinne's circular letter dated December 31, 1903.

[28] See, however, L. Janssens, "Leon XIII et Pie X," *RBén* 20 (1903): 337–50.

[29] APr, Collegio II II I. Obituary, *StudMitt* 27 (1906): 773–76.

ied at Sant'Anselmo from 1891 where, after three years, he received a doctorate in philosophy. Already at this time he showed his particular love for Semitic languages, as a result of which he was soon entrusted with the teaching of these at Sant'Anselmo. In 1894–1895, with a view to perfecting his knowledge of the languages, he visited the Middle East. On his return to Sant'Anselmo, his prestige as an Orientalist rose rapidly. One after the other he accumulated an impressive collection of works in Hebrew, some of them rare. He had many Jewish friends, among them the Chief Rabbi of Rome, Vittorio Castiglioni, who honored Weikert's memory with an obituary in an Italian Jewish periodical.[30] The most important of Weikert's scholarly publications is a grammar of the Hebrew language, written in Latin, which reflects his excellent knowledge of the most refined aspects of the style of the language.[31] Weikert's publications demonstrated not only a deep knowledge of the Old Testament but also the profoundest study of rabbinical literature. Thus, it was inevitable that he came to the notice of the Roman Curia. In 1903 he was appointed one of the first members of the newly founded Papal Biblical Commission. A factor in his appointment may have been his tendency toward exegetical conservatism. During the summer vacation, Fr. Thomas used to leave Rome for Lourdes where he spent some months as a confessor. His knowledge of several modern languages made him particularly suited for this service at that much-visited center of pilgrimage. On June 30, 1906, he left Rome for Lourdes as usual. In the small French town of Les Arcs sur Argens, where he had broken his journey, he died suddenly on July 9. The cause of death could not be established with certainty—typhus or meningitis were possibilities. He was forty two years old.[32]

[30] *Il Vessillo Israelitico*, no. 54 (1906): 587–89.

[31] Th. A. Weikert, *Grammatica linguae hebraicae cum chrestomatihia et golssario studiis academicis accomodata necnon in usum domesticae disciplinae* (Rome, 1904).

[32] In the night of April 25 to 26, 1906, the death took place suddenly in the college of the first prior of Sant'Anselmo, Fr. Adalbert Miller (Müller). Born in 1842 in Baden, Miller emigrated at an early age to America and there entered St. Vincent in 1858. Boniface Wimmer sent him to Rome for studies where he obtained a doctorate in philosophy and the natural sciences. Ordained priest in 1865, he was novice master at St. Vincent before being sent back to Rome in 1887 as one of the founding monks of the new Sant'Anselmo. Gifted in many areas and universally esteemed for his modesty and happy disposition, he served Sant'Anselmo not only as prior but also as a teacher in several disciplines: philosophy, the natural sciences, Hebrew, biblical exegesis, dogmatic and moral theology. One fruit of his lectures is his book, *Hermeneutica sacra, Lectiones habitae mensibus Nov. et Dec. MCMI in Collegio*

The rector of Sant'Anselmo at the time was Fr. Laurentius Janssens from Maredsous.[33] His lectures in dogmatic theology, always delivered in brilliant and expressive Latin, followed strictly the Thomist neo-scholasticism prescribed for all Catholic theologians by Leo XIII and even more strongly by Pius X. Janssens, however, avoided extreme positions and opened up his explanations of the *Summa* of St. Thomas with references to the ancient fathers, in particular to Augustine and Anselm of Canterbury. The result of this teaching activity is Janssens' wide-ranging, if not very profound, commentary on the *Summa Theologiae*, which he published in no fewer than nine impressive volumes. The best of these, volumes one to seven, appeared between 1899 and 1905; the remainder, after a long interval, between 1918 and 1921.[34]

Sant'Anselmo, a destination for day-trippers

S. Anselmi de Urbe (Rome, 1902). Cf. obituaries, *Messager de S. Benoît* 8 (1906): 56; and *StudMitt* 27 (1906): 567.

[33] O. Rousseau, "Sa Grandeur Mgr. Janssens O.S.B.," *RLM* 10 (1925): 285–92; J. Alt, "Laurentius (Heinrich) Janssens," *Verbum* vol. 5 (1963): 301–8; G. Ghysens, *Bibliographie nationale . . . de Belgique*, 38 (Brussels, 1973), coll. 353–58 (list of publications).

[34] *Summa theologica ad modum commentarii in Aquinatis Summam praesentis aevi studiis aptatam*, vols. 1–3 (*De Deo uno*) (Rome, 1899); vol. 3, *De Deo trino* (Freiburg-im-Breisgau, 1900); vols. 4–5, *De Deo-Homine* (Freiburg-im-Breisgau, 1900–1902); vol. 6, *De Deo Creatore* (Freiburg-im-Breisgau), 1905; vols. 7–8, *De Homine* (Rome, 1918–1919); vol. 9, *De gratia Dei et Christi* (Freiburg-im-Breisgau), 1921. The work was not completed.

Already under Leo XIII the versatile Belgian had executed commissions for the Roman Curia. In October 1908 Pius X appointed him secretary of the newly created Congregation of Religious. With this appointment, Janssens left the teaching body of Sant'Anselmo and prepared himself for a career in the Roma Curia. A few months later, he was already titular abbot of Mont-Blandin in Ghent. All the signs seemed to favor the path toward a red hat as a matter of course. Then in 1910 Janssens committed a faux pas that changed the direction of his life.

The former president of the United States, Theodore Roosevelt, had requested via the ambassador of the United States at the Quirinale a private audience with Pius X. If the displeasure of the Vatican had already been aroused by the "detour" via the embassy to the Italian State, the mistrust was increased by the behavior of the former vice-president Charles Warren Fairbanks who, shortly after a private audience with the pope, delivered a strongly anti-Catholic lecture at the Methodist center in Rome. Pius X informed Roosevelt that he would grant an audience only if the former president would promise not to visit the Roman Methodists. As a result of this, Roosevelt, himself a Protestant, abandoned the idea of meeting the pope.[35]

Laurentius Janssens as a titular abbot

Laurentius Janssens, however, thought that making a private visit to Roosevelt would help to mend the "broken porcelain."[36] He did not meet Roosevelt in the latter's hotel but left his card with a message, thanking Roosevelt for his benevolence toward the Catholic Church in the United States and particularly toward Benedictines in North America. News of Janssens's behavior spread like wildfire as far as America and caused reactions of all kinds. On April 21 the cardinal secretary of state, Merry del Val, informed the apostolic delegate in the United States, Archbishop D. Falconio, by telegram that Janssens had offered his resignation as secretary of the Congregation of Religious and that this had been immediately accepted by the pope. In fact, on April 8, immediately after the incident, Pius X had summoned Janssens. Following the audience, Janssens was no longer secretary of the

[35] Concerning this incident see, *CivCatt* vol. 61, pt. 2 (1910), 232–37. Also, J. Schmidlin, *Papstgeschichte der neuesten Zeit* 3 (Munich, 1936): 66. Further, Fr. J. Zierlein, *Theodore Roosevelt and Catholics*, 1882–1919 (St. Louis: V. T. Suren, 1956), 343–49.

[36] Regarding what follows, cf., ASV, Segr. di Stato, year 1910, Rubr. 251, fasc. 2.

above-mentioned Vatican Congregation. Given the state of siege in which the papacy considered itself, Pius X reacted vigorously against even the suspicion that any member of the clergy might criticize the decisions of the Holy See.

Despite this éclat, Janssens was allowed to remain in Rome and continued to work for the Curia. In the Annuario Pontificio he was described as "Rettore emerito di S.Anselmo" (rector emeritus of Sant'Anselmo). He resumed his teaching activity in the college. In 1921, Pope Benedict XV, who did not continue the integrist policies of his predecessor, made Janssens titular bishop of Bethsaida, a sign of personal esteem by the pope and perhaps also a small gesture of compensation. Janssens was consecrated bishop in Sant'Anselmo by Cardinal van Rossum. Although his health and capacity for work seemed to be unbroken, he had only a short time to live. On July 17, 1925, following a short illness, he died at the motherhouse of the Scheut missionaries near Brussels.

Fr. Hartmann Strohsacker (1870–1946)

Janssens was an unusually gifted man. The ease with which he spoke Latin, English, German, and Italian, his talent as a speaker, and his sparkling wit quickly brought him into contact with many persons, many of whom, however, could be hurt by his mockery. He seemed enchanted by many areas of knowledge and art, poetry, drawing, photography, but above all, music. He was one of the pioneers of Gregorian chant during the period of renewal of church music, and as rector he directed the schola with skill and passion. As a theologian he was also a fighter. A verdict on the extent to which, as second secretary of the Pontifical Biblical Commission for many years, he was responsible for the markedly conservative decisions during the pontificate of Pius X must be left to future research.

In 1908 Hemptinne appointed Fr. Hartmann Strohsacker of Göttweig in Austria as rector of Sant'Anselmo in succession to Janssens.[37] Following his promotion as doctor of theology at Innsbruck in 1899, Strohsacker came to Sant'Anselmo where he taught dogmatic and pastoral theology and patristics. From 1906 he was also subprior. Academically he did not distinguish himself. Already in 1913 he was recalled to

[37] Strohsacker was born on July 6, 1870, professed on October 15, 1889, and ordained priest on July 16, 1893.

Göttweig *ob penuriam sacerdotum sui monasterii* (because of the lack of priests in his monastery).[38]

The first year of the new rector coincided with the spectacular event of the eight-hundredth anniversary of the death of St. Anselm of Canterbury.[39] In contrast to the way in which such centenaries are celebrated today, the centenary of 1909 was almost purely liturgical but celebrated with great pomp. The actual feast day of April 21 was preceded by a triduum that began on Sunday, April 18. Each of the three preparatory days was marked by pontifical Mass and pontifical Vespers. Vespers was followed by a special sermon presenting different aspects of the saint. This was followed on each of the days by solemn Benediction of the Blessed Sacrament in a packed church, given by Cardinals Rinaldi, Vincenzo Vanutelli, Satolli, and Rampolla. The pontifical Mass on the morning of April 19 caused particular interest in Rome since it was celebrated according to the Greek rite, the musical accompaniment being provided by the students of the Greek college.[40] The festal sermon by Laurentius Janssens won particularly high praise. He underlined the role of St. Anselm as a Doctor of the Church and showed his relevance, "particularly in the intellectual and religious disputes and challenges of the present time."[41]

For the actual feast day, Pius X had sent his vicar general, Cardinal Pietro Respighi, to celebrate the pontifical Mass at Sant'Anselmo in the presence of twenty-five bishops and abbots from many lands. In the afternoon, before the closing pontifical Vespers, there took place a so-called Festive Academy, greatly favored at this period. "Under the direction of the subprior, Fr. Suitbert Birkle of Seckau, the students played pieces by Haydn, Handel, Mozart, and Wagner with perfect artistry."[42]

[38] *AOSB* (1913): 31. In 1930 the chapter of Göttweig elected him abbot. Having survived the bitter period of the dissolution of the monastery by National Socialist oppression, he died on December 3, 1946, at Göttweig. See Cl. A. Lashofer, "Professbuch des Benediktinerstiftes Göttweig," in *StudMitt*, Supplementary vol. 26 (St. Ottilien, 1983): 201–87.

[39] *StudMitt* 30 (1909): 259–62. Also *SBSt* 33 (1909): 201–6.

[40] In 1897, Pope Leo XIII had entrusted the Greek college to the Benedictines. Abbot Primate Hemptinne was the actual superior until 1910. He agreed with Leo XIII's plans to foster closer relations with the Greek Church, but this was opposed by the Italo-Albanians. Pope Pius X did nothing to encourage Hemptinne's *activité orientale*. Hemptinne's successor, Stotzingen, was extremely reserved toward the Eastern Churches. Cf. Cl. Soetens, "Le Primat de Hemptinne et les Bénédictins au Collège Grec 1897–1912," in *Il Collegio greco di Roma. Ricerche sugli alunni, la direzione, l'attività*, ed. A. Fyrigos (Rome: Pontificio Collegio Greco, 1983), 201–87.

[41] *SBSt* 33 (1908): 204.

[42] *StudMitt* 30 (1909): 262.

Students arriving at the College

Sant'Anselmo knew how to organize brilliant celebrations! Again and again reports of these are to be found in the sources. Clearly they were a welcome change from the strict monastic rhythm of life in the college. Hemptinne had a wide network of connections in society, in particular with the nobility. There was no lack of opportunities to stage a celebration. Thus, in November 1908, the college joined all of Catholic Rome in celebrating the golden jubilee of the priestly ordination of Pius X with illuminations of the house and a festive academy.[43] In the refectory on November 17 were present not only cardinals and bishops but also Baron von Schorlemer, extraordinary ambassador of the German emperor; Prince Johannes Hohenlohe-Bartenstein, envoy of the Prince Regent of Bavaria; Count Smet de Waeger, the Belgian extraordinary envoy; and several others. "A deep silence reigned when the Primate began a brilliant speech in French in which he extended words of greeting and welcome on behalf of the Benedictines of Sant'Anselmo to the

[43] *StudMitt* 29 (1908): 750ff.

illustrious guests and to the sovereigns who had sent them to the Eternal City." The chronicler reported that "he expressed fine words of homage for the noble emperor of the German people, who had in so many ways demonstrated his favor toward and admiration for the Benedictine Order." Such words and gestures were still possible before the outbreak of the tragic world war!

Fr. Suitbert Birkle at a musical interlude in Sant'Anselmo

The annals for the same year report the celebration at Sant'Anselmo on December 3 of the diamond jubilee of the reign of Emperor Francis Joseph of Austria-Hungary. This took place in the presence of Cardinals Agliardi and Rinadli, the Austro-Hungarian ambassador to the Holy See, Count Szechen, and other guests. In the hall, decorated with a portrait of the emperor and with many flowers, a festive academy was held at noon during which the students, under the direction of Fr. Suitbert Birkle, performed pieces by Schosser, Tinel, and Haydn. The new secretary of the Congregation of Religious, Laurentius Janssens, gave masterly performances of pieces by Beethoven and Schubert on the cello with piano accompaniment, "and once the Radetzky March had been played, the anthem 'God save the Emperor' filled the hall, sung with enthusiasm by the young voices of the students." During the lunch that followed, the Abbot Primate celebrated Austria and its emperor. "Ambassador Count Szechen raised his glass to the health of the Benedictine Order and the guests remained gathered for a long time in animated conversation in Sant'Anselmo."[44]

In the summer of 1910, Hemptinne spent several months in the United States visiting the monasteries there.[45] He returned an ill man, "broken, with the hand of one suffering from fever, he described his experiences in the New World and was almost unable to climb the stairs anymore."[46] From then on his health visibly declined. Following a stroke in October 1912, he asked Pius X to allow him to resign. The pope, however, did not accept the resignation but ordered instead the

[44] "Festfeier anläßlich des 60-jähigen Regierungsjubiläums Sr. Majestät des Kaisers Franz Josef von Österreich," *StudMitt* 29 (1908): 752.

[45] *AOSB* (1911): 27–29, with a list of places visited.

[46] Cf. Pl. Glogger, *BenM* 16 (1943): 138.

The Congress of Abbots of 1913 before the election of the Abbot Primate

election of a coadjutor. The rector of Sant'Anselmo, Fr. Hartmann Strohsacker, received a papal instruction to summon a Congress of Abbots to be held at Sant'Anselmo.[47] The congress took place at Sant'Anselmo during the academic year from May 12–14, within the octave of Pentecost. Seventy-four of the 101 entitled to vote had come in response to the rector's invitation. Most of the absent electors were represented by procurators. Already in the first ballot the abbot of Einsiedeln, Thomas Bossart, who from 1895 to 1896 had been a universally appreciated professor of dogmatic theology at Sant'Anselmo, received eighty-four of the ninety-eight votes.[48]

Hemptinne on the boat to the United States in 1910

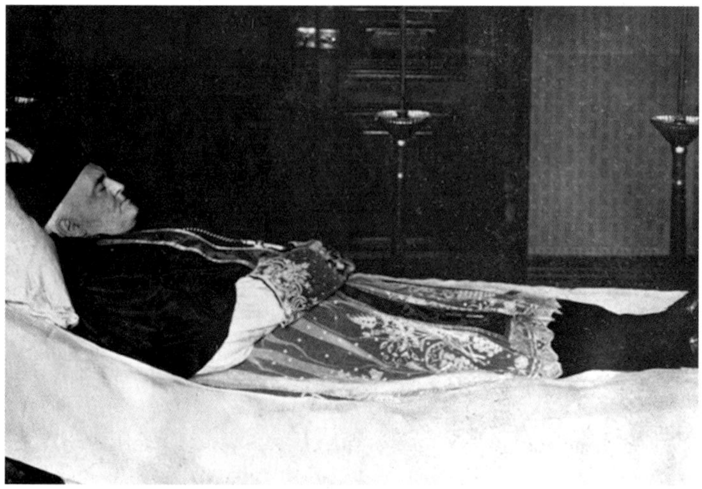

Hemptinne lying in state at Beuron in 1913

Bossart, however, did not accept the election. At the suggestion of the rector, the decision was left to the pope, who on the following day through the cardinal secretary of state, Merry del Val, replied that he did not wish to deprive Bossart of his freedom. If the latter was still determined to refuse, then a new scrutiny should take place. This then took place. In a new ballot on the afternoon of Pentecost Tuesday, the abbot of Maria Laach, Fidelis von Stotzingen, received seventy-five of the ninety-nine votes cast. He accepted election as coadjutor and shortly afterward resigned as abbot of his home monastery. Some months later,

[47] APr, Congr. Abb. 1913; Electio Coadjutoris 1913; Renner, 253f.

[48] On Th. Bossart (1858–1923), see R. Henggler, *Professbuch der Fürst. Benediktinerabtei U.L. Frau zu Einsiedeln* (Einsiedeln, 1933), 217–21.

on August 13, 1913, Hildebrand de Hemptinne died at Beuron, his original monastery of profession. Thus began the period of office of the second Abbot Primate, whose views on the role of the Collegium Anselmianum within the Order and of its monastic-academic character hardly differed from those of his predecessor. Both were Beuronese and both were noble.

Fidelis Franz Wilhelm Baron von Stotzingen belonged to the ancient Swabian nobility of the knightly class.[49] The family had formerly been in the service of the House of Habsburg when the territory of West Austria (Vorderösterreich) belonged to that house. The future Primate was born on May 1, 1871, in Steißlingen in Baden, the son of Baron Roderich von Stotzingen and his wife, Karoline, née Countess von Rechberg und Rothenlöwen. Having completed his secondary education at Würzburg, Fidelis, not yet twenty years old, entered Beuron in 1891. He was a straggly youth with bad posture and lacked a musical ear. He was, however, polite, with exquisite manners and deep faith. From 1892 to 1898 the young monk studied theology and philosophy at Sant'Anselmo. He was an excellent student, mostly notable for his industry. In September 1898 he took over the readership in dogmatic theology at the Beuronese theological school, having been ordained to the priesthood a year previously.

Abbot Thomas Bossart (1858–1923)

Fr. Odo Casel (1886–1948)

[49] Regarding what follows, see ArchMaria Laach, Obituary of Abbot Primate Fidelis von Stotzingen. Further, G. Bartsch in *BenM* 23 (1947): 18–20; B. Neunheuser, *Liturgie u. Mönchtum* 2 (1948), 57–63; L. Eberle, "Abbot Primate Fidelis von Stotzingen," *ABenR* 4 (1953): 101–14.

The second important period of his life following his entry at Beuron began in 1901. Barely thirty years of age and in his absence, on the morning of October 31, following a rapid ballot, the monks of Maria Laach elected him second abbot of the restored monastery in succession to the saintly Wilibrord Benzler who had become bishop of Metz. Stotzingen's significance for Maria Laach and what he did for this monastery are not part of the history of Sant'Anselmo. Suffice it to say that his abbacy was a period of extraordinary flowering both inside the monastery (he professed sixty-three monks) and high esteem from outside. A frequent visitor was the German emperor, William II. For all his unshaken fidelity to Beuronese observance, Abbot Fidelis was the first to overcome the Beuronese mistrust of university studies for monks, and in 1904, he was the first to send a priest for scientific studies at a state university.

Stotzingen felt that in Laach he was in the right place, and many abbots in the Order may have quietly envied him his blossoming monastery in the Eifel, full of young monks. Without a doubt, the transfer to Rome was also a bitter sacrifice for Abbot Fidelis. The office of Abbot Primate was new to the Order and its position, "peculiarly floating, in the final analysis of undefinable character, delicate and difficult regarding the monasteries and especially difficult also in regard to the Roman Curia."[50]

Fidelis von Stotzingen stuck to this post for thirty-three years. Unlike the first Primate, he was not creative by nature, his talents were more limited, his judgment narrower, and his manner of procedure more cautious and timid. He was, however, "a man of absolute fidelity to the monastic ideal and unglamorous detail of day-to-day administration."[51] If in the following years far fewer brilliant celebrations took place at Sant'Anselmo than had been the case under the worldly wise and vivacious Hemptinne, this was partly because of the more introverted personality of the second Primate, who avoided appearances in society. Another reason was the greater poverty of Sant'Anselmo in the postwar years.

Up to the outbreak of the First World War, despite slight fluctuations, the number of students constantly grew. In 1900 there were sixty-one Benedictine students, while in 1910 there were seventy-two. In addition, there were three Cistercian students and six from the Mercedarian Order.[52] One of the students in 1910 was Odo Casel from Maria Laach. He

[50] Neunheuser, *Liturgie u. Mönchtum*, 60.

[51] Obituary, p. 22.

[52] Hemptinne, circular letter dated October 4, 1910.

was at Sant'Anselmo from 1908 to 1913 when he completed his studies with a doctorate in theology.[53] His dissertation, which was published—a rare distinction at the time—dealt with the eucharistic doctrine of St. Justin Martyr.[54]

Fidelis von Stotzingen as abbot of Maria Laach

In 1914 the college had seventy-five Benedictine students. In addition, there were six Cistercians, one Camaldolese, and one Olivetan. The main theology course, *Theologia maior*, had thirty-eight inscribed students and the nonacademic *Theologia minor*, twenty-eight. There were eight inscriptions for canon law and the same number for the *Philosophia maior* course while *Philosophia minor* had thirteen. Several students were simultaneously registered for different courses.

There were eleven professors to teach these students. Following the departure of Fr. Hartmann Strohsacker, the new Primate appointed Fr. Suitbert Birkle from Seckau as pro-rector.[55] He had been teaching dogmatics at Sant'Anselmo since 1908, was subprior, instructor of lay brothers, and chanter. The second professor of dogmatic theology was Fr. Ambrose Kohlbeck from St. Vincent. Fr. Hildebrand Höpfl from

[53] From the many works written about Casel—constantly reviewed in *ALW*—it is sufficient here to mention B. Neunheuser, *Casel, Odo,* in *TRE* 7 (1981): 643–47; and A. Schilson, *Theologie als Sakramentaltheologie. Die Mysterientheologie Odo Casels* (Mainz, 1982).

[54] O. Casel, "Die Eucharistielehre des hl. Justinus Martyr," *Der Katholik* 94, no. 13 (1914): 153–76, 243–63, 331–55, 414–36.

[55] Stotzingen, circular letter dated July 20, 1914, *AOSB* (1913): 31f.; and *AOSB* (1914–1919), 61–67.

Fr. Ambrosius Kohlbeck (1869–1931)

Fr. Ildefons Schuster (1880–1954)

Fr. Chysostomus Baur (1876–1962)

Emmaus/Prague taught exegesis and introduction to the Bible, moral and pastoral theology and homiletics were in the hands of Fr. Kallistus Kohler of Beuron; while Fr. Ildefonso Schuster of St. Paul Outside the Walls was a new member of the teaching body as lecturer in ecclesiastical history,[56] replacing the patrologist Fr. Chrysostomus Baur who had returned to Seckau.[57] Another new face was Fr. Bonaventura Ubach of Montserrat, an excellent Orientalist, who took over the teaching of Hebrew and Arabic. Philosophy was represented by Fr. Josef Gredt of Seckau and Fr. Ramiro Marcone of S. Giulano at Genoa. Legal studies were the responsibility of Fr. Augustine Bachofen of Conception Abbey and Fr. Justinian Serédi from Pannonhlama for canon law along with Fr. Constantin von Hohenlohe-Schillingsfurst of Seckau for *Jus civile Romanum*. To complete the list of the community of Sant'Anselmo for 1914, it should also be mentioned that there were three officials.

[56] T. Leccisotti's comprehensive but unfortunately too hagiographical biography of Schuster, *Il Cardinale Schuster*, 2 vols. (Milan, 1969), says nothing about Schuster's activity as a professor at Sant'Anselmo. Nor is there anything but scant mention of Schutser's studies at Sant'Anselmo (cf. vol. 1, pp. 46–50). More valuable is the series of articles by B. Baur, *Aus dem Leben des Kard. Ildefons Schuster von Mailand*, *BenM* 32 (1956): 275–81, 367–72, 457–64. Cf. also Baur, *BenM* 33 (1957): 10–23, 101–20. Further, R. Beron, ²*LThK* 9 (1964): 521. Schuster completed his studies at Sant'Anselmo in 1903 with a doctorate in philosophy, along with Fr. Alcuin Deutsch, later abbot of Collegeville and a great benefactor of the college.

[57] V. Redlich, "Zum Tod von P. Chrysostomus Baur von Seckau," *EuA* 38 (1962): 155.

Fr. Hilarius Walter of Beuron was secretary to the Abbot Primate, master of ceremonies, librarian, archivist, and annalist. Fr. Lambert Courtois from Afflighem was cellarer, infirmarian, and guest master, while Fr. Daniel Feuling of Beuron was second secretary to the Abbot Primate and sacristan. All physical work in the house, kitchen, and garden was performed by sixteen lay brothers, all of whom—with one exception, Br. Alexius Mathian, 1871–1933, who, unique in history, had made profession for Sant'Anselmo—were members of the Beuronese Congregation.

This presentation of the personnel of Sant'Anselmo provides a picture of the situation in the years before the First World War, but also the background to the decision by Pope Pius X to confirm by *Motu Proprio* Sant'Anselmo's right to confer academic degrees, including doctoral decrees, in philosophy, theology, and canon law.[58] With this *Motu Proprio* not only was a legal uncertainty removed—hitherto degrees had been granted on the basis of a verbal permission from Pope Leo XIII and a rescript of 1891 from the Congregation for Studies—but also the privilege granted by Pius X went further in that it specifically gave Sant'Anselmo the same status as the other Roman papal universities and recognized canon law as a separate course. The essential section of the *Motu Proprio* reads:

Fr. Augustin Bachofen (1872–1943)

Fr. Kallistus Kohler (1880–1947)

Fr. Hilarius Walter (1871–1940)

[58] *Motu Proprio* "Praeclara inter opera," June 24, 1914, *AAS* vol. 6 (1914): 333–35. See also *AOSB* (1914–1919): 8–9.

> After mature deliberation on the situation and having consulted our beloved son the Cardinal Prefect of the Congregation for Studies, we decree by our apostolic authority and on our own initiative that the Benedictine College of Sant'Anselmo in Rome, like the other academies in the city, should possess for ever the privilege of conferring academic degrees in philosophy as well as sacred theology and canon law on its students from both the secular and regular clergy who have studied in the above-mentioned college and successfully completed examinations to the satisfaction of a majority of its professors.
>
> In order that this privilege will bear greater fruit not only to the Order but also to the Church, it is our wish and command that the professors of the college of Sant'Anselmo, when treating of philosophical as well as theological material, always follow the teaching of St. Thomas Aquinas and that the text used as the basis for lectures for students whose goal is an academic degree should be that of St. Thomas. Departure from [the teaching of] Thomas Aquinas, particularly in philosophy and in theology, cannot, as we have already said, but lead to great damage. To follow him is the surest way to acquire a deep knowledge of things divine.[59]

[59] "Itaque re mature perpensa, collatisque consiliis cum dilecto Filio Nostro, Cardinali S. Congregationi Studiorum Praefecto, apostolica Nostra auctoritate ac Motu Proprio statuimus, ut Collegium Benedictinorum S. Anselmi de Urbe ad instar aliarum academiarum in Urbe existentium, perpetuo privilegium obtineat conferendi omnes gradus academicos cum in philosophia, tum in sacra theologia, tum in jure canonico alumnis utriusque cleri, saecularis ac regularis, qui rite laudati Collegii scholas in memoratis facultatibus frequentaverint et, periculo coram Collegii professoribus facto, majorem suffragiorum partem retulerint. Quo autem salubriores hoc privilegium et Ordini et Ecclesiae fructus ferat, volumus et praecipimus, ut professores Collegii Anselmiani in re tum philosophica tum theologica doctrinam semper sequantur Aquinatis, atque in praelectionibus sacrae theolgiae pro alumnis, qui ad academicos gradus contendunt, ipsum textum S.Thomae ad hibeant. Aquinatem enim deserere, in re philosophica praesertim et theologica, uti jam diximus, non sine magno detrimento esse potest; ipsum sequi tutissima est via ad profundam divinarum rerum cognitionem" (*ASS* 6 [1914]: 35). Pius X's *Motu Proprio* must be seen in the context of his other legislation regarding studies, which entered into great detail and even prescribed the daily timetable for Italian seminaries; cf. *ASS* 40 (1907): 336–43; *ASS* 41 (1908): 212–42. On June 29, 1914, a few days after the *Motu Proprio* for Sant'Anselmo, Pius X issued the *Motu Proprio* "Doctoris Angelici," which renewed the preeminence of Thomism and compelled theological faculties to base their teaching on the *Summa* of Thomas Aquinas. See *AAS* 6 (1914): 336–41.

View of the College from the east

The *Motu Proprio* is dated June 24, 1914. Some days previously, Pius X, on the feast of Corpus Christi, invited the whole college—professors, officials, students, and lay brothers—to a private audience in the Vatican.

When the academic year came to its usual end on the feast of Saints Peter and Paul and professors and students had departed for the well-deserved vacation, no one could have guessed that the First World War would break out and that Pius X would die on August 20, 1914. On the outbreak of war, the Primate returned immediately to Rome, arriving on August 18. As soon as the pope heard of his return, he summoned Stotzingen to an audience for August 19. This audience, however, never took place.[60]

[60] *AOSB* (1914–1919): 67.

Monument to Abbot Primate Hildebrand de Hemptinne in the cloister of Sant'Anselmo erected by the "grateful abbots." The coats of arms in mosaic are those of the Congregations belonging to the Confederation at that time. In a circle from left above to right above: The Cassinese Congregation, the Hungarian Congregation, the Brazilian Congregation, the American-Cassinese Congregation, the Congregation of Sankt Ottilien, the Austrian Congregation of St. Joseph, the Austrian Congregation of the Immaculate Conception, the Swiss Congregation, the Congregation of Subiaco, the Swiss-American Congregation, the Congregation of the Annunciation, the Beuronese Congregation, the Congregation of Solesmes, the Bavarian Congregation, the English Congregation.

Chapter 3

Sant'Anselmo from 1914 to 1945

1. The College as a Military Hospital and Afterward

Although it still seemed in August and September 1914 that the new academic year in Rome could not begin, the new pope, Benedict XV, pressed for the reopening of the Roman colleges as in peacetime. Thus, on October 1 the Abbot Primate sent a circular letter to the abbots whose clerics had been studying at Sant'Anselmo, informing them that the school year would commence as usual.[1] Because of the delay in sending the news and the uncertainty of the political situation, few of the students had arrived when the academic year began on November 1, 1914. Soon, however, the number rose to sixty, even if students from the belligerent powers were few. Fr. Hildebrand Höpfl, professor of scriptural sciences, did not arrive in Rome until December 8. At the outbreak of war he had been at Montserrat, and it was only as a result of the intervention of Cardinal Pietro Gasparri and carrying a letter of recommendation from the British embassy in Madrid that he was able to return to Italy.

Once the war had begun, Italy still wavered between the two sides, undecided whether to support the Allies or the Axis powers. Officially, Italy was still neutral, but already the Abbot Primate and Sant'Anselmo were attacked by the Italian public, the former as "a friend of the Kaiser," the latter as a nest of "Tedeschi" (Germans). The wildest rumors circulated, such as Sant'Anselmo was one great depot for German weapons. At the insistence of the Abbot Primate, the Italian police searched the house from top to bottom. Naturally, nothing was found, not even a single pistol.[2]

[1] *AOSB* (1914–1919): 67f.

[2] L. Eberle, "Abbot Primate Fidelis von Stotzingen," in *AbenR* 4 (1953): 101–14; cf. ibid., 109.

Sant'Anselmo with the neighboring Generalate of the Dominicans at Santa Sabina

Already on January 9, 1915, Pope Benedict XV granted the whole college a first private audience in the throne room of the Vatican. The pope underlined that not only did he want to be called protector of the Benedictine Order but also wanted actually to be that. "The new college, it is true, has existed for only a few years, but its fame is not negligible. Not to mention the studies which are pursued in this college with traditional Benedictine thoroughness, one need only refer to the happy reform of Church music originating in the Aventine and the promising work of the Commission on the new edition of the Vulgate."[3]

The latter reference of the pope was to a task that Pius X had entrusted to the Benedictine Order in 1907. The commission, under the leadership of the then-president of the English Congregation, Dom Aidan Gasquet, established its seat at Sant'Anselmo in November 1907. Since, however, the number of students at Sant'Anselmo was increasing every year, a new location for the Vulgate commission and its valuable specialized library had to be found. Abbot Gasquet, who had been made a cardinal in 1913, rented a part of the Palazzo S. Callisto in Trastevere, which belonged to the Benedictines of St. Paul's Outside the Walls, and in December 1914, the commission moved to this new accommodation. At that time the commission was composed of seven members, all exceptionally learned members of the Order from several countries. In 1933,

[3] Cf. *StudMitt* 36 (1915): 325.

Pius XI reorganized the work of the commission and erected the Abbey of St. Jerome for it.[4]

Abbot Primate Fidelis von Stotzingen

The feast of St. Joseph, which in 1915 fell on April 21, was once more marked by a glittering celebration at Sant'Anselmo. On this day D. Gregorio Grasso, the abbot of Montevergine who had been appointed archbishop of Salerno, was consecrated bishop. As a former student of Sant'Anselmo, he wanted the ceremony to be held on the Aventine. Several bishops and twelve abbots took part in the consecration, and there were nearly five hundred guests at the reception that followed in the refectory of the college. The shadows of war, however, were already cast over Sant'Anselmo. At the end of April, on the instructions of the German consulate, all Germans eligible for military service were ordered to return home. Seven clerics and one lay brother were affected by this order. "Soon ever more serious reports began to arrive from all quarters so that the Vatican and the ambassadors advised in the first days of May that citizens of the Austrian and German Empires should be sent home."[5] On May 5, 1915, the Abbot Primate bowed to the inevitable. After supper, he announced without any further explanation that the college had been closed for an indefinite period. On the following day, almost all the professors, students, and lay brothers left the house. Among those who remained behind were two American professors, Fr. Augustine Bachofen of Conception Abbey and Fr. Ambrose Kohlbeck of St. Vincent. On May 8 they succumbed to curiosity about the feeling in a Rome gripped by war fever. As protection they both carried small American flags in their hands. Fr. Bachofen reported later that when they returned to Sant'Anselmo in the evening they met the Abbot Primate in the atrium. In great fear the Primate begged them on his knees to leave Rome immediately. He could no longer guarantee their safety. He himself intended to remain at Sant'Anselmo regardless of what might happen. Thus, on the following day, both Americans left the college and traveled via Milan to Switzerland. Some days later, watching the trains arriving at the station in Lugano, they suddenly discovered Abbot Primate Fidelis in

[4] See "Die Vulgata-Revision im Jahre 1913," *StudMitt* 35 (1914): 405f.; also, "S. Callisto in Rom, die Abtei der Vulgata-Kommission," *StudMitt* 36 (1915): 328f.; J. Schildenberger, "Arbeit an der lateinischen Bibel," *BenM* 17 (1935): 401–8; P. Salmon, "San Girolamo, Abbazia di," in *Enciclopedia Cattolica,* vol. 10 (1953), coll. 1770f.

[5] Cf. *StudMitt* 36 (1915): 326.

the crowd. When asked why he had left Rome despite his intention to remain, he replied with his usual simplicity, "because the Secretary of State—Cardinal Gasparri—ordered me to do so."[6] It was May 12, 1915. The Primate found refuge in the monastery of Einsiedeln, where he lived for the next four years. Before his departure from Rome, he had transferred the administration of Sant'Anselmo to the abbot general of the Congregation of Subiaco, Don Mauro Serafini. For this reason, the latter lived in Sant'Anselmo until 1919. In addition, the college was supervised by Fr. Pierre Bastien of Maredsous, who maintained contacts with the Roman Curia, and by Fr. Bonaventura Ubach of Montserrat, who took over the task of cellarer or, more accurately, that of factotum.[7] There was a fourth "watchman" in the person of the titular Abbot Paolo Ferretti of the Subiaco Congregation who had been lecturing on Gregorian chant at the papal musical institute "Musica Sacra" since 1911 and was to become its president in 1922. In the place of the Beuronese lay brothers who had been withdrawn, services in the college were taken over by three brothers from the Congregation of Subiaco who had had to leave Palestine as a result of the war there. Despite the small number of residents in the large house, the monks gave great importance to the recitation of at least part of the Divine Office in choir.

Fr. Philibert Schmitz (1888–1963)

Abbot Ildefons Schuster as Abbot of St. Paul's Outside the Wall at study

[6] Eberle, "Abbot Primate Fidelis von Stotzingen," pp.109f.

[7] R. M. Diaz, *Dom Bonaventura Ubach. L'homo, el monjo, el biblista* (Barcelona, 1962), 86f.

From the spring of 1916 the Italian government began to transform schools and public buildings into military hospitals. Since the threat of confiscation also lay over Sant'Anselmo, those responsible for the college, with the agreement of the Holy See, voluntarily offered the government the greater part of the house for use as a military hospital. At the end of September 1916, following some necessary building alterations, including the erection of a wall separating the hospital from the area reserved for the monks, the first patients arrived. D. Lorenzo Salvi was appointed military chaplain of Sant'Anselmo. In 1917 Salvi became the first Abbot Ordinary of Subiaco, following Pope Benedict XV's renunciation of the centuries-old papal office of commendatory abbot of the Abbey of St. Scholastica. Other monks of the Subiaco Congregation who had been called up for military service worked as medical orderlies in the hospital. Thus, the number of Benedictines at Sant'Anselmo gradually rose again so that it became possible to celebrate the liturgy, particularly on the great feasts such as Christmas, with a certain solemnity and with the participation of doctors, nurses, and patients. Sant'Anselmo continued to be used as a military hospital until July 1919.

Following the closure of the college, several abbots had expressed the wish that students who had begun their studies at Sant'Anselmo should be given the opportunity of completing these studies according to the Roman system in an Austrian monastery. Thus in the autumn of 1915, a replacement for Sant'Anselmo was opened at the monastery of Seckau in the Steiremark. This was intended primarily for Austrian Benedictine students, but there were also some clerics from the Beuronese Congregation, from Switzerland, and even from North America. In addition, the Capuchins of the Steiermark sent seven friars for studies, so the number of students quickly rose to forty-two. The rector of the temporary college was Fr. Suitbert Birkle of Seckau, assisted by Fr. Josef Gredt, Fr. Hildebrand Höpfl, and others from the Beuronese Congregation. The full philosophical and theological courses were continued until June 1917. Only then were they suspended, pending the reopening of Sant'Anselmo in Rome.[8]

On the first Sunday of 1919, the day had arrived. The number of students who had come for the new academic year amounted to nearly forty. The Abbot Primate, however, justifiably wrote in his circular letter for Christmas 1919, "Hardly anyone can fail to recognize that the war has greatly changed our college of St. Anselm and the whole Order." These changes were noticeable at Sant'Anselmo by quite a change in the

[8] Cf. *StudMitt* 37 (1916): 641f. See also, *AOSB* (1914–1919): 69–72.

Professors and students in 1921

professorial body. The former rector, Fr. Suitbert Birkle, did not return to Rome.[9] The Primate had to find a replacement. His first choice was Fr. Romuald Simó of Montserrat, but by the academic year 1920–1921, Simó was replaced by Fr. Patrick Cummins from Conception Abbey. Otherwise in these years there was a noticeable fluctuation in the membership of the teaching body.

At the Synod of Abbots President in 1920, the Primate urgently requested the abbots to provide suitable teachers. In order to maintain the philosophical, theological, and canon law courses as required by the regulations, a minimum of fifteen professors would be needed.[10] There was a particular lack of teachers of philosophy and dogmatic theology. Too often, competent teachers were recalled to their home monasteries; thus, Fr. Karl Jellouschek of the Schotten monastery in Vienna was recalled after having taught dogmatics for only one year. Again, Fr. Simon Landersdorfer of Scheyern was elected abbot of his

[9] Sent to Brazil in 1921 to help the Brazilian Congregation, Fr. Suitbert Birkle ran that Congregation's theological school for four years until his election as abbot of Seckau in 1925. He died suddenly on February 27, 1926. See AOSB (1920–1926): 238f.

[10] *Protocollum Synodi Revmorum el Illmorum Abbatum Praesidum Congregationum Confoederatarum O.S.B. mense Maio anni 1920 in aedibus S. Anselmi de Urbe habitae* (Rome: Typis Polyglottis Vaticanis, 1920), 25.

monastery just as Fr. Ildefonso Schuster had been elected abbot of St. Paul's Outside the Walls—though in this case the abbot continued to give lectures on liturgy. Others could not cope with the Roman climate or had to leave the college for health reasons. Among these were Fr. Philibert Schmitz of Maredsous, later to become a famous historian of the Order, who had taught ecclesiastical history from 1920 to 1924 at Sant'Anselmo and had taken care of the library. He was a former student of Sant'Anselmo who in 1913 had obtained a doctorate in theology with a thesis on Rupert von Deutz. Because of a disease that affected his voice, he had to abandon his teaching career in Sant'Anselmo. In later years he was hardly ever capable of speaking in public.[11]

Fr. Bonaventura Ubach (1879–1960)

A great loss to Sant'Anselmo was the return to Montserrat in 1924 of Fr. Bonaventura Ubach. In him the college lost one of its most competent and versatile professors.[12] He was temperamentally the complete opposite of Fr. Philibert Schmitz. If the latter was naturally very reserved, almost shy and not interested in travel, Fr. Bonaventura Ubach not only possessed, in addition to an astonishing capacity for work, a gregariousness and eagerness to learn about other peoples and cultures and a delight in long and arduous journeys. Ubach was born in Barcelona in 1879. He came to Montserrat at the age of twelve to the then-college for overseas missions (Colegio de Misioneros de Ultramar). At the age of fifteen he was already a novice and made first profession at sixteen. During his years as a cleric he already showed his preference for Bible studies and in particular for Oriental languages. Following his ordination to the priesthood in 1902, he began to lecture on the introduction to Scripture and taught Hebrew to his younger colleagues at Montserrat's own theological school. He was able to visit Jerusalem for the first time in 1906, registering for three courses at the Dominican Bible school.

[11] In 1928 he became editor of the RBén in Maredsous, a post he held until 1957, as well as librarian until 1953. The first two volumes of the *Histoire de l'Ordre de S. Benoît* appeared in 1942, the seventh volume in 1957. Schmitz died at Maredsous in 1963. For obituaries, see Th. Delforge, *EuA* 40 (1964): 75–77; P. Verbraken, *StMon* 6 (1964): 218–20; D. Misonne, *Yermo* 2 (1964): 71–73; D. Misonne. *RHE* 59 (1964): 260f.; T. Moral, *ABenR* 15 (1964): 458–65 (with bibliography).

[12] R. M. Diaz, in *Miscellanea Biblica B. Ubach,* Scripta et Documenta 1 (Montserrat, 1953), 1–14; ibid., Dom Bonaventura Ubach (A. 7), 73–78.

Here, he met the famous exegete Fr. M. J. Lagrange. This was the first of many journeys to biblical lands which at that time retained many of their original characteristics. The result of these journeys was, above all, a comprehensive collection of artifacts connected with the Bible that is preserved today in the Bible Museum at Montserrat. At this time, too, Fr. Ubach began a series of publications in which he attempted to explain the Bible in the light of archaeology and the customs of the Bedouin he had studied. Meetings with Arabs were easy for him since in 1908 and 1909 he had learned both spoken and literary Arabic in Lebanon.

Ubach came to Sant'Anselmo in 1913 as professor of Oriental languages. The fruit of his teaching activity is a two-volume Hebrew grammar titled *Legisne Toram*? ("Can you read the Torah?") that was published in 1918–1919.[13] A German reviewer rightly emphasized the novelty of Ubach's method, "which is usually employed only in a conversation-grammar for a modern language."[14] In 1917 Pope Benedict XV had established the Oriental Institute in Rome. Fr. Ubach was one of its first professors, initially of Syriac, later also of Hebrew. At this time he began, at the express wish of Benedict XV, to initiate contacts with the Syrian Orthodox Christians separated from Rome. These conversations were continued under Pius XI. For this purpose he spent time in the Middle East during 1922–1923. He also received permission to celebrate in the Syrian-Antiochean Rite. This involvement with Eastern Churches did not mean that his interest in biblical archaeology suffered. His thirst for knowledge brought him as far as Mesopotamia and Persia. He taught Hebrew for the last time at Sant'Anselmo in the academic year 1923–1924. Behind his departure from Rome was his extensive project to publish a Catalan version of the Bible with commentary and scientifically useful illustrations. This *Bíblia de Montserrat* became his life's work, which was not yet completed on his death in 1960.[15]

In 1925, a year after Ubach's departure from Sant'Anselmo, the college once more suffered the loss of an excellent teacher and one much loved by the students when Fr. Lambert Beauduin returned to his home monastery of Mont César in Louvain.[16] He had taught for only a few years at Sant'Anselmo, since 1921, but they were influential years in

[13] B. Ubach, *Legisne Toram? Grammatica practica lingue hebraicae seminaris scholisque publicis accomodata,* 2 vols. (Montserrat, 1918–1919).

[14] B. Vandenhoff, *ThRv* 27 (1928): 172.

[15] J. Schildenberger, "Das Bibelwerk der Abtei Montserrat," *BenM* 34 (1958): 38–41.

[16] On Lambert Beauduin (1873–1960) see the obituaries by O. Rousseau, *Irén.* 33 (1960): 3–28 (with bibliography); also, V. Fiala, *EuA* 36 (1960): 139–45. Further, the article "Beauduin" in *The Oxford Dictionary of the Christian Church,* 2nd. ed., ed. F.

his life and had a special significance beyond the confines of Sant'Anselmo. Beauduin taught fundamental theology at the college. In the Primate's circular letter, his departure was explained by "pressing needs" of his home monastery.[17] These laconic words concealed more exciting realties than an unsuspecting reader at the time might have imagined.

Fr. Lambert Beauduin (1973–1960) circa 1922

Lambert Beauduin was already a workers' chaplain when he entered the monastery of Mont César at Louvain in 1906. Mont César was a foundation of Maredsous and at that time still belonged to the Beuronese Congregation. Early on, Beauduin realized that the liturgy which was celebrated so solemnly in Beuronese monasteries ought not to be a privilege of an educated elite but must become the soul of the spiritual life of a parish. Further, the treasures of the Missal should be made available to and understood by ordinary people, and the active participation of all the faithful in the liturgy should be promoted. On September 29, 1909, at the Catholic Congress in Malines, Beauduin outlined this idea, as simple as it was correct, so convincingly that his hearers reacted with delighted applause. This "Event at Malines" is one of the milestones of the liturgical movement.[18]

The First World War interrupted Beauduin's pastoral-liturgical apostolate that had begun so promisingly. He spent the war years in exile in Ireland. By the time he returned to Louvain he had already identified another goal worth fighting for. Beauduin was a man of stormy temperament and irrepressible speech who did not make life easy for his superiors. The new idea to which he now devoted his energies was the simplification of monastic life. Thus, Abbot Robert de Kerchove, abbot of Mont Cèsar, a man strongly attached to Beuronese observance, must have been relieved when Abbot Primate Fidelis von Stotzingen

L. Cross and E. A. Livingstone (London, 1983), 147. See also *Catholicisme hier, aujourd'hui, demain*, vol. 9 (Paris, 1982), col. 1518.

[17] "Insuper decursu huius anni scholastici ob urgente necessitates revocati sunt ad propria monasteria R. P. D. Lambertus Beauduin, lector Theologiae fundamentalis et R. P. D. Gabriel Tissot, qui Patrologiam et S. Liturgiam tradebat," in circular letter from Stotzingen dated June 30, 1925.

[18] B. Fischer, "Das 'Mechelner Ereignis' vom 23. September, 1909," *Liturg. Jahrbuch* 9 (1959): 203–19.

requested the services of this monk, bubbling with ideas, as a professor at Sant'Anselmo.[19]

Fr. Lambert began his lectures in October 1921. They were to become—for all and unexpectedly for himself also—the foundation of his ecumenical vocation. Beauduin as a novice professor remembered the advice of one of his old teachers at a seminar in Louvain, "Do not rely on the handbooks but go back to the sources!" Beauduin's task as professor of fundamental theology at Sant'Anselmo was to compare the Catholic teaching of the Church with that of the Churches separated from Rome. In doing this he was amazed to discover how many errors concerning the Eastern Churches were contained even in the classical Catholic handbooks. Thus he began increasingly to study the life and teaching of the Orthodox Church from the ground up. Already in Louvain he had come to know the Ukranian Metropolitan of Lwow, Count Andreas Szeptyćkyj, and he met him once more in Rome. Szeptyćkyj had no difficulty in convincing Pius XI, who was thinking much about Russia, that the surest way to the soul of the Russian Church and its reunion with Rome lay in Benedictine monasticism. The contact with Szeptyćkyj, along with his own studies, led to the development in Beauduin's easily ignited mind the idea of a Benedictine foundation that would be completely devoted to the unity of the Church. In thinking about this, Beauduin, to his surprise, discovered similar but long-forgotten plans that Leo XIII had for Sant'Anselmo. In fact, from the very beginning, no one among the Benedictines, neither Bernardi nor his successors, believed in the pope's dream of Sant'Anselmo as a bridge to the Eastern Churches. Indeed, Abbot Primate Stotzingen was firmly opposed to such a goal for the college. When Beauduin made no secret of his "discovery," the Primate summoned the restless Belgian to tell him with absolute frankness that hitherto everyone had avoided raising this delicate matter. It was a utopian idea; Benedictines belonged to the West and, in short, Leo XIII's idea must be quietly buried. But it was already too late. Through the offices of the new rector of the Oriental Institute, Fr. Michel d'Herbigny, SJ, Pope Pius XI had already become aware of the monk from Louvain. The pope saw in Beauduin's plans, which d'Herbigny had already outlined to him, a welcome help toward the realization of his favorite idea of the reunification of the Russian Church with Rome—although Beauduin did not wish to commit his

[19] For what follows, see, R. Aubert, "Dom Lambert Beauduin dans le monde et l'Église de son temps," *Unité des Chrétiens* 28 (1978): 2–4; and O. Rousseau, "La naissance d'Amay," *Unité des Chrètiens* 28 (1978): 7f. The complete issue of January 1978 is dedicated to Beauduin.

future monastery one-sidedly to Russia. For the time being, however, this difference of goals was of little importance and Beauduin was more interested in obtaining the pope's basic approval for the project.[20]

When in May 1924 Abbot Primate Stotzingen received a letter in Latin (*Equidem verba*) from the pope, dated March 21, he was faced with an acute dilemma.[21] Because the contents of the letter displeased him, he first did everything to delay its publication. It remains an open question whether or not the strange fact that *Equidem verba* did not appear in the *Acta Apostolicae Sedis* can be attributed to intrigue on the part of the Primate. Beauduin himself, however, who naturally was not unaware of its existence, made sure that the letter was widely distributed.

In his letter to the Primate, Pius XI wrote that he expected every Benedictine Congregation, or at least in every country, to have a monastery that would make the unity of the Church—and in particular the reunification of the Christians of Russia with Rome—its special interest. Monks should pursue this great goal by means of study of the language, history, customs, mentality, and above all the theology and liturgy of the East.

This was not all of what Beauduin had been hoping for, but he was satisfied that the pope had expressed such approval at all.

The lukewarm response from the Benedictine Order to this exhortation of Pius XI is well known.[22] In Germany only the Abbey of Gerleve took an interest and for a time published German translations of liturgical texts of the Eastern Church. At Beauduin's urging, a different approach was taken in Belgium. No existing Belgian monastery was entrusted with the task of working for union with the East, but in December 1925, in a former Carmelite house, Fr. Lambert Beauduin, with the support of Cardinal Mercier of Malines and along with several

[20] E. Fouilloux, *Les catholiques et l'unité chrétienne du XIXe et XXe siècle. Itinéraires européèns d'expression française* (Paris, 1982), 143–50, particularly 147.

[21] "Epistola ad Rmum D. Fidelem de Stotzingen, Abbatem Primatem O.S.B. de preparendis monachis pro future opere unionis Russiae cum Ecclesia Caholica," *AOSB* (1920–1926): 76–78; German translation, *BenM* 6 (1924): 295f. Significantly, the pope's letter is mentioned neither in the official chronicle of Sant'Anselmo (i.e., in the *AOSB*) nor in Stoztingen's circular letters!

[22] The reference to this by the Primate in the *Quaestiones Congressui Revmorum Abbatum proponendae* (Rome, 1925), 28, is devoid of any enthusiasm: "Opus unioni Ecclesiae Orientalis, imprimis apud varios Russiae populos, destinatum et a Summo Pontifice Pio P, XI gloriose regnante per litteras d.d. 21.martii 1924 datae nobis specialiter commissum enixe R.mis Patribus commendatur." It is clear that at the congress itself this hot topic was quickly dropped. Paragraph 30 of the *Protocollum* does not even mention the pope's letter.

Belgian Benedictines from various monasteries, founded the "Monastery of Unity" at Amay-sur-Meuse, which later transferred to Chevetogne. Already in January 1925, Abbot Primate Stotzingen had tried by means of a strictly confidential letter to persuade the abbot of Louvain to refuse permission for this foundation because of Beauduin's "extravagant temperament and lack of balance."[23] Fortunately, Kerchove did not allow himself to be influenced by this.

The foundation of Amay also meant the end of Beauduin's connection with Sant'Anselmo. The rest of his life, rich in trials caused by the misunderstandings he encountered, is not the concern of this study.

2. Clouds on the Horizon

Stoztingen had not been idle during his year of exile in Switzerland. He used his stay in a neutral country to trace Benedictines who were missing, dead, or imprisoned. In many hundreds of cases he was able to transmit news and letters to and from the various countries that were at war and bring consolation to relatives of those involved. In this way the Primate, by his integrity and humanity, not only gained widespread respect and high esteem even among non-Germans but also prepared the ground on which Sant'Anselmo was able quickly to flourish soon after the end of the war. The eminent English historian Dom David Knowles, who as a monk of Downside studied at Sant'Anselmo for a year in 1922–1923, gave high praise to the college. Three years after the Treaty of Versailles that ended a war in which monks had fought and suffered on different sides, the unity in thought and feeling at Sant'Anselmo was far greater than in any other Roman college.[24]

Everything, however, was not well. In the postwar years the Abbot Primate's problems were not confined to obtaining suitable professors. The financial basis of the college was far from secure. In addition there were constant doubts concerning the justification of the college's right to exist or at least concerning the style of life at Sant'Anselmo.[25]

[23] L. Bouyer, *Dom Lambert Beauduin, un homme d'Église* (Tournai, 1964), 122f.; M. Cappuyns, "Dom Lambert Beauduin (1873–1960). Quelques documents et souvenirs," *RHE* 6 (1966): 424–54, in particular 449f.

[24] D. Knowles, *The Benedictines* (London, 1929), 64, as quoted in *The Historian and Character and Other Essays* (Cambridge, 1963), xxi.

[25] In a confidential letter written in German and dated February 26, 1913, Fr. Hilarius Walter of Beuron, secretary to the Abbot Primate, expressly denied accusations raised by A.G. (= Aidan Gasquet, then president of the English Congregation) against Sant'Anselmo. Gasquet had said, "Whatever may be said of the studies, the place is not ideal from the point of view of the religious." Gasquet criticized the

At the Congress of Abbots in 1913, the then-rector, Fr. Hartmann Strohsacker, presented an open, clear overview of the college's finances to the abbots.[26] In addition to what the abbots had heard from Hemptinne himself in 1900, they now heard that as well as the cost of the buildings, Leo XIII had donated a further 1,000,000 lire for the maintenance of Sant'Anselmo—though with the provisio that Sant'Anselmo should support the Greek college with an annual sum of 40,000 lire. The sum donated by Leo XIII was used to buy a farm, "Campo Vecchio" at Grottaferrata, but this had to be sold after a few years. A further source of regular income were the payments by the firm, Le Grand Bros. at Fécamps in France for permission to use the name "Bénédictine" for their world-famous liqueur. These royalties amounted every year to 12,500 lire. Apart from the annual contribution to the Greek College, Sant'Anselmo had no further liabilities or debts. Since, according to the cellarer, current running-costs could be covered by the fees paid by the students and contributions from guests, the aim, Strohsacker continued, should be to create a sinking fund from which a future Primate could live with dignity (*decenter vivere*)—the current Primate was supported by personal contributions from outside—and make possible the funding of major repairs as well as necessary acquisitions for the church, sacristy, and library. A beginning had already been made by lodging contributions from individual monasteries and the annual royalties from Fécamps, but the annual contribution to the Greek college was an unpleasant

---

fact that the students received "no training in the religious life," and in this regard praised the situation that had been obtained under Bernardi. Walter countered, "The 'religious life' under Bernardi consisted of Prime and Compline, a short daily meditation, as well as two conferences per week. It is true that the daily meditation is no longer held in common, but the reason for this is that the celebration of the full Divine Office, the great number of Masses—about forty a day—at which the students must serve, make it impossible to find time for common meditation. Over against this, since 1893 the full Divine Office is celebrated, indeed solemnly on feast days; the two weekly conferences take place regularly, and in addition, on Thursdays a *capitulum culpae* for the students. Further, it should be emphasized that the students conscientiously practice daily meditation, if privatim—I know this from the students' spiritual directors—and that they receive detailed instruction from their directors." Despite the constant increase in the number of students since 1893, continues Walter, the Abbot Primate has given regular conferences, has met weekly with the rector and the master of clerics to discuss the state of the college, and "in addition personally directed a large number of students in spiritualibus. And he did this until as a result of his illness and on the express instructions of his doctor and the infirmarian, he had to ask publically that he be excused"; cf. APr, Congr. Abb. 1913.

[26] APr, Congr. Abb. 1913. Published in Renner, 254ff.

burden. Above all, the original sum of 1 million lire must be retrieved. For this and for the cessation of payments to the Greek college not more than 400,000 lire would be needed. If in this way a solid fund could be established, future subsidies from the monasteries would not be necessary. One could, indeed, achieve this goal with the sum of only 300,000 lire. Further, this could be even further reduced if the Fécamps royalties could be transformed into shares. If, however, the abbots president wished to pay the professors an appropriate stipend—a development, by the way, much to be welcomed—then the sum of 400,000 lire must stand. As it turned out, professors, officials, and brothers received no recompense for their work at the college. They lived at the expense of their home monasteries.

It had already been considered how such a sinking fund or endowment might be created. The rector mentioned the suggestion from the president of the Austrian Congregation of the Blessed Virgin Mary, Abbot Adalbert Dungel of Göttweig, that a bank loan of between 500,000 and 700,000 lire be taken. In the case of the latter figure, every monastery would pay 7,000 lire, and an additional yearly 600 lire for interest and depreciation, but would be freed from the need to pay any further subsidy. Within thirty years the full debt would be cleared and Sant'Anselmo would have a secure financial base without needing constantly to beg from monasteries and other benefactors. This well-thought-out plan soon came to nothing because of the outbreak of the First World War.

At the Synod of Abbots President in 1920, Abbot Primate Stotzingen provided "strictly confidential" information concerning the financial situation of Sant'Anselmo following the war.[27] The situation had become threatening. For this reason the Primate had gone to the pope in 1919 and presented the plight of Sant'Anselmo. Benedict XV showed great understanding and immediately canceled the annual payment to the Greek college with a once-off severance contribution of 400,000 lire. The American-Cassinese Congregation made a generous extraordinary contribution of 70,000 lire. The Italian government transferred 73,000 Lire by way of compensation for the use of the building as a military hospital. Nevertheless, underlined the Primate, when all income was taken into account, there remained a yearly deficit of about 55,000 lire. To raise this sum there was no alternative to the introduction of a subsidy to be paid equally by all Congregations and abbeys. Once the economic climate had improved, other methods for financing the college would have to be found. Perhaps every Congregation could establish its own

[27] APr, Congressus Praesidum 1920. Tit. IV, De Collegio Anselmiano.

fund, the interest on which could be used to cover the yearly subsidy required by Sant'Anselmo.

One notices that the plan for a common fund had already been abandoned. The capital to be invested by each Congregation would remain in the hands of that Congregation. This, too, reflects the shattered unity of nations that resulted from the First World War.

In fact, in the following decades no "Sant'Anselmo Foundation" was ever established. To this day, the greater part of the funding for the college and Athenaeum comes from the annual subsidy from the monasteries of the Benedictine Confederation. Any extraordinary expenses or special projects must be financed by additional begging letters from the Abbot Primate—not exactly a happy state of affairs!

There was, however, an even more serious and more fundamental problem with which the Abbot Primate had to wrestle in the first years after the World War. Since this problem persists, if in varying forms, right up to today, it is worth examining it more closely.

Doubts concerning the sense and objectives of Sant'Anselmo are as old as the college itself. Since the actual existence of Sant'Anselmo was no longer a subject of debate—the college having been built and opened—the unease of some abbots expressed itself in murmurings about the observance of the college.

In 1919 the Abbot Primate had the customs hitherto observed in the college printed in the form of statutes for presentation to the Synod of Abbots President in 1920.[28] During the discussion at the synod the *quaestio fundamentalis de indole et natura Collegii* (the fundamental question of the specific character and nature of the college) arose.[29] One of the participants (his name is not given, but it was possibly the archabbot of Pannonhlama) vigorously defended the idea that Sant'Anselmo was purely a house of studies and neither an abbey nor a monastery. Thus, everything must be removed from the statutes that made the college resemble a monastery. For example, the Divine Office should be celebrated in common only on Sundays and feast days, and the students' rooms should be cleaned by the lay brothers. If these changes were not made, teachers and students, suggested the critics, would not have the necessary time for study and thus the college could not keep up with the other Roman universities.

[28] *Statuta in Collegio Sancti Anselmi de Urbe observanda.* Manuscripti instar (Subiaco: Typis Proto-Coenobii), 1919.

[29] *Protocollum Synodi Revmorum et Illmorum Abbatum Praesidum Congregationum Confoederatarum O.S.B., mense Maio anno 1920 in aedibus S. Anselmi de Urbe habitae* (Rome: Typis Polyglottis Vaticanis, 1920), 16f.

Since this intervention openly placed a question mark over the constitution of Sant'Anselmo, there followed a lively discussion among the presidents. The result of this, however, was a clear endorsement of how the college had functioned to date. The abbots declared:

1. The College of Sant'Anselmo is not an abbey nor a monastery in the juridical sense, since it was neither canonically erected as such nor possessed a community of its own nor a novitiate;
2. nevertheless, Sant'Anselmo is not merely a house of studies. The Benedictine students of the college should not only be trained in the sacred sciences but also should also progress in the spiritual life and the practice of the monastic virtues. Otherwise, it would make no sense for the Confederation to maintain such a house at great expense;
3. therefore, the whole Office is to be prayed every day in choir, even if in a simplified form.
   Many participants testified that they had heard from Hemptinne himself that he had visited Leo XIII specifically to discuss the matter of the Office. The pope replied that the full Office was to be prayed in choir. In order to make this possible, the founder of the college (i.e., Leo XIII), granted the privilege of always praying ferial Matins on weekdays;
4. if the monastic life is not observed and the religious instruction of the clerics is not completed, then abbots should not send any more students to the College of Sant'Anselmo, since there would be a danger that they would lose their vocations;
5. although concern for the spiritual formation of the young monks is a priority, care must be taken that both teachers and students have the necessary time for studies.

A further result of the presidents' discussion of the statutes was the decision that in the future, Sant'Anselmo should be described as the "International Benedictine College." In place of the title "subprior," the title of "vice rector" was introduced.[30]

Finally, the presidents declared that the statutes hitherto observed should, with a few changes they desired, be legally binding until the next Congress of Abbots or the next synod of abbots president. The ques-

[30] "Quod singula statuta attinet Patres congregati quaedam modificanda putant; ita consentiunt in titulo statutorum nomini 'Collegii' addendum est praedicatum 'internationalis'; loco tituli Subprioris nomen Vicerectoris adhibendum esse; retinendum vero esse nomen Magistri alumnorum." *Protocollum Synodi* 17.

tion of whether or not the presidents had the right to approve statutes for Sant'Anselmo was answered in the affirmative, since in 1906 Pius X had empowered the Abbot Primate to call the presidents together so that they could lay down and decide everything that would be for the good of the Order and of the College of Sant'Anselmo.[31]

With this, the uncertainty concerning the status of Sant'Anselmo seemed to have been resolved. The next few years, however, were to make it abundantly clear that doubts remained about the legality of the course adopted.

On July 6, 1925, the liberal "Neue Zürcher Zeitung," under the heading "Foreign News in Brief," published an unsigned article titled "Disagreements in the Benedictine Order." The astonished reader learned from a well-informed correspondent that:

> Shortly before Pentecost the abbeys of the Order received a circular letter from the rector of the Anselminum, canvassing support for the idea—in view of the forthcoming election of a new Abbot Primate in the autumn—that the office of the abbot of Sant'Anselmo in Rome should be combined with that of the rector of the academy.
>
> There is no reason why the Abbot Primate as the mere representative of the Order to the Holy See should be abbot of the Anselmianum as has been the case up to now. If the circular letter does not expressly contain a personal jibe against the present Abbot Primate, the aristocratic Baron von Stotzingen, it does, nevertheless, express a secret dissatisfaction with the present state of affairs which we can formulate as a latent struggle between federalism and centralism in the Order.

The reporter then gives an overview—mostly accurate if also prejudiced—of the attitudes of the most important Benedictine Congregations and, naturally, those of the Roman Curia to the "openly or secretly conducted campaign to centralize the Order" and concludes, "In any case, at the election of an Abbot Primate in autumn, whether the person elected remains Abbot of Sant'Anselmo or not and whether it results in

[31] "Ex audientia Ssmi . . . Eadem Sanctitas Sua benigne excipiens preces Rmi Primatis OSB. Et Abbatis S. Anselmi de Urbe, declarare dignatus est posse eundem Primatem sexto quoque anno Praesides omnium Congregationis Ordinis Romam advocare, ut collatis consiliis, quidquid in bonum eiusdem Ordinis et Collegii Anselmiani vertere potest, statuant atque decernant." Rescript of the Congregation of Bishops and Religious dated December 2, 1906, *AOSB* (1893–1908): 57f. "Neque proinde dubium esse potest, Praesidibus Congregatis ius competere, de quo quaeritur." *Protocollum Synodi* 19.

Fr. Patrick Cummins
(1880–1868)

the reelection of Baron von Stotzingen, unpopular in several quarters, the electors will be somewhat influenced by Benedictine federalism and Jesuit centralism."

What had happened? In May 1925, Fr. Patrick Cummins of Conception Abbey in the United States, who had been rector of Sant'Anselmo since 1912, sent a short letter in Latin to the abbots, and this without consulting either the Abbot Primate or his own abbot. In the letter, Fr. Cummins claimed that on the basis of Leo XIII's brief *Summum Semper*, it was the rector and not the Abbot Primate who was responsible for Sant'Anselmo and was its head. Hitherto, for the sake of peace, he, Fr. Cummins had left everything to the decision of the Primate. Now, however, the Congress of Abbots was approaching and the time had come for the competent authorities to clarify matters. The rector summed up his own views in four points:

1. Since the College of Sant'Anselmo was a papal university, the person who is its head, must, as is the case in every university, have the title of rector;
2. one could question the advisability of retaining the title of "abbot of Sant'Anselmo," despite the fact that it was not an abbey. If the title were to be retained, then it should be held by the rector;
3. in order to make clear to the whole Order, the legal rights and position of the rector, he should be elected by all the abbots;
4. immediately following his election, the rector should nominate a pro-rector who, in the event of a vacancy, would enjoy all the rights of the rector until the next election.[32]

[32] APr, Cong. Abbatum 1925, I 13/B 3, Ia. Printed below in appendix 8. On May 26, 1925, Cummins wrote the following astonishing letter to Abbot Primate Stotzingen: "I would gladly give my life if I could spare you the pain that the enclosed letter is likely to cause you [i.e., Cummins's circular letter in Latin]. Only once before in my life has a matter been so difficult for me—namely, when my conscience forced me to cause similar pain to my father in Christ, Abbot Frowin of blessed memory. He forgave me, even though he could not accept my ideas, but I shall carry the pain of this incident with me to the grave. And now, I must repeat this sacrifice whose object is a man who is consuming his whole life in the service of the Order, a friend who has shown me such trust—one on whom I must inflict such a blow.

The circular letter caused an uproar in the Order that is hardly understandable today. Before the Congress of Abbots both the rector and the Abbot Primate received letters of approval as well as disapproval.

One of the first replies to the rector came from Abbot Willibald Wolfsteiner of Ettal.[33] This letter shows that it was well understood within the Order that here the basic issue was not a power struggle between rector and Abbot Primate but the fundamental structure of Sant'Anselmo. Wolfsteiner is not only convinced of the significance of Sant'Anselmo for the Order and for the Church but also feels himself personally bound to the college. As abbot of the restored monastery at Ettal he has shown his love for Sant'Anselmo by the fact that, "in the few years since Ettal has existed once more, he has already entrusted twelve students to the college."[34] He rejoices over the good monastic and academic development that have characterized Sant'Anselmo from its foundation and then emphasizes that

> The Anselmianum must be Benedictine in every way and must not allow itself in its constitution and way of life to be influenced by other orders such as the Franciscans, Dominicans, and Jesuits and the way they run their academic institutions. Most of the students come [to Sant'Anselmo] after completing their short year of novitiate and thus, despite the fact that contemporary trends might not understand this, are even more in need of a deepening of the monastic spirit. However, it is part of Benedictine education that the house should have an abbot at its head . . . but two abbots or two superiors with jurisdictio ordinaria cannot be superiors of one and the same house of the Benedictine Order." Wolfsteiner concedes that there are still some issues to be clarified regarding

---

Dear Father Abbot Primate, it would have been a joy to serve you all my life. I will never be happy about what I now have to do. I ask only one thing: my conscience alone and [not the influence of] others has brought me to this step. I emphasize this because at the time Abbot Frowin was of the opinion that I had fallen victim to the *murmurantibus*. "A temetipsum hoc dicis? An alii tibi dixerunt de me?" Thus, he concluded his reply and never looked at me again. No, coram Deo, I may have made a mistake and now once again I may be making a mistake. But what I have done, and what I am now doing, is not prompted by disloyalty, but the slowly ripened fruit of my own, imperfect indeed, but nevertheless loyal service in the spirit of our common father Benedictus. Fatigue in this service forced me to turn to the Mother of God. And this is where you will find me. Yours obediently in the Divine heart, D. Patrizio, OSB." APr, Cong. Abbatum 1925, I 13/B 3, Ib.

[33] K. Gross, Willibald Wolfsteiner, "Mönch und Abt 1855–1942," *Ettal* (1950): 117f. For what follows see also Renner, 259–62.

[34] APr, Congr. Abb. 1925, letter from Wolfsteiner of June 2, 1925.

Abbot Willibald Wolfsteiner (1855–1942)

the relationship of the Primate to the college, but "My concern and indeed that of many other abbots is primarily that in the training of our students in the Anselmianum, the spirit and special character of our Order be guaranteed in every aspect."[35]

Did all Bavarian abbots think this way? One can have one's doubts. Consultations held by the abbots of the Bavarian Congregation along with the abbots of Münsterschwarzach, Neresheim, and Schweiklberg on June 6, 1925, on the occasion of the consecration of the abbey church at Schweiklberg, indicate otherwise.[36] The aims of the twelve points drawn up by the Bavarian abbots[37] become clear from the notes made almost at the same time by Abbot President Placidus Glogger (St. Stephan in Augsburg): "Personally, I have always *not* approved of the fact that the rector [of Sant'Anselmo] was made prior. From many years of experience here and from tradition, I know that a clear separation between teaching and house (i.e., monastery) is best."[38]

On the other hand, the respected canon lawyer, Abbot Raphael Molitor (Gerleve) completely disagreed with this position: "I am not pleased with the twelve points [of the Bavarians] formulated against the rector's circular. Clearly, the Bavarians find the solution in terms of the relations that exist between secondary school and abbey in their Congregation. This [solution], however, cannot be applied to our situation because we have to take completely different preconditions into account."[39] This was undoubtedly the case: Sant'Anselmo was not a monastery to which an academic institution had been entrusted as a task but was, rather, a center for the training of young monks at the seat of the Abbot Primate who, in addition, held the title of "abbot of Sant'Anselmo." But what did that mean?

[35] Archabbot Norbert Weber of St. Ottilien wrote in a similar vein on August 4, 1925 (APr, Congr. Abb. 1925).

[36] APr, Cong. Abb. 1925, I 13/A 3 g (Letter from Abbot Pl. Gloggers of June 8, 1925).

[37] *Resolutiones proponendae Synodo Abbatum.* APr, Congr. Abb. 1925, A 13/A 3 g.

[38] On the rector's circular letter of May 27, 1925, see *Gedanken von Abt Placidus Glogger Augsburg*: APr, Congr. Abb. 1925.

[39] APr, Congr. Abb. 1925, I 13/B 3, 2a.

A conference of German abbots held on June 23, 1925, at St. Boniface in Munich soon demonstrated that what was at stake was less the person of the rector than the definition of the status and role of the Primate.[40]

Thus, when the Congress of Abbots opened on October 1, 1925, in Sant'Anselmo, it was no surprise that the first item on the agenda was questions concerning the Confederation and the office of the Primate. The second item on the agenda (*De Collegio Sancti Anselmi*) was not dealt with until October 5.[41] The following is a brief summary of the results: The personal union of rector and prior was strengthened. The majority of the abbots decided that at Sant'Anselmo, the rector had the same status under the Abbot Primate as the (claustral) prior in other monasteries. With this, the second attempt to alter the established structure of Sant'Anselmo and to separate the university and college was rejected. Clearly, the abbots were afraid that such a division into two entities could damage the monastic lives of young monks.

The congress decided that the statutes did not require the confirmation of the Holy See, and that the congress itself could decree the binding character both of the statutes of the college as well as the program of studies (*Ratio studiorum*).[42]

In effect, this was based on the draft that had been approved by the presidents in 1920 and which was accepted almost without any amendments. This program of studies, which appeared in print in 1928, represents the final and only legal provision on the part of the Congress of Abbots for the shape of studies at the Anselmianum. A few years later, with the constitution *Deus scientiarum Dominus* of Pius XI, which subjected all ecclesiastical academies, programs of study, and the appointment of professors to strict control by the Congregation for Studies, the Order lost this privilege.

Although the finances of Sant'Anselmo remained limited, there were no major worries in this area. The Abbot Primate thanked all abbots who helped Sant'Anselmo financially with donations, Mass intentions,

[40] APr, Congr. Abb. 1925, I 13/B 3, 2b: Minutes of the conference of abbots of June 23, 1925.

[41] *Protocollum seu Relatio de Sessionibus quas R.mi et Ill. Abbates Congregationum Confoederatarum O.S.B. habuerunt in aedibus S. Anselmi mense Octobri 1925* (Romae: ex typographia "Campitelli," 1925), 16f.; cf. "Äbteversammlung und Primaswahl (Rom, 1–11 Oktober 1925)," *BenM* (1926): 74–80.

[42] "Demum R.mus Praeses Congressus quaestionem movet, utrum Statuta S. Sedi confirmanda proponantur, an probatio R.morum Abbatum interim sufficiat. Omnes congregati censent approbationemn S. Sedis non esse petendam, sed ipsum Congressum Abbatum jam sua auctoritate et Statuta Collegii et Rationem studiorum confirmare, additis variationibus nunc deliberandis." *Protocollum* (A. 41), 25.

and the services of lay brothers. The constant stream of Benedictine students from all over the world was a joy. The Primate suggested that, in accepting students, preference—available places permitting—should be given to those aspiring to academic degrees before considering other applicants, *Quod ab omnibus approbatur* (Which was approved by all).

3. The Blossoming of Sant'Anselmo

Fr. Athanasius Staub (1864–1955)

On October 6, 1926, during the Congress of Abbots, the abbot of Muri-Gries recommended to the participants that they should request the abbot of Einsiedeln for the services of the dean (prior) of Einsiedeln, Fr. Athanasius Staub, as *Senior spiritualis* for Sant'Anselmo.[43] This suggestion was greeted with enthusiastic applause, yet another proof that for the abbots the spiritual care of the students was more important than the academic.

Fr. Athanasius Staub was not unknown in Sant'Anselmo. From 1895 to 1902 he had been a lecturer in fundamental theology as well as master of clerics. He had left Rome with a heavy heart when obedience summoned him back to Einsiedeln. His home monastery needed his services as a popular missioner. His greatest burden was his appointment in 1903 as prefect of the monastery's boarding school. Exactly two years later—"after the purgatory of the prefectship"—Fr. Athanasius was appointed dean in succession to Thomas Bossart, who had been elected abbot. In the judgment of the annalist of Einsiedeln, "What Fr. Athanasius achieved in fully twenty years is worthy of highest admiration. The fate of the house at that time lay in good hands. The two superiors, abbot and dean, were strong personalities, even if very different in education and character, but nonetheless devoted to each other in genuine trust, happily complementing each other. Thus, there were years during which many believed that Fr. Athanasius would one day wear the abbatial chain. But this was not to be."[44] Abbot Ignaz Staub gave his dean to Sant'Anselmo, and so Fr. Athanasius went once more to Rome. In Sant'Anselmo he took over not only the role of prefect of clerics but also the office of rector in place of Fr. Patrick Cummins, the loser in the rector/prior dispute whom the Primate sent back to Con-

[43] *Protocollum* 27.

[44] L. Räber, *St. Meinrads Raben* 44 (1955): 141–46; cf. 143.

ception Abbey. In addition, he taught sacramental theology during the academic year 1926–1927. In later years he took over pastoral theology, which was more suited to his practical bent.

From 1925 until his departure from Sant'Anselmo at the outbreak of World War II, Athanasius Staub was one of the most remarkable characters in the college. "Fr. Athanasius filled his job, not on the basis of great learning, which he never possessed and never pretended to have, but with the force of his personality." The Einsiedeln annalist wrote,

> He was rather domineering, somewhat like the mayor of a canton in Inner Switzerland, with much of the diplomatic skill of his fellow Niedrwaldner Melchior Lussy (the wily diplomat at the Council of Trent), but also with the delightful cheerfulness of the true children of God. This superiority was accepted by people of very different levels of learning and from different backgrounds. And so it happened that Don Atanasio was not just an undisputed personality in Sant'Anselmo but that all of Rome knew this short, strongly built Swiss Father, who with a swift gait and astonishingly winning ways went in and out of countless doors and offices. The doors of the Vatican were also open to him at any time of the day. There were years during which week after week Fr. Athanasius was consulted by the Secretariat of State of Cardinal Pacelli and later Pius XII. Only the departed confrere knows how many matters in the Church of God were settled with his advice. In any case, there were many and very decisive matters. It is clear that there was no lack of those who envied this man. However, he was also able to laugh about this: he wanted nothing for himself, his work and efforts were all for the Church—*dilexit Ecclesiam* (epitaph of Cardinal Mermillod).

Fr. Athanasius Staub was already sixty-one years old when he became rector of Sant'Anselmo. His robust health allowed him to plunge fully into his new and varied responsibilities. He did not consider it beneath his dignity to personally take care of all the secretarial work of the college. He was greatly loved by the professors and was for the students an example of a life lived in accordance with the Rule and a rector who showed great understanding for the young members of the Order entrusted to him. "Despite completely different characters, he had the best of relationships with his superior, Abbot Primate Fidelis von Stotzingen. His genuinely Swiss democratic manner was a happy complement to the rather reserved demeanor of his aristocratic superior."[45]

[45] L. Räber, *BenM* 31 (1955): 470.

The Old Library, later Aula IV, now assembly hall

What was the academic ideal at Sant'Anselmo when Fr. Athanasius Staub became rector? What was it able to offer? It is worth taking a look at the *Ratio Studiorum* which was backed by the authority of the Congress of Abbots of the Benedictine Confederation.[46]

The "International College of Sant'Anselmo" (*Collegium Internationale S. Anselmi de Urbe*)[47] saw itself primarily as a *Studium Generale* and in particular for the training of Benedictine priests in philosophy, theology, and canon law. It was, however, also open to diocesan clerics and those of other orders. Leadership of the college rested with the rector and the academic council (*Consilium Aademicum*), which was composed of all

[46] *Ordo et Ratio Studiorum Collegii internationalis S. Anselmi de Urbe.* Manuscripti instar (Subiaco: Typus Proto-Coenobii, 1928).

[47] In subsequent years there were frequent discussions concerning the exact title of the college, e.g., *AAt*, Libellus Actorum, 384ff. Finally, in 1933 the Curia itself used the title "Pont. Institutum Academicum Collegii International is S. Anselmi de Urbe." AAt, Libellus Actorum, 415.

the professors of the college.[48] Particularly important decisions had to be presented by the rector to the Abbot Primate for confirmation. The *Studium Generale* of Sant'Anselmo consisted in three faculties, of which two (those of philosophy and theology) as well as the *cursus maior*, alone led to an academic degree; each offered in addition a *cursus minor* which was a sufficient precondition for priestly ordination.

For philosophy three years were required for the doctorate. One was obliged to enroll for lectures in:

1. scholastic philosophy in the areas of logic, natural philosophy and psychology, metaphysics, and ethics (linked with sociology);
2. the history of philosophy;
3. review courses on the experimental sciences (*Psychologia experimentalis* and an overview of the natural sciences).

In addition, selected texts from Aristotle (in Greek) and St. Thomas were read and explained.

At the end of the first year, the baccalaureat could be obtained followed by the license at the end of the second year. In both cases, the examinations were lengthy and demanding.

Admission to the course in theology was permitted only to those who *expresse et ex professo* (specifically and correctly) had studied scholastic philosophy.

The *cursus maior* in theology took five years: two years to the baccalaureat with the license following after the third year. The doctorate in theology could be obtained at the earliest after the fifth year. The material was divided into compulsory lectures (with compulsory examinations at the end) and supplementary lectures (*cursus supplementarii*), which were compulsory but without obligatory examinations and voluntary courses, open to students from all faculties.

The compulsory courses were: fundamental theology, special dogmatic theology according to the *Summa* of St. Thomas, biblical science, Hebrew, ecclesiastical history, patrology, moral and pastoral theology, liturgical science, and canon law.

[48] The Abbot Primate always presided over the meetings of the Consilium (Concilium) Professorum. Stotzingen signed the minutes as *Abbas Primas*. In earlier years he often added, *Praeses Concilii*. Later, the minutes were also signed by the rector. Following the new legislation on studies of 1931, Stotzingen signed with *Magnus Cancellarius Instituti*. Cf. AAt, Libellus Actorum.

In supplementary lectures individual exegetical topics were treated along with biblical Greek (knowledge of classical Greek was a prerequisite for enrollment) and theological methodology.

Voluntary subjects provided the opportunity to learn another Oriental language: Aramaic, Syriac, or Arabic, the latter an old specialization at Sant'Anselmo, and in addition introductions to Christian archaeology, to particular patristic or liturgical topics, to historical methodology, and several other subjects. Naturally, these voluntary courses tended to change radically and rapidly, but the obligatory courses remained virtually unaltered.

Officially, the course in canon law took three years, with lectures on texts from the *Codex Iuris Canonici*, the philosophy of law, the history of canon law, and introduction to Roman law. A student who had already studied canon law for two years as part of a course in theology, however, was permitted to enroll for certain lectures in canon law, thus shortening his course. Nevertheless, to obtain a doctoral degree a student was required to have spent at least two years after theology exclusively studying canon law.

In accordance with ancient Roman practice, attendance at lectures was strictly obligatory. Whoever during the academic year missed ten lectures for which he was enrolled without good reason—to be decided by the rector—or without excuse was considered to have forfeited that year and was not permitted to take the examinations.

In addition to the lectures, regular disputations were held in the different faculties. Further, "Solemn Disputations" were held several times a year, all members of the college being obliged to attend. One needs to explain only to students of our time that all of this, naturally, took place in Latin.

To obtain a doctoral degree, in addition to a final examination (in theology, lasting fifty minutes and covering all of dogmatic theology) the presentation of a dissertation was required. This had to be at least sixty pages long and written in Latin. If this dissertation was considered by the Academic Council to be of sufficient merit, it could subsequently be published "honorably" (*honorifice*) in printed form.

Such a program of studies, respectable when viewed as a whole, naturally stood or fell on how it was realized by good professors and capable students. Sant'Anselmo possessed both, but the question remained: were there enough of both? This question posed the greatest threat to the faculty of canon law, but it was precisely this faculty that was to be honored in an unexpected way.

Sant'Anselmo had now been in existence for several decades, but no member of the professorial staff had yet been created cardinal. In fact, at the time the conferral of the red hat on a member of the teaching body was regarded as the highest honor that a papal university could receive. Thus, it is understandable that from time to time the question arose—almost impossible to understand today—of who would be the first cardinal from Sant'Anselmo.[49] In 1927 the time had come. The first professor to become a cardinal was Justinian Serédi from the Archabbey of Pannonhalma.[50]

George Serédi was born on April 24, 1884, near Bratislava, the youngest of eleven children of a working-class family. In 1901 he entered Pannonhalma and received the name Justinian. In 1904, having completed secondary school, his superiors sent him to study theology at Sant'Anselmo where he remained until 1908. In that same year, however, the young priest was recalled to Rome. At that time in Rome work on the new text of canon law, announced by Pius X in 1904, was in full swing. The head of the commission entrusted with this task was Cardinal Pietro Gasparri, whose extraordinary legal talent and organizational competence had predestined him for this role. His assistant was Fr. Pierre Bastien, professor of canon law at Sant'Anselmo, an excellent canonist and, in addition, a skilled diplomat. Bastien's brief was to support the new canons with relevant texts from historical legal sources.

The work, however, was making little progress. This may have been because the task was not suited to Bastien's temperament and interests. Thus, Gasparri looked around for another assistant and Bastien recommended his young pupil, the twenty-four-year-old, newly ordained Hungarian priest Justinian Serédi for the post. Serédi's responsibility was to cull through the mass of legal sources to find and assemble all the material from which the new canons were drawn or which played a role in the interpretation of the law. "Since at the beginning the text of the canons was in constant fluctuation and subject to alternation, the inclusion of every new canon brought with it the need to omit an old one or the alteration of one that had already been included. All of this required the discovery of new sources, as well as in some cases the elimination or changing of existing sources. One can safely say that in the whole college of consultors there was no other who had so profound an insight into the process of codification and such comprehensive knowledge of its development than the same Serédi." To give some idea of the extent of the work, it is enough to say that the number of sources referred to amounted to 10,500 in all. Since reference was made several

[49] L. Hanser, "Justinian Serédy," *StudMitt* 46 (1928): 136.

[50] J. Bánk, "De Justiniano Cardinali Serédi," *Monitor ecclesiasticus* 81 (1956): 463–81; J. Bánk, "Kardinal Serédi, der Kanonist," *ZRG*, 44, no. 1 (1958): 209–36.

times to each source, however, the number of references rose to about 26,000. One must also bear in mind that many cards, since every source to which reference was made had its own card.

Serédi devoted ten years to this work. For three full years of this time, he lived in the Vatican as the personal guest of Cardinal Gasparri, the secretary of state. The reason for this is that it was feared that Serédi, as a citizen of an enemy state, would be interned by the Italian government. The manuscript that was finally handed over to Cardinal Gasparri ended with the words: *"Finis I.O.Gl.D." (In omnibus glorificetur Deus*—The End. That in all things God may be glorified). In his own hand, Gasparri added the words *"Tibi gratulationes meas porrigo, etsi indigne P.C.* [Petrus Cardinalis]. *Ad multos annos. Vale."* (Though unworthy, I congratulate you, Cardinal Peter. Hail, and may you have a long life!) The work was finished in 1917, in the middle of the First World War. Serédi traveled to Hungary with a papal diplomatic passport, there to rest and to engage in pastoral work and minister to Italian prisoners of war. In 1920 he was once more in Rome, this time as professor of canon law in Sant'Anselmo. In addition, he soon took on lectures in the Vatican School for Archives, was adviser in canon law to the Hungarian embassy to the Holy See, procurator general of the Hungarian Benedictine Congregation as well as a procurator of the Hungarian bishops to the Roman dicasteries, consultor of the Commission of Cardinals for the authentic interpretation of the *Codex Iuris Canonici*, and, finally, the editor of the sources underlying this text of the Church's law. This was an immense collection of diverse and dispersed legal texts from all ages, carefully gathered together under the title: *Codici Iuris Canonici Fontes*. During his time in Rome Serédi was able to publish the first four impressive volumes of this work. The fifth volume appeared in 1930, with the ninth and last not appearing until 1939.

In the middle of these many activities there arrived the news of the death of the prince-primate of Hungary, Johan Czernoch. Although Serédi was mentioned among the candidates for the succession, this was not taken particularly seriously at Sant'Anselmo. When rumor began to have it that Serédi would be made a cardinal, Abbot Primate Fidelis summoned Father Justinian and warned him: "Just put out of your head any idea that you will ever be a cardinal." In reality, Serédi had already received written notice from Cardinal Gasparri of his nomination, but with the injunction to keep this secret for the time being. A few days later, on November 30, 1927, the Primate invited all professors and students to the "Red Room" near the refectory in Sant'Anselmo, usually used for formal celebrations. Here, the Primate announced, in ascending importance, the news had arrived that Father Justinian had

Georg Justinian Cardinal Serédi (1884–1945)

been appointed archbishop of Esztergom, Primate of Hungary and cardinal of the Roman Church.[51]

The appointment of Serédi was by no means the cause of unalloyed joy in Hungary. The government had its own candidate. Indeed, the minister for religious affairs, Count Kuno Kleibesberg, was sent secretly to Rome with the task of having the nomination reversed, were this possible. But it was to no avail. Under these circumstances, the early period in office of the new and youthful prince primate—he was only forty-three years old—was not easy. By nature inclined to be reserved, Serédi preferred the calm of his study to the unavoidable public appearances and receptions; in addition, he was not a good speaker. These deficiencies were compensated for, however, by his upright character, personal modesty, attention to duty, and his devotion to the needs of his diocese and the interests of his country. His reputation among jurists was unassailable. In 1936 the faculty of laws of the University of Oxford conferred on him an honorary doctorate in laws.

During the upheavals of the Second World War he gave instructions: every priest was to remain at his post at whatever cost. He himself, despite illness and bomb attacks, remained at his post, dying at Esztergom on March 29, 1945, as the Russian troops were occupying the city. The conquerors who broke into the Primate's palace found only his corpse.

Ironically, in the same year that a canonist from Sant'Anselmo—certainly because of his professional knowledge and his devotion to the service of the Holy See—received the honor of the cardinalate, the faculty of canon law of that university had ceased its lectures due to lack of students. Already in 1923 the Abbot Primate had appealed to the abbots to release students to study canon law. In 1926 the call for help was dramatic and pressing, given the fact that at the beginning of the academic year only two students were registered for the major course—the consequences being that the full course could no longer be offered. In 1927 the Abbot Primate issued his final appeal to the abbots not to let the faculty of canon law die out. One must bear in mind that at the same time the house was flooded with requests from students seeking admission to philosophy and theology.[52] From the academic year 1927–1928 on, because of the lack of students, the faculty of canon

[51] A description of the complicated ceremonies connected with the elevation to the cardinalate can be found in G. Locher, "Kardinal Georg Justinian Serédi," *BenM* 10 (1928): 171–75. See also K. Gross, *StudMitt* 46 (1928): 25–28.

[52] Stotzingen, circular letters dated June 24, 1928, and May 13, 1926. On July 2, 1927, he wrote: "Vere tamen dolendum est, numerum alumnorum, cursu (!) majori juris cononici adscriptorum, vere exiguum fuisse, imo timendum est, ne anno

law at Sant'Anselmo had to cease to operate. In subsequent years it was hoped again and again to start anew, but to this day this has not proved possible, even if the rights to such a faculty in Sant'Anselmo have never been renounced. The last person to receive the doctorate in canon law from Sant'Anselmo was Basilius Ebel, later abbot of Maria Laach. This was in 1925. In 1927 the last license in canon law was awarded to Matthias Quatember, O.Cist, who subsequently became abbot general of the Cistercian Order.

While the faculty of canon law was closing down, the ascent of the theological faculty began. Soon it was to attain a prominent position among the other Roman universities.

In 1924, Fr. Matthäus Rothenhäusler from Gerleve succeeded Fr. Philibert Schmitz as professor of ecclesiastical history and soon, by means of his seminars, organized along the model of those at German universities, had a lasting influence on the quality of studies at Sant'Anselmo. Biblical sciences were well represented by Fr. Hildebrand Höpfl, whose three-volume introduction to the study of the Bible, which appeared in 1921, rapidly went through several editions.

Again, the area of biblical studies was strengthened by Fr. Athanasius Miller from Beuron, who arrived in Rome in 1922 and created great enthusiasm, particularly as a teacher. Since 1925, Oriental languages were taught by Fr. Luis Palacios from Montserrat. His lectures resulted in the publication of both a Syriac and biblical Aramaic grammar in 1931 and 1933, respectively. Of these, the second particularly is used to this day and has been republished several times.[53] The most valuable addition to Sant'Anselmo in the 1920s, however, was in the area of dogmatic theology, for which it was possible to "win" Fr. Anselm Stoltz of Gerleve. During the academic year 1927–1928 Fr. Anselm had to replace, at short notice, Fr. Richard Schutte of Oosterhout who, after a long illness, had finally to return to his monastery. From 1928, Fr. Philipp Oppenheim of Gerleve taught liturgy and patristics and, beginning in 1921, the veteran canonist, Fr. Pierre Bastien, was supported by Fr. Gerhard Oesterle, also from Gerleve.[54]

---

sequenti, deficientibus quasi ex toto auditoribus, cursus tanti momenti supprimi debeat."

[53] L. Palacios, *Grammatica syriaca ad usum scholarum* (Montserrat, 1931); 2nd rev. ed. V. Camps (Montserrat, 1954); L. Palacios, *Grammatica aramaico-biblica ad usum scholarum*, 5th ed. (Montserrat, 1980).

[54] Here it should also be mentioned that Dom Augustin Genestout (1888–1969), a monk of Solesmes and procurator general of the French Congregation, lived from 1926 as a permanent guest at Sant'Anselmo and here, in the 1930s, developed in

While it was only in later years that the capabilities of these new teachers were to come to the notice of a wider public, nevertheless the faculty was well manned when on May 24, 1931, Pope Pius XI issued the apostolic constitution *Deus scientiarum Dominus*, which contained new, strict guidelines for the raising of academic standards in all ecclesiastical higher teaching establishments. Specific guidelines for the implementation of the constitution followed on June 12, 1931.[55]

In May 1931, the Primate had already informed the Synod of Abbots President of the new law and of the sacrifices that this would demand of the Order. The constitution deliberately made it more difficult to obtain degrees: now, a minimum of four years was required for a doctorate in philosophy, and in the case of theology, five years. The Primate made it known that by the academic year 1932–1933, Sant'Anselmo, if it wished to continue conferring academic degrees, would have to comply with all the regulations of the constitution.[56] Was the Confederation able and willing to make these sacrifices? According to the requirements of the prescribed disciplines, the faculty of philosophy would have to have six professors; theology, thirteen. Thus, the number of teachers of philosophy would have to be increased by two and of theology by one. The Primate went on to say that there was no lack of students, but the house could accommodate only between eighty and eighty-five. For this reason, preference would be given to those applying for academic courses. The new regulations meant that any revival of the faculty of canon law receded further into the future, since this would require at least five professors and an annual enrollment of at least ten students.[57]

---

strict secrecy his revolutionary theory of the priority of the Rule of the Master over the Rule of Benedict. Because he was only a guest in Sant'Anselmo, his name does not appear in any of the usual Sant'Anselmo records for the period, nor in the lists of the "Familia Anselmiana." It is certain, however, that he was present in Sant'Anselmo, a fact that is supported by the various editions of the *Annuario Pontificio*. On Genestout, see B. Jaspert, *Die Regula Benedicti Regula Magistri-Kontroverse*, Regulae Benedicti Studia 3 (Hildesheim, 1975), 8–16.

[55] *AAS* 23 (1931): 241–52. "Ordinationes ad Consitutionem Apostolicam 'Deus Scientiarum Dominus' de Universitatibus et Facultatibus Studiorum ecclesiasticorum rite exsequendam," ibid., 263–84. See also *AOSB* (1931): 7–35.

[56] *Protocollum seu Relatio de Sessionibus quas Reverendissimi et Illustrissimi Abbates Praesides Congregationum, Confoederatarum OSB habuerunt in aedibus S. Anselmi mense Maio 1931* (Subiaco, 1931), 12–17. Stoztingen, circular letters dated June 29, 1931, and July 11, 1932.

[57] During the discussions on the implementation of the new constitution, the Primate and the professors of Sant' Anselmo thought about the *Characteristica Collegii*: the Primate mentioned as *distinctiva*: (1) a firm commitment to Thomism in philosophy and theology; (2) "iuxta traditiones O.N. Historia Ecclesiastica necnon

The new constitution required highly qualified professors. These were now divided into ordinary professors, extraordinary professors, and "docenti." Appointments to the first two categories were reserved to the Congregation for Studies. Higher standards were also prescribed by Pius XI for aspiring students. From now on they must not only possess a qualification that would permit them to pursue a course of academic study in their countries of origin, but the regulations for implementation also provided a list of subjects that qualified for such a course. At the top of the list were Latin and Greek.

If in the 1930s Sant'Anselmo reached a high academic level, this is without doubt because of the excellent and almost identical secondary education that the students, in particular those from German-speaking countries, brought with them to Rome. The academic level of a faculty depends not only on the quality of its professors but also on the quality of its students! This is a fact that is often forgotten.

While it was with great difficulty that Sant'Anselmo was able to conform to the new legislation on studies, this legislation was in no way an attempt to deprive the college of oxygen. Pius XI's goodwill toward Benedictines and Sant'Anselmo remained undiminished, a fact that was demonstrated on more than one occasion. At the end of 1932 he received the whole college, led by the Primate, in a private audience in the Aula Clementina and used this opportunity to honor the college by conferring on it the title "Pontifical," at the time and for long afterward a very particular mark of distinction.[58]

After the death of the pope, an alumnus of Sant'Anselmo wrote that during his pontificate, Pius XI had received the Abbot Primate around ninety times in audience. "And the college too, as such, at least in the early years of the pontificate, had an annual audience—later this was

---

et Patrologia et Institutiones Liturgicae specialiter evolvuntur." AAt, Libellus Actorum, 424f. Thus, in the regulations for studies approved in 1933, under Tit. I, Art. I, it is decreed: "Specialis Anselmiani Instituti indoles sequitur ex supralaudato Pii Pp. X Motu Proprio, quo doctrina Aquinatis, immo ipse S. Thomae textus in praelectionibus sacrae theologiae adhibendus praescribitur, necnon ex optimis Ordinis S. Benedicti traditionibus, quibus monachi documenta venerandae antiquitatis speciali studio investigare docentur. Alumni ergo Instituti tam in rebus speculativis quam in disciplinis positivis, Doctore Angelico duce, ita instituantur, ut ad altiorem sacrarum scientiarum cognitionem adducti, ad fontium Studium, ad investigationis laborisque scientifici usum, ad magisterium exercendum sint instructi necnon sacram scientiam sive docendo sive scribendo excolere, promovere atque defendere valeant." P. Inst. Acad. S.Anselmi, de Urbe Statuta (Rome, 1934), 9.

[58] *AOSB* 1932, Decree of the Congregation for Studies dated January 15, 1933, conferring the title "pontifical": cf. ibid., 22.

not the case since because of illness the Holy Father had to curtail the number of audiences. Usually on these occasions he wanted to hear us singing a piece of Gregorian chant."[59] It was also Pius XI who regularly invited the community of Sant'Anselmo to the great ceremonies in St. Peter's to adorn these celebrations with its "Canto Gregoriano." This happened for the first time at the Eucharistic Congress of 1922. All from Sant'Anselmo who were present on Easter Day 1937 had the unforgettable experience of standing behind the pope as he gave the blessing Urbi et Orbi, looking over the heads of the cardinals as the gathered crowds knelt in St. Peter's Square. In addition, a schola of twenty from Sant'Anselmo sang at the coronation of Pius XII in St. Peter's. As a reward for this involvement, members of the college had already under Pius XI received free admission to the Vatican museums.

Fr. Anselme Burgy (1893–1942)

Adaptation to the new regulations for studies took place surprisingly quickly at Sant'Anselmo. As early as April 21, 1934, the Congregation for Studies definitively approved the statutes of the *Pontificium Institutum Academicum Collegii Internationalis Sancti Anselmi de Urbe*.[60]

The papal legislation not only tightened up academic requirements but also created new titles and offices. From that time, the Abbot Primate carried the title *Magnus Cancellarius* of the university and the rector acquired the designation *Magnificus*. Deans had to be provided for the individual faculties, and for the first time Sant'Anselmo had a secretary of the college.[61]

[59] APr, Ateneo IV: Pubblicazioni. Scintillae Anselmianae I, 3 (Martius, 1939), 3. The "Scintillae Anselmianae" was a short-lived student journal of Sant'Anselmo of which four numbers appear from November 1938 to July 1939. The originator of the project was Br. Erminold Füssel of Metten. The colorful mixture of news from the life of the college, as well as some reviews of books published by the professors, appeared in German, English, French, and Italian or Latin.

[60] APr, II 13. Documenta varia. Cf. *AOSB* (1934): 22. For the printed version of the statutes see: *Pontificii instituti Academici Sancti Anselmi de Urbe Statuta* (Romae: ex Typographia "Madre di Dio," 1934).

[61] AAt, Libellus Actorum, pp. 429f. Rescript of the Congregation for Studies dated November 29, 1932, with the nomination of Fr. Athanas Staub as *Rector Magnificus*, Athenaei S. Anselmi; *AOSB* (1932): 22. Stotzingen, circular letter dated July 11, 1933. The first secretary of the college was Fr. Benoît Beguiriztain from Belloc. He was

Having consulted the rector and the faculty, the Primate appointed the biblicist Fr. Hildebrand Höpfl as first dean of the theological faculty. Following Höpfl's unexpected death in 1934, he was succeeded by the historian Fr. Matthäus Rothenhäusler who remained in office until 1951 when he was succeeded by Fr. Cyprian Vagaggini. The first dean of the philosophical faculty was Fr. Josef Gredt.

In retrospect, it can be admitted that a few years after the demise of the faculty of canon law, and certainly influenced by the new regulations governing studies, complaints began to arise concerning the drop in student numbers in the philosophical faculty. For the first time, we read in the Primate's circular letter dated July 11, 1933, that the number of students enrolled for the main course in philosophy left much to be desired. "It would be a cause of great regret if the major course in philosophy, which has been offered with great success over so many years at the Institutum Anselmianum and which is very highly regarded in Rome, should have to be discontinued because of the small number of students."[62] In an attempt to make it attractive for abbots to send students for higher philosophical studies, the Primate reminded them that a license could be completed in three years that would qualify the candidate to teach in nonacademic institutions. "In practice, this license can almost be compared to the old doctorate." Of course, the Primate suggested, it would be even better if as many Benedictines as possible were to complete doctorates in philosophy. Such doctorates would take four years to complete.

The Primate did not mention a fact known to all and which is still the case, that is, that many monasteries could not afford to send their monks for lengthy periods of study. The longer studies lasted, the fewer were the clerics released for lengthy specialized training.

In the following year and once again in 1935, the Abbot Primate repeated his warning: "There is a growing danger that the *cursus maior* in this faculty will have to be suspended because of the lack of students."[63] In fact, in 1935 there were only eleven students enrolled in the main course, of which six alone were Mechitarists. Nevertheless, the two

---

soon replaced, however, by Father Anselme Burgy from La Pierre-qui-vire, who simultaneously assumed the office of master of clerics.

[62] "Valde profecto dolendum esset, si cursus major philosophicus, qui per tot annos in Instituto Anselmiano maximo cum successu tradebatur et magna in Urbe gaudet aestimatione, propter minimum alumnorum numerum esset suspendendus." Stotzingen, circular letter dated July 11, 1933.

[63] "Ita periculum augetur, ne cursus major hujus facultatis suspendi debeat ob penuriam auditorum." Stotzingen, circular letter dated July 11, 1935.

Fr. Matthias Thiel (1884–1962)

doctoral students in the year later made names for themselves as scholars. These were Fr. Zeno Bucher of Sankt Ottilien and Fr. Viktor Warnach of Maria Laach.

It is possible that this first crisis in the faculty of philosophy—the main cause of which was undoubtedly the stricter requirements for studies—was also a symptom of an uneasiness over the one-sided neoscholastic orientation of that faculty, Gredt being its most decided representative. Other ways of thinking, which even then were already being discussed by Catholic philosophers—for example, M. Scheler's value philosophy—ran up against a wall of neo-Thomist rejection.

Gredt's predecessor, Fr. Beda Adlhoch from Metten, had attempted a wider interpretation of scholasticism—the latter being unavoidable for Catholic theologians of the period. In doing so, he appealed not only to Anselm of Canterbury but also to the early Middle Ages before Anselm.[64] During an audience of the college with Leo XIII he was asked by the pope, "Do you follow St. Thomas?" Adlhoch's adroit answer was, "*Sequor principia, quae Sanctitas Vestra proclamavit, et traditionem Benedictinam.* [I follow the principles proclaimed by Your Holiness as well as the Benedictine tradition.] The chief teacher of Christendom was happy, as one could see clearly enough."[65] Although Leo XIII himself subscribed to Thomism and did all he could to further it, he was nevertheless free from one-sidedness and intolerance. In contrast, under Pius X philosophers, too, were kept on a tighter rein.

In the 1930s, along with Gredt, Fr. Matthias Thiel from Maria Laach (1884–1962), who had studied in Freiburg under Geyser and Husserl,[66] taught philosophy at Sant'Anselmo. The chronicler of Maria Laach

[64] On B. Adlhoch (b. November 19, 1854; professed, September 28, 1880; priest, June 28, 1878, from 1891 to 1898 professor at Sant'Anselmo, died March 3, 1910, at Metten) see W. Raucher, *StudMitt* 31 (1910): 379–83. A fruit of his teaching activity in Sant'Anselmo is the original small book *Praefationes ad Artis Scholasticae inter Occidentales fata* (Brünn, 1896), in which Adlhoch bases his understanding of philosophical scholasticism on J. Hergenröther's *Handbuch der allgemeinen Kirchengeschichte* II, 3rd ed. (Freiburg im Breisgau, 1885), 448.

[65] B. Adlhoch, *StudMitt* 14 (1893): 464f.

[66] ArchMariaLaach, Obituary from Maria Laach of Father Matthias Thiel, died May 14, 1962.

describes Thiel thus: "Fr. Matthias was a philosopher but in a particularly austere way. He was not endowed with a lively imagination. He was totally devoted to St. Thomas and to the Aristotelian-Thomistic system." In his publications, Thiel demonstrated a multifaceted philosophical interest. But in the lectures of this small, slightly misshapen, gentle but humorless monk, this interest was not apparent and its spark was not communicated to his hearers.

Fr. Beat Reiser (1880–1940)

The third ordinary professor of the philosophical faculty was Fr. Beat Reiser from Einsiedeln (1880–1940).[67] This native of Swabia had received a doctorate in philosophy at Sant'Anselmo in 1904 and since then had taught philosophy and rhetoric in the abbey school at Einsiedeln. In the autumn of 1920 he began to teach alongside his revered mentor Josef Gredt, an activity to which he devoted himself with fiery zeal and success. He, too, was a convinced Thomist. With ten years of hard work, including research expeditions to France and Spain, he produced a three-volume edition of the philosophical writings of the Spanish Dominican Johannes a Sancto Thoma (1589–1644), the main pillar of Gredt's interpretation of St. Thomas.[68]

Reiser, however, became known in Rome and far beyond not primarily as a philosopher nor as a historian of philosophy but rather as a musician and in particular a proponent of *Musica sacra*. His *Laudes festivae* were and are appreciated and used by cognoscenti.[69] These are also a reflection of the rich liturgical life at Sant'Anselmo in the 1930s. For many years, Reiser, gifted with a pleasant singing voice, was master of the choir there. For relaxation he played the harp, a talent for which he was famous: the secretary of state, Cardinal Pacelli, liked to invite him to come to sing German Christmas songs accompanied on the harp. In the 1930s, Reiser's musical knowledge and activity made Sant'Anselmo a center of Gregorian chant. Reiser's enthusiasm for Gregorian chant and his rejection of polyphony, however, met with resistance, not least in his own monastery with its own rich musical tradition. As the Einsiedeln

[67] "Hochw. Dr. P. Beat Reiser, OSB," *Einsiedler Anzeiger*, September 10, 1940.

[68] Ioannis a S. Toma, *Cursus philosophicus thomisticus*, ed. B. Reiser, 3 vols. (Turin, 1930–1937).

[69] B. Reiser, *Laudes Festivae. Lectionarium et Cantarium pro diversitate temporum et festorum* (Typis Polyglottis Vaticanis²), 1940.

chronicler noted elegantly, "Dear Fr. Beat experienced his happiest hours thanks to the *philosophia perennis* and to *musica sacra*—but also, almost inevitably, his bitterest disappointments."

At the end of his foreword to the last volume of the above-mentioned edition of the works of the Spanish scholastic Johannes a Sancto Thoma, Reiser, well aware that his tastes were not shared by all, summed up, "What is presented in this course is like old wine. Others offer a sweeter wine, which indeed is more welcome to the palate. But let us not despise the old wine! Even if its taste is more bitter, it is better for the stomach."[70]

Fr. Beda Thum (1901–2000)

A fourth teacher of philosophy must be mentioned here—but not assessed—who did not fit into the format of the faculty as hitherto described. This is Fr. Beda Thum of Metten, who came to Sant'Anselmo in 1931.[71] Coming originally from the natural sciences, he was at first entrusted with the teaching of natural philosophical subjects. It was only in the years following the Second World War that his profile as a metaphysician became more pronounced—and as a metaphysician who made no secret of his opposition to the strict Thomism which was traditional in Sant'Anselmo.[72]

In 1936 the theological faculty acquired a second historian in the person of Dom Charles Poulet from the abbey of Wisques.[73] He was

[70] "Quae hoc cursu philosophico apponuntur, sunt sicut vinum antiquum. Alii vinum dulcius offerunt palatoque certo iucundius, at ne spernendum censeamus vinum antiquum, magis amarum palato, stomacho magis salubre." B. Reiser, *Ioannis a S. Thoma*, vol. 3 (Turin, 1937), x.

[71] Fr. Beda Thum, born on December 12, 1901, professed at Metten on May 3, 1923, and ordained priest on April 10, 1926. See introduction and bibliography in *Symphilosophie. Gesammelte Studien von Beda Thum*, ed. U. Faust and J. Hofmann (Salzburg, 1981).

[72] Beda Thum was also involved in organizing the academic program for the commemoration of the jubilee of the Venerable Bede at Sant'Anselmo in 1935; *AOSB* (1935): 62f.; *RLM* 21 (1935–1936): 174f. The lectures by Abbot B. Cappelle of Mont-César of Fr. M. Iguanez of Monte Cassino, and Fr. Beda Thum of Metten were published in *S.Beda Venerabilis*, StAns, vol. 6 (Rome, 1936).

[73] ArchWisques, Obituary of Dom Charles Poulet. Born on October 27, 1887, in Avesnes sur Helpe (North), he attended the minor seminary at Cambrai. In October 1908, he became student prefect in the College St. Pierre in Fournier. In 1910 he asked to enter Oosterhout in the Netherlands, where the Wisques community was living in exile. He made simple profession on July 2, 1912. He was briefly a soldier in the

almost fifty years of age when he came to Sant'Anselmo and already had an established reputation as an ecclesiastical historian, above all for his two-volume *Histoire de l'Eglise*. Published in 1926, this work went through numerous editions and was used as a textbook in many French seminaries. Poulet was an unusually energetic worker, "extremely jealous of his time." He loved the withdrawn monastic life, whose particular characteristic for him expressed itself in an almost fearful observance of the vow of poverty. Travel appeared to him as merely the cause of unnecessary expense, and he was completely lacking in that curiosity that is essential for the traveler. The only things that could captivate him were books. Indeed, he was scarcely familiar with the great artistic and historical monuments in Rome that stimulate most historians. At Sant'Anselmo his task was to teach medieval and early modern church history. He did not find teaching easy, and it was also a lack that, not being an Old Anselmian, he was not used to speaking Latin. Despite this, students enjoyed his lectures, which were spiced with anecdotes, while his "French" Latin, with its often incorrect placement of accent, was a constant source of amusement.

Fr. Charles Poulet (1887–1950)

Without a doubt, Fr. Matthäus Rothenhäusler surpassed Poulet in historical-philological training and sureness of touch in the use of the tools of the historical craft. Poulet, however, made no claims to being a researcher. His talent lay elsewhere. In the spirit of Guéranger, his aim was to transmit to Catholic friends of history the story of the development of the Church of Jesus Christ from unlikely beginnings to its contemporary greatness—and in this he succeeded. He saw this transmission as his main task during his time at Sant'Anselmo and also enjoyed the greater leisure that the life in the college offered him

First World War, but in 1916 he was discharged on health grounds. On September 20, 1919, he was ordained priest. As a historian he was self-taught. His main works are: *Guelfs et Gibelins*, 2 vols. (Bruxelles, 1922); *Histoire de l'Eglise*, 2 vols. (Paris, 1926). This had repeated editions up to the 1950s. In 1960, Dom L. Gaillard prepared a revised version: *Histoire du Christianisme,* 5 vols. (= in 39 fascicles of which the last contributions were written by others) (Paris: Beauchesne, 1923–1961); *Histoire de l'Eglise de France*, vol. 1, *Moyen Age* (Paris, 1946); vol. 2, *Temps modernes* (Paris, 1946); vol. 3, *L'époque contemporaine* (Paris, 1944–1946); *La sainteté française contemporaine. Sous le signe de Marie* (Paris, 1946).

Fr. Petrus Sedlmayr (1884–1961)

Fr. Benedikt Baur (1877–1963)

compared with the daily rhythm of a "normal" abbey. The life in Sant'Anselmo appeared to him to be eminently suitable for the preparation of his wide-ranging *Histoire du Christianisme*, which appeared in fascicles from 1932 on. With this goal in mind, he accepted the burden of lectures. By the time of Poulet's death, the project had grown to four large quarto volumes and was not yet finished. For the lay reader it was too wide-ranging and for the expert it presented too little that was new. Then came the Second World War. As a Frenchman, Dom Poulet could not and did not want to remain in a country that was at war with his homeland and in a college where most of the residents were German. Thus, he took himself to the South of France to the spa town of St. Jean-de-Luz, where an English widow—a Benedictine oblate—owned a villa with a private chapel. After the war, he returned to Rome, but his health was already undermined. On February 17, 1950, he died suddenly during a visit to St. Jean-de-Luz. He was sixty-three years old. His desk at St. Jean-de-Luz was covered with notes and record cards relevant to his great historical project.

In the 1930s two other teachers joined the professorial staff at Sant'Anselmo, Fr. Petrus Sedlmayr of Ettal (1884–1961) and Fr. Benedikt Baur from Beuron (1877–1963). The former taught fundamental theology from 1934 "with conscientious dedication,"[74] but without sparkle. Fr. Bauer was not unknown in Rome. Born in 1877, he had been appointed rector of the Greek college by Pius X in

[74] ArchEttal, Obituary of Fr. Petrus (Josef) Sedlmayr. Born on May 4, 1884, in Tegernsee, ordained priest on June 19, 1909, in Freising, entered Ettal in 1916, and made simple profession on March 4, 1917. In 1926, after years of pastoral work, he was appointed master of novices at Ettal, becoming in addition subprior and master of lay brothers there in 1927. He was a professor at Sant'Anselmo from 1934 to 1946. In 1947 he returned to Ettal where he was librarian until 1955. He died on February 5, 1961.

1912.[75] The chronicle relates that at that time, Benedikt Baur grew an impressive beard, but the latter did not make a convinced Latin monk into an equally convinced archimandrite. When Italy joined the war against Germany in 1915, he and the whole Greek college left Rome and went into exile at Einsiedeln. One of his students, who remained in lifelong contact with him, was the later Cardinal Acacio Coussa, who died in 1962. After the First World War, Father Benedikt taught philosophy at Engelberg in Switzerland and then dogmatic theology for some years in Beuron. Finally he became spiritual director at the newly established Benedictine college in Salzburg.

One can have doubts about Baur's suitability for teaching dogmatic theology in Sant'Anselmo alongside Anselm Stolz. His strength did not lie in academic theology but rather in the care of souls. Even while a professor at Sant'Anselmo, he developed an immense activity as retreat master and spiritual director, which made him well-known in German-speaking countries as well as in Italy. The fruit of this activity, mostly undertaken for women religious, was a series of publications, almost all of which enjoyed high print runs and were translated into several languages. Here it suffices to mention only his meditations on the Church's year under the title *Werde Licht* ("Let there be Light") in four volumes, which appeared in nine editions and in six languages.

Fr. Burkhard Neunheuser (1904–2004)

In 1938 Baur's time in Rome came to an end when the Curia appointed him archabbot of Beuron. As he knew well, this was for him the beginning of a period of suffering. At Sant'Anselmo he was succeeded as a teacher of dogmatic theology by the then-thirty-five-year-old Fr. Burkhard Neunheuser from Maria Laach. As their students soon and correctly noticed, Neunheuser proved a happy counterbalance to Anselm Stolz, three years older and a former classmate. One of the students from 1938–1939 gives an account of the teaching

[75] ArchBeuron, Obituary of Archabbot Benedikt (Karl) Baur. M. Eckardt, Christi pascimur cruce. Das Kreuz Christi nährt uns. Zum silbernen Abtsjubiläum von Benedikt Bauer, Erzabt von Beuron (1938–1955) am 24. Feb. 1963, in *Konradsblatt*, February 17, 1963; V. Fiala, *Erzabt Benedikt Baur, gestorben am 10. November, 1963*, *EuA* 40 (1964): 70–75; bibliography in, S. Mayer, *Beuroner Bibliographie 1863–1963* (Beuron, 1963), 20–22.

of both professors, which, despite its linguistic deficiencies, accurately reflects this complementarity:

> When the house bell rings at 8:45, Fr. Anselm Stolz, a monk of Gerleve, enters the classroom, a bundle of books under his arm, to introduce us to dogmatic theology. He has been teaching this subject for ten years and in this time has developed his own theological method. He is convinced that the work of a Catholic theologian does not consist primarily in the rehearsal of an already completed schema which provides the occasional opportunity to get lost in minutiae, most of which are of a purely philosophical nature which no longer have any close connection with the truths of revelation.
>
> The methodology of Catholic theology must also be more Catholic, i.e., it must attempt to encompass the whole of dogma, not merely specific definitions but, above all, the ordinary magisterium of the Church. It is precisely the fact that it finds its sources in the Tradition of the Church that differentiates theology from every other science. Were one to confine oneself to the fruits of a particular historical period, this would mean that the fruits of preceding and succeeding periods would be renounced, with the result that the material chosen would be incapable of transmitting a rounded picture of Catholic truth. Here, the object is to discover by means of dedicated and detailed research, what Tradition has said over the centuries concerning the individual truths of the Faith, what the Fathers said in their time, to understand how problems were presented in contemporary debate and how to accept with gratitude the harvest thereby obtained as a contribution toward a better understanding of revealed Truth.
>
> By proceeding thus, the theologian has the best chance of avoiding two mistakes. Not only will he avoid falling into one-sided scholastic speculation in the mistaken view that scholasticism represents the absolute apogee of the achievable, while what went before were imperfections, but he will also not get lost in the pure history of dogma. Rather, he will combine both, that is, positive and speculative theology, in a balanced and organic way.
>
> This is the way that Fr. Anselm shows us, in clear, well thought-out presentations. Our pens rush over the paper as we endeavor to record what we have heard. Soon it will be easier since it has been announced that Herder will publish the dogmatic treatises. That on the Trinity will appear already this month.
>
> Alongside Fr. Anselm, in the evenings we have lectures in the major course in dogmatics from Fr. Burkhard Neunheuser of Maria Laach. He follows the same method as Fr. Anselm except that he

concentrates more on Sacred Scripture and on the background to the development of dogma in the Catholic interpretation. This is only Fr. Burkhard's second year as a professor here, since the Most Revd. Archabbot Benedikt Baur, following his nomination as abbot, had to return to Beuron.

Both Fr. Anselm and Fr. Burkhard are former students of Sant'Anselmo. Thus, gradually, a house tradition is being built up—true to the founding principles of our patron: *Non tento, Domine, penetrare altitudinem tuam, quia nullatenus comparo illi intellectum meum, sed desidero aliquatenus intelligere veritatem tuam, quam credit et amat cor meum* [Lord, I do not attempt to plumb your depths, then in no measure can my intellect measure up to this task; I desire, however, to understand a little of your truth, a truth which my heart believes and loves] (Monologion).

Since many former students of Sant'Anselmo will, perhaps, be interested in what we cover in our seminars, what follows is a short account.

For a long time, now, Fr. Anselm has occupied himself in research of the mystical tradition. Years ago he studied the works of St. Anselm. In the last academic year he investigated the Moralia of St. Gregory. This year the seminar in dogmatics is dealing with the transfer to the modern understanding of mysticism.

Along with this Fr. Burkhard offers in a special course an introduction to contemporary questions in sacramental theology.[76]

Unfortunately, in that same year Fr. Burkhard Neunheuser had to stop teaching at Sant'Anselmo because, following the accidental death of a young lecturer in philosophy in his home monastery, he was needed as a teacher there. It was only more than twenty years later, in 1961, that he was able to resume his teaching activities at Sant'Anselmo in the newly established liturgical institute.[77]

In October 1937 the second twelve-year mandate of Abbot Primate Fidelis von Stotzingen expired. This required the Primate to summon a meeting of the Congress of Abbots at Sant'Anselmo for September 21. The solemn opening Mass was celebrated by Father Athanasius Staub, rector magnificus of Sant'Anselmo, in the presence of one hundred

[76] APr, Ateneo IV: Pubblicazioni. Scintillae Anselmianae I 2 (January 1939): 6f.

[77] On B. Neunheuser, see: E. v. Severus, "Utilis Frater. Bibliographie Dr. theol. Burkhard Neunheuser OSB," *ALW* 15 (1973): 123–64. The Pontifical Liturgical Institute dedicated a festschrift to him as its president from 1972 to 1978: *Eulogia, Miscellanea Liturgica*, StAns, vol. 68 (Rome, 1979).

abbots.[78] The reason for this honor lay in the fact the college was celebrating its golden jubilee, a fact expressly mentioned by the Primate in a speech to the second plenary session of the congress.[79] After a short review of the history of the college, the speaker quickly came to the unsolved—or unsolvable?—issues that the institute presented to the Primate and the Benedictine Order.

The most pressing was, as always, the unsatisfactory financial provision for the college. It was true that there were no outstanding debts, but the house lived from hand to mouth. Fortunately, all the manual work in house and garden was performed by the roughly fifteen lay brothers of the Beuronese Congregation who worked quietly and loyally without payment or recompense to their home monasteries.

The Abbot Primate did not forget to refer to this inestimable service which "could hardly have been rendered by highly paid employees." Further, these brothers were a shining example to all in the house—professors, officials, and students—by their exemplary monastic lives.

But, the professors, too, worked without payment, receiving only a modest subsidy toward their traveling expenses. Nevertheless, an increase in fees for the students as well as the *subsidium* payable by the individual monasteries was unavoidable. The abbots understood the difficulty and approved the proposal.

A second main problem for Sant'Anselmo was, according to the Primate, the difficulty of attracting suitable professors. He observed correctly that this problem arose *ex intima Ordinis nostri natura provenit* (from the special nature of our Order).

It could in fact happen that the Primate was suddenly faced with the need to find someone to fill a professorial chair. From where was a suitable person to come at short notice? It was easier to fill such a need in a centralized order than in the extremely federalized structure of the Benedictine Confederation.[80] Further, Fidelis von Stotzingen was far too upright and loyal to have undertaken secret moves toward centraliza-

[78] Eyewitness report by PL Glogger, "Pax Benedictina (Zur Primaswahl 1937)," *StudMitt* 55 (1937): 17–20. Also, Renner, 264–69.

[79] APr, Congr. Abb. 1937, I 15/D 1°, Tit. V. De Collegio S. Anselmi de Urbe.

[80] Stotzingen had already outlined the problem of the recruitment of suitable professors in his circular letter dated July 11, 1935. In Article 21 of the constitution *Deus scientiarum Dominus*, the prerequisites for conceding the right to teach were significantly increased. As Stotzingen wrote to the abbots, "Abbas Primas cum proprios monachos non habeat, quos ad tale officium praeparare posit, considerata intima Ordinis nostri natura, unica via, qua finis supra memoratus obtineatur, et futurus professorum senates condigne in tuto collocetur, in eo esse videtur ut Rmi Abbates eorumque monasteria pro futuro Obligationem adsumant unum alterumve

tion, even if such might have been for the good of Sant'Anselmo. The matter of the need to replace a professor at short notice did, in fact, arise in 1937. At the Congress of Abbots the Primate appealed for a suitable replacement for Fr. Luis Palacios, *qui in persecutione hispanica pro fide obiit* (who died for the Faith in the Spanish persecution).[81]

In July 1936, Fr. Luis Palacios of Montserrat, who for eleven years had been a lecturer in Oriental languages at Sant'Anselmo, returned home to Spain at the end of the academic year. He had hardly arrived home in his monastery when he and his confreres were caught up in the wave of suffering that was the Spanish Civil War. Palacios, who was resting in a neighboring property of the monastery, fled before the actions of revolutionaries in a nearby village. He was accompanied by another priest and both were probably trying to escape abroad. They were arrested, however, by left-wing troops and taken to Barcelona where they were imprisoned. Every effort was made from abroad to obtain their release but without success. At the end of November 1936, despite severe angina that he had contracted in prison, he was led away by members of the militia. Since that time there had been no trace of him. In all likelihood he and his confrere were murdered that same night, both for the same reason: they were monks.[82]

Fr. Edmund Beck (1902–1991)

It was only in 1939 that the Primate was able to find a successor for Palacio in the person of the young Fr. Edmund Beck from Metten, who was later to far surpass his predecessor as a scholar. Beck could be spared by Metten because the Nazi regime had just closed the monastery school.

To the surprise of many and the disappointment of some, the 1937 Congress of Abbots ended with the reelection of the already ailing Fidelis von Stotzingen. It had, however, been useful to the college that Stotzingen had drawn the attention of the abbots to the golden jubilee and with that to the problems of Sant'Anselmo.

---

monachum ad normas modo indicates formandi atque Collegio Anselmiano, si requiritur, adsignandi."

[81] *Protoccollum seu Relatio de Sessionibus quas Revmi et Illmi Abbates Congregationum Confoederatarum OSB habuerunt in aedibus S. Anselmi 1937* (Subiaco, 1937), 13f.

[82] "Tarrconen. Beatificationis seu Declarationis Martyrii Servorum Dei Emmanuel Borras Ferri episcopi auxiliaris et sociorum." (Tarragona, 1952), 14–19.

The jubilee itself was celebrated on January 4, 1938.[83] On the evening of January 3, the Primate invited the professors and students to a commemorative celebration accompanied by music provided by instrumentalists and singers from the house. At nine o'clock the following morning there was a solemn Mass of thanksgiving in honor of the Holy Trinity. The High Mass was sung by the vice rector of the college, who fifty years before had participated in the opening of the college as one of its first students.

In keeping with the grave circumstances of the time, the public celebrations were modest. Little or nothing remained of the brilliance and pomp of earlier celebrations on the Aventine. Nonetheless, from the Vatican, Pius XI kept in touch with what was happening. On the evening of the feast he sent two monsignori from his immediate entourage to Sant'Anselmo to convey his blessing and to present a portrait of himself with the following handwritten dedication, *Gratulabundus Augurabundus Pius PP. XI* (with heartfelt good wishes and blessing, Pope Pius XI). In addition, the pope instructed the secretary of state, Cardinal Pacelli, to send his own letter of congratulation.

4. During the Second World War

In a circular letter dated July 11, 1939, Abbot Primate Fidelis von Stotzingen reported on the academic year 1938–1939. Despite the restlessness of the times, wrote the Primate, in Sant'Anselmo it had been possible for everything to continue in peace and quiet. The number of students registered for the year was 106. Of these, twenty-seven were from outside the college, made up of a strong group of Augustinians, then Mechitarists, Salesians, Somaschi, and others. In addition, eight Benedictines lived in Sant'Anselmo who attended other Roman academies. The professorial body was made up of twenty-two persons, of whom two were not Benedictines, one being a Dominican from the Angelicum who taught sociology, and Enrico Josi, a professor at the Pontifical Institute for Christian Archaeology who for several years had been lecturing in Sant'Anselmo on the archaeology of early Christian Rome. The manual work in the house was entrusted to fifteen lay brothers from different monasteries of the Beuronese Congregation.

In the circular the Primate once again drew attention to the need to send a greater number of students for the major course in philosophy.

[83] G. Locher, "Jubelfeier—Fünfzig Jahre Neu-St. Anselm," *BenM* 20 (1938): 142–47; 217–23.

"The number of such students has so fallen that there is a danger that lectures in the faculty of philosophy may have to be suspended. This would greatly damage our Order and the institute of Sant'Anselmo. All the more would this be regrettable given that in the coming year seven excellent professors were to teach in this faculty."[84]

The Primate announced in the same circular that at the end of June, Fr. Pierre Bastien had returned for good to his home monastery of Maredsous. Pierre Bastien[85] was one of the pillars of Sant'Anselmo. Since 1925 he had been vice rector of the college. Born on October 5, 1866, although not directly in the Ardennes, in the opinion of his Belgian confreres Bastien had the character of a *vrai ardennais*—reliable, persistent, hard-working, and ready to help. He could be frank to the point of brusqueness but this was appreciated by his friends. He had entered Maredsous at the age of twenty and made profession to Abbot Placidus Wolter. As was usual in the Beuronese Congregation at the time, he was sent immediately after the novitiate to Seckau where the Congregation's school of philosophy was located. From 1887 to 1891 he studied theology at the "Old Sant'Anselmo" near St. Peter's. Following his return to Maredsous, the young priest was sent first for a few years to work in the abbey school but then was given responsibility for the clericate which was in Louvain where the superior was Dom Columba Marmion. In Louvain he studied canon law. Soon his reputation as a canonist began to spread. As a result he came to Rome in 1905 as a member of the commission for the revision of canon law. For several years he published with other Benedictines the "Collectanea" of the Roman Congregation for Bishops and Religious, was a consultor for several of the Roman dicasteries, and was even for a while responsible for the publication of the *Acta Apostolicae Sedis*. In addition to all of this, he lectured on the canon law of religious life at Sant'Anselmo as well as occasionally in moral theology. His special area

Fr. Pierre Bastien (1866–1940)

[84] "Numerus enim horum alumnorum ita diminutus est, ut periculum adsit, ne cursus facultatis philosophicae suspendantur, quod profecto magnum esset damnum pro Ordine nostro, pro Instituto Anselmiano, quidque eo magis dolendum esset, cum septem optima professors munus docendi in hac faculate anno proximo exercebunt." Stotzingen, circular letter dated July 11, 1939.

[85] H. De Moreau, "Dom Pierre Bastien (1866–1940)," *RLM* 25 (1939–1940): 153–57.

of competence was canon law of the religious life, of which he had an unsurpassed knowledge. He knew "everything" about the legal position of institutes with simple vows. In his obituary he thus was described, "More than any Mother Superior he appeared as [the personification of] divine providence, as the guardian angel of the institute." The fruit of this hectic activity was his much-used "Directoire canonique à l'usage des Congrégations à voeux simples," which appeared first at Maredsous in 1911 and was translated into German. According to one who knew the subject well, this was "the first complete and updated presentation of canon law as it affected religious institutes of both men and women with simple vows."[86]

As has already been suggested, Fr. Pierre Bastien was not a desk-bound canonist like Justinian Serédi but a practical lawyer. At the request of the Holy See, he was apostolic visitator in Bosnia and Herzegovina from 1910 until November 1914 where his task was to mediate in the bitter, longstanding conflicts among Catholics and between the secular and regular clergy in those regions. While there, not far from Sarajevo, he was overtaken by the outbreak of the First World War.

Fr. Pierre Bastien was a convinced Beuronese monk who loved the liturgy and Gregorian chant. Who would have imagined that before he began to publish in canon law he had already written a practical introduction to Gregorian chant?[87]

When in 1939 he was forced by a painful illness to return to Maredsous, he found leaving Rome very difficult. He was granted only a few months of rest in his home monastery, where he died on February 20, 1940. At the same time that his funeral was taking place at Maredsous, a solemn liturgy was being celebrated in Sant'Anselmo, presided over by the Abbot Primate in the presence of Cardinal La Puma, several abbots, senior officials of the Roman Curia, the Belgian ambassador, and members of the Belgian colony in Rome.

The Second World War had already broken out when Fr. Bastien died. This war was to have serious consequences for the continued existence of Sant'Anselmo as an international college. Should lectures be suspended as they had been during the First World War? Abbot Primate von Stotzingen decided to continue as hitherto. At the first meeting of the academic council held on October 31, 1939, the Primate informed

[86] P. Bastien, *Directoire Canonique à l'usage des Congrégations à Voeux Simples* (Bruges: Abbaye de Maredsous, Ch. Beyaert, 1933); quotation above taken from review of *Kirchenrechtliches Handbuch für die religiösen Gemeinschaften mit einfachen Gelübden*, by K. Elfner in *DT*, vol. 18 (Freiburg-im-Breisgau, 1911), vii.

[87] *Méthode élémentaire du Chant grégorien* (Rome-Tournai[1], 1907).

the professors of the resignation on grounds of age of the rector, Fr. Anselm Staub. At the same session he announced that the Congregation for Studies had confirmed the appointment as rector of Fr. Ulrich Beste from Collegeville. The Primate announced in addition the appointment of Fr. Matthäus Rothenhäusler of Gerleve as vice rector in place of the deceased Fr. Pierre Bastien.[88]

Since initially the professorial body was almost complete—only Fr. Charles Poulet from Wisques did not return to Rome for the academic year 1940–1941—it was possible to continue teaching activities undisturbed for at least the first years of the war. In the very first year of the war, however, Sant'Anselmo lost two professors with the deaths of Fr. Josef Gredt and Fr. Beat Reiser.

Fr. Gredt's strength had been declining for over a year, but nothing could prevent him from returning to Rome, where he had worked for over forty years, for the beginning of the academic year 1939–1940.[89] It was true that he no longer taught any obligatory courses, but he announced that he would deliver voluntary lectures *de diversis materiis philosophiae* (on various philosophical topics). He was, however, scarcely able to do this. Although the decline caused by his advanced age had become clearly visible, when the end came it was so swift that those around him did not think his death imminent even one hour before it happened. Stomach pains caused by an undiagnosed ulcer began to trouble him seriously and increase his debility only in the last weeks before his death. His energy did not permit him simply to rest in his cell and he was unwilling to recognize the seriousness of his situation. He still celebrated Mass on the day before his death; that evening he was walking around the house. The obituary stated, "He expressed the wish to celebrate in the second cycle of Masses on the following day and, already retired to bed, he asked for his rosary which he had not said that day."[90] In the late evening he suffered a hemorrhage. The infirmarian stayed with him until the pain let up and until he managed to sleep around two o'clock in the morning. The following morning Fr. Josef insisted on rising with the help of the infirmarian, but this led to a complete collapse. It was now clear to all that there was no time to lose. The infirmarian, Fr. Georg Bartsch from Emauzy, anointed him, the Abbot Primate and professors rushed to his room to recite the prayers for the dying, and half-an-hour later Fr. Josef Gredt died peacefully. The

[88] AAt., Libellus Actorum, 527.

[89] ArchSt. Matthias, Obituary from the Abbey of St. Eucharius (St. Matthias), R. P. Josef Gredt, died on January 29, 1940.

[90] Ibid.

annalist writes, "This was an extremely beautiful homecoming for him since in the last few months he had suffered so much from an unusual and pressing anxiety and admitted even to a great fear of death." It was January 29, 1940. Gredt was in his seventy-seventh year.

Some months later the dean of the philosophical faculty, Fr. Beat Reiser from Einsiedeln, suffered a stroke that led to progressive paralysis of his right side. This necessitated his return to Switzerland where he died in the hospital at Einsiedeln on September 8, 1940.

While the office of dean was filled by Fr. Matthias Thiel of Maria Laach, the actual successor of Fr. Josef Gredt was his confrere from Trier, Petrus Borne.[91] Gredt himself had groomed him for the succession and in turn Fr. Petrus revered his confrere and teacher and helped him in many practical matters. Until his election as abbot of St. Mattias in Trier in 1947, Petrus Borne acted as guardian of Gredt's philosophical patrimony.

Fr. Petrus Borne (1910–1976)

Two innovations introduced in Sant'Anselmo during the war years were undisputed gains. The first was the possibility of submitting dissertations in one's mother tongue instead of in Latin. Along with this was the transfer of all philosophical and theological lectures to the morning as well as the reduction in the number of these lectures.

The first change was occasioned by the request of an Italian Franciscan student for permission to write his dissertation in Italian.[92] At their meeting

[91] ArchTholey, Tholeyer Brief Ostern 1978. Petrus (Johannes) Borne, born on February 12, 1910, in Prümzurlay (district of Birburg), came to St. Matthias at Trier in 1923, from which he attended a public secondary school. Following his final school certificate, he was received into the novitiate at St. Matthias where he took triennial vows in 1930. He did his philosophical and theological studies in the diocesan seminary at Trier. In 1935 he was ordained priest in Trier cathedral and in 1936 Laurentius Zeller sent him to Sant'Anselmo to study under Gredt. Following the award of his doctorate in philosophy in 1938, he began to teach philosophy at Sant'Anselmo. On February 13, 1947, the community at St. Matthias elected him abbot, and on March 9 he received the abbatial blessing in the church at Sant'Anselmo from Abbot-Bishop Lorezo Salvi of Subiaco, assisted by Abbots Pierre Salmon of St. Jerome in Rome and Matthäus Quatember, procurator general of the Cistercian Order. In 1950 he transferred with part of the community of St. Matthias to Tholey in the Saarland. From 1965 until his death he was president of the Beuronese Congregation. He died at Tholey on March 3, 1976.

[92] AAt, Acta Fac. Theol. 34 and 37.

on December 5, 1939, the professors of the theological faculty supported this, *ratio est tum ne Professori incumbat arduum sat saepe munus corrigendi paginam per paginam locutiones latinas Alumnorum, tum praesertim quia etiam in aliis Urbis Academiis Pontificiis variae linguae admissae sunt* (so that the professors be relieved of the frequent and burdensome task of correcting the students' Latin, page for page, but also and especially because different languages are permitted in the other Roman pontifical academies). On March 14, 1940, the faculty agreed unanimously to a relevant revision of the statutes in this regard and the Congregation for Studies was petitioned to sanction this revision.

The second change was prompted by conditions in the years 1944–1945 when Rome was besieged and no public transport was available to external students. Thus, all compulsory lectures were transferred to the morning while at the same time the number of such lectures was increased from four to five each day. Despite this, some cuts had to be made in the material treated because it was not possible to cover everything in these morning lectures.[93]

On the recommendation of the Congregation for Studies, the examinations in the first year of the war were brought forward because several of the students had to reckon with being mobilized.[94] This possibility applied above all to the Germans. Nevertheless, the institute still had fifty-three registered students at the beginning of the academic year 1941–1942, and thirty-nine Benedictines resided in the house. Six students attended other pontifical institutes in the city. Indeed, the number of those obtaining academic degrees actually increased. In the academic year 1941–1942, no fewer than six Benedictines, following the publication of their theses, obtained the doctorate in theology. These were Gerard Békés from Pannonhalma, Viktor Schönbächler of Disentis, Augustin Mayer from Metten, Albrecht Wagner of Sankt Ottilien, Paulus Hörger (also from Sankt Ottilien), and Bonifatius Fischer of Beuron. In the same year a further eight students passed the doctoral examinations in theology. Even the faculty of philosophy was able to confer two doctoral certificates. Three students were classified as *Doctores approbati*. The Abbot Primate was justified in referring on July 7, 1942, to this success which—augmented by the publications of professors of Sant'Anselmo—contributed to the prestige of the college, already high in Roman estimation.[95]

[93] Ibid., 116.

[94] AAt, Libellus Actorum, 528.

[95] AAt, Libellus Actorum Concilii Professorum Pont. Inst. Acad. S. Anselmi de Urbe 1940/1941–1944/1945, 18.

Stotzingen was very careful to ensure that no national factions arose among the Benedictines in the college that could endanger the unity and the survival of the house. As early as May 30, 1940, at a meeting of the academic council, he reminded all of their duty to avoid the formation of factions in the college. The war was not to be given entry to the house. It was precisely for this reason that the distribution of students into *camerate* was strictly maintained, *ne quos congregavit in unum Christi amor, praesentes res adversae dissicent* (so that the current difficult circumstances would not divide those whom the love of Christ had brought together).[96]

The *camerate*, from the Latin *decuriae*, were much like what today, once more, are called deaneries. These were groups of resident students led by senior students known as *capi* or *decani* appointed by the Abbot Primate after consultation with the rector and the master of clerics.[97] The deans were not religious superiors and the *camerate* were not "basic communities." Their sole function was to organize students' recreation and common life. Twice a month the master of clerics divided the resident students into new *camerate*. In this exercise great care was taken that no one language group would predominate in any *camerata*. It was expressly intended that during periods of recreation students would have the chance to learn other languages. At that time lectures were not held in the present lecture theatres but in rooms on the upper floors of the house. The present aulas I and II were one large recreation room for students divided by partitions in order to give each *camerata* its own space. A particular task of the *capi* was to plan the group's weekly *exeat* into the city. Neither professors nor students could simply leave the house at will. The longer walks were usually confined to Sunday afternoons and to Thursday, a day on which there were no lectures. Each *camerata* had to go into the city as a group under the leadership of its *capo*. In addition to these regular excursions, there was an organized program for visiting the main Roman architectural monuments and art treasures—the dates of such visits were announced by the master of clerics at the beginning of the academic year.

Despite the Primate's warnings, there were, inevitably, national tensions among professors and students. In particular, those who came from countries in the West invaded by the German army regarded Germans with suspicion. This was not justified, as soon became clear when in Germany an undisguised campaign against the Church got under

[96] AAt, Libellus Actorum, 529.

[97] *Statuta in Collegia internationali Benedictinorum Sancti Anselmi de Urbe observanda* (Subiaco, 1939), nos. 64–65.

way and monasteries were closed by the Gestapo, German professors and students thereby losing their monastic homes.[98]

Fr. Hermann Keller (1905–1970)

Suspicion was justified in only one case, but very few were aware of his activities. The person in question was Fr. Hermann Keller of Beuron, who, however, did not teach at Sant'Anselmo but only turned up from time to time.[99] Keller, the favorite pupil and evil genius of Anselm Stolz, had the task of helping the latter in producing the new handbook of dogmatics. Although his name appears as coauthor on every fascicle that appeared, however, he did not in fact contribute a single line.

Fr. Hermann Keller was a man of exceptional intelligence. In 1931 he obtained a doctorate in theology at Sant'Anselmo with a dissertation on Origin's concept of the Church that greatly impressed his teachers.[100] But as a person Keller was unstable, ambitious, and inscrutable. Already at the beginning of the war he was working with the Gestapo and his activities as an agent in Rome did great damage to the German resistance to Hitler. Fortunately for Sant'Anselmo, Admiral Canaris, the wily head of German foreign counterintelligence and an opponent of Hitler, found a way of removing Keller quickly from Rome.

Keller went to Paris. "In the city on the Seine he soon achieved a certain notoriety among the freeloaders profiting from the occupying regime."[101]

In the academic year 1942–1943, the absence of students from abroad meant that numbers in the house were already much reduced. Resident

[98] Letter from Fr. Paulus Hörger of Sankt Ottilien to the author, dated April 18, 1986.

[99] Fr. Herman Keller was born on June 21, 1905; professed at Beuron on June 29, 1925; ordained priest on July 6, 1930.

[100] "Thesis ejus [= Keller, *Origines quemnam de Ecclesia habuerit conceptum*] propter adhibitam diligentiam, maturum judicium et acutam erudtionem juxta judicum sententiam digna est qualificatione 'eminenter.' Etiam quoad profundam speculationen dogmaticam laudatur." AAt, Libellus Actorum, 356.

[101] H. C. Deutsch, *Verschwörung gegen den Krieg. Der Widerstand in den Jahren 1939–1940* (Munich, 1969), 136–44; cf. p. 144 for the quotation above. After the war, Keller laid low for a while, after which he was chaplain to the Benedictine nuns of Mariendonk in the Lower Rhine, where he died on March 17, 1970. After his death the nuns of Mariendonk published a collection of his spiritual conferences under the title, *Herr, lehre uns beten* Kempen: Abtei Mariendonk, 1972).

students numbered twenty-five and external students twenty-eight. It was thanks to the Italian monasteries and, later, to the clerical society "Pia Società di S. Paolo" that teaching did not stop for lack of students. Also, since there were enough professors available, the situation did not appear immediately threatening.

Just before the start of the academic year 1942–1943, however, Sant'Anselmo received a blow with which no one had reckoned and that caused acute pain to many: the early death of Fr. Anselm Stolz.[102] At the end of the previous academic year, the abbess of the Benedictine nuns of Sorrento had asked the Abbot Primate if one of the professors of Sant'Anselmo could replace their chaplain during the holiday period. Fr. Anselm Stolz willingly accepted this task. He loved the south of Italy. The nuns of Sorrento were known for their translations of German scholarly works into Italian. Fr. Anselm's duties were to consist in taking over the conferences for the community along with the High Mass and sermon on Sundays as well as the usual devotions. This left him with an abundance of time for the recuperation he so badly needed. He had worked very hard over the last few years. On July 9 he went to Sorrento and returned to Rome on September 24. He pronounced himself most satisfied with his sojourn in the south. For the immediate future he had committed himself to give some lectures at the monastery in Camaldoli near Arrezo and after that to preach a retreat to the Camaldolese monks at Fonte Avellana. He found this last engagement difficult, but the monks pressed him so insistently that he did not want to refuse. On the second day after his return from Sorrento he was already not feeling well but was not quite sure what was wrong. Was it the change of climate, food, a slight cold caught on the journey, or a touch of influenza? He certainly did not think that there was anything seriously wrong. Thus, on September 28 he went to Camaldoli and then on to Fonte Avellana.

Throughout his time in Fonte Avellana he showed signs of fever. Because he was being pressed to continue with his talks, he was unwilling to interrupt them. During the return journey to Rome he already felt extremely unwell. On the following morning he was unable to leave his bed. He was shown to have a temperature of 40.5 degrees Celsius but the feeling was that he was suffering from a heavy cold. On the second day, despite his protests, his confreres called the doctor. The doctor

[102] For what follows see, ArchGerleve, Sterbechronik des RP Anselm Stolz, gestorben am 19. Oktober 1942. This obituary was based on a report from Fr. M. Rothenhäusler.

expressed concern that Fr. Anselm had not called him immediately on his return from Sorrento but hoped for a speedy recovery and ordered blood tests and an investigation of the kidneys. The fever remained high. Soon the clinic sent the results of the tests—acute typhus and kidney disease. Since Roman hospitals were not adequately equipped to receive such cases, Fr. Anselm remained at Sant'Anselmo in the care of Br. Berthold Wusthorn of Beuron, who was a trained nurse, and of the infirmarian, Fr. Athanasius Miller. The doctor visited daily, but from the very first day the patient took little nourishment despite the urgings of the doctor that he should take as much as possible, in particular milk. But it was precisely this that the patient refused, believing that coffee or tea would help him. Under these circumstances he was bound to become ever weaker and soon his powers of resistance were exhausted. And so he received the anointing of the sick and the sacrament of penance, the latter of which he received three times during his illness. He received Holy Communion every day with the exception of the last few days before he died. For the most part the patient was conscious but so weak that he could not speak. Despite all of this, no one thought that the end was so near since, according to the doctor, the illness was taking a perfectly normal course. The crisis came on October 18 and the infirmarians recognized that the patient was in great danger. Fr. Athanasius Miller and Br. Berthold spent the night at the bedside of the dying monk. He was conscious up to shortly before his death and made it clear by small signs that he was participating in the prayers for the dying. In the early morning of October 18, 1942, his sufferings were over. On the instructions of the authorities, the burial took place on the following day. Although it had not been possible to inform many of the death and of the time of burial in the cemetery of Campo Verano, and although the ecclesiastical schools were still on vacation, many more mourners than expected appeared. Among them were the archaeologist Ludwig Curtius and Fr. Anselm's friend, the theologian Erik Peterson. It was difficult or indeed impossible to replace Fr. Anselm Stolz, who had taught at Sant'Anselmo and who was loved by his students for the clarity and depth of his theology. The Abbot Primate named as successor Fr. Cipriano Vagaggini, an Italian but a monk of the Abbey of Saint-André near Bruges in Belgium. Fr. Vagaggini had already been teaching Oriental theology at Sant'Anselmo since 1940–1941.[103] As was

[103] AAt. Libellus Actorum . . . 1940/1941, 19, "In conferentia in capitulari aula habita ad initium anni Illmus D. Abbas Primas in necrologio personam et opus tum RPD Anselmi Burgy, Magistri Alumnorum et Actuarii Concilii, depinxit . . . tum RPD Anselmi Stolz, qui et ipse ab Alumnis valde amatus propter claram et

to become evident in the years that followed, it would not have been possible to find a better successor.

Despite the constantly diminishing number of students, life at Sant'Anselmo continued as normal until the autumn of 1943. At this point several non-German professors were absent or were unable to return to Italy.[104] The younger lay brothers were called up to the German army, which made it necessary, from 1943 onward, to transfer responsibility for the kitchen to German sisters of the Society of the Blessed Virgin Mary. Soon food began to become scarce. Professors and students cooperated in growing as many vegetables as possible in the garden at Sant'Anselmo, and for this purpose the terraces on the south and west were irrigated.[105]

In October 1943, Sant'Anselmo was first affected by the events surrounding Monte Cassino.

The German military authorities had been able to persuade a justifiably reluctant Archabbot Gregorio Diamare and the monks of Monte Cassino that the movable art treasures and the archives of the monastery were in extreme danger and that for this reason they should be removed north to a safe place. In addition, the evacuation of the monastic community had become inevitable. On October 19, 1943, Fr. Tommaso

---

profundam doctrinam dogmaticum, quam per plus 14 annos tradidit, nuncusque loquitur in variis suis operibus theologicis, partim in alias linguas versis." AAt, Acta Fac. Theol. 49, "In sermone suo inaugurali diei 5 Novembris 1942 Rev.ms D. Abbas Primas vi facultatum sibi a Sancta Sede et per Statuta Pontificii nostri Instituti Academici concessarum, qua Cancellarius Magnus Instituti in numerum Professorum ordinariorum Facultatis Theologicae assumpsit RPD Philippum Oppenheim OSB (Gerleve), hucusque Professorem extraordinarium.; RPD Cyprianum Vagaggini OSB. (St. André) iamiam Professorem extraordinarium Theologiae Orientalium, confirmavit eique, loco defunct RPD Anselmi Stolz, cathedram dogmaticum matutinam dedit."

[104] Up to the end of the war, the following professors lived at Sant'Anselmo [NB: this list includes the offices held as well as the subjects taught by the individuals.]: U. Beste (rector, pastoral theology); M. Rothenhäusler (vice rector, dean of the faculties of theology and philosophy, ecclesiastical history); G. Oesterle (canon law); A. Miller (Old Testament); G. Manise (moral theology); Ph. Oppenheim (liturgy); B.Thum (philosophy); E. Beck (languages); J. Müller (history of philosophy); C. Vagaggini (dogmatic theology); P. Borne (philosophy); A. Metzinger (New Testament); L. Thiry (philosophy); A. Mayer (dogmatic theology). E. Josi (archaeology) was an external teacher. Ch. Poulet and, since 1943, Cyrill Janota (Pannonhalma, dogmatic theology) were absent. Cf. Kalendarium Lectionum . . . 1943–1944 (Rome, 1943), 38–40, Libellus Actorum . . . 1940/1942, annus acad. 1943–1944.

[105] Letter from Fr. Paulus Hörger of Sankt Ottilien to the author dated April 18, 1986.

Lecisotti personally briefed the Abbot Primate on the situation.[106] Fidelis von Stotzingen responded very hesitantly to a request for hospitality because he saw no possibility of feeding more than twenty-five extra people. When on December 8, 1943, the manuscripts and archives of the monastery of St. Benedict came from Spoleto and were handed over by the Germans to the monks in front of the Castel Sant'Angelo in Rome, the Abbot Primate sent Fr. Athasasius Miller and Fr. Augustin Mayer to receive the treasures in his name.[107] Following the complete destruction of his monastery, the aged, stooped, Archabbot Diamare went on February 14, 1944, to Sant'Anselmo with a part of his community. He remained there until 1945 when he went with some of his monks to S. Elia, close to Monte Cassino, so that his diocese would no longer lack its shepherd.[108]

Already by then and into the first years following the war, the American abbots—in particular Abbot Alcuin Deutsch of Collegeville and Abbot Columban Thuis of St. Joseph's Abbey—energetically but unobtrusively supported Sant'Anselmo, low on food and cut off from its sources of income, by sending money via the Vatican, especially in the form of Mass stipends. Later, Mount Angel was particularly active in sending supplies of food.[109] When the long-awaited end to the war came and the Allies wanted to intern the German priests and brothers, this was able to be prevented by the rector, Fr. Ulrich Beste, an American.

5. Biographical Sketches of Some Professors

Fr. Hildebrand Höpfl (1872–1934)

If in the interwar period Sant'Anselmo enjoyed a solid reputation in the Catholic world as a center for biblical studies, the basis for this esteem is to be found in the work of Fr. Hildebrand Höpfl.[110]

[106] Diary of Tomasso Lecisotti in *Il Bombardamento di Montecassino. Diario di E. Grossetti—M. Matronola con altre testimonianze e documenti*, ed. F. Avagliano, Misc. Cassinese, vol. 41 (Monte Cassino, 1980), 113–37.

[107] Conversation with Cardinal Augustin Mayer on May 9, 1986.

[108] Stotzingen, circular letter dated August 1, 1946.

[109] Ibid., and conversation with Cardinal Augustin Mayer on May 9, 1986.

[110] ArchGrüssau, Obituary from Grüssau, P. Hildebrand Höpfl, died on February 14, 1934. An extract from this obituary is to be found in *StudMitt* 52 (1934): 31ff. Signed by S.S., i.e., Salesius Schmitt. The most important works of H. Höpfl are: (1) *Die höhere Bibelkritik. Studie über die modern rationalistische Behandlung der Hl. Schrift* (Paderborn, 1901, ^{2}1905); (2) *Das Buch der Bücher. Gedanken über Lektüre und*

Höpfl was born in Ledau in Bohemia on November 25, 1872, the son of a master baker. His baptismal name was Gustav. He was orphaned at an early age, losing both parents and all of his siblings at the age of five. His grandmother took responsibility for the rearing of the gifted and sensitive boy. In the autumn of 1887, having attended the local primary school, he came to the recently opened oblates' school of the Beuronese Congregation at the monastery of Emmaus in Prague. Three years later he graduated to the senior branch of the school, which was located at Seckau in Austria, where he spent a further three years. Gustav was tall, taller than his fellows, and was a good student. He had a quick grasp and was gifted with an unusually good memory. Thus, his grades were always the best, as they continued to be in his later studies.

In the summer of 1893, the "sixth-formers"—as the first graduating class of the oblates' school was called and who had been permitted to skip the final year of humanities—were permitted to enter the monasteries for which they were intended. In Höpfl's case this was Emmaus, where on the feast of the Birth of the Virgin Mary he was received into the canonical novitiate. One year later, on the same feast, he made profession. Br. Hildebrand studied philosophy in his home monastery, following which, in 1896, he was sent by Abbot Benedikt Sauer to Sant'Anselmo for theological studies. In 1900 he completed these studies with a doctorate in theology. He worked for only a short time at Emmaus because in the following year he was appointed lecturer in Scripture at his Congregation's theological school at Beuron, where he remained for two years. In 1903 he was appointed to the same position at Sant'Anselmo. From that year on until his death, apart from the interruption during the First World War, he worked as an exegete at Sant'Anselmo.

When the First World War broke out, Fr. Hildebrand happened to be on a holiday visit at Montserrat in Spain. Even though he was able, with a letter of recommendation from the British Embassy, to return to Rome, he could not work there for long. Following the closure of

---

Studium der Heiligen Schrift (Freiburg-im-Breisgau, 1904); (3) "Kardinal Wilhelm Sirlets Annotationes zum Neuen Testament. Eine Verteidigung der Vulgata gegen Valla und Erasmus. Nach ungedruckten Quellen bearbeitet von . . . ," in *Biblische Studien XIII*, 2 (Freiburg-im-Breisgau, 1908) (4) "Beiträge zur Geschichte der sixto-klementinischen Vulgata. Nach gedruckten und ungedruckten Quellen," in *Bibl. Studien XVIII*, 1–3 (Freiburg-im-Breisgau, 1913); (5) *Die Stationen des heiligen Kreuzweges nach Jerusalem* (Freiburg-im-Breisgau, 1914); (6) *Introductionis in Sacros utriusque Testamenti libros Compendium*, vol. 1, *Introductio generalis* (Rome, 1922), vol. 2, *Introductio specialis in libros V.T.* (Subiaco, 1921), vol. 3, *Introductio specialis in libros N.T.* (Subiaco, 1922); (7) *Tractatus de inspiratione Sacrae Scripturae et Compendium hermeneuticae biblicae catholicae* (Rome, 1923, ^{2}1929).

the college in 1915, he returned first to Emmaus but then worked for a year in Sant'Anselmo's wartime refuge at Seckau. In December 1916, his superiors sent him to Jerusalem. This entailed a difficult, weeklong overland journey across Asia Minor. For three years Höpfl lived at the Abbey of the Dormition of the Virgin in Jerusalem, teaching in the seminary of the Latin patriarchate. On the basis of his teaching activity, the Latin patriarchate was able to intervene on his behalf and he was permitted to remain in Jerusalem when the monks of Dormition were accused of espionage, deported to Egypt, and interned there by the English authorities on November 24, 1918. For a time, Fr. Hildebrand was the sole guardian of the monastery on Mount Sion. In January 1920, he was able to return to the reopened Sant'Anselmo. When the community of Emmaus was divided on national-ethnic grounds, Fr. Hildebrand opted for the reestablished monastery of Grüssau in Silesia, which he saw for the first time in the summer of 1921.

From then on he had a great affection for this monastery, even though his duties in Rome meant that he was never often there nor for any length of time. The only time available was during the summer vacation, the latter part of which he always spent in the sunny monastery of Mur-Gries near Bolzano in the South Tyrol. He seldom spent his holidays elsewhere. When, however, he was in Grüssau, he never missed choir and was happy to give conferences to the brothers and novices.

In the summer of 1933, he had to receive treatment in Zurich for diabetes. There did not appear to be any grounds for concern. In February 1934, he had influenza for some days but did not think much of this. Following an attack of sneezing, however, his nasal cavity became inflamed and this quickly developed into facial erysipelas which, because of his diabetes, could only be treated with difficulty. He died on February 14, 1934. The Abbot Primate wrote of him, "Particularly in the days of his final illness he proved himself a monk of deep faith and piety. Again and again he repeated that his only and total desire was that God's will for him would be done." When he died, he was not yet sixty-two years old.

The annalist at Grüssau described Höpfl's person and work as follows:

> All of those who knew Fr. Hildebrand well will remember him as a kindly man and an exemplary priest and religious. He used the great gifts of mind and heart that God had given him in constant service of God and neighbor. While one cannot doubt that he would equally have given himself wholeheartedly had he been asked to serve elsewhere, one can safely say that Providence so arranged matters that he was placed in situations that best corresponded to his own talents. For fully three decades Fr. Hildebrand worked at

> the education of young Benedictines from all countries and congregations as a teacher of Sacred Scripture at the international College of Sant'Anselmo in Rome. It is here that his real life's work was anchored, a work in which he achieved much of significance. In addition to encyclopedic knowledge, his rare gifts as a teacher made him suitable for these charges. Himself thoroughly permeated by Sacred Scripture, he knew how to awaken in his students that enthusiasm and love for the Word of God which gave wings to his own soul.
>
> His lectures flowed easily, always clear and lively, frequently spiced with amusing anecdotes. Fr. Hildebrand spoke without notes, being bound to no script or book. He could depend completely on his faultless memory. Indeed, he knew the Bible by heart. His competence in Latin, the language of instruction, was such that he was able effortlessly to speak as if in his mother tongue. He never got lost in examining fruitless details but, nevertheless, was never superficial and knew how to distinguish between what was useful for life and unnecessary ballast. Fr. Hildebrand was a master in every area of biblical science. He taught in turn, Introduction to the Old and New Testaments; exegesis of the Old and New Testaments as well as biblical languages. If necessity demanded it, he could also be relied on to teach nonbiblical subjects. Thus, for a time he taught philosophy and moral theology, both of these, again, with his usual mastery of the material and his own special clarity.[111]

By means of his scholarly publications, Fr. Hildebrand's influence and reputation reached beyond Sant'Anselmo where he became the first dean of the faculty of theology, following the reorganization of ecclesiastical studies under Pius XI. His publications since 1900 showed him to be a scholar of unconcealed conservatism in biblical studies but possessed of great knowledge and extraordinary industry. He gained recognition, deservedly so, mainly through his three-volume handbook on the introduction to the Bible. From 1921 on it appeared in several editions and was used, in revised form, by Höpfl's successors right up until the early 1960s.[112]

[111] It is perhaps the case that this presentation of Höpfl's personality is painted in too strident colors. Former students of his who are still alive remember another side: a rather pedantic teacher of occasionally narrow views, particularly when compared with Fr. Athanasius Miller, and one not free from vanity. Such criticisms, however, do not lessen his importance for Sant'Anselmo.

[112] The last edition, *Introductio generalis in sacram Scripturam, editio sexta noviter recensita quam curavit P. Ludovicus Leloir OSB* (Naples-Rome, 1958). *Introductio specialis*

Fr. Hildebrand did not publish only scholarly works. He was also able to write in an accessible way about biblical matters and wrote exciting accounts of his travels. In addition to the three-year sojourn in Jerusalem mentioned earlier, in the years 1908 and 1911 he traveled, for study purposes, in Greece, Asia Minor, Syria, Palestine, and Egypt. In those days such journeys were a rarity, and it was not a superfluous exercise to write about them. Höpfl's reports reflect his delight in nature and his sensitivity for the life and customs of the people in the places he visited.[113]

In addition to his activities as a professor, Höpfl worked for several Congregations in the Roman Curia. In 1905, Pius X appointed him a consultor of the Pontifical Biblical Commission, and in 1913 consultor at the Congregation of the Index. Furthermore, Benedict XV made him a *qualificator* of the Holy Office in 1917 and in 1918 a consultor for the Oriental Congregation.

His gregariousness and readiness to help prompted Höpfl to obtain permission to hear confessions in Rome, a permission not easily granted in those days. This enabled him to help in the parish of Testaccio at the foot of Sant'Anselmo.

At the head of his obituary, the annalist at Grüssau used the motto "He did everything well" from Mark 7:37. Fr. Hildebrand himself had once used this sentence in gratitude to the Lord when looking back on all the events of his varied life.

Fr. Josef Gredt (1863–1940)

The outward course of the life of the most important philosopher of Sant'Anselmo is of a simplicity that shows that Gredt had been able to devote himself totally and without digression to the task with which he was entrusted.[114]

---

in Vetus Testamentum, editio sexta quam curavit P. Sebastian Bovo OSB (Naples, 1963). *Introductio specialis in Novum Testamentum, editio sexta quam curavit P. Adalbertus Metzinger OSB* (Naples, 1962).

[113] "Reiseerinnungen aus Kleinasien," *SBSt* 33 (1909): 376–86, 416–24, 460–73; *SBSt* 34 (1910): 24–32; "Cholera an Bord," *SBSt* 35 (1911): 294–99.

[114] ArchSt. Matthias, Obituary from the abbey of St. Eucharius (= St. Matthias): *R.P. Josef Gredt, gestorben am 29. Januar 1940*. For a short account of his life and a bibliography, see *Miscellanea Philosophica R. P. Josepho Gredt O.S.B. completis LXXV annis oblata. Cura Facultatis philosophicae Pontificii Instituti S. Anselmi de Urbe OSB*, StAns (Rome, 1938), 7–8. See also, an obituary by P. Borne, in *Acta Pont. Acadamiae Romanae S. Thomae Aq. Et Religionis Catholicae N.S.* 6 (1939–1940): 266–71, and G. M. Manser, *DT* 18 (1940): 3–4.

Gredt was born on July 30, 1863, in Luxembourg, the son of the secondary-school headmaster Dr. Nikolaus Gredt and his wife, Franziska Hofmann. He was baptized Johann Nikolaus August. The boy received a solid humanistic education and at an early age felt himself drawn to the priesthood. He came in touch with Thomism for the first time in the seminary in Luxembourg through the lectures of Johannes Woltrink, professor of dogmatic theology. On August 24, 1886, he was ordained priest by Bishop Johann Josef Koppes in Luxembourg cathedral under the image of Our Lady of Consolation. Gredt went to Rome for further studies and there heard two important Thomists, Francesco Satolli, later cardinal, and the future Master of the Sacred Palace, Fr. Alberto Lepidi, OP. In Rome Gredt obtained a doctorate in theology. Subsequently, he learned Syriac, Hebrew, Aramaic, and Arabic in Innsbruck under Professor Gustav Bickell. In addition he studied Oriental archaeology and attended lectures and exercises in the natural sciences.

During the first Easter vacation he joined a fellow student from Switzerland on a hike from Innsbruck to the South Tyrol. He was less enchanted when his friend chose the abbey of Muri-Gries as the base for their excursions. Perhaps he wanted to suppress a latent attraction toward the monastic life. Already, in Rome, Gredt had come to know something about Benedictine monachism through Fr. Chrysostom Stelzer, an acquaintance that had stimulated reflection. In any case, it would appear that the stay in Muri-Gries led to Gredt's breaking off his studies in Innsbruck and requesting entry to the Abbey of Seckau in Styria. He made profession on May 18, 1891, and was immediately given the task of introducing his younger confreres to Thomistic-Aristotelian philosophy which at that time was experiencing a new upsurge.

In 1896 Gredt was summoned to Sant'Anselmo. With that, he began a work to which, until the end of his life, "he devoted himself so completely and with such success, that his name became a watchword for thousands in our monasteries and way beyond. One had only to attend one of his lectures to acquire an indelible impression of the extent to which he was restlessly absorbed by the matter immediately under discussion, of the degree to which he was one with the subject. In truth, he was possessed by that strict, intellectual eros that since Plato has characterized all genuine teachers of philosophy." Gredt epitomized the phrase from Aristotle's lost *Protrepitkos*, "Under every circumstance one must philosophize."[115] Gredt's *Elementa philosophiae aristotelico-*

[115] *Aristotelis qui ferebantur Librorum fragmenta*, collegit V. Rose, Bibl. scriptor. graec. et roman, Teubneriana (Leipzig, 1886), no. 51.

thomisticae, "his book," was a product of his work as a teacher and in outline already existed from his time in Seckau. Working on it relentlessly, Gredt perfected this work in the seven editions that appeared during his lifetime.[116]

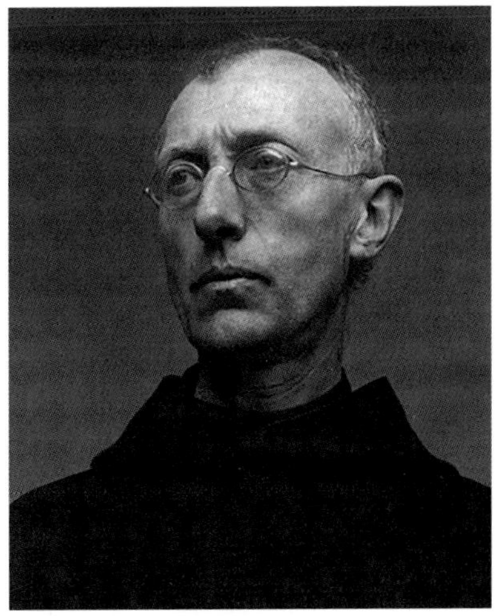

Fr. Josef Gredt (1863–1940)

The structure of the work followed the usual pattern of the material in question, i.e., logic, natural philosophy with psychology, metaphysics, and ethics, along with natural law. "A specific aesthetic as a philosophy of the beautiful is lacking—there are only hints of this in [the treatment of] metaphysics."[117] If logic was seen not so much as a science or method of thought but above all as a theoretical, speculative discipline and if in the area of natural philosophy the emphasis was not on the individual datum arrived at by a process of induction but rather on questions concerning ultimate being and the interior structure of objects, it was Gredt's treatment of metaphysics that revealed where he felt most at ease.

A particular feature of Gredt's handbook, evident from the first edition on, is that it did not merely present the teachings of Aristotle and Thomas Aquinas but aimed at leading the reader and student immediately to these great masters of philosophy. This explains the many extensive quotations from sources that accompanied the topics and theses under discussion.

Gredt wrote in a clear, simple, Latin devoid of rhetorical flourishes: "The austere but at the same time beautiful law of clear unconditional objectivity ruled." Gredt was able indeed to speak, half in jest, half seriously, about the "poetry" of his work. "If someone asked him for personal advice on a philosophical difficulty, he was able to open the book and read a relevant passage, slowly, word-for-word, since it seemed to him that in the book he had said everything so well, clearly, and to the point that he could not otherwise say it better."[118]

The demands he made on students were not few, "and it seemed to him that it was totally in keeping with the *pulchritudo universi* (the beauty of the universe), as he liked to joke, if the less gifted or the less

[116] The first edition appeared in Rome between 1899 and 1901. The thirteenth and last edition, *Editio decima tertia recognita et aucta ab Euchario Zenzen OSB*, appeared in two volumes in Barcelona in 1961.

[117] D. Feuling, "Eine aristotelisch-thomistische Philosophie," *BenM* 9 (1927): 66.

[118] ArchSt. Matthias, Obituary, p. 4.

diligent did not reach the goal." His academic activity, however, was not exhausted in training young students to think or in the communication of knowledge. Much more, he was a research philosopher. The stylistic objectivity of his philosophical idiom was simply an expression of a pronounced objectivity of thought characteristic of Gredt's philosophical method. It is precisely in this concern to deal solely with the topic in hand that Gredt showed himself to be a true pupil of St. Thomas Aquinas—which was always what he wanted to be. He showed this too in his treatment of opinions different from his own. He never became personal, relying rather on the strength of reason and argument. Such an objectivity and love of the truth led to great depth. But already, even then, a commissioned critic observed the darker side of these virtues. Not everyone was willing to follow him into the heights and depths of his abstractions and, particularly at the beginning of his career, his concise mode of expressing himself made it considerably difficult for him to make himself understood. It is true that the critic conceded, "Indeed, whoever performs this work [i.e., thoroughly works through the *Elementa*] is offered real treasures of the intellect. One would search long to find such riches of clearly polished concepts and carefully crafted overviews and divisions for such a system."[119] Gredt could not foresee that it was precisely this systematization that would be objected to in an era suspicious of all "systems."

Gredt was deeply convinced of the truth of Thomist teaching, awakened to new life by Pope Leo XIII. In trying to enter deeper into Thomist thinking, he tried to complement the interpretations of Cardinal Cajetan (d. 1534) and Franciscus Sylvester of Ferrara (d. 1528), who at that time were the only ones accepted in Rome and whom he himself had long followed, by considering other masters in the exegesis of the writings of St. Thomas. Specifically, he became a follower of the late Thomist John of St. Thomas (d. 1644), a Spaniard whose works were later to be newly edited by Gredt's pupil Beat Reiser.

Gredt, however, was also convinced that the philosophical system to which he subscribed, and which the Church in his day time and again proclaimed to be the most suitable instrument for acquiring a deeper understanding of the truths of the faith, was sufficiently broad to encompass all of that which existed without distortion or reduction. For this reason he followed contemporary developments in the natural sciences, for example, Einstein's theory of special relativity, with excited attention and tried to incorporate their results organically into the pre-

[119] Feuling, "Eine aristotelisch-thomistische Philosophie," supra, 67.

Fr. Daniel Feuling (1882–1947)

cisely defined Thomist system he had devised. But for him, Thomist doctrine always remained the starting point and signpost.

In the 1930s, however, Fr. Daniel Feuling of Beuron began to express misgivings about Gredt's philosophical method.[120] Feuling accused Gredt of not treating St. Thomas's principles in the same way as the philosophical conclusion of the contemporary natural sciences, "thoroughly, radically, and constantly to sift these principles in the light of overall conditions of common human as well as scientific experience and research." In Fueling's opinion, "If the method of Fr. Gredt's life's work had permitted him to grasp and live in a more original way the psychological, mathematical, physical, cultural sciences and human modes of experience, his work would have taken on an essentially different shape."

One should add that in order even to begin to operate as suggested above, Gredt would have to have had a different temperament and different interests. In fact, he lived on the abstract heights of metaphysics and it was only there that he was happy. This was in keeping with the fact that, while extremely undemanding in any area that went beyond his really modest needs, he was astonishingly inept in the area of the practicalities of life. Born with difficulties of vision and hearing as well as an exaggerated timidity in religious matters, already evident in his childhood, he was prevented from acquiring any pastoral experience. Nevertheless, in dealing with others he was affable, constantly cheerful, and full of genuine gratitude for any small help or kindness shown him. He liked to spend the holidays walking in the mountains where he could indulge his strong sensibility for nature. This gaunt monk with a tough constitution also particularly liked mountain climbing, very often climbing alone.

As his reputation spread beyond the confines of the Benedictine Confederation, recognition was not long in coming. On February 1, 1908, he was coopted as a member of the Roman Academy of St. Thomas, which had been founded by Leo XIII. On his seventy-fifth birthday the government of Luxembourg made him an officer of the Order of the

[120] D. Feuling, "Joseph Gredt's deutsche Philsophie," *BenM* 17 (1935): 319–21, quotation on p. 321.

Oaken Crown, and a year later the Grand Duchess made him a knight of the House Order of Nassau. He was, however, almost completely ignored by German university philosophers, even if it was suggested that Nicolai Hartmann had tried to find him a chair so that finally a "full-blooded Thomist" with whom one could have a genuine debate would find a place at a German university.

Gredt's task was and remained Sant'Anselmo and the education of young Benedictines in the strict school of the *philosophia perennis*. Dom Jean Mabillon would have been astonished to see incarnated in Gredt the synthesis between scholastic philosophy and monastic life which he, Mabillon, had believed to be scarcely possible.

Fr. Anselm Stolz (1900–1942)

Fr. Anselm Stolz (1900–1942)

Anselm Stolz came from the Rhineland.[121] He could not deny this, nor did he want to. His intellectual agility, which constantly led him to other shores, his love for the neighboring French civilization, his spirited humor, and the sparkling bonmots of which he was capable, remind one a little of his fellow Dusseldorfer Heinrich Heine—with the difference that unlike the latter, he had not abandoned his roots.

Born on January 28, 1900, in Ekrath near Düsseldorf, the son of a headmaster, his baptismal name was Julius. His elder brother, Arno Heinrich Constantin, born in 1895, having completed his secondary education at the oblates' school of the Beuronese Congregation at Seckau, had entered

[121] The most important source is, ArchGerleve, *Sterbechronik des RP Anselm Stolz, gestorben am 19. Oktober 1942*. This was written by Fr. Pius Buddenborg, prior of the Abbey of Gerleve, which at the time had been closed by the Gestapo. Buddenborg, subsequently abbot of Gerleve, had completed a doctorate in theology at Sant'Anselmo, *summa cum laude*, in 1930. He also wrote an obituary, "Pater Anselm Stolz zum Gedächtnis," *Sactificatio Nostra. Religiöse Zeitschrift für den katholischen Klerus* 14 (1943): 45–47. See also, A. Gabbiani, "Omaggio a Stolz," *L'Osservatore Romano*, November 21, 1942, p. 3; St. Bettencort, "D. Anselmo Stolz OSB," *VCr* 15 (1943): 160–70; O. Rousseau, "Introduction," in A. Stolz, *Theologie de la mystique*, 2nd ed. (Chevetogne, 1947), iv–xi; E. Salmann, "Gnadenerfahrung im Gebet. Zur Theorie der Mystik be A. Stolz un A. Mager," theological diss. (Münster, 1979), 449–52. For a complete bibliography of the works of A. Stolz, see appendix 1 of this work. The numbers used here refer to this bibliography.

the Abbey of St. Joseph in Gerleve at the age of eighteen. On August 11, 1914, he made profession there as Frater Benedikt. Ordained a priest in 1920, Fr. Benedikt was one of those monks of Gerleve who was sent to support Dormition Abbey in Jerusalem. He lived and worked there for over sixty-five years, known to many as the prior of the abbey in difficult times. He died on April 26, 1986, at the biblical age of ninety-two.[122]

The annalist at Gerleve wrote after Fr. Anselm's death that the older monks of Gerleve still remembered the small Julius Stolz, who already as a young secondary school pupil often came to visit his elder brother in St. Joseph's during the holidays. "Bright and lively as only a young Düsseldorfer can be, he mixed with the monks, helped during the summer in the garden and in the fields, during which work he was often allowed to lead the Rosary, loudly, with his bell-like voice." Thus, it came as no surprise that immediately following his graduation from secondary school in his hometown of Düsseldorf, he asked to enter Gerleve. After several months, however, he had to interrupt the novitiate which he had begun under the patronage of St. Anslem. Shortly before the end of the First World War, he was called up for military service. Fortunately he was not sent to the front, but in the retreat from Belgium he had to make the journey from Malines to Düsseldorf on foot. From that time on, he detested all forms of military activity.

Regularly demobilized in Düsseldorf, he immediately asked in writing to be permitted to recommence the novitiate. "I have not improved," he wrote to his novice master, "on the contrary, many rough edges need to be knocked off. But the will is there. That I can swear on my honor and with a good conscience." Thus, once more he began the monastic journey from the beginning. He did not always find it easy, but the novice was able to seal his trust in the grace of God by making profession on February 29, 1920. In October 1921, following the completion of his philosophical studies in Maria Laach and Gerleve, Abbot Raphael Molitor sent him to Sant'Anselmo to study theology. With this began five years of the richest development of the young monk's talents. Beyond the prescribed theological course, his limpid intelligence sought and found much stimulation in the lectures of, and through personal cooperation with, Fr. Josef Gredt. Above all, he learned from the works of Thomas Aquinas, whose *Summa Theologiae*, he admitted himself, he worked through four times. In addition to the lectures at Sant'Anselmo, he attended those of Fr. M. de la Taille, SJ, at the Gregorian University, and those of Fr. R. Garrigou-Lagrange, OP, in the Angelicum. In his

[122] ArchDormition Abbey, Death Notice of Benedikt Stolz.

Fr. Anselm at study

final year he took part in the *cursus magistralis* in the Gregorian, from which he learned much that was helpful in his later work as a teacher.

At the end of May 1926, he obtained a doctorate in theology at Sant'Anselmo. His dissertation did not pass over the hurdles on the way to approval without difficulties, changes, and excisions. On February 19, 1926, the rector, Fr. Athanasius Staub, reported to the Concilium Professorum that Fr. Anselm Stolz's work had been read by no fewer than four professors, all of whom were of the opinion that it contained teaching that was, to say the least, dangerous. For this reason, the thesis must be rejected.[123] Under these circumstances Stolz asked to be permitted to write a new, shorter, dissertation. The Concilium agreed. This new dissertation, which he completed in a few months, earned him the degree of doctor in theology on May 27, 1926.[124]

In the rejected thesis Stolz had examined the theory of the French Jesuit Fr. Rousselot, who died in 1915, concerning the act of faith. Over against a rational, not to say rationalistic, Catholic apologetic that pretended to prove the divine character of Christianity as one might prove the existence of Caesar or Alexander, Rousselot wished to emphasize the absolute necessity of the supernatural illumination of the grace of faith and had said that there simply was no natural certainty for doctrines and facts of faith. Whether or not Stolz tended too much toward this view, he had to choose a new, if related, topic: "The Act of Faith according to the Teaching of the [First] Vatican Council."

[123] "Hanc thesim iam quatuor Professores legerunt, qui omnes conveniunt in hoc quod reputent ibidem propugnari doctrinam saltem periculosam et propterea thesim reprobandum esse. . . . Concilium autem habita consideration magni laboris, quo D. Anselmus in priori thesi conficienda insudavit, eidem concede aliam de novo thesim 30 vel 40 paginarum exarare posse, sub directione tamen alicuius Professoris et hac conditione quod thesis reprobate in archivio asservetur simul cum censura reprobationis." AAt, Libellus Actorum, 237.

[124] "Convocatis Professoribus, Adm. Rev. PD. Rector ut Praeses Concilii, declaret D. Anselmum Stolz (S. Joseph, Gerleve) suam novam thesim doctoralem 'De actu fidei iuxta Concilium Vaticanum' iam publice defendisse et quaerit utrum huisumodi thesis ad lauream doctoralem in s. Theologia acquirendam admitti posit. Audiuntur in primis duo Professores qui thesim legerunt: ipsi thesim adprobant eamque dicunt ad lauream doctoralem sufficere; alii omnes consentiunt et ideo D. Anselmo Stolz cum omnibus conditionibus requisitis satisfecerit, laurea doctoralis in s. Theologia conceditur." Ibid., 241.

In 1933 he published his first book.[125] While the topic was borrowed from his rejected thesis, the content dealt only indirectly with Rousselot. Stolz was more interested in discovering historically what Thomas Aquinas, to whom all appealed, had actually said on the subject. In his investigation Stolz discovered how Thomas in his teaching on the act of faith was still close to the general understanding of the fathers. This mystical element, still present in Thomas, had been almost completely forgotten by later schoolmen. Already in this first work of the young theologian there are indications of certain traits which were to appear in all of his later writings, if in differing forms. Among these are: an intimate knowledge of the works of Aquinas, an intuitive attraction to the theology of the fathers and prescholastics, as well as an understanding of the mystical dimension of Christianity.

In the summer of 1926 Stolz returned to his home monastery where he was immediately given the task of teaching philosophy to the clerics. At the same time he went every week to Münster where he attended, as a guest auditor, the seminar of Fr. Diekamp, professor of dogmatic theology in the theological faculty of Münster University. According to a later student of his, it was here that Stolz became aware of the danger posed to young students by a one-sided rational theology. For this reason he always subsequently recommended that both philosophers and theologians should read Sacred Scripture regularly.

After only two years the Abbot Primate requested the services of the young monk of Gerleve for the vacant chair of dogmatic theology at Sant'Anselmo. At that time Gerleve did not have many vocations and to release Stolz for Rome was a sacrifice that Abbot Raphael Molitor was willing to make only in the light of the needs of the Benedictine Order. Thus, in April 1928, Fr. Anselm Stolz returned to Rome. The annalist at Gerleve reported,

> His pupils at that time had, for the most part, been fellow students. They will all remember the significant moment when Fr. Anselm took the professorial chair for the first time. Recalling him as a student with his Rehnish humor, sometimes bordering on high spirits, they were now surprised and struck by the seriousness with which the young professor stood at the threshold of his life's work. His consciousness of the great responsibility with which he had been entrusted gave him the words and bearing to present an impressive

[125] Anselm Stolz, *Glaubensgnade und Glaubenslicht nach Thomas von Aquin* [The grace of faith and the light of faith according to Thomas Aquinas], StAns, vol. 1 (Rome, 1933).

> and convincing lecture. From the first day his lectures shone with a wonderful clarity of thought and simplicity of language. One recognized at once that Fr. Anselm had found the right place.

With his great linguistic gifts and competence, Stolz soon made friends and contacts among the professors of theology in the Roman academies. Above all, his frequent exchange of ideas with Erik Peterson in the 1930s made a deep impression. Peterson (1890–1961), who had been a respected professor of ecclesiastical history and New Testament exegesis at the Protestant theological faculty in Bonn, caused a sensation by his conversion to Catholicism in St. Peter's at Christmas 1929. He remained in Rome in precarious financial circumstances. From 1937 on he lectured on ancient Christian literature at the Papal Institute for Christian Archaeology.[126]

In his more than fourteen years of activity in Rome, Anselm Stolz published with consistent hard work a series of monographs and longer articles in the various German and foreign specialist reviews, dealing with topics that covered the whole ambit of theology. As a young teacher of dogmatic theology he had thought about writing a commentary on the *Summa* of St. Thomas Aquinas, but the very first *tractatus* he had to teach—*De Deo Uno*—led him in a different direction. He did, it is true, contribute commentaries to volumes 2 and 3 of the German edition of St. Thomas—"Gottes Leben, sein Erkennen und Wollen" (God's life, his knowledge and will), in 1934, and "Gott, der Dreifaltige" (The triune God), in 1939. Under Peterson's influence, however, and convinced by his intensive study of the patristic sources of St. Thomas, he saw that his life's work lay in making the theological richness of the oldest and frequently overlooked doctrinal tradition of the fathers fruitful for contemporary theological thinking and with this to lead out of the narrowness of neoscholastic discourse.

Already in 1933, coming from a background in speculative theology, Stolz warned, "In the long run our dogmatic theology cannot any longer close itself to the already established and speculatively extremely

[126] On Peterson, see P. Testini, *RivAc* 37 (1961): 185–88 (includes a bibliography); H. Schlier *Hochl.* 53 (1960–1961): 283–86; A. A. Dempf, "Erik Petersons Rolle in der Geisteswissenschaft," *Hochl.* 54 (1961–1962): 24–31. As E. V. Severus correctly underlines in *ALW* 28, no. 1 (1986): 157, Stolz and also Peterson were both influenced by the ecclesiological awakening of the 1930s. According to Severus, who had discussions about this with Stolz in 1935 and 1938, the latter frequently pointed out the inner connection in the Apostles' Creed between the articles on belief in the Holy Spirit and belief in the holy Church.

fruitful results of the historical investigation of dogma" (No. 18). Thus, the idea ripened within him of writing a new handbook of dogmatic theology that, "doing justice to the [current] state of scholarly historical research, would embrace the theology of the fathers as well as that of the scholastics."[127] Nothing came of the plan to cooperate in this project with his former student Fr. Hermann Keller, in whom he placed great trust. All the four fasicles that appeared during his lifetime were written by Stolz himself. At his death, he had read the first galley proofs of the fifth fascicle (*De sacramentis*) and the manuscript of the sixth fascicle was with the printers. Alas, the handbook, new and stimulating in its theological methodology, was not completed after Fr. Anselm's death. Perhaps it was better so. The work was too marked by Stolz's way of thinking, too much the immediate fruit of his lectures.

This can be said because Anselm Stolz's significance lay more in his activities as a teacher than in his literary work. As the son of a competent headmaster, he brought with him from his family an unusual talent for teaching. Crystal clear in his thinking, precise and simple in his presentation, he was convincing in his lectures and knew how to place his listeners quickly under his spell. But his success with his students on the Aventine and with those who listened to his conferences elsewhere did not rest either on his complete mastery of his material or on his accomplished rhetorical skills. His success was based on the radiance of his personality. Since for Stolz theology is the science of faith, i.e., its subject matter is supernatural, the theologian must be a person of faith who needs the particular support of the Holy Spirit for his task. Without this charism, a person cannot be a theologian in the narrowest sense of this word. "The task of proclaiming and explaining God's word belongs to the 'prophets.' The theologian as teacher participates in this task" (no. 47). Expressions such as these reflect Stolz's musings on his intellectual position. From these he drew two conclusions:[128]

1) Theology requires an openness to the workings of grace, a firm faith, incessant prayer, and purity of heart. "Faith is more necessary to the theologian than sharpness of intellect."[129] "If the theologian

[127] "Hoc modo summa quaedam theologiae orta est, quae, statui scientiae historicae satisfaciens, theologiam Patrum et Scholae complectitur." Preface to Anselm Stolz, *Introductio in Sacram Theologiam* (Freiburg-im-Breisgau, 1941).

[128] Cf. *Introductio in S. Theologiam,* 126–38.

[129] "Fides necessarior est theologo quam acumen mentis," in ibid., 126. This phrase was quoted by Pope Paul VI, referring to Stolz, in his address to the International Congress of Theologians in Rome on October 1, 1966, *AAS* 58 (1966): 895f.

is searching for understanding of faith (*intellectus fidei*), it is not sufficient to sharpen the intellect alone and to rely on study. The theologian must also strive for perfection." Like Anselm of Canterbury, Stolz emphasized that the study of theology, the practice of acsesis, and contemplation belong together. All those who knew Anselm Stolz witness that in his own life and up to his final days he practiced this with ever-growing seriousness.

2) Theology as a God-given charism must serve the benefit and consolation of the pilgrim Church. For this reason, the theologian must have a particularly keen eye for the anthropological and soteriological value of the truth of Revelation. Theology presses forward toward love. With regard to God, the theologian is the observer of eternal truth; with regard to other persons, however, the theologian has pastoral obligations. In his innermost being, the theologian is one who proclaims the Faith. It is this point of view that explains Stolz's total unwillingness to recognize the distinction—made above all in his time by the Jesuits at Innsbruck—between a special theology of proclamation, i.e., kerygmatic theology, and academic theology.

Witnesses are unanimous in stating that Stolz conscientiously followed the demands of his second principle outlined above and there were many who entrusted themselves to his spiritual guidance, particularly in his later years.[130]

From what has been said up to now one can understand Stolz's particular and early affinity with mysticism. From a magisterial series of lectures delivered at the Salzburg University Week in 1935 appeared his most significant and also, perhaps, his most controversial work, *Theologie der Mystik* of 1936. In contrast with a psychologizing interpretation of mysticism as well as an exaggeration of phenomena associated with individual mystics, Stolz's aim was to rediscover the basic theological structure of the experience of God, of the life in and from Christ that every Christian has already received as a gift in baptism. He was stubborn in his refusal to explain Christian experiences of faith in psychological categories or even to compare the one with the other. He

[130] The historian Hubert Jedin, who for reasons of racial persecution found refuge in the Campo Sancto Teutonico for the duration of the Second World War, wrote on March 31, 1942, to Cardinal Bertram of Breslau, "Over the last three days the priests of Campo Santo made their annual retreat under the direction of Fr. Anselm Stolz, OSB, professor of dogmatics at Sant'Anselmo. This retreat was the most serious and stimulating that I have hitherto experienced as a priest." See Hubert Jedin, *Lebensbericht*, ed. K. Repgen, in Veröff. d. Komm. f. Zeitgesch., A: Quellen, vol. 35 (Mainz, 1984), 249.

consciously clung to the paradoxical term "trans-psychological experience," coined by himself, as more appropriate to the subject matter.

It is not possible here to engage in a contemporary assessment of the riches of Stolz's thought. The historian, however, will glimpse the fact that Stolz was intuitively on the way toward a "monastic theology" long before his pupil, the medievalist Dom Jean Leclercq, formulated the term. "Monastic theology" is something other than the "theology of monasticism," about which Stolz had also reflected on, particularly in his later years and especially in his last book, *L'ascesi cristiana*, which contained certain very debatable theses. Stolz wanted much more to practice theology in a prescholastic manner that had been buried for centuries. In this, his model was Anselm of Canterbury. "For Anselm," he wrote in 1937, "there is no difference between philosophical and theological thinking and, consequently, no dualism between learning and piety. He prays as a theologian and theologizes in prayer" (No. 3). The theology Stolz visualized saw its essence neither in a dialectical treatment of the teachings of the faith nor in a systematic compendium of these teachings but rather in a loving and mystical immersion of oneself in the content and ground of the faith. Here lies Stolz's greatness as a theologian—and also his limits.

His greatness lay in the fact that had he lived longer and had had more students, a genuine Benedictine theology would have had a chance to grow at Sant'Anselmo and in the Order, which would have been an enrichment for the Church and provided a firm intellectual and spiritual foundation for the vocations of young monks. That Stolz himself was able to strike out on this path was also without doubt thanks to the monastic character of Sant'Anselmo. At the same time, his thinking certainly—perhaps to a greater extent than he himself was aware—met the expectations of Catholic theology in Germany and France following the First World War. If up to that point the German Catholic theological faculties had promoted historical-critical research and rational thought, both proofs of the "scientific" character of theology as an academic discipline and a defense of the "reasonableness" of faith in the face of liberal and late-Enlightenment attacks, the students of the twenties and thirties were demanding something different. They were motivated more by the religious dimension of the study of theology, which found expression in a renewal of ecclesial awareness and a deeper understanding of the liturgy as a joint cultic activity of priest and community.[131]

[131] Cf. L. Scheffczyk in *Handbuch der Kirchengeschichte*, ed. H. Jedin, vol. 7 (Freiburg-im-Breisgau, 1979), 267; and in the memoirs of B. Kötting in *Frümittelalterl*, Studien 18 (1984): 4–13, here p. 9.

Anselm Stolz was the first to establish this new direction in Catholic theology at Sant'Anselmo in the years between the two world wars. The secret of Anselm Stolz's success as a teacher lies not least in his convincing response to the contemporary religious questioning of the young students of the time.

At the same time, however, this would appear to mark the limits of his importance. In the meantime, the pendulum has swung once more from the experience of the values of dogmatic theology in actual human living back to the values of "reason." The wind of skeptical secularization has turned chillier, and the awareness of the social and political responsibility of Christian theology more pronounced. Had the wind not already begun to change during the last years of Stolz's life? Was the alternative he proposed in the face of the idolization of race and power in the Third Reich, that is, the mysticism of the "joyful configuration with the Lord, the witness to the truth" to the point of willingness to suffer,[132] theologically adequate?

[132] "De theologo valet, et quidem in sensu speciali, propter maiorem assimilationem ad Dominum testificantem veritatem, promissio Christi, quam S. Matthaeus refert (5, 12): Gaudete et exsultate." In *Introductio in S. Theologiam*, 130.

The church at Sant'Anselmo before the reordering in 1952

Chapter 4

A New Flowering: 1946–1965

1. The First Postwar Years

Long since exhausted and plagued by illness, Abbot Primate Fidelis von Stotzingen died at Sant'Anselmo on January 9, 1947. For months he had been able to celebrate Mass only with great difficulty and assisted by a priest-confrere.[1] "Not wanting to be absent from the common meals, he had himself carried to the refectory on a stretcher." Finally, however, infirmity overcame his strong will and unbending sense of duty. Since more than a month before Christmas he had been unable to celebrate Mass. On Christmas Eve he suffered a first stroke, a second following on January 7. He died at noon on January 9. Five minutes before noon he opened his eyes, which had been mostly closed during his illness, and raised his head slightly from the pillow. A friendly smile—one like the familiar smile he made when he was in full health—crossed his pain-filled face. At that moment the clock in the room struck twelve. The patient sank back, closed his eyes and mouth, and died. During this time, the community was singing Sext and None in the church, the end not having been expected so soon. The only person present at the death was the brother infirmarian.

Abbot Primate Fidelis von Stotzingen

The destructive war had seriously hindered contacts between the Primate and the monasteries of the Order, indeed in some cases had made them completely impossible. It was true that most of the mon-

[1] ArchMaria Laach, Necrology of Abbot Primate Fidelis von Stotzingen. Stotzingen's last circular letter is dated August 1, 1946.

asteries closed down by the Nazis were reopened after the war, but in countries where communists seized power a second closure followed. This was the fate of the Abbey of Grüssau in Silesia, the monastic home of Fr. Franciscus Silesius Schmitt, who had lived as a guest at Sant'Anselmo for more than ten years and there produced the greater part of his famous edition of the works of St. Anselm of Canterbury.[2] Nobody, not least the Abbot Primate, could prevent the closure of Grüssau. Stotzingen's great achievement, indeed, was to lead the college undamaged through the war with a staff of almost exclusively German professors and officials and a student body composed for the most part of Italians. For the academic year 1945–1946 there were no fewer than sixty-one students on the books, of whom the smallest group were Benedictines, resident at Sant'Anselmo.

On February 10, 1947, invitations to the first postwar Congress of Abbots were issued by the rector, Fr. Ulrich Beste, following a personal instruction by Pope Pius XII.[3] In preparation for the congress, Beste sent a questionnaire to the abbots that also dealt with matters concerning Sant'Anselmo. These were questions always ancient and always new: How can Sant'Anselmo find sufficient and suitable professors in the Order? Where were students to come from and what form should monastic discipline take? What about the studies themselves? How was the whole thing to be financed?

Already before the congress and on the basis of replies that were coming in, Beste articulated some reflections that are not superfluous

[2] Volumes 2 to 4 of the *Opera Omnia of St. Anselm* were printed in Rome. Cf. F. S. Schmitt, "La nuova edizione delle opera di S. Anselmo d'Aosta," in *Relazioni e Comuicazioni al XXXI Congresso storico subalpino* (Aosta: September 9–11, 1956), 947–60; F. S. Schmitt, "Zur neuen Gesamtausgabe der Werke des hl. Anselm von Canterbury," *EuA* 37 (1961): 116–28; ArchGrüssau, Necrology of P. Franciscus Salesius Schmitt, 1894–1972. Schmitt, who had studied theology at Sant'Anselmo, obtaining a doctorate in that discipline, received a decisive impulse in the choice of his life's work from Prof. B. Geyer of Breslau. Cf. H. Kohlenberger, "Erfülltes Leben im Dienste von Wissenschaft und Kirche," *Sophia* 41 (1973): 136–38.

[3] "Iuxta Leonis XIII litteras apostolicas 'Summum Semper' d.d. 12 Iulii 1893, post obitum Abbatis Primatis erit Rectoris Colegii Sancti Anselmi de Urbe, omnes Congregationum Confoederatarum Praesides cunctosque Abbates regiminis de mandato Summi Pontificis convocare ad electionem successoris intra sex menses celebrandam. Adorando igitur Divinae Providentiae consilio cum Reverendissimus et Illustrissimus Dominus Fidelis de Stotzingen, Abbas Primas Ordinis nostri, d. 9 Januarii huius anni 1947 beata morte in Domino quieverit, prasentium tenore de mandate Pii XII feliciter regnantis in audientia d. 1 Februarii accepto, Te, Reverendissime Pater, invitamus et arcessimus ad congressum Abbatum." APr, Congr. Abb. 1947.

to present here.[4] In the matter of acquiring professors Beste noted, "Experience shows that personal astuteness and wise discretion on the part of the Primate are not sufficient [to obtain sufficient professors from the Order for Sant'Anselmo]. A pontifical institute of the dignity and importance of Sant'Anselmo should not lack the appropriate juridical constitution. For this reason, the college as a pontifical academic institution should be so constituted and structured that it should be capable of survival and of achieving the goal set it by several popes and to meet the needs of the whole Benedictine Order. The individual Congregations should be compelled to fulfill, in fraternal charity, their strict obligation to provide, via their respective presidents, two or three suitable monks . . . and no such monk who thus forms part of the body of professors or officials should be recalled without the consent of the Primate."

With regard to the number of students, he observed that, "should the college not receive effective assistance and resources, there is also a great danger that the faculty of philosophy will have to be closed, as has already happened in the case of the faculty of canon law. Such a closure would really be a shame for our Order."

In the matter of how the course of studies might be improved, it is worth mentioning the urgings of some abbots that the monastic and liturgical content of these studies be more strongly emphasized and promoted than hitherto.

As soon, however, as money was mentioned, all the abbots to whom the rector wrote maintained a low profile. On this Beste wrote, "The three questions of students, studies, and the subsidium are intrinsically related." The rector saw, rightly, that if the faculty of canon law were to be reopened—as some abbots wished—or if disciplines such as liturgy, monastic studies, or patristics were to be developed, this would require new living accommodation, new lecture theatres, and a new library. Who should pay for these if not the Congregations and the monasteries? In fact, for the first time the idea of an *aula magna* "worthy of the college" appears in the minutes of the congress of 1947.

With a strong majority of eighty-six votes but against a significant minority of twenty-three and ten spoiled votes, the congress approved Beste's proposal that the Primate should be conceded greater rights in the matter of the appointment of professors from the Order. *Jus atque fas est* (the Primate is fully within his rights) to require every Congregation

[4] APr, Congr. Abb. 1947. This is an anonymous memorandum, but undoubtedly from U. Beste, as was confirmed to the author of this history by Cardinal Augustin Mayer on June 9, 1986, on the basis of comparison of samples of Beste's handwriting.

to provide two or three monks whom he considers suitable, though not more than one from any given monastery. Abbots are warned not to close themselves to the requests of the Abbot Primate. In the case of a dispute, however, the Primate may summon a monk to Sant'Anselmo even against the will of his own abbot—an extreme provision the employment of which in subsequent decades has always been avoided by successive Abbots Primate.[5] No one would suggest that this decision, included in the "Lex Propria," the Constitution of the Benedictine Confederation, in 1952, noticeably altered the behavior of monasteries with regard to Sant'Anselmo.[6]

The main reason for summoning the congress of 1947 was, of course, the election of a new Abbot Primate. It is known that the Curia supported the candidacy of the rector of Sant'Anselmo. But the abbots decided otherwise. Perhaps they feared that Beste as Primate would press a centralizing agenda too far. Thus the congress's first choice fell on Benno Gut, the recently elected abbot of Einsiedeln. When Pius XII refused to accept this postulation, the congress elected another Swiss abbot, the sixty-year-old Abbot of Muri-Gries, Bernhard Kälin.[7]

Bernhard Kälin—abbot of Muri-Gries since 1945—was a schoolmaster of long standing.[8] He could not shed this persona when he came to Sant'Anselmo. From 1913 to 1945 Kälin had taught philosophy at the

[5] *Protocollum seu Relatio de Sessionibus quas Smi et Illmi Abbates Congregationum Confoederatarum habuerunt in aedibus S. Anselmi de Urbe a die 9 Septembris usque as 16 Septembris anno iubilaeo gloriosi transitus S.P.N. Benecicti 1947* (Norcia), 17f.

[6] "Ius atque fas est Abbati Primati servata cum monacorum numero singularum Congregationum proportione monachos pro praedictis muneribus in Collegio gerendis seligere, ita tamen ut ex eodem monasterio unus tantum exigi potest. Abbati Primati sic petenti omnes superiores morem gerant. Si in aliquo casu circa cooptationem professoris vel officialis inter se confligant iudicium superioris et postulatio Abbatis Primatis, et hic, consultis Rectore Magnifico et Consilio Primatiali, in postulando candidato insistendum censuerit, votis Abbatis Primatis cedere oportet er nominationi annuere." "Lex Propria Confoederationis Congregationum monasticarum O.S.B., nr. 153," in S. Mayer, *Confoederatio Benedictina*. Fontes (in textu originali et in versione Germanica) ad historiam et ius vigens Confoederationis Benedictinae (Beuron, 1956), 150–52. On the *Lex Propria* in general, cf. Schmitz, 247–52, and Renner, 275–81.

[7] Election protocol in *Protocollum seu Relatio* (A. 6), pp. 32–35.

[8] On Kälin, see J. Uttenweiler, "Abt Bernhard Kälin von Muri-Gries, der dritte Abtptimas des Benediktinerordens und sein erster Besuch in Beuron," *BenM* 24 (1948): 212–16. Also, P. Blättler, *Sarner Kollegi-Chronik* 24 (1962): 98–105; P. Blättler, *Jahresbericht der kantonalen Lehranstalt Sarnen* 9 (1962–1963): 105–11. P. Blättler, B. Egli, *EuA* 38 (1962): 511–15; G. Oesterle, "Erinnerungen an den verstorbenen Abt Primas Dr. Bernhard Kälin," *EuA* 39 (1963): 63–67.

The refectory at Sant'Anselmo with the reader's pulpit at the entrance

cantonal college at Sarnen, the Benedictine secondary school of Muri-Gries. Since 1929 he was, in addition, rector of the college at Sarnen. "There was, it is true, nothing fascinating about his teaching methods, nor was spontaneity or originality part of his makeup. His strength lay in solid, objective knowledge that he presented with persistence and faithfulness to his principles."[9] It was this period at Sarnen that saw the production of his two-volume introduction to scholastic philosophy which appeared in several editions.[10] Indeed, so full of work were these years that Kälin was able to cope only thanks to his boundless energy and healthy constitution. Kälin's textbook was popular among philosophy students at Sant'Anselmo, for whom Gredt's handbook was difficult to understand—and this not only because of the style of Latin in which it was written.

With Kälin, the leadership of Sant'Anselmo was for the first time since the days of Abbot Bernardi in the hands of a Benedictine who was not a member of the Beuronese Congregation. It soon became clear, however, that Kälin had no desire to overturn or to modify in any way

[9] Blättler, *Sarner Kollegi-Chronik* 24, supra, pp. 99f.

[10] B. Kälin, *Lehrbuch der Philosophie*, 4th ed., ed. R. Fäh (Sarnen, 1950).

the monastic customs of the house marked as they were by the Beuronese observance. One innovation introduced in 1948 did not come from him but originated, rather, in an instruction from the Congregation for Studies. From then on, the academic year was not to begin as heretofore in November, following a three-day retreat for the whole Anselmian community and accompanied by forty hours of eucharistic adoration. Instead, the year was to begin in a markedly simplified fashion on October 15 with a Mass of the Holy Spirit. The academic year, and with it community life, was to end on the feast of SS. Peter and Paul.[11]

Abbot Primate Bernhard Kälin

In his second year as Primate, Kälin made a long journey through the United States, still a strenuous undertaking at that time, visiting about one hundred Benedictine houses of men and women.[12] For half a century, since the time of Hildebrand de Hemptinne, no Primate had visited an American monastery. Kälin's journey was undertaken certainly not because he enjoyed traveling. Nor can one suggest that he understood the peculiarities of American Benedictines better than Stotzingen. But in the preceding year, the Americans had generously supported Sant'Anselmo with money and food. This had to be acknowledged and made known to the whole Order. In addition, the Primate hoped that by appealing personally he could obtain further help in undertaking the repairs and renovations urgently required at Sant'Anselmo. Thus, the main reason for the visit that lasted from August 1948 to March 1949 was Sant'Anselmo. And, in fact, thanks to the help of American Benedictine monasteries of men and women, it was possible immediately to begin building renovations.[13] Up to then, the lecture theatres had been situated in the upper floors of the house. These were now transferred to what had hitherto been recreation rooms opening off the cloister. This was the first step in the direction of a visual separation of the Benedictine college and the university. From then on, the upper floors were reserved for the use of Benedictine residents alone.

At the same time, the Abbot Primate moved from his apartment in the smaller courtyard, where his secretariat and the infirmary were also situated, into the virtually unused "cardinal's suite" overlooking Testaccio.

[11] Kälin, circular dated August 15, 1948.

[12] Kälin, circular of 1949.

[13] Kälin, circular dated June 29, 1950.

The spaces vacated in the former Primate's wing were turned into cells, admittedly small, for students and lay brothers. In this way, extra rooms were provided just in time for the rush of new Benedictine students to Sant'Anselmo.[14] Already in 1951–1952 there were 101 resident students from all the Congregations that then belonged to the Confederation. In the year 1955–1956, there were no fewer than 117, while in the following year the record number of 121 residents was reached, most of these residents also studying at Sant'Anselmo. But Sant'Anselmo did not have sufficient rooms for these numbers. Leo XIII had built for eighty students. For this reason, two and even three students had occasionally to share rooms. While the student body fully reflected the international character of the Order and of Sant'Anselmo itself, the professorial body continued for a long time yet to have a Beuronese majority.

In the academic year 1953–1954 the three new lecture theatres off the cloister acquired appropriate, even splendid, seating. It had been possible to acquire the solid walnut benches of the Italian Senate and distribute these among the three lecture theatres.[15] The students sitting in these chairs, which were upholstered in red velvet, each with a wide desk and sheltered in front by a balustrade, could survive an unproductive lecture without physical discomfort. According to the old custom, attendance at lectures was still obligatory. Furthermore, since, according to the Roman regulations for studies still in force, professors in the main disciplines were obliged to provide survey courses of the material in question rather than a monographic treatment of individual topics or problems (as is both usual and possible in Germany), it was not possible for teachers to confine themselves to what they found attractive or interesting. This was difficult for students from countries other than Italy. As Goethe, looking back at his own time as a student at Leipzig, said, "Youth prefers to be stimulated rather than instructed."[16]

In 1952 the renovation and reordering of the church according to the plans of Zurich architect Fritz Metzger was also completed. Up to then the monks had sat on pews in the nave of the church, an arrangement that greatly restricted the space available to those of the Roman faithful

[14] The following statistics are taken from the Abbot Primate's circular letters.

[15] "Durante anno academico tres aulae lectionum novis subsellis instructae sunt, ex aulis Senatus Reipublicae Italicae acquista." Kälin, circular dated July 15, 1954. This seating was finally removed in 1972 as part of a renovation of the lecture theatres. Already in 1964 Aula I was altered in order to accommodate the many students of the liturgical institute.

[16] J. W. von Goethe, Aus meinem Leben. Dichtung und Wahrheit, II, Berlin Edition, vol. 13 (Berlin, 1976), 355.

who came to the liturgy. Abbot Primate Kälin had a proper choir installed, filling the transepts of the basilica. The ugly high altar with its wooden ciborium was replaced by a table-shaped altar positioned closer to the triumphal arch that made Mass facing the people possible. This alteration followed the example of many ancient Roman churches but was by no means usual in the liturgy of the time. Originally, the apse had three windows. These were now closed and the spaces between the pillars of the apse were filled with panels of costly marble. A new organ, built by the Lübeck firm of Kemper, was placed in the semicircle that had previously been occupied by the high altar. Mosaics in the style of a Roman basilica were designed by the artist Br. Radbod Commandeur of Maria Laach for the vaulting of the apse. In the middle there was a gemmed cross with a circular halo carried by two angels, on the right, St. Anselm and on the left, St. Benedict. The mosaics on the two side altars are also by Radbod Commandeur.[17]

On April 19, 1953, Cardinal Ildefonso Schuster consecrated the new high altar.[18] As a boy in the oblates' school at St. Paul's Outside the

The artist Br. Radbod Commandeur working on a mosaic

[17] W. Buchowiecki, Handbuch der Kirchen Roms, vol. 1 (Vienna, 1967), 401ff. In the academic year 1956–1957, Sant'Anselmo also received a gift of four bells. Up to then there had only been two bells that had come from the Roman monastery of Carmelite nuns, Regina Coeli, closed in the previous century. The bronze statue of St. Anselm of Canterbury, which stands in the atrium of the basilica, is by the Swiss artist Albert Wider and dates from 1966.

[18] Kälin, circular letter dated June 19, 1953. The Blessed Sacrament altar was consecrated by Bishop Placido Nicolini, and the Lady Altar, by Abbot Primate Kälin.

Reordering of church: Installation of choir stalls, a freestanding altar at the crossing, and an organ in the apse

The reordered church

Walls, Schuster had been present at the laying of the foundation stone of Sant'Anselmo and as Frater Ildefonso had attended the solemn consecration of the church in 1900. Now, a year before his death, it was granted to him to consecrate the high altar in the renovated church. The success of the renovation and reordering of the church at Sant'Anselmo can only be properly appreciated today. Following the Second Vatican Council, which resulted in architectural interventions to most churches, almost nothing had to be changed in Sant'Anselmo. Under Abbot Primate Benno Gut, the organ found a new position in order to make room in the apse for a chief celebrant's chair and seating for concelebrants.[19]

[19] "A pluribus benefactoribus privatis adiutus organum nostris necessitatibus melius respondentem (!) et aptiore in loco collocatum Ecclesiae Anselmianae tribuere potui; eadem occasione eodemque adiutorio ecclesiae nostrae presbyterium et apsis ita transformari potuerunt ut decori domus Dei et celebrationibus liturgicis secundum novas normas ordinatis melius provideretur." Gut, circular letter for the feast of the Sacred Heart, 1966. This was the third organ at Sant'Anselmo. The first, built by Klais of Bonn and a gift of a certain "Domina Postley," was placed in the left aisle in 1911. This organ, following its blessing on May 25, 1911, by Cardinal B. Lorenzelli, was presented to many invited guests in a concert of works by

On the other hand, the attempt made over many years to build a new *aula magna* in the garden at Sant'Anselmo was a singular failure.[20] Again and again it was hoped that the state and municipal authorities would grant planning permission—indeed, foundations were dug in the hope that such planning permission was about to materialize. In the end, however, it had to be accepted with resignation that the exposed position of Sant'Anselmo, so close to the historic center of Rome, would be an obstacle to any further building.[21]

Fr. Ulrich Beste had often asked to be relieved of his office of rector. At the end of the academic year 1948–1949, Abbot Primate Kälin granted his wish, but Beste stayed on in Sant'Anselmo to teach moral

Bach, Guilmant, Rheinberger, Bossi, and Widor. The organist was Ulisse Matthey, the cathedral organist of Loreto. This concert inspired the chronicler to a veritable rhapsody of praise: "Quanta enim vis et virtus, cum cunctae organi tubae clangore magnifico spatiosum adimplent templum; quam suavis vero 'vocis coelestis' et dulciter vibrantis 'undae maris' sonus necnon variorum tibiarum clarus cantus; quanta iterum in variandis, crescentibus et decrescentibus vocibus facilitas; quam mira tandem modestia, qua hae voces se accommodant Gregoriano cantui, eumque sustentant elevantque!" *AOSB* (1911): 29–31.

[20] The wish to build an *aula magna*, quae Athenaei nostri digna sit was first expressed by the rector U. Beste at the Abbots' Congress of 1947. Cf. *Protocollum seu Relatio*, 19. Since 1960, Abbot Primate Benno Gut pursued a plan to build an aula in the garden on the western tip of the Aventine. In the circular letters in the following years, the hope was constantly expressed that planning permission would be obtained.

[21] Other, less visible, alterations of the buildings were still possible in the first postwar years. Thus, beginning on January 1, 1958, it was possible to build a motor workshop and garage at the foot of the Aventine on the Via Marmorata. The initiator of the project was the then-cellarer of Sant'Anselmo, Fr. Thomas Rückert. The latter had other ideas of how Sant'Anselmo could make additional and regular income from letting spaces to business concerns. Most of these schemes, however, were rejected. Fr. Thomas Rückert, born on November 6, 1911, professed at Münsterschwarzach on May 14, 1933, having studied for a year in St. Ottilien, studied philosophy and theology at Sant'Anselmo from 1934 to 1938 as auditor ad gradus academicos non adspirant. He was ordained priest on March 31, 1938. A year later he began the study of civil and canon law at Lateran University. This lasted until 1942 when he was called up for military service. After the war, he completed his studies in 1947 with a doctorate utriusque iuris. In 1948, Abbot Primate Kälin appointed the competent and affable Rückert, a well-versed lawyer, as cellarer of Sant'Anselmo. He held this office until 1970. During this period, Fr. Thomas became completely "Roman." Following a heart attack, but also because of differences with the new Abbot Primate Rembert Weakland, he returned to Germany where from 1971 he was an energetic and well-loved chaplain in Bad Brückenau. He died on September 24, 1980. Cf. ArchMünsterschwarzach, Necrology P. Thomas Rückert.

theology and, later, canon law.[22] Ulrich Conrad Beste was born in 1885 in Freeport, Minnesota, to a farming family of German origin. He was one of eighteen children of Conrad Beste and Clara Woeste. At home, the family spoke German. Later, when Beste was a student at Saint John's Abbey, he was for a time secretary and then vice president of a students' German literary society. As a student he was always one of the best in the various subjects and regularly received the annual prizes in Latin, Greek, religion, and also for "good conduct." In 1907, following his completion of the classical course, he was accepted into the novitiate of Collegeville, receiving the name Ulrich. One year later he made simple profession and in 1911 made solemn profession at Engelberg Abbey in Switzerland. By that time he had already been for a year in Europe, studying theology at Sant'Anselmo. Subsequently he continued at Sant'Anselmo in the faculty of canon law, obtaining the doctorate *iuris utriusque* in 1915. In the summer of that year he returned to the United States and until 1939 taught canon law, moral theology, and languages at Saint John's seminary and university. In 1923 he became rector of the seminary, a post he held until he was appointed to Sant'Anselmo.

Fr. Ulrich Beste (1885–1976)

When he went to Rome, Fr. Ulrich had already made a name for himself with his *Introductio in Codicem*, the first edition of which appeared in 1938. This was a comprehensive commentary in Latin on the Church's official legal compendium. For over thirty years Beste's *Introductio*, which he constantly updated, was a standard textbook in many theological faculties all over the world. The book appeared in six editions, the last copies being sold in 1967. It was not only Americans who joked, "In canon law, the best is Beste."

As the newly appointed *Rector Magnificus* of Sant'Anselmo, Fr. Ulrich soon came in contact with officials of the Roman Curia who immediately recognized his fund of knowledge. In 1941 he became a consultor of the Holy Office. In this capacity he composed over 450 written opinions on marriage cases submitted to the Holy Office for discussion and to the pope for his signature. His friendship with Cardinal Alfredo Ottaviani dated from this period. In 1963, when Beste celebrated his golden jubilee of priesthood, Ottaviani did not fail to attend the formal luncheon

[22] ArchCollegeville, personal file of U. Beste.

at Sant'Anselmo and to honor the jubilarian with an elegant and witty speech.

Later, Fr. Ulrich told how on the morning of the day on which the conclave began, he had spoken in the garden of the Holy Office with Cardinal Roncalli who emerged from that conclave as Pope John XXIII. In 1960, John XXIII named Ulrich Beste a member of the Preparatory Commission for the Second Vatican Council. Further, in 1962 he was made a *peritus* for the council, one of the first to be named for this post.

Beste had been entrusted with other important tasks. In 1953 the Holy See appointed him to preside over the general chapter of the Pallotines and the election of their superior general. Writing about this, he said, "It was a delicate mission at a critical time." At that juncture, the Pallotines were deeply divided on the matter of the Schönstatt movement.

As rector of Sant'Anselmo, Fr. Ulrich was popular among professors and students. He said later, "Even though I was an American, I was never bothered by the Germans." At the end of the war it was a blessing for Sant'Anselmo that the rector was an American. This made many matters possible and easier. Until he died, the tall, strongly built farmer's son, with large hands, clung firmly to the traditions he regarded as proven and correct. He loved Latin and spoke it in his lectures with evident pleasure. To the last he conscientiously followed the old customs of the American-Cassinese Congregation and was wary of several of the postconciliar developments in American monasteries. Even-tempered as he was, this suspicion did not result in his withdrawal into a self-imposed isolation. In 1966 he ceased his activity as a teacher at Sant'Anselmo. Shortly afterward he returned forever to his home monastery, where he died in 1976 at the advanced age of nearly ninety-one. Without fear of contradiction, one can say that Fr. Ulrich Beste was one of the professors who contributed most to Sant'Anselmo.

On August 8, 1949, before Ulrich Beste's successor as rector, Fr. Augustin Mayer, could take up office, Fr. Philipp Oppenheim of Gerleve, who had taught liturgy at Sant'Anselmo for twenty years, died suddenly in his home monastery. Since Fr. Oppenheim was really the initiator of the academic study of liturgy at Sant'Anselmo and with him the college's influence in this discipline began to spread beyond its walls, his life and work deserve to be remembered at this point.[23]

Born in 1899, Philipp Emil Oppenheim came in contact with the neighboring Abbey of Gerleve while a young student of theology at

[23] ArchGerleve, Necrology of Gerleve, R. P. Philippus Oppenheim, died on August 8, 1949. Obituary by H. Engberding, *EL* 64 (1950): 80ff., with selected bibliography.

Fr. Philipp Oppenheim (1899–1949)

Münster in Westphalia. In September 1919 he entered the monastery as a postulant. Following his studies in Gerleve and at the Congregation's school of theology at Beuron, and after his ordination to the priesthood in 1923, Abbot Raphael Molitor allowed him, starting in 1926, to attend Franz Josef Dölger's lectures in church history and the history of the liturgy at Münster. The purpose of the exercise was to teach Fr. Philipp how to work in an academic milieu.[24] When Dölger was called to the University of Breslau, Fr. Philipp followed him and in 1928 was awarded a doctorate in theology for a wide-ranging dissertation on "Das Mönchskleid im christlichen Altertum" (The Monastic Habit in Christian Antiquity). At the end of that same year, with the purpose of broadening and deepening his knowledge, particularly in the area of Christian archaeology, his abbot sent Fr. Philipp to Rome where he lived as a guest at Sant'Anselmo. In March 1929, almost as a matter of course, Fr. Philipp took over the lectures in liturgy and patristics from Fr. Heinrich Louwerse from Oosterhout who had fallen ill. Initially this was intended to be a temporary assignment to fill a gap, but in the long term it became his official area of work. Appointed extraordinary professor in 1932, in 1942 he was made ordinary professor for historical-systematic liturgy at Sant'Anselmo. There followed, in 1945, his nomination to the chair of liturgy at the Pontifical Lateran University and in 1946 to the chair at the University of Propaganda Fide. In the following year Pope Pius XII appointed him a consultor at the Congregation of Rites and a member of the Liturgical Commission. Already in 1942, the Pontifical Liturgical Academy had chosen him as a censor.

Thus Philipp Oppenheim, as a teacher of liturgy, had to give lectures at three universities, conduct seminars, and act as adviser and moderator to many candidates for the degrees of license and doctor. His positions in the Curia, though an honor, entailed much extra work. On top of this, he was for thirteen years secretary to the Athenaeum. But Oppenheim also felt impelled to become involved in pastoral activity. Every Sunday he celebrated and preached for the Salesian sisters in

[24] On Dölger, see Th. Klauser, "Franz Josef Dölger, 1879–1940. Sein Leben und sein Forschungsprogramm 'Antike und Christentum,'" *Jahrbuch für Antike und Christentum*, extra vol. 7 (1980).

Testaccio. He was a much sought-after confessor for the 750 vocational, technical, and secondary students in the neighboring Institute of Pius IX. Frequently he gave introductions to the liturgy of the greater feasts to young male academics resident on the Greater and Lesser Aventine. In addition, he taught languages during the German and later the American occupations.

But not even this exhausted his capacity and appetite for work. From the completion of his studies at Breslau and up until the time of his death, there appeared in periodicals and specialist encyclopedias an unbelievable flood of independent studies and articles. During the first years of his teaching activity in Rome, he developed the daring plan of gathering and presenting the whole ambit of liturgical studies in one great collective work. According to this plan, which had been thoroughly thought through and finalized, about forty volumes were to be produced which would cover all introductory topics to the liturgy, all the basic terminology, as well as the individual areas of liturgical academic investigation. The first volume of this *Institutiones systematrico-historicae in sacram Liturgiam*, which appeared in 1937, published by Marietti of Turin, was well received. Ten further volumes appeared in quick succession up to the time of Oppenheim's death. The intervening war brought its own obstacles and difficulties. In 1949, the author was only fifty years old and after twenty years as a teacher had a thorough knowledge of his subject and all the source material he needed in the great Roman libraries. Thus, despite initial doubts, one could expect that this wide-ranging work would reach a happy conclusion. Parallel to this project, Oppenheim also published other liturgical studies, among them several of independent scholarship. It suffices to mention only his *Pro Christo legatione fungimur*, a spiritual commentary on the individual stages of wisdom that appeared in 1949.

After Oppenheim's death, one of his confreres at Gerleve, himself a recognized specialist in the area of liturgy, made the following assessment: "The particular strength of Fr. Oppenheim's talent undoubtedly lay in his ability to gather material, in putting order into and publishing this material. . . . One can only marvel that he processed so much material and the speed at which he worked."[25] But already at that time, Oppenheim's method of working and its results were subject to much criticism. The annalist at Gerleve could not resist remarking that "his works seldom go beyond an extensive and cleverly organized collection of material. A more thorough intellectual penetration and digestion

[25] See obituary by H. Engbeding, p. 80.

of this material might perhaps have reduced the number and scope of his books, but increased their value. This, however, was neither his way nor, indeed, in keeping with his academic training and any well-meaning and critical comments could not change this."[26] Oppenheim, in his turn, did not allow himself to become embittered by the criticism of his publications. On the contrary, he was a particularly kind-hearted person who radiated his own special warmth wherever he was. Certainly, he sometimes found things difficult, for example, when his superiors tried to dampen his ardor and often kept him waiting a long time before granting requests for permission to print. But he passed these tests of obedience and humility in an exemplary manner. Sant'Anselmo has much for which to thank him, the first significant liturgist of the college after Ildefonso Schuster.

2. The Rectorship of Fr. Augustin Mayer: Studies and Life in the College from 1949 until the Second Vatican Council

When Augustin Mayer, since 1939 second professor of dogmatic theology and master of clerics at Sant'Anselmo, was appointed *Rector Magnificus*, the university had eighty-six resident Benedictine students and sixty external students. The only real worry was the small number of those taking the "academic course" in the faculty of philosophy. All in all, the professorial body was composed of first-rate individuals.

Further, in the first years of the new rector, Sant'Anselmo had the good fortune of attracting several outstanding new teachers. Thus, a still young and unknown historian, Fr. Kassius Hallinger of Münsterschwarzach, came to Rome to replace Dom Charles Poulet who had died suddenly on February 17, 1950. The credit for drawing attention to Hallinger and energetically furthering his cause belongs to Fr. Matthäus Rothenhäusler. Hallinger had just finished a wide-ranging dissertation on Benedictine reform movements from the tenth to the twelfth centuries with a doctorate in theology from the University of Würzburg. Rothenhäusler, having read the dissertation, immediately recognized its great value and smoothed the way for its publication in the series *Studia Anselmiana*, having from the beginning full confidence in the academic competence of the writer. Today, more than fifty years later, one can say that Hallinger's first work, *Gorze-Kluny. Studien zu den Reformgegensätzen des Hochmittelalters*, is one of the most important monographs on the

[26] Necrology, p. 6.

history of Benedictinism in the Middle Ages to have been published in the twentieth century.

Fr. Sebastiano Bovo from Praglia succeeded Fr. Athanasius Millar in the chair of Old Testament. For eleven years, until his recall to Praglia in 1960, Bovo taught Old Testament at Sant'Anselmo with great success.[27] He was greatly liked and esteemed by his students because, as well as teaching the absolutely necessary literary criticism of the Old Testament, he laid particular worth on communicating its theology.

Following a brief intermezzo during which the chair was held by Fr. Petrus Siffrin of Jerusalem, Oppenheim was succeeded by Fr. Cunibert Mohlberg from Maria Laach who had been in Rome for a long time, knew it well, and was a proven scholar.

Following the nomination as prior of St. Matthias in Trier, Eucharius Zenzen, who was himself one of Gredt's students and succeeded him as professor, Fr. Gabriel Büki of Pannonhalma took over this prestigious chair.[28]

[27] Sebastiano Nunzio Bovo, born on April 1, 1922, in Praglia, made profession in the monastery there on October 13, 1939, and was ordained priest on September 2, 1945. Having studied at Sant'Anselmo during the war, he went on to study at the Biblical Institute. His dissertation for the doctorate in theology, under Fr. Matthäeus Rothenhäusler, examined "Il Commento all'Apocalisse di Ambrogio Autberto." Part of this dissertation was published in StAns, vol. 28 (Rome, 1951), 372–403, under the title *Le fonti del Commento di Ambrogio Autperto nell'Apocalisse*. On December 18, 1965, Bovo was elected abbot of Parma. Shortly after his appointment as visitator of the Italian province of the Subiaco Congregation, he resigned as abbot. In 1981 he became vicar for religious in the Diocese of Parma. He died on October 18, 1983. See an obituary by A. Galletti in *Ben*. vol. 31 (1984): 201–3.

[28] Eucharius Zenzen, born in Andernach on October 17, 1903, entered the diocesan seminary in Trier in 1922. In 1925 he was clothed as a novice of the recently restored Abbey of St. Matthias. Following his ordination to the priesthood he was sent to Sant'Anselmo in 1929 to study philosophy. With J. Gredt as moderator, he completed this study in 1932 with a doctorate in philosophy, summa cum laude. On his return to Trier, Zenzen worked first as a youth chaplain, from 1936 in the Catholic "Jugendhaus" in Dusseldorf. Zenzen avoided the Nazi takeover and prohibition of all Catholic activity with young people by studying social economics and sociology at Paris and Lille. During the war, Zenzen was, from 1941, chaplain to a home for physically handicapped boys. After the war he resumed his general pastoral work among young people in Haus Altenberg, the new diocesan center for the pastoral care of the young. In 1947 he received the summons to Sant'Anselmo. When in 1950 the continued existence of St. Matthias again became an issue, Zenzen intervened energetically with Pius XII on behalf of the abbey in Trier. As a result, the Holy See appointed him prior and administrator of the part of the community that opted to remain in Trier. From 1951, he continued to teach philosophy, first as a guest professor and later as an honorary professor in the theological faculty of

The three professors from Metten at Sant'Anselmo—(from left) Fr. Edmund Beck, Fr. Augustin Mayer, Fr. Beda Thum

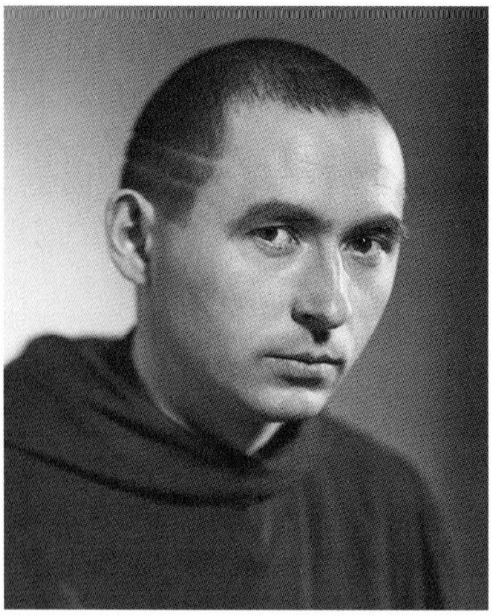

Fr. Eucharius Zenzen (1903–1963)

*Fr. Gabriel Büki (*1924)*

In the meantime, the constant lament over the paucity of students in the faculty of philosophy continued throughout the years, even at a period during which Sant'Anselmo was literally overflowing with Benedictine students. Certainly, the reasons for this lay not only in Sant'Anselmo itself. At a meeting of the Congregation for Studies with the rectors of the Roman academies in 1957, the danger to the Church, if the trend of the decline in the numbers of those studying philosophy were to continue, was lamented.[29] Already in 1950 the Abbot Primate had warned that, "particularly in our days, in which so many ideologies are circulating and being promoted, a solid and healthy philosophical training is absolutely necessary."[30] He said the same thing in 1957. As Abbot Primate, Benno Gut joined in this chorus of lament. In 1964 he reprimanded the lack of esteem for the study of philosophy evidenced in the Order. It had become clear during the Second Vatican Council how important a thorough grounding in philosophy was for contemporary intellectual discourse. "In particular, it is precisely the professors of the faculty of theology who more than once have asserted that those students who, before they begin their theological studies, complete the *cursus maior* in philosophy, demonstrate greatest security in understanding and making judgments on the topics in question."[31]

---

the University of Trier. In 1961, the community of St. Matthias elected him abbot. He died at Dinklage in Oldenburg on April 16, 1963. Cf. J. Aengenvoort, *Musik und Altar* (July 1963): 98–101; E. Brammertz, *Trierischer Volksfreund* (April 18, 1963): 4.

[29] "Mense Februarii huius anni S.C. de Seminariis et Studiorum Universitatibus Rectores Athenaeorum Urbis semel atque iterum ad consilia conferenda convocavit. In talibus colloquiis a pluribus notabatur quoque quantum damnum Ecclesiae immineret, si numerus alumnorum studiis philosophcis destinatus mensura hoc ultimo decenno observata decrescere pergeret." Kälin, circular letter dated July 18, 1957.

[30] Ibid.

[31] "Dum Facultas Theologica et Pontificium Institutum Liturgicam a crescente in annos auditorum numero frequentantur, quoad studia philosophica in nostra Confoederatione persistere videtur quaedam veluti minor aestimatio. Quod sane

But no amount of entreaty or lament was of any help. One might ask if this lack of interest was based on the kind of philosophy taught at Sant'Anselmo, a neoscholastic philosophy increasingly perceived as obsolete and incapable of either accepting or providing new impulses. Seen in this light, the departure of Fr. Beda Thum, called to the philosophical institute of Salzburg University in 1960, was not only a heavy loss for philosophy at Sant'Anselmo but also a signal, since Beda Thum was the one who had been most capable of introducing new ideas and a new questioning to philosophical discourse in the Athenaeum. When shortly afterward Thum moved to Vienna University and ceased all lectures at Sant'Anselmo, Abbot Primate Benno wrote with great concern to the abbots, pointing out that in the meantime there were so few *Philosophiae magistri* left in the Order that the only faculty of philosophy the Order had been entrusted with was in danger.[32] We shall meet these admonitions and warnings yet again at a later stage.

Right at the beginning of Augustin Mayer's period as rector, two decisions were taken that still affect academic life at Sant'Anselmo. The first decision was the establishment in 1950 of a liturgical institute, the purpose of which was not the teaching of liturgy but, rather, to serve academic research by the publication of sources that were important to the history of the liturgy. Fr. Cunibert Mohlberg was appointed head of the new institute.[33]

The Abbot Primate announced the second initiative in May 1952. This was the establishment of a *Studiorum Monasticorum Institutum*.[34]

---

magnopere dolendum est, cum iam in universa Ecclesiae vita et maxime in ipso Concilio Oecumenico eluceat, quanti momenti in hodierna multarum idearum colluctatione sit solida conformatio philosophica. Ipsi Facultatis Theologiae professores non semel attestantur eos alumnos securitate quaestiones penetrandi et diiudicandi eminere qui ante studia teologica cursum maiorem Facultatis Philosophicae absolverint." Gut, circular letter of June 1964.

[32] "Parcite mihi, Colendissimi Domini, si hac occasione iterum et instantius moneo, studiis philosophicis profunde excolendis in Ordine nostro numerum nimis exiguum iuvenum monachorum destinari. Quodsi pro Abbate Primate difficile est, magistros obtinere pro cathedris anselmianis, peculiari ratione id evenit in magisteri pro Facultate Philiosophica accersendis. Tam pauci sunt in nostro Ordine Philosophiae magistri, ut unica Facultas philosophica nobis concredita in discrimine versetur." Cf. Gut, circular letter dated June 29, 1962.

[33] Kälin, circular letter dated June 29, 1951. The original title was, "Societas Anselmiana studiis cultus christiani augendis." In addition to Mohlberg, the first members were: Fr. Petrus Siffrin of Dormition Abbey, Jerusalem, Fr. Anselm Strittmatter of St. Anselm's, Washington, and Fr. Leo Eizenhöfer of Neuburg.

[34] Kälin, circular letter dated May 26, 1952. Lectures were to be offered in "Historia spiritualitatis antiquae ante S. Benedictum, RB, Historia generalis OSB, Jus

Group photograph of the College in the 1950s. 1. Fr. Augustin Mayer, 2. Rector Fr. Ulrich Beste, 3. Abbot Primate Bernhard Kälin, 4. Vice-Rector Fr. Matthäus Rothenhäusler, 5. Cellarer Fr. Thomas Rückert, 6. Fr. Georg Bartsch, 7. Fr. Charles Poulet, 8. Fr. Johannes Müller, 9. Fr. Beda Thum

Unlike the liturgical institute, the monastic institute was intended not only to conduct research but also to train students. Their target group were young monks who had already completed their theological studies. These were to be offered a two-year course *in doctrina monastica* at Sant'Anselmo. As announced by the Abbot Primate to the abbots, lectures were to cover, in addition to the historical disciplines, Benedictine proper law, the theology of the spiritual life, and *liturgia theologica.* From the beginning, however, interest in this new institute was meager. The main group for which the course had been intended were future novice masters. Were abbots scared off by this? For the academic year 1953–1954, the institute had eleven students, of whom five were guests. Lectures in certain disciplines such as the theology of the liturgy, the history of spirituality, and topics from the Rule of Benedict, however, attracted students from the regular courses in theology and philosophy. This pattern was continued in later years when leadership of the institute was assumed by Fr. Basilius Steidle of Beuron. Starting in the academic year 1955–1956, Dom Jean Leclercq of Clervaux came for many years to Rome for one semester to lecture and conduct seminars on medieval monastic theology.

---

proprium benedictinum, Historia spiritualitatis benedictinae a S. Gregorio M. usque hodie, Historia spiritualitatis recentioris non benedictinae a s. XII/XIII usque hodie, Theologia ascetica et mystica theoretica, Liturgia theologica."

At least in the case of the faculty of theology, the 1950s were, after the 1930s, a period of new flowering at Sant'Anselmo.

Because of the great number of Benedictine students from all over the world, monks from the United States and from German-speaking monasteries being the largest groups, it was possible to make high intellectual and monastic demands on the students. But as far back as the early 1950s, the first complaints about the students' inadequate mastery of Latin had begun to be heard.[35] Above all it was the students from the United States who often—though not always—had considerable difficulties in following lectures delivered in Latin as well as in the written and oral examinations held in that language. This barrier awakened in the Americans, whose school system was different from that of the Continental Europeans, disquiet about Sant'Anselmo and feelings of inferiority which some years later were to prove explosive in the college.

At this period the professorial body was composed of significant scholars and some excellent teachers. In philosophy, Fr. Beda Thum was considered a deep thinker who made no concessions to his students but who convinced by the power and audacity of his speculation.

The first chair of dogmatics was held by Fr. Cyprian Vagaggini, who had been a pupil of Stolz and excelled both as an astute thinker and a teacher capable of firing his students with enthusiasm.[36] His tractatus on the Trinity demanded hard work from his students. His prize lecture, however, was his introduction to theological methodology, with its broad view of the history of modern thought, which he held every four years in accordance with the then-usual cycle of lectures. He had the capacity to express himself in lively, fluent Latin, incorporating, seemingly as a matter of course, quotations in Greek from the New Testament.

In his lectures Vagaggini dealt less with the liturgy, only to do so much more in his publications, looking on his subject matter from the perspective of a dogmatic theologian. The happiest result of this activity is his study *Il senso teologico della liturgia*, which appeared in 1956 and rightly attracted immediate attention. This book can be called "Benedictine" in

[35] "Quod studia attinet, experientia non semper laeta iterum edocemur almnos Athenaei linguam latinam probe sciant oportet. Cum disciplinae in scholis nostris latine tradantur, tempus frustra tereretur, si alumnus magistros intelligere non potest." Kälin, circular letter dated August 15, 1954.

[36] For Vagaggini's biographical details, see. *Lex orandi, lex credendi, Miscellanea in onore di P. Cipriano Vagaggini, OSB*, ed. G. J. Békés and G. Farnedi, StAns, vol. 79 (Rome, 1980), 7; also, L. De Lorenzi and M. Löhrer, "Una celebrazione significativa: I 70 anni di P. Cipriano Vagaggini," *Ben* vol. 27 (1980): 283–88. See also pp. 263–67 infra.

Fr. Anselm Günthör
*(*1911)*

Fr. Jean Leclercq
(1911–1993)
Receiving a doctorate honoris causa *at the University of Louvain in 1962*

the best sense—a successful attempt to grasp lived liturgy in a theological way while maintaining a thoroughly personal emphasis.[37]

The second section of the course in dogmatic theology was taught by the rector himself, Fr. Augustin Mayer. The author of this study remembers very clearly Mayer's lucid presentation of the extremely complicated history of the sacrament of penance. Those who lived at Sant'Anselmo will agree that of all the professors, Augustin Mayer spoke the most brilliant Latin.

At Sant'Anselmo, research into the history of the Church and of the Benedictine Order was represented by two scholars of international repute, of whom one could not have been more different from the other. These were Kassius Hallinger and Jean Leclercq. As in his book *Gorze-Cluny*, Hallinger, insistent on a precise and rigorous use of the tools of the historian's craft, loved to underline the contrasts, dazzling emphases, and memorable formulations which his students did not easily forget.[38] Full of fighting spirit, Hallinger divined opposition where often what was involved was more a difference of emphasis or a different way of posing the question. Foreign to him was any interest in the theological element of ecclesiastical history. In contrast, the latter was Jean Leclercq's dominating interest.[39] Leclercq,

[37] An English edition appeared in 1959 but was followed in 1976 by a further edition based on the fourth Italian edition and revised by Vagaggini. See *Theological Dimensions of the Liturgy*, trans. L. J. Doyle and W. A. Jurgens (Collegeville, MN, 1976).

[38] On Hallinger's biography and bibliography, see *Consuetudines Monasticae. Eine Festgabe für Kassius Hallinger aus Anlass seine 70. Geburtstages*, ed. J. F. Angerer and L. Lenzenweger, StAns, vol. 85 (Rome, 1982), 19–22; also, C. Elvert, *Aus der Werkstatt des Corpus Conduetudinem Monasticarum*, in StAns, vol. 85 (Rome, 1982), 423–35. See also pp. 253–60 infra.

[39] Jean Leclercq studied theology at Sant'Anselmo from 1933 to 1937. The topic of his dissertation for the doctorate in theology at the Institut Catholique in Paris in 1940, on Jean Quidort, was suggested by Dom Charles Poulet. See *Bernard of Clairvaux: Studies Presented to Dom Jean Leclercq*, Cistercian Studies Series, vol. 23

who could be just as spirited as Hallinger, was fascinated by a topic scarcely touched in the wide field of medieval monasticism, namely, its (prescholastic) theology. For this French monk, who knew many monasteries all over the world, this was not only a subject for scholarly research as described and justified in his countless publications but also a challenge and stimulus for contemporary theology. In Leclercq, the impulse received from his teacher, Anselm Stolz, had a powerful effect. The finest fruit of Leclercq's teaching activity in Sant'Anselmo is his book, *L'amour des Lettres et le désir de Dieu*, which appeared in 1957 and was published in English under the title *The Love of Learning and the Desire for God*. To this day, this remains a standard work for all who wish to become involved in and gain an understanding of the area of the "monastic theology" of the Middle Ages.[40]

In moral theology, Fr. Anselm Günthör from Weingarten, an experienced pastor, attempted to combine the biblical basis of Christian morality with a presentation of what were then the most recent positions of the Church on current questions such as situation ethics. Günthör's moral theology, like his pastoral theology, was always practical. It was astonishing how he managed to include in his lectures references to the latest publications in this field. He was also outstanding as a teacher of homiletics.[41]

(Washington, DC, 1973) [includes a bibliography]; see also additional bibliogprahy from 1978 to 1982 by Jean-Marie Christiaens in L. Freeman, ed., *Volume in Honor of Dom Jean Leclercq*, Monastic Studies No.16 (Montreal: Benedictine Priory, 1985), 253–60. Leclercq began to lecture at Sant'Anselmo in October 1955.

[40] A third historian who began a long and many-sided career as a teacher at Sant'Anselmo in the academic year 1960–1961 was the Cistercian Fr. Polycarp Zakar. He had just completed a brilliant thesis under the moderatorship of Fr. Kassius Hallinger on the strict observance in the Cistercian Order, a thorny problem in the history of the Order in seventeenth-century France. Beginning in 1961, Zakar took over the area of the history of the early Church, which since 1955 had been taught with great success by Fr. Anscar Mundó of Montserrat. Unfortunately, in 1959 Mundó left Sant'Anselmo and the Order. From 1966, Zakar taught modern Church history and, from 1971, canon law. In 1978 he was elected dean of the faculty of theology at Sant'Anselmo, a novelty since this was the first time that a non-Benedictine held this office. In 1985 Zakar was elected for a third term but had to resign in the same year and finish his teaching activity at Sant'Anselmo, having been elected abbot general of the Cistercian Order.

[41] A. Günthör, Die Predigt. *Theoretische und praktische theologische Wegweisung* (Freibug-im-Breisgau, 1963).

Fr. Gerhard Oesterle (1879–1963)

Despite these positive aspects, a constant source of worry for the Primate and rector was the provision of suitable professors for the chairs of Old and New Testament. This left a critical gap in the theological training of students at Sant'Anselmo at a time of biblical reawakening in the Catholic Church. The frequent change in personnel meant a breach in a tradition that in previous decades had made Sant'Anselmo widely known. Competent teachers such as Fr. Louis Leloir of Clervaux or Fr. Notker Füglister remained only for a few years. Attempts to recruit Fr. Jacques Dupont of St. André were unsuccessful, his only involvement in Sant'Anselmo being the delivery of some of the lectures in New Testament during the academic year 1954–1955.

The regulations then in force offered those beginning their theological studies a wealth of impulses that were no longer available later when the timetable was trimmed and the material to be covered was divided into "cycles." Thus, Fr. Edmund Beck was able to continue a tradition of Oriental studies that reached back to the first years of the college, with introductions to Syriac, Coptic, and Arabic, along with seminars that even dealt with such topics as the Koran in its original language. Fr. Emmanuel Lanne of Chevetogne gave insights into Byzantine theology, Enrico Josi taught Christian archaeology,[42] and Dom Eugène Cardine of

[42] Enrici Josi, 1885–1975, was for decades a distinctive, jovial, figure among the often monastically dour Benedictine professors. He had a wide knowledge of his area of competence that was justifiably recognized internationally—among other distinctions, he held honorary doctorates from the universities of Strasbourg, Louvain, and Freibug-im-Breisgau. The guided tours of the catacombs which he held for the students of Sant'Anselmo were famous. Although he was a consummate conversationalist, he totally lacked any talent for teaching. This was compensated for by his "friendliness" in the examinations. The nobility of character of this great and learned man is reflected in an extract from a letter to the then-rector, Fr. Basil Studer, dated July 7, 1968: "I was invited to Sant'Anselmo to teach Christian archaeology by two learned and late-lamented abbots, D. Ildefonso Schuster and D. Henri Quentin. I confess that with time such an honor made me proud, having found that the many Benedictine students were always attentive to my lectures and worked hard. During the academic year 1967–1968, when my course in Christian archaeology did not have a single Benedictine student but only two students from the Society of the Divine Word and two Somaschi, I had to examine my conscience and recognize that the absence of Benedictines was solely my fault because, as the Rule of St. Benedict teaches in Chapter 7, 'qui se exaltat humiliabitur.' For this

Fr. Eugène Cardine (1905–1988)

Fr. Louis Leloir (1911–1992)

Fr. Petrus Siffrin (1998–1963)

Solesmes gave a sensitive introduction to the structure and interpretation of Gregorian chant, based on neumes found in early medieval manuscripts.[43]

Outside the college, Sant'Anselmo was known above all for its publications. The most important of these were "Studia Anselmiana," with its subgroup "Analecta monastic"; Mohlberg's liturgical editions and

reason, mea culpa." AAt, Professori anziani I-Z. On March 7, 1969, the Athenaeum conferred on him an honorary doctorate in theology. On Zosi, cf. A. Ferrua, *Studi Romani*, no. 23 (1975): 494f. For his bibliography, see *RivAc*, no. 51 (1975): 5–23.

[43] The work of Fr. Gerhard Oesterle (1879–1963), from Gerleve, should also not be forgotten. He lived at Sant'Anselmo from 1921 to 1959. From 1932 he was ordinary professor of canon law. Having received the doctorate from the faculty of canon law at Sant'Anselmo in 1909, Oesterle was well known in Rome not only as a canonist. He was quintessentially a pastor who understood as part of the apostolate his involvement as a consultor, both for the Oriental Congregation and that of the sacraments, as judge of the Roman synodal courts from 1939 to 1949, as procurator for many years of the Benedictine Congregations of Beuron and Switzerland, and, finally, as postulator in three processes for beatification. As a jurist and pastor, rich in experience garnered from the Roman marriage tribunal, the Rota, he helped many of those damaged by their experience of marriage and who sought his help. It is virtually impossible to count the number of articles he published in pastoral and juridical journals, mostly based on concrete legal cases. Among his more important works are, *Praelectiones iuris canonici*, vol. 1 (1931), the only volume to appear, and, *Consultationes de jure matrimoniali* (Rome, 1942). Cf. ArchGerleve, Gerleve Necrology, R. P. Gerhard Oesterle died on September 4, 1963. Obituary by S. Senger, *EuA* 39 (1963): 515f.

those of his coworkers, Fr. Petrus Siffirn[44] and Fr. Leo Eizenhöfer[45] of Neuburg in the series *Rerum ecclesiasticarum documenta*; and finally, the great project for the publication of medieval monastic customaries, the *Corpus Consuetudinem Monasticarum*, inspired by Fr. Kassius Hallinger in 1955 and to which he later dedicated his energies more and more exclusively. The first volume of this series, now world famous among medievalists, appeared in 1963.

Fr. Emmanuel Lanne (1923–2010)

Of decisive importance for the future of Sant'Anselmo was the establishment of a new liturgical institute. It was announced by the Abbot Primate to the abbots of the Confederation on July 3, 1961. The reader will remember that since 1951 there existed an *Institutum Liturgicum Anselmia-*

[44] Fr. Petrus Siffrin was born on October 1, 1888, in Bildstock in the Saar. On August 1, 1928, he was ordained priest of the Diocese of Trier. One year later he asked to enter the Abbey of Gerleve, where he made profession on March 22, 1915. From 1928 to 1936 he was in Dormition Abbey on Mount Sion in Jerusalem, transferring his stability there. Later he was in St. Matthias in Trier without ever officially belonging to this monastery. During the Nazi period, following the dispersal of the community of St. Matthias, he was a pastor in the Saarland until 1948 in the parish of Schwarzenholz. From early on he became versed in the history of the liturgy in the West. For this reason, following the sudden death of Fr. Philipp Oppenheim of Gerleve, he was entrusted in 1949 with the teaching of liturgy at Sant'Anselmo. But this lasted only for a short time. Small in stature and of irascible temperament, he could not get on with his students. From 1950 he was Fr. Cunibert Mohlberg's closest coworker, rendering inestimable assistance in the latter's edition of the sacramentaries. In 1960 he returned to St. Matthias. In 1961 the theological faculty at Trier conferred on him an honorary doctorate. He died at Trier on June 6, 1963. Cf. Obituary with bibliography by L. Eizenhöfer, *EL*, no. 78 (1964): 63–65; also, V. Fiala, *EuA*, no. 39 (1963): 336–39. Information from Fr. Petrus Becker of St. Matthias at Trier, dated December 31, 1986.

[45] Fr. Leo Eizenöfer was at Sant'Anselmo from 1950 until 1956. He was born on August 15, 1907. Following four years of theology at Innsbruck, he entered the Abbey of Neuburg near Heidelberg in 1931. He made profession on April 9, 1933, and, following a further year of theology at Beuron, was ordained priest on July 25, 1936. From 1936 to 1941 he studied ancient philology in Heidelberg, completing this study with a doctorate in 1942. From 1941 to 1950 he was rector of the chapel at Neuburg's property, "Neersdommer Mühle," near Kempen on the Lower Rhine. He died on July 25, 1981, in Heidelberg. ArchNeuburg, *Wort in die Zeit*, no. 124 (Advent 1982): 5–15. For his bibliography up to 1977, cf. Kl. Gamber S. Rehle, *Textus patristici et liturgici*, vol. 13 (Regensburg, 1977), 166ff. Obituary by R. Baroffio, *RivLi* no. 68 (1982): 287–92.

num that occupied itself only with the editing of the ancient sacramentaries. This had by no means been the original idea of Cunibert Mohlberg, but the confinement to research had been forced on him by the faculty of theology at Sant'Anselmo, driven in particular by Fr. Matthäus Rothenhäusler. On December 7, 1949, Mohlberg had written to Abbot Primate Kälin, "It made a strange impression on me that express reference was made to a provision that the institute was not for students. What, however, if one or two should wish specifically to be trained for academic research in liturgy? When it comes to dealing with important issues such as the unsuccessful theology of Odo Casel, for which no historical basis exists, or 'the development of the sanctoral calendar,' important for the reform of the Breviary, must I, as has already happened in the past, look for outside scholars? Under these circumstances, the *Institutum Liturgicum Anselmianum* already seems to me to be a stillborn infant. My idea is and remains an *Institutum Liturgicum Benedictinum* situated in Sant'Anselmo, widely structured according to my plans which are based on those made in his day by Cabrol."[46]

Fr. Leo Eizenhöfer (1907–1981)

In 1960 the idea of a refoundation or broadening of the liturgical institute at Sant'Anselmo was in the air. In general, help was expected from the Benedictines in the hoped-for renewal of the liturgy. Above all, dioceses need experts in liturgy. Could Sant'Anselmo not offer a service to the universal Church in this area? Fr. Cipriano Vagaggini was already a consultor to the Liturgy Commission of the Second Vatican Council. But in Rome non-Benedictines had begun to interest themselves in the liturgy as, for example, Fr. H. Schmidt, SJ, of the Gregorian University. The Lateran University was planning the establishment of a liturgical institute. Sant'Anselmo wanted to forestall this. Fr. Cipriano Vagaggini was the driving force behind the project and was quickly able to win Abbot Primate Benno Gut and the rector, Augustin Mayer, for the idea.[47] Nevertheless, there was no lack of critical voices. The question of finance still remained the least problem to be surmounted. More important was the anxious question, would it be possible to find sufficient Benedictines

[46] Letter from C. Mohlberg to Abbot Primate Kälin dated July 7, 1949, cf. AAt, Professori anziani I-Z.

[47] Acta Synodi Abbatum Praesidum 1962, pp. 27ff.; S. Marsili, "Un Istituto Pontificio Liturgico a Roma," *RivLi* 48 (1961): 220–22.

The glittering opening of the Pontifical Liturgical Institute in the refectory of the College on December 9, 1961

who would be free to study liturgy for two years? Experiences of the monastic institute advised caution. In fact, from the very beginning, Benedictines were a tiny minority among the students of the liturgical institute. But if the majority of students were non-Benedictines, would this not change the character of Sant'Anselmo?[48]

[48] APr, Visitatio canonica in Collegio S. Anselmi peracta mense Martio 1962, "Institutum Liturgicum nunc est fundatum et apertum et causa finita est. Cum hoc factum sit cum consensu Praesidum, duobus vel tribus exceptis, non est, cur adhuc vituperetur, sed omni sagacitate curandum est, ut Institutum floreat et crescat." But—according to a handwritten note—the visitator, Archabbot B. Reetz of Bueron, qualified this by a verbal observation at the Synod of Abbots President on October 5, 1962, "Fatendum tamen est indolem Athenaei S. Anselmi per fundationem huius instituti liturgici aliqualiter mutatum esse, quia collegium, quod hucusque monachis reservatum erat, nunc apertum est omnibus alumnis aliorum Athenaeorum Urbis.

These reservations were to be taken seriously but were outweighed, even by the presidents of the Benedictine Congregations consulted, by optimism and by a willingness to risk the project. It was a strong encouragement that on June 17, 1961, the Roman Congregation not only approved what was planned but also, in a signal display of trust, conferred the title "pontifical" on the institute about to be established.[49]

The solemn opening of the new *Pontificium Institutum Liturgicum* took place on December 9, 1961.[50] Lectures at the institute which, like the monastic institute, formed part of the faculty of theology, had already begun almost two months before with six professors and forty-two students.

Fr. Salvatore Marsili (1910–1983)

The formal opening session took place in the presence of thirteen cardinals, nine ambassadors, representatives of the city of Rome, high officials of the Roman Curia, religious superiors, and other invited guests, altogether about 250 people. For the occasion, the refectory had been cleared. The centerpiece was a comprehensive lecture by Cipriano Vagaggini on the connection between liturgy and theology in the first half of the twentieth century. The cardinal secretary of state, Amleto Cicognani, had sent a congratulatory letter in Latin from Pope John XXIII to Abbot Primate Benno Gut.

Vagaggini would have seemed to be the predestined head of the new institute, but he refused the post. Thus, the first moderator was Fr. Salvatore Marsili from Finalpia, a liturgical scholar well-known particularly in Italy.[51] Salvatore Marino Marsili came from the village of Affile near Subiaco, a village known as Enfide to the readers of the second book of

Praeterea dimidia tantum pars professorum sunt monachi OSB." Cf. also, Acta Synodi Praesidum, 1962, p. 29.

[49] Decree of the Congregation for Studies dated June 17, 1961, *AAS* 54 (1962): 113f.

[50] Gut, circular letter dated June 29, 1962; *Liturgia e pensiero teologico recente. Inaugurazione del Pontificio Istutituto Liturgico* (Rome, 1961); S, Marsili, "Inaugurazione del Pontificio Istituto Liturgico," *RivLi* 49 (1962): 69–72.

[51] "Mysterion. Miscellanea Liturgica in occasione dei 10 anni dell'Abate Salvatore Marsili," in *Quaderni di RivLi* N.S. [=New Series], vol. 5 (Turin, 1981), ix–xvi; Bibliography in ibid., xvii–xxxiii; AA.VV.; "In memoriam Ab. Dom Salvatore Marsili (1910–1983)," *RivLi* 71 (1984): 131–43; B. Neunheuser, *Don Salvatore Marsili: Personalità e attività scientifica*, in Riforma liturgica tra passato e futuro. Atti della XIII Settimana di studio dell'Associazione Professoru di Liturgia, Cassano Murge, Bari, 27–31 agosto, 1984, Casale Monferrato, 1985, pp. 139–53; *Paschale mysterium.*

the so-called *Dialogues* of Gregory the Great. As a seventy-year-old, he was still marked by peasant steadfastness and stubbornness. He was born on August 10, 1910. At that time in the Subiaco area there were many young persons considered suitable for the religious life but, in general, in order to avoid the establishment of family cliques among future monks, such potential candidates were distributed among other monasteries of the Congregation. And so, the ten-year-old Marino went to the oblates' school at the Abbey of Finalpia on the finest stretch of coast on the Ligurian Riviera. On January 1, 1927, not yet seventeen years old, Marsili made his first profession. For two years he studied philosophy at the seminary in Subiaco, then his abbot sent him to Sant'Anselmo where, under the strict tutelage of Fr. Matthäus Rothenhäusler, he completed his theological studies in 1934 with a dissertation on Cassian and Evagrius Ponticus.[52] He had been ordained priest on July 16, 1933, in the monastery church of Sacro Speco at Subiaco.

For Marsili, however, the crucial experience of his life was the time spent at Maria Laach. From November 1934 until July 1935 he studied there at the Benedictine academy that had been established by Abbot Ildefons Herwegen. At that time, it was most unusual for an Italian Benedictine to go abroad for studies—and above all to go to Germany. The idea came from the breadth of vision of Abbot Bonifcaio Bolognani of Finalpia, who in 1914, despite limited resources both of personnel and finance, had the courage to found the "Rivista Liturgica," the oldest such journal in Italy. It was now his ambition to have competent young monks fully trained for this purpose. The year in this great Rhineland monastery gave direction to Marsili's life. He always spoke of Abbot Ildefons Herwegen with great esteem. But at Maria Laach, Marsili found not only the great theme of his life, but it was there, too, that he became a convinced adherent of Odo Casel's theology of mystery.[53] Marsili's

---

Studi in memoria dell'abate Prof. Salvatore Marsili (1910–1983), ed. G. Farnedi, StAns, vol. 91 (Rome, 1986).

[52] "Giovanni Cassiano ed Evagrio Pontico." Dottrina sulla carità e contemplazione, StAns, vol. 5 (Rome, 1936), reprinted 1980. For this dissertation, however, Marsili received a mere *bene probatus*. AAT, acta Fac. Theol, 11. Later, he tried without success to have this mark improved, "Rms. P. Rector Concilio proponit deinde, ex parte D. Salvatoris Marsilii petitionem melioris qualificationis laureae doctoralis. Concilium censet qualificationem sic de jure et juste datam mutari non posse." AAt, Libellus Actorum, 513.

[53] One of Marsili's last articles dealt with Casel's theory, "Das Gedächtnis des Herrn in der Theologie der Gegenwart, besonders in der Schau Odo Casels," *ALW* 22 (1980): 9–29.

life's work as a scholar is essentially a development and clarification of Casel's theory concerning the presence of the Christian mystery of salvation in the celebration of the liturgy.

Back in Finalpia, Marsili began to publish scholarly articles in the "Rivista Liturgica." Then came the Second World War. Like many other Italian priests, Marsili spent the war, beginning in 1942, as a chaplain, but in his case in the particularly prestigious position of chaplain to the staff of his uncle, Marshal Rodolfo Graziani. He remained at his uncle's side in the later phases of the war when Mussolini made Graziani commander-in-chief of the army of the "Republic of Salò," the short-lived fascist state that existed only by the grace of Hitler. Given this background it was advisable for Marsili at the end of the war to vanish from the scene. He withdrew to the Abbey of Noci in southern Italy where nobody knew him.

Nevertheless, as early as 1947 he was entrusted with the editorship of the "Rivista Liturgica," a commission that brought him back to northern Italy. His involvement in pastoral liturgy, which had never been small, increased enormously. Then, in 1948, his life took another unexpected turn. Emmanuele Caronti, abbot general of the Congregation of Subiaco, to which Finalpia belongs, forbade Marsili to publish or say anything connected with liturgy. One can only speculate over the reasons for Caronti's harsh prohibition. Was it Marsili's fondness for Casel's theology that was being strongly contested at the time? Was it his sympathy for Ildefons Herwegen, whose commentary on the Rule of Benedict was condemned by Caronti as well as several other abbots? Or did the abbot general see in Marsili a secret liturgical revolutionary—an opinion which, looking back, was not totally mistaken? With exemplary obedience Marsili maintained this enforced silence. He went once more to Noci where he worked in the monastery and in the parish, but above all he used this quiet time to make many translations from French and German.

Under a new abbot general, Celestino Gusi, a Spaniard, Marsili's long silence came to an end. Gusi sent him to Sant'Anselmo, which just then was searching for a new liturgist. Thus in 1960—such is the irony of history—Marsili became the successor of Cunibert Mohlberg, a person of quite different temperament and opinions. When in 1981 the pontifical liturgical institute was founded with Marsili's help, as first moderator he promoted it with all his energy. But above all, he devoted himself with a passion to the theology of the liturgy, a subject that to the end of his life he never abandoned. Soon he was teaching at other Roman institutes, continued to edit the "Rivista Liturgica," and began, with other experts, to produce a modern scholarly handbook of liturgy which was to appear in several volumes, three of which he lived to see and jointly write.[54]

In 1972, his confreres at Finalpia elected Marsili their abbot, an office he held until 1979. In fact, it was difficult to imagine Marsili as an abbot. He certainly did not possess the kind of balancing temperament desirable in a superior. Thus, following his resignation, he was glad to resume his teaching at Sant'Anselmo, which, in fact, he had never completely abandoned. Following a short illness, he died on November 27, 1983, death taking him in the middle of his work.

Fr. Adalhard Heitmann (1907–2001)

Marsili was decidedly a fighter by nature. Opposition particularly provoked him to creative thought. His acute understanding made him able immediately to understand the central point of an issue but misled him to an exaggerated formulation and an often too polemical presentation of opinions that made them untenable. In addition, since he lacked that jovial friendliness that the whole world believes Italians to possess, this highly gifted, personally modest and undemanding, but completely undiplomatic, person constantly met with much rejection.

This presentation of studies at Sant'Anselmo has brought us ahead of events. No less important in reaching a verdict on the period before the Second Vatican Council is a glance at the more monastic aspects of life in the college.

Fr. Adalbert Metzinger (1910–1984)

In the 1950s, the monastic observance at Sant'Anselmo, despite the presence of two consecutive Swiss Abbots Primate, was strongly marked by the old Beuronese customs. This was most clearly evident in the liturgy, in the esteem in which it was held, and in the way it was celebrated. The full, unshortened Benedictine Office was prayed daily in common in the abbey church. The liturgical celebrations were firmly under the leadership of Beuronese masters of ceremonies,

[54] *Anamnesis. Introduzione storio-teologica alla Liturgia*, a cura dei professori del Pontificio Istituto Liturgico S. Anselmo di Roma, direzione di S. Marsili (Casale Monferrato, 1974).

the first of whom was Fr. Adalbert Metzinger of Beuron itself,[55] the second being Fr. Adalhard Heitmann of Gerleve.[56]

Particularly on the great feasts of the church year, and mainly at Christmas and in Holy Week, the liturgy at the college was characterized by great brilliance and beauty and regarded as a model for all of Rome. Holy Week and the Paschal Triduum of 1952 were celebrated in the crypt of Sant'Anselmo, the main church being closed for renovation, and were broadcast live by Vatican Radio with the express purpose of offering the consolation of the universal Catholic liturgy to the persecuted Christians in Communist countries.[57] At that time there were 150 Benedictines resident at Sant'Anselmo. The large community, the presence of which was taken for granted on the major feasts, offered in fact a unique opportunity to develop the full riches of form and music of the liturgy as it was then.

Ordinary workdays were more prosaic.[58] On days when lectures were held, rising was at 4:55. At 5:15, Lauds, Prime, and Terce were recited one after the other, without singing, in the church, which in winter was bitterly cold. This was followed by private Masses in the crypt, served by the nonpriests who until the early 1960s formed the majority of the community. Communion was received at these Masses. During the first or second cycle of Masses—the crypt did not have sufficient altars for all priests to celebrate at the same time—those who were not celebrating

[55] Fr. Adalbert Metzinger was born on March 17, 1910. He made profession at Beuron on May 25, 1930, and from 1932 studied at Sant'Anselmo where he obtained a doctorate in theology, following this with a license from the Pontifical Biblical Institute. He was ordained priest on July 28, 1935. From 1939 he was professor of Old Testament at Sant'Anselmo and from 1942, as successor of Benno Gut, professor of New Testament. In addition, he was chanter and master of ceremonies at Sant'Anselmo. From 1959 until 1974 he lived in Beuron's foundation of Las Condes in Chile, during which period he taught New Testament at the Catholic University in Santiago. He was conventual prior of Las Condes from 1966 to 1970. In 1975, following his return to Beuron, he was elected abbot of Weingarten. He died on October 11, 1984. ArchWeingarten, "Annals of the Abbey of Weingarten for the years 1980–1986," pp. 36ff.

[56] From 1957, Fr. Adlahard Heitmann of Gerleve was extraordinary professor for theologia naturalis—and from 1961–1962 et psychologiae—at the faculty of philosophy of Sant'Anselmo. He returned to Gerleve in 1970.

[57] "Divini ritus, Maiore Hebdomada ac festo Paschalis ibidem celebrtati, a Sede radiophonica Vaticana per aetheris undas sunt transmissi ut praesertim a fratribus et sororibus in Christo, Russicae dominationi subiectis, possent audiri." Kälin, circular letter dated June 29, 1952.

[58] For what follows, see *Statuta in Collegio Internationali Benedictinorum Sancti Anselmi de Urbe observanda 1962*.

The group of lay brothers circa 1960. Front row: Br. Pankratius Schnapp (Beuron), Br. Constantin Aanini (Beuron), Abbot Primate Benno Gut, Fr. Anselm Günthör (Weingarten), Br. Avelin Stengel (Maria Laach), Br. Rupert Heidl (Seckau). Back row: Br. Gerold Gassmann (Einsiedeln), Br. Philipp Amberg (Einsiedeln), Br. Marold Grätz (Münsterschwarzach), Br. Orlando Ott (Sankt Ottilien), Br. Heimrad Seibel (Münsterschwarzach), Br. Germar Bolch (Münsterschwarzach), Br. Wilhelm Lang (Sankt Ottilien), Br. Justin Gruber (Schwieklberg), Br. Gerold Bruch (Beuron)

or serving remained in choir for thirty minutes of meditation. The next liturgy in common was at 12:40 with Sext and None. Directly after lunch, during which there was usually reading, Vespers was recited in the church. On Sundays and feasts, Vespers was sung at 3:00. At 6:45 p.m. Matins was recited—or at 6:30 when the following day was a feast with twelve lessons. This was followed by supper, then recreation, which one was not permitted to spend in one's cell. The day ended at 8:30 p.m. with Compline. The rector paid close attention to the regular attendance of all professors and students at all hours of the Divine Office.

The crypt of Sant'Anselmo with sixteen altars for individual Masses. Now the library.

On days in which there were no lectures, rising was somewhat later, i.e., at 5:25. At least once a month the Abbot Primate or the rector delivered a spiritual conference to the whole *familia Anselmiana*, either in Latin—this particularly at the beginning of the academic year—or in Italian. There was also a regular chapter of faults held separately for professors, officials, and students. Apart from the regular exeats on Sundays and Thursdays, to go into the city was possible only with special permission. Students received such permission seldom and only *gravi de causa*—for important reasons. Students had to ask a blessing, kneeling, from the master of clerics; professors and officials, also kneeling, from the Abbot Primate or the rector. As a matter of course, the monastic habit was always worn by everyone both inside and outside of the house. Smoking in public was taboo and permitted in their rooms only to those in whose monasteries smoking was allowed. The need for monastic silence was constantly emphasized, if not always with success.

Today, this regime, which was already a relaxation of the one in force in the 1930s, is a cause of astonishment and incomprehension for a different generation. But the customs of Sant'Anselmo were without a doubt an expression of serious monastic intent. Naturally, they were only a framework to support the spiritual life, but not one that could create that life. One might ask how many of the long recited prayers, particularly those in the evening after a demanding day of study, the individual monk could really pray with his heart and how many were mere routine and lip service. Who can say? The strict organization of the day encouraged a recollection that was beneficial both for study and prayer but made it difficult, however, to participate in cultural activities in the city. It was forbidden to go to the cinema or theater—a prohibition common to all Roman colleges. Many of these regulations were certainly small-minded and their general tenor discouraged any spontaneity. But already, even then, the customs of Sant'Anselmo were not unchallenged.

In a circular letter to abbots dated July 18, 1957, Abbot Primate Kälin discussed efforts to transform Sant'Anselmo into a house of studies devoid of monastic character, or at least to shorten the Divine Office in the college. To do the first would, according to the Primate, be a fundamental contradiction of Leo XIII's vision for the house. The second suggestion should be rejected because Sant'Anselmo was a house for young monks and not for future secular priests. Were the Benedictine students at Sant'Anselmo, day in and day out, year in and year out, dispensed from the choral or indeed the private praying of the *Officium divinum*, they would gradually acquire "a false opinion on the hierarchy of values regarding the Divine Office and study." Kälin's reasoning was not without foundation: that young monks, who during their five-year theological training were not tested in the effort of common prayer and had not decided in its favor would look for the same or wider dispensations once they were faced later with new and greater burdens. How then would they reconcile this with the fundamental Benedictine principle that nothing is to be preferred to the work of God?[59]

Fr. Polycarp Sherwood (1912–1969)

[59] "Si adolescentes monachi tempore studiorum, et quidem per circiter 5 annos a recitatione Officii Divini, sive privata, aut tantummodo chorali ex parte per totum annum scholasticum dispensarentur, *paulatim falsum indicium de hierarchia valorum*, sc. de Officio Div. Et de studio Litterarum in eorum mente oriretur, et si, absolutis studiis philosophicis et theologicis, aliis officiis et muneribus occupantur, et saepe ita ut onera sustinenda non minuantur, immo augeantur, sine dubio easdem vel maiores dispensationes a chorali recitatione Off. div. a Superioribus petent. Sed quid dicendum de monachis S.P.B. qui maxima ex parte alia officia Operi Dei praeponunt, cum ipse Legifer filiis suis valde serio inculcet: Operi Dei nihil praeponatur." Kälin, circular letter dated July 18, 1957.

The cause of this *apologia* of the Primate was the dissatisfaction, particularly of American students, with the style of life and teaching methods at Sant'Anselmo. Two American confreres, the master of clerics, Fr. Virgil O'Neill of Collegeville, and the professor of patristics and biblical Greek, Fr. Polycarp Sherwood of St. Meinrad, became the spokesmen of these students.[60] Both accused Sant'Anselmo of having too solemn and too much liturgy, of spending too much money on beautifying the church and too little on the renovation of the house, of allowing students too little time for private study, overfeeding them instead with too many lectures. In a long memorandum, Sherwood dealt with basic problems, finding fault above all with "the ambiguity as to the nature of Sant'Anselmo."[61] In fact, there was no clear division between college and university. The rector of the university was simultaneously prior of the "Primatial Abbey" of St. Anselm, dependent as an official solely on the Primate and appointed by him.

News of the disturbance expressed in this fashion by O'Neill and Sherwood in Sant'Anselmo soon crossed the Atlantic and led to various interventions from American abbots.[62] Abbot Primate Kälin thought it necessary to present his view of the situation in a special circular let-

[60] Fr. Polycarp Sherwood of St. Meinrad was born on November 3, 1912, professed on August 6, 1940, and ordained priest on September 21, 1943. He taught at Sant'Anselmo from 1946, at first fundamental theology and later patristics and biblical Greek. On his arrival in Rome, he only had a license in theology, not obtaining the doctorate—at the Gregorian University—until 1955 with the dissertation "The Earlier Ambigua of Saint Maximus the Confessor and his Refutation of Origenism," printed in StAns, vol. 36, in 1955. A further fruit of his interest in Maximus the Confessor is his excellent translation and introduction, *St. Maximus the Confessor—Four Centuries on Charity—the Ascetical Life*, Ancient Christian Writers, vol. 21 (Westminster: MD, 1955). Sherwood died on February 9, 1969. ArchSt. Meinrad, Curriculum vitae and bibliography of P. Sherwood.

[61] APr, Collegio Varia 1956–1957. Sherwood outlined his ideas in a thirty-five-page memorandum dated May 30, 1957. Titled "Analysis Anselmiana," his criticisms culminate in three accusations which he blames for the dissatisfaction of many—American—students: "(1) ambiguity both as to the purpose of the college and its fundamental regime; (2) lack of adequate contact and consultation between and among the various elements that constitute the complete S. Anselmo; (3) overloading alike of the academic schedule and of the monastic observance."

[62] On November 13, 1957, Abbots L. Schwinn of Holy Cross, C. McDonald of Atchison, B. Dworschak of Collegeville, and B. Luibel of St. Bernard met in Chicago to discuss the problems of Sant'Anselmo. Among other things, they criticized the "lack of time for study" and "liturgy receives too much emphasis." APr, Collegio Varia 1956–1957.

Congress of Abbots 1953 received by Pope Pius XII

Congress of Abbots 1959

ter to all Benedictine superiors in the United States.[63] For his part, Fr. Augustin Mayer, the main target of O'Neill's attack, even visited these American monasteries. At the end of the academic year 1957 the two "troublemakers," O'Neill and Sherwood, were deported to their home monasteries. With this, the "conservatives" at Sant'Anselmo had gained a victory. The clear parallels between this and the ominous Cummins case of 1925, however, prompts the thought that this time the desire for change on the part of the Americans, including many abbots, was incomparably stronger and more insistent than in the 1920s. How long would it be possible to maintain the inherited observance?

It would, however, be incorrect to view those responsible in Sant'Anselmo as dark reactionaries, determined to defend an untenable position with tooth and claw against the will of the Confederation. Against such a notion is the undiminished stream of Benedictine students sent by their abbots to Rome to the college on the Aventine, surely not only for the intellectual training it provided. Further evidence is provided by the spirited defense of the "Anselmian liberties" by the rector, Augustin Mayer, at the Congess of Abbots in 1953 against the exaggerated attacks of the narrow-minded Abbot General Caronti of the Subiaco Congregation on the leadership of the college because students had played football without wearing the monastic habit.[64]

Abbot Emanuele Caronti (1882–1866)

At the last Congress of Abbots held before the Second Vatican Council, which took place from September 18 to 25, 1959, at Sant'Anselmo, Augustin Mayer was justified in presenting a generally satisfactory picture of the academic and monastic/disciplinary situation of the college.[65] He mentioned that it was desirable more consciously to encourage those who had obtained the license to proceed to the doctorate. Further, greater care should be given to those who had completed their basic theological studies elsewhere and now wished to obtain the license at Sant'Anselmo.

[63] APr, Collegio Varia 1956–1957, cf. Kälin's letter dated April 26, 1957, to all OSB abbots in the United States.

[64] *Protocollum seu Relatio de Sessionibus quas Rmi et Illmi Abbates Congregationum Confoederatarum O.S.B. habuerunt ia aedibus S. Anselmi* 1953, nn51–56ff.

[65] *Protocollum seu Relatio de Sessionibus quas Rmi et Illmi Abbates Congregationum Confoederatarum O.S.B. habuerunt ia aedibus S. Anselmi* 1959, nn24ff., 28ff.

Again, the library needed to be expanded and, finally, an *aula magna* should be built.

The rector conceded that not all the disciplines in philosophy and theology were pursued or taught in the best possible way at Sant'Anselmo. Not every professor was a leading light in his field. But the Athenaeum could only offer what it had received from the Confederation. The Abbot Primate had always had the greatest difficulties when he needed a new teacher for Sant'Anselmo. Every Congregation should play its part in this common task of the Order. Mayer admitted that indeed too much emphasis was placed on lectures and oral examinations, but the number of lectures had already been reduced. With a clear reference to O'Neill's and Sherwood's rejected proposals for change—without, however, mentioning them by name—the rector reaffirmed his conviction that Sant'Anselmo needed a unified leadership, i.e., the rector and prior should be the same person. This had been the wish of the Synod of Abbots President in 1920 and was approved by the Congress of Abbots of 1925. At that time also, the recitation of the full *Officium divinum* had been expressly approved. The term *Collegium monasteriale* was an accurate expression of the nature of the college. In this term, the two constitutive elements of Anselmian life were taken into account. The daily timetable could never fulfill the wishes of all, and its specific details should be left to those responsible for running the house. Further, a precondition should be a climate of trust between Sant'Anselmo and the monasteries of the Confederation. Mayer lamented the tendency of some students to play off several superiors against one another in an attempt to obtain greater freedom; the spirit of destructive criticism evident in some; occasional extravagance in the use of money and offenses against monastic silence. All in all, these were small criticisms, and the rector admitted that one could also rejoice over so many good and "truly obedient, meek, and willing" students.[66]

Fr. Johannes Müller, dean of the faculty of philosophy, offered the abbots a broad description of the faculty's program of studies, making a particular plea for the main academic course.[67] Who did one consider to be candidates for this *cursus superior*? Primarily it would be future teachers of courses held in the monasteries themselves but also candidates for philosophical chairs at Sant'Anselmo itself and the philosophical institute at Salzburg, which had a particular relationship with Sant'Anselmo and the Benedictine Order.

[66] *oboedientes, mites et patientes*, cf. RB 2.25.

[67] Ibid., no. 26ff.

The discussion among the abbots that followed these reports showed that most were happy with Sant'Anselmo. There were few critical voices. This was rather strange, given what had been going through American heads in the previous two years. In all, 133 abbots voted in favor of the motion, "The College of Sant'Anselmo has the character of a monastic college where the students are instructed not only in the sacred sciences but also in the spiritual life."[68] Only eleven abbots voted against this declaration. Similarly unanimous was the decision of the congress that the full Divine Office was to be celebrated in choir—allowing, however, the Primate and rector the freedom to grant necessary dispensations.[69] At that time no one could have imagined how differently the succeeding Congress of Abbots would think about this matter!

In 1959, however, the great surprise was the election of the Primate. It had generally been expected that Bernhard Kälin would be confirmed in office, but on the third ballot, on September 24, Benno Gut, the abbot of Einsiedeln, received 123 of 167 votes. Once again, as in 1947, Gut was postulated by the abbots, an impressive indication of the esteem in which the lively and enthusiastic abbot of Einsiedeln enjoyed in the Order. In 1947 Pius XII refused to permit the fifty-year-old and only recently nominated abbot nullius to accept the election. Now, John XXIII allowed the sixty-two-year-old to do so. Perhaps it would have been better for Sant'Anselmo if Gut had become Primate in 1947 instead of the pedantic and overcautious Kälin. In 1959, Gut was already showing signs of the results of demanding years at Einsiedeln and in the service of the Church in Switzerland.[70] But Gut was glad to return to Sant'Anselmo, which he had known as a student from 1920 to 1923 and where he had been a professor from 1930 to 1942, first for fundamental theology and—following his license at the Biblical Institute—for New Testament exegesis. "He knew how to enthuse his students. He explained and interpreted the Sacred Scriptures to them as a rule of life. As a teacher at Sant'Anselmo he won the esteem of many students from all over the

[68] "Collegium S. Anselmi habet indolem collegii monasterialis ubi alumni non tantum in sacris scientiis, sed etiam in vita spirituali instituantur." Ibid., no. 62.

[69] "Totum officium in choro recitandum est, ita tamen ut usus fiat privilegii Collegio concessi et officium—inquantum fieri potest—sive de feria, sive in ritu duplici minori recitetur. Dispensationes opportunae sive ab Abbate Primate sive a Rectore concedantur." Ibid.

[70] On B. Gut, see obituary by G. Holzherr in *Schweizer. Kirchenzeitung*, no. 138 (1970): 725f. The quotations above are taken from this; Alos, K. Etter, *Meinradsraben* 60 (1971): 39–48; ArchEinsiedeln, Abtbiographien, 58f.

Pope John XXIII at Sant'Anselmo on September 25, 1959, in conversation with the former Abbot Primate Bernhard Kälin (left) and his successor, Benno Gut (center)

world. From this period he knew most of the abbots of the Order even before he became Primate."

Benno Gut was a man of many talents both of intellect and of the heart. "Not least, he was a great lover of music. He had a great sensitivity to people, a memory for faces and names, and the gift of appreciating the special character of the other." He loved to make others happy and had great difficulty refusing a request. With that, he was more easily hurt and more sensitive than his humor might have led one to suspect. "His repeated severe illnesses and ongoing health problems give one the impression that he did not take his responsibilities lightly." Mercifully, the burden of his new dignity as Primate did not strike him immediately. His taking office coincided with a hitherto unknown high point in the history of Sant'Anselmo, the first visit of a pope to the college.

Just one day after Gut's postulation and immediately after the confirmation from the Congregation of the Consistory, Pope John XXIII visited Sant'Anselmo on the afternoon of September 25.[71] Today's reader must bear in mind that Pope Pius XII was not yet dead for one year. Surrounded by centuries-old court ceremonial, that pontiff had, since the war, left the Vatican only for his annual summer sojourn at Castel Gandolfo. When John XXIII began cautiously to leave the Vatican for a few hours in order to come closer to people, it was almost sensational. For this reason, the pope's visit to Sant'Anselmo in 1959 made a deep impression on the participants at the Congress of Abbots, unlike that of any meeting with a pope today. This impression was reinforced by the spontaneous and friendly manner in which John XXIII spoke to the individual abbots in the chapter room following the formal ceremony in the church—behavior which was not usual, at least for more recent popes.

The time of the Second Vatican Council arrived. This was experienced close up and with full hearts by the professors and students of Sant'Anselmo. Of the forty-one council fathers who belonged to the Benedictine Order, twenty-four lived at Sant'Anselmo during the sessions. This entailed a noticeable reduction in comfort at the college as well as much additional work.[72] But this was compensated for by the immediate experience, the proximity of the discussions at the council, and the opportunity to ask those council fathers who lived for weeks at a time in the college about their impressions and opinions. Rector

[71] *L'Osservatore Romano*, June 27, 1959, p. 1.

[72] Cf. Gut's circular letter, *infra octavam Pentecostes*, 1963, with a list of Benedictines present at the council.

Visit of Pope John XXIII to Sant'Anselmo on September 25, 1959

Augustin Mayer was even elected secretary of the Conciliar Commission for Seminaries and Studies.

On several occasions the schola from Sant'Anselmo sang Gregorian chant in the council hall at St. Peter's. This writer will never forget the closing Mass of the first session of the council on December 8, 1962, when, under the direction of Fr. Egidio Zaramella of Praglia, two thousand council fathers sang the *Missa de Angelis*, alternating with the small group of cantors from Sant'Anselmo. At the end of the liturgy as the already seriously ill Pope John left the gathering, many felt that he had spoken to the council for the last time.[73]

This was time of great excitement, but perhaps not the best of times for study, which requires peace and quiet and detachment. There followed years of restless change. Under the surface there was a ferment not only in the day-to-day life of those at Sant'Anselmo and not only in Benedictine monasteries all over the world. This became obvious to all

[73] *Acta Synodalis SS. Concilii Oecumenici Vaticani II*, vol. 1, pars 4 (Typis Polyglottis Vaticanis, 1971), 645.

Benedictine bishops, territorial abbots, and abbots president who resided at Sant'Anselmo. Council Fathers at the end of 1962: First row, seated from left to right: Abbot-Bishop Viktor Hälg of Ndanda, Former Abbot-Bishop Joachin Amman of Ndanda, Archbishop José Floriberto Cornelis of Elisabethville, Abbot Primate Benno Gut, Bishop Simon Landersdorfer of Passau, Bishop Paul Leonard Hagarty of Nassau, Abbot-Bishop Aurelian Bilgeri of Eshowe, Abbot-Bishop Eberhard Spiess of Peramiho. Second row, standing: Abbot Jerome Weber of Muenster, Archabbot Denis Strittmatter of St. Vincent, Abbot Raymund Tschudi of Einsiedeln, Abbot Gilbert Hess of Blue Cloud, Abbot Placidus Staeb of Bahia, Abbot Christopher Butler of Downside, Archabbot Benedikt Reetz Of Beuron, Abbot Johannes Maria Hoeck of Scheyern, Abbot Anselmo Tranfaglia of Montevergine, Abbot Maurus Riha of Michaelbeuren, Bishop James Komba of Songea, Abbot Godefroid Dayez of Maredsous, Abbot Gregory Gomez of New Norcia, Abbot Basilius Niederberger of Mariastein, Archabbot Suso Brechter of Sankt Ottilien, Abbot Martinho Michler of Rio de Janeiro, Abbot Walter Coggin of Belmont

when the next Congress of Abbots opened on September 18, 1966. This congress was completely marked by the council that had just ended.

3. Further Biographical Sketches of Professors

Fr. Matthäus Rothenhäusler (1874–1958)

Fr. Matthäus Rothenhäusler came from the Ravensburg district of Württemberg and was the second of ten children.[74] "The Rothenhäuslers were all physically delicate and sure to survive only after they had gone beyond thirty years of age. This was particularly the case with Franz-Joseph, only that he remained delicate even beyond this." Nonetheless, while always in delicate health, he survived to eighty-four. His ability became evident at an early stage. Right from the beginning, his parents and an uncle, who was parish priest in a village near Tettnang and prepared the boy for secondary schooling, expected him to become a priest. But for a long time he thought of becoming a writer instead. In fact, Rothenhäusler had "something of the artist about him. Not only did he have a sound judgment in matters of art but had himself an artistic style, had artistic handwriting and an undoubtedly strong poetic talent that, unfortunately, was too little developed and glimmered only in poems for special occasions, but then hinted at the possibilities slumbering under the surface." Having completed his secondary education, Rothenhäusler decided against a career as an artist and instead, in the autumn of 1892, entered Beuron where on January 1, 1894, he took perpetual simple vows. The necrologist at Gerleve wrote, "The philosophical and theological studies that were now begun had to be interrupted again and again by periods of total exhaustion." This meant that he was not able to be ordained priest until August 15, 1902, in Beuron.

Fr. Matthäus Rothenhäusler (1874–1958)

Even then, the long years of illness and the enforced, patient waiting permitted in the young monk a ripening of that interior and exterior monastic attitude that stamped him for the rest of his life and helped him to overcome the physical weakness that dogged him until his death. Later, indeed, he lamented that he had been unable in those years to give his whole energy to the study of philosophy and

[74] ArchGerleve, Necrology of R. P. Matthäus Rothenhäusler, died on July 31, 1958. [In what follows, quotations not specifically identified are taken from this necrology]; obituary in *StudMitt* 69 (1958): 95–99; see bibliography in appendix 2 of this work.

theology. "Often he expressed his conviction that a really well-trained and competent theologian had to make a strenuous effort fully to master philosophy and systematic theology in addition to his special field of study as well as having an overview of the whole."

In 1904, Archabbot Placidus Wolter sent Fr. Matthäus to Beuron's new foundation in the Westphalia, the Abbey of St. Joseph at Gerleve. On December 11, 1911, with the transfer of stability, he bound himself forever to this young monastery. Although many of the priest-monks of this still small and above all poor monastery were often absent on pastoral assignments, the first abbot of Gerleve, the young Raphael Molitor, freed Rothenhäusler for several years' study in Bonn. For four years, beginning in the late autumn of 1906, he lived in Maria Laach's house of studies in Bonn, attending lectures in church history by Heinrich Schrörs and in the history of law by Ulrich Stutz, "in whose school he received a solid historico-legal formation." Rothenhäusler completed his studies in Bonn with the publication in 1912 of a study on "The Order of the Reception of Brethren in the Regula S. Benedicti." In this he investigated the "formal act of reception," but in the second and third sections, beginning with the second promise of profession, i.e., *conversatio morum*, "the fundamental concepts and premises that could lead to a deeper insight into the nature of Benedictine profession." When a reviewer of this work wrote in 1913 that the study offered surprising insights into the world of early monasticism and—beyond its proclaimed subject—was also valuable in the fields of asceticism and mysticism, this verdict sums up what Fr. Matthäus himself always proclaimed as his scholarly ideal, namely, while beginning with a special topic, to present an overview that embraced other fields of theology.

The other characteristic of Rothenhäusler's later research had already been recognized by his teacher, Stutz, who spoke about "an investigation conducted with meticulous care and the highest circumspection and prudence."[75] In this first study, Fr. Matthäus had already found what was to be the great theme of his life: research into early Christian, monastic, and Benedictine spirituality, in particular into the origins of monastic profession.

In 1924 he was entrusted with a new task that fundamentally stamped his life from then on. In this year he was appointed professor of church history at Sant'Anselmo. He worked there for twenty-eight years as a gifted and highly esteemed teacher of church history, being appointed full professor in 1932. For many years he taught all of church history;

[75] *ZSRG.K* 2 (1912): 379.

later, when Dom Poulet came to Rome, he concentrated mainly on the history of the early Church and on patrology. Both formally and from the point of content, his lectures were distinguished. According to the verdict of his pupil Fr. Augustin Mayer, of all the Anselmian professors, Matthäus Rothenhäusler spoke the most perfect Latin. Rothenhäusler, however, did not see his lectures as his principal task but, rather, the seminars in which he unsparingly insisted on faultless scholarly work and a conscientious use of historical method. "It was not easy to please him; and to work with him on a doctoral dissertation was indeed hard labor." Conditioned by his constant physical debility, the number of his publications remained small. But what he did write was of consequence. His two studies on Diadochus of Photike, fruit of many years of work on this author and of seminars at Sant'Anselmo, ought not to be forgotten. In 1934, Abbot Primate Stotzingen appointed him dean of the faculty of theology. In addition, from 1939 he was vice rector of the college.

"Significant as a scholar and teacher, Fr. Matthäus had, perhaps, an even deeper and more long-lasting effect by his monastic example. What he wrote and taught about monasticism, he also lived in an exemplary fashion." He found for himself an impressive synthesis of monastic vocation and scholarly research in which the latter constantly offered him new stimulus and nourishment for his spiritual life. He remains in the memory of those who knew him, an extremely disciplined, inwardly directed, and decidedly "spiritual" person, "who was accustomed to see and assess in the light of Christ his own life and all else that happened. . . . In 1952 the seventy-eight-year-old returned to Gerleve where he willingly shared his rich treasures with his confreres." On the occasion of his diamond jubilee of profession at the beginning of 1954, he received a particular honor when Rector Augustin Mayer brought him the news in Gerleve that the University of Sant'Anselmo had conferred on him an honorary doctorate in theology.[76]

Rector Augustin Mayer and Abbot Primate Benno Gut in 1962

"While his physical strength ebbed more and more, his mind always remained fresh, flexible, often indeed bubbling and sparkling. He al-

[76] AAt, Acta Fac. Theol. Nn. 94–94bis. On November 22, 1953, the faculty praised him as, "indagatorem spiritualitatis antiquae indefessum, consiliarem studiorum sagacem, Collegii columnam."

ways remained interested in what was new—and not only in the field of theology—a careful and benevolent observer and helper of his younger confreres, while also a passionate defender of old ways. A few hours before his death he asked that he be read to from the book *Blühende Wüste* (Flowering Desert) about the life of early monks."[77]

Fr. Athanasius Miller (1881–1963)

Fr. Athanasius Miller (1881–1963)

Among the professors described in this book, Fr. Athanasius Miller is, among all of those who knew him, surely the most esteemed and loved.[78] There are many proofs of this both during his lifetime and after his death. Those who met him during his life met a gentle and modest person, aware of his own faults; with a mischievous eye; an almost self-evidently pious monk who made no display of this; a priest and pastor who, not without reason, was a sought-after confessor to cardinals, bishops, abbots, and countless nuns. Personally undemanding, with his superiors' permission and especially during the war, he helped the poor, above all many destitute monasteries of women, with considerable donations of US dollars that he knew how to collect. But however great his willingness to help, he was also marked by a sober realism, particularly in his pastoral work. His was a well-known saying, "The devil can lurk even behind a hundred Communions."

The necrology of Beuron continues, "It was in January 1962. Fr. Athanasius was resting in his monastic cell at Sant'Anselmo after the exertions of one of the many farewell celebrations held in his honor. He said, looking back on his productive life, 'I could do without all the

[77] *StudMitt* 69 (1958): 97. The book mentioned is S. Feldhohn, *Blühende Wüste. Aus dem Leben palästinensicher und ägiptischer Mönche des 5. u. 6. Jahrhunderts* (Düsseldorf, 1957).

[78] ArchBeuron, Necrology from Beuron, P. Athanasius Maximillian Miller. [Following quotations not specifically identified are taken from this necrology; D. Zähringer, P. Athanasius Miller von Beuron, *BenM* 25 (1949): 384ff.; A. Metzinger, "Eine Festschrift für P. Athanasius Miller," *BenM* 28 (1952): 242–46; B. Schwank, "Zum Tode von P. Athanasius Miller am 17. April 1963," *EuA* 39 (1963): 251ff.; P. G. Duncker, "Dom Atanasio Miller OSB, Secretario della Pontifica Commissione Biblica," in *Mélanges Eugène Tisserant*, vol. 1, Studi e Testi 231 (Città del Vaticano, 1964), 197–208.

Fr. Athanasius Miller during a lecture

books I have written. There is just one single book that I should still like to write and that would be called, God is good!' "

Fr. Athanasius Miller came from Upper Swabia. He was born on September 22, 1881, in Wolfartsdweiler near Salgau, one of ten children of a farming family. No fewer than five of these children, three girls and two boys, entered the monastery. The first to enter was Maximilian, the next was Fr. Athanasius. Many decades later, in a poem which appeared as a booklet, he described how he came to the monastery—initially the Abbey of Emauzy in Prague. The title of the poem was "The Seven Swabians or the Journey to the Monastery, an Adventure Story told by M. Schwäble." In the list of Fr. Athanasius's publications contained in the festschrift presented to him on his seventieth birthday in 1951, this booklet is only mentioned in a footnote.[79] "Indeed, even Pope Pius XII knew about it and mentioned 'The Journey of the Seven Swabians to the Monastery' to the newly appointed secretary of the Bible Commission at his first audience in 1949."[80] First published in installments in the

[79] *Miscellanea Biblica et Orientalia R.P. Athanasio Miller OSB, Secretario Pontificae Commissione Biblicae completis LXX annis oblata*, ed. A. Metzinger, StAns, vols. 27, 28 (Rome, 1951), 1; cf. also S. Mayer, *Beuroner Bibliographie. Schriftsteller und Künstler während der ersten Jahre des Benediktinerklosters Beuron 1862–1963* (Beuron, 1963), 101–5.

[80] Cf. *EuA* 39 (1963): 252.

Katholischen Sonntagsblatt (Catholic Sunday Paper) in Stuttgart in 1921, then as an independent booklet in several editions, the foreword, signed by M. (i.e,. Max) Schwäble, explains why the poem was composed. "Nearly eight years ago, as the writer of this story found himself, because of overwork, unable to do anything worthwhile, began to make a draft. He found this exercise so refreshing and amusing that it became a source of enjoyable recuperation."[81]

The booklet describes, in a lively and sparklingly humorous way, how in 1897 the young Max Miller—called "Gondola Swabian" in the story because of his shoes bent in the shape of a gondola—made his way to Prague with six other boys from his native southern Germany to be received at the oblates' school of the Beuronese Congregation at Emmaus Abbey (today Emauzy Abbey). He spent two years in Prague and a further two years in the monastery school at Seckau in Styria. In September 1901, he went to Beuron and began his monastic life under the name Athanasius. Following his profession on October 15, 1902, he studied philosophy for two years at Maria Laach and after that, theology at Sant'Anselmo where he obtained the doctorate in theology in 1908. He was ordained priest on September 22, 1909.

Since his superiors had envisioned him as a lecturer in biblical sciences at the theological institute in Beuron, from 1908 to 1909 he continued his training in Oriental languages and exegetical methodology at the University of Strasbourg. Professor Faulhaber, later archbishop and cardinal of Munich, made a deep impression on him. In 1909 Miller transferred to the newly established Biblical Institute in Rome. By the spring of 1910 we see him accompanying the archabbot of Beuron, Ildefons Schober, to Jerusalem for the blessing of the Abbey of the Dormition of the BVM on Mount Sion. Miller remained in Jerusalem until the autumn of 1911. While there, he attended the Dominican École Biblique. He also used this time for study trips throughout Palestine, Phoenicia, Syria, the Sinai Peninsula, and Egypt. During these excursions he collected many objects from the biblical world that subsequently were gathered together in Beuron to form a small biblical museum of illustrative material for theological studies. Another fruit of this sojourn in biblical locations was a series of pictures on the geography and history of the Near East that was later expanded and published at Stuttgart in 1925. In October 1911 Fr. Athanasius took over the lectures on the introduction to the Old Testament and, from 1914, those on Old Testament exegesis. In addition, from 1912 he was master of clerics, an office he exercised with great conscientiousness.

[81] Quoted from the 5th ed. (Beuron, 1957).

In 1914 he was able once again to travel to the Middle East, this time with Abbot Raphael Molitor of Gerleve, who was to conduct the canonical visitation on Mount Sion. Fr. Athanasius was again able to travel beyond Palestine into Syria and Egypt. The necrologist notes,

> Fr. Athanasius traveled with open eyes through the Holy Land. Thus, in many conferences, some illustrated with photographic transparencies, he was able to report vividly about the holy places to the community at Beuron. But he had taken on too much and strained his bodily resources. In July 1915, he suffered a complete collapse from the consequences of which he recovered only with difficulty. He had to withdraw from work for an extended period and undergo various medical treatments and procedures. As he began to more or less recover, he was called up into the army—we are now in the middle of the First World War—and became a medical orderly, later becoming a hospital chaplain in Karlsruhe. In January 1919, Fr. Athanasius was able to resume his teaching at Beuron.

But his work there soon came to an end. In 1922, Abbot Primate Fidelis von Stotzingen was able to win him for Sant'Anselmo as a teacher of Old Testament. Until his appointment in 1949 as secretary of the Pontifical Biblical Commission, and with the exception of a third year, 1930–1931, in Jerusalem, where he taught in the seminary of the Latin patriarchate, Fr. Athanasius held the chair of Old Testament at Sant'Anselmo.

Athanasius Miller was the complete teacher. He was not a scholar in the sense of a researcher who enriched biblical science with new ideas or insights. But for all that, he was a fascinating teacher. "His lectures remain unforgettable, each one a masterpiece of its kind. His lecture theater was always full to the last place. His delivery was simple, full of imagination, his words bringing alive even the driest Old Testament report. Whoever experienced, heard, and observed Fr. Athanasius when, for example, he described the death of King Eglon of Moab at the hand of the judge Ehud in Judges 3, will retain indelible memories of this teacher of the science of Sacred Scripture." In his scholarly publications, always well-researched, Fr. Athanasius's first aim was to transmit his enthusiasm for the Old Testament. The psalms were his main area of interest, certainly a most fitting object of reflection for a monk. His translation of the psalms and canticles of the Breviary first appeared in 1920 and went through fifteen editions. Personally, the psalms had become familiar prayers to him. In an introduction to the psalms published in 1924, he expressed his conviction that these old prayers could become, "still for us today, a sublime, deeply felt expression of our thoughts and feelings in every situation, in all sorrows and needs."[82] In his later years he admitted often that "when things are going badly, I remember a word from the psalms and hold fast to it."[83]

When in 1940 Athanasius Miller was appointed a consultor to the biblical commission, the study of the Bible in the Catholic Church was about to experience a new flowering after the serious setbacks of the beginning of the century.[84] A freer, less prejudiced spirit was finding its way and was expressly promoted by Pius XII:

- In 1941, the need to study the Bible in the original languages—and not only in the Latin Vulgate—was emphasized.
- In 1943, with the great encyclical *Divino Afflante Spiritu*, the "liberation encyclical" of Catholic exegetes, the condemnation of the employment of modern scholarly methods in the study of the Bible, hitherto in force, was abandoned.
- In 1948, the letter of the biblical commission to Cardinal Suhard, in which the assertion of Moses' authorship of the Pentateuch and a literal understanding of the first eleven chapters of the book of Genesis were abandoned.

Fr. Athanasius was one of the authors of this latter document that rescued Old Testament scholarship among Catholics from decades of paralysis. Today the biblical commission plays hardly any role in the life of the Church. In earlier times this was not the case. Established by Pope Leo XIII in 1902, the Pontificia Commissio de re Biblica had the task of "promoting the study of the Bible by assessing the useful results of modern research, of defending Sacred Scripture with the weapons of healthy criticism and of solving matters of dispute."[85] Pius X not only gave the commission the right to confer academic degrees but also increased the authority of its decisions by placing them on the same level as those of the Roman Congregations. As was the case with these curial Congregations, the members of the commission were composed of cardinals and consultors, only some of whom resided in Rome. Today, following the incorporation of the commission into the Congregation for the Defense of the Faith by Paul VI on June 27, 1971, it is difficult to

[82] *Die Psalmen. Einführung in deren Geschichte, Geist und liturgiche Verwendung* (Freiburg-im-Breisgau, 1924), 229.

[83] *EuA* 39 (1963): 251.

[84] Cf. Duncker, "Dom Atanasio Miller OSB, Secretario della Pontifica Commissione Biblica," 202ff.

[85] H. Höpfl, *LThK* 2 (1931): 286.

grasp the strong and often feared influence of the biblical commission on Catholic theology in the preconciliar era.

On May 8, 1949, Pius XII, possibly on the advice of Cardinal Augustin Bea, appointed Fr. Athanasius secretary of the Pontifical Biblical Commission in succession to the Dominican Fr. Vosté, recently deceased.[86] Athanasius Miller exercised this delicate task with much skill and tact. Not only had he to draft the decrees of the commission and produce the final versions but also keep himself informed on the progress of biblical studies in the Catholic world; read, advise on, and reply to the many reports, queries, and complaints. Finally, along with others from the body of consultors, he had to conduct the extremely difficult examinations of the biblical commission that were regarded as equal to those of the Pontifical Biblical Institute. Miller devoted himself to this task, which was not always appreciated. His sense of humor helped him to overcome many difficulties.

In his later years, "he suffered from diabetes, his weakened eyes made reading ever more difficult, he suffered strong rheumatic pain which often deprived him of sleep for much of the night. In all of this, he would not hear of painkillers or sleeping tablets."[87] Increasing blindness led him in 1962 to request Pope John XXIII to release him from office. In the summer of that year, the eighty-one-year-old returned to Beuron after forty years of work in Rome. Weakened by age and illness, he died on April 17, 1963, in the hospital at Leutkirch in the Allgau. He would have liked to have died in Beuron.

Fr. Cunibert Mohlberg (1878–1963)

Following Mohlberg's death[88]—far from his beloved Rome in his home monastery of Maria Laach to which his abbot, Basilius Ebel, had personally accompanied him some months previously—the well-known archaeologist Fr. Engelbert Kirschbaum, SJ, wrote to Rector Augustin Mayer:

[86] J. Schildenberger, *EuA* 57 (1981): 255f.

[87] *EuA* 39 (1963): 251.

[88] ArchMaria Laach, P. P. Kunibert Mohlberg, † May 21, 1963, Necrology. Obituaries: *RivAC* 40 (1966): 7–9 [Mohlberg's bibliography, on pp. 9–16]; E. V. Severus, *ALW* 8, no. 1 (1963): v–viii; J. B. Villiger, Offprint from the *Schweizerische Kirchenzeitung*, 131, nos. 32 and 33 (1963); Offprint from the *Zuger Nachrichten* of May 29, 1963; V. Fiala, *EuA* 39 (1963): 336–39; B. Neunheuser, *EL* 78 (1964): 58–62. For bibliographical notes and bibliography, see also *Miscellanea liturgica in honorem L. Cuniberti Mohlberg*, vol. 1 (Rome, 1948), ix–xxxix.

> Permit me to express to you and your Athenaeum my sincere condolences on the death of Fr. Cunibert whom I so greatly revered. Despite his many quirks I always held him in high esteem and genuinely liked him. I feel his loss keenly. His dear personality with all its human sides was, for decades, part of my life in Rome. I am certain that this "great child" has reached the good Lord and that from above he will loyally remember us. His work was significant and was a credit both to his Order and to the scholarly life. I write this in full awareness of his peculiarities. But when one looks at this man and his work as a whole one cannot speak otherwise. It is to your great credit that you made his later works possible and made him feel at home during the last decades of his life. It is only now from above that he will recognize this and thank you for it.[89]

Fr. Cunibert Mohlberg wearing the insignia of the Order of Merit of the German Federal Republic

With these words, not only is Fr. Cunibert Mohlberg's person succinctly summed up but also his special relationship with Sant'Anselmo is mentioned.

When in 1950 Abbot Primate Bernhard Kälin appointed Mohlberg to the newly erected chair of liturgy and he came to reside at Sant'Anselmo, he had already lived in the Eternal City for twenty years. During the lifetime of Abbot Primate Fidelis von Stotzingen, Sant'Anselmo had been closed to him. Why? Today it is difficult to discover the reasons. One reason may have been Mohlberg's alienation from his home monastery of Maria Laach, a Laach that had completely subscribed to the theology of Odo Casel, a theology passionately rejected by Mohlberg. Another reason may have been the stormy temperament and free lifestyle—for those days—of the self-confident Rheinlander. Fr. Cunibert, who had a mocking tongue, could on his part ask, "Why was I never wanted in Sant'Anselmo? I could have rubbed my sinful skin clean on the holiness of my confreres and been edified through a growth in virtue!"[90] In another letter to the Primate he crowed, "In any case, the reason why [in Fidelis von Stotzingen's version] one wanted with every means to prevent my inclusion in Sant'Anselmo, because one was afraid of a fight with [Fr. Philipp] Oppenheim, has been triumphantly refuted. At that

[89] AAt. Professori anziani I Z.

[90] Ibid., letter from Mohlberg to Kälin dated January 25, 1950.

time the hens were laughing, today it is the calves who are doing so as well."[91] In fact, until his transfer to Sant'Anselmo, Mohlberg, who had held the chair of special history of the early Church at the Pontifical Institute for Christian Archaeology since 1929, had lived with the Lazarists in the Via Pompeo Magno. Among other things, this caused him to speak of himself as "Magno Pompeo." Since his death, Mohlberg's academic career and work has been recounted and evaluated. Here, a summary will suffice.

Born on April 17, 1878, of an artisan family—his father was a village blacksmith—in Efferen near Cologne, Leonhard Mohlberg first attended the tradition-steeped "Apostelgymnasium" in Cologne, then the oblates' school of the Beuronese Congregation in Seckau, after which, aged nineteen, he entered Maria Laach. In 1902, he made solemn profession for Laach at Beuron, where he had been sent for his theological studies. According to the practice of the Beuronese Congregation at the time, he also received the subdiaconate, diaconate, and was ordained priest in the archabbey. When he had completed his theological studies, Fidelis von Stotzingen, still at that time abbot of Maria Laach, sent him to the Catholic University of Louvain where the gifted young priest read archaeology, history, and philosophy. His actual mentor in the discipline of historical methodology was Alfred Cauchie (1860–1922). The latter opened for him the methodological path into research of historico-liturgical sources that was to determine the course of Mohlberg's later life. In 1911, he became a "Docteur en sciences morales et historiques," with a brilliant dissertation on the then-half-forgotten Radulph de Rivo, "the last representative of the old Roman liturgy."

When the young monk from Laach began to make the opening up of liturgico-historical sources his life's work, liturgical renewal was in its early stages. But Mohlberg brought some impulses for Maria Laach with him from Louvain. Thirty years later, in an autobiographical retrospective, "Confidences from my Dealings with Medieval Manuscripts," he described how at that time the various streams of liturgical scholarship came together.[92] There were meetings with scholars such as Franz Joseph Dölger, Adolf Rücker, Anton Baumstark, and, above all, the friendship with Romano Guardini, which were seminal. Liturgy ought not only to be based on history but also should develop into an independent theological discipline according to the motto *Fontes et Ordo*—the liturgy must be the source and program of life. Along with Guardini and others,

[91] Ibid., letter dated November 20, 1949.

[92] *Miscellanea historica in honorem Alberti de Meyer*, vol. 2 (Brussels, 1946), 1314–1340.

Sant'Anselmo's vault (in foreground) at the Campo Verano Graveyard, opposite the Basilica of St. Lawrence

Fr. Cunibert Mohlberg with a student

Mohlberg was in fact one of the pioneers of the liturgical movement.

Fr. Cunibert came early to Rome. In 1924, at the instigation of the then-prefect of the Vatican Library, Giovanni Mercati, he had been entrusted with the classification of the library's important holdings of liturgical manuscripts. In 1929, he took over the chair of early church history at the Pontifical Institute for Christian Archaeology, a chair which up to then had been held by Dom Henri Quentin. Mohlberg taught there for more than three decades. His lectures, like those later in Sant'Anselmo, were if anything somewhat disappointing, overflowing with ideas and anecdotes but without order. Mohlberg's strengths lay elsewhere, namely, in personal direction of his students and in methodologically faultless scholarly work.

He loved to spend the holidays in Switzerland. In Zurich, from 1930, he continued in the months of August to October the cataloguing of the medieval manuscripts of the Central Library originally begun by Dom Germain Morin, OSB. The impressive catalogue finally appeared in 1950. At Sant'Anselmo he continued his scholarly editions of liturgical sources, first with Fr. Leo Eizenhöfer of Neuburg and Fr. Petrus Siffrin of Jerusalem, then, with the latter as his loyal assistant, on his own.

There was no lack of honorable recognition. He accepted these honors with humor and modesty. In 1956 he was awarded the Grand Cross of the Order of Merit German Federal Republic, having been nominated a *Socius Ordinarius* of the German Archaeological Institute in Berlin in 1955. In 1958 he was made an honorary member of the Swiss Association of Catholic Historians, receiving in the same year an honorary doctorate from the faculty of philosophy of the University of Zurich on the occasion of the 125th anniversary of that institution. He received many other distinctions, among which it suffices to mention here only the honorary citizenship of his native town and the naming of a street after him in 1958.

How multifaceted Fr. Cunibert's personality was is indicated by his interest in radiesthesia, the practice of the use of dowsing rods and pendulums, to which he attributed mysterious powers—and caused many confreres to shake their heads in suspicion. Under a nom de plume, Fr. Cunibert even wrote a book on this subject titled "Briefe an Tschü. Anleitung zu radiästhetischen Studien" (Letter to Tschü. An Introduction to the Study of Radiesthesia.)[93]

He was not always easy to get on with. He did not hesitate to criticize and his candor often overstepped the boundaries of good manners. But, deep down, Fr. Cunibert, who possessed a palpable joie de vivre, was a good and generous person who had a pronounced love of animals. "He regarded the donkey—which he imagined to be standing near his deathbed—as a particularly apt model for the monastic life. Of this animal he said that it is fed little, can be heaped up with burdens, is beaten often, but obstinately puts up with all of this."

He retained a grateful respect for the Abbot Primate who opened Sant'Anselmo to him. In a letter to Kälin on the eve of the Epiphany 1950, we read, "My field being the early Church, for me, as for the Church of the East, the Epiphany is the great feast next to Easter. And so, I should like to bring to you along with the three camels from which the three Kings have already dismounted, yet a fourth—no myrrh, because I think you already have enough of that. . . . How right was my real spiritual father Columba [Marmion] when he suggested that if one needed to do penance for murdering his mother-in-law, he should be made abbot. . . . You will receive enough incense. And so, all that remains to me is gold, but real gold, the gold of my loyalty which I have always promised you through thick and thin."[94]

[93] Mohlberg's nom de plume, under which this book appeared for the first time in 1945 and in a fourth revised edition in 1959, in the Arkana publishing house at Ulm, was Candi.

[94] AAt, Professori anziani [Former Professors], I-Z, letter from Mohlberg to Kälin dated January 5, 1950.

For all his urbanity, Mohlberg possessed a childlike piety. Every morning, also during the holiday months, he rose early, performed his meditation, and then celebrated Mass with great recollection. He had received his spiritual formation during his years at Louvain at the hands of the saintly Dom Columba Marmion, who died in 1923 as abbot of Maredsous. Mohlberg spoke of Marmion to his pupils with a great warmth of heart that could only have come from someone who in the depth of his being was a person of faith and piety.

Fr. Jean-Pierre Müller (1904–1979)

Fr. Johannes Müller—as he was known to German-speaking Anselmians and as he called himself in the years before the Second World War since his native language was German—was a man to whom Sant'Anselmo owes exceptional gratitude.[95] He was a Luxembourgeois, born on February 24, 1904, at Hollerich, the third of five children of an exemplary Christian family. His father finished his career as president of the board of administrators of the St. Paul Printing Company and of the "Luxemburger Wort." It was from his father that Fr. Johannes undoubtedly inherited his resolute and straightforward character, combined with the politeness that distinguished his behavior. At the age of nineteen, having brilliantly concluded his secondary schooling, he asked to be admitted to Clervaux. On August 6, 1925, he made profession. From the beginning he studied philosophy and theology at Sant'Anselmo. It was there that he met another Luxembourgeois, Fr. Josef Gredt. He studied Aristotle and Thomas under this teacher, but at the same time differentiated himself from Gredt by his strong interest in questions of the history of philosophy. Already in 1929 he received the doctorate "summa cum laude" and was ordained priest in the following year.

Fr. Jean-Pierre Müller (1904–1979)

[95] J. Gribomont, *Dom Jean-Pierre Muller OSB in memoriam*, Luxemburger Wort, January 11, 1980, with a bibliography; B. Neunheuser, "Erinnerungen an Dom Jean-Pierre Müller" [died November 2, 1979], *EuA* 56 (1980): 74–76. Cf. also Theodor Wolfram Köhler, *Sapientiae Procerum Amore. Mélanges Médiévistes offerts à Dom Jean-Pierre Müller O.S.B. à l'occasion de son 70ème anniversaire (24 février 1974)*, StAns, vol. 63 (Rome, 1974).

From 1932 to 1934 he taught philosophy in his home monastery of Clervaux to the house's clerics and in 1934–1935 taught dogmatics. This teaching ended when he was called to Sant'Anselmo as professor of the history of philosophy. He became a full professor in 1942, conscientiously fulfilling the obligations of this chair until 1976. For a quarter of a century Müller was also the librarian of Sant'Anselmo. He filled this time-consuming charge meticulously and during this period acquired, above all, valuable source material on the history of medieval philosophy. In 1942 he became director of "Studia Anselmiana" which series he continued with the many volumes that appeared under his supervision and which helped these scholarly publications to achieve a high esteem in the world of learning. As a scholar himself he contributed through his critical editions of medieval philosophical texts. His main area of interest was the discussions in the universities in the era of St. Thomas Aquinas. In particular he concentrated on the Dominican scholar Johannes Quidort of Paris, whose thought he opened up anew. This work demanded that he bring into play his many competencies: a comprehensive knowledge of the world of thought of high scholasticism and a sure judgment of its philosophy had to go hand in hand with a mastery of the historian's craft. Johannes Müller was equal to this task. His words had great weight among colleagues, while his professional criticism was also feared.

In 1951 he became dean of the faculty of philosophy. When in 1966 Rector Augustin Mayer was elected abbot of Metten, Fr. Johannes Müller became pro-rector of Sant'Anselmo for a year and a half. In 1967 the Luxembourg embassy to the Holy See appointed him religious counselor, an office that demanded much sensitivity in balancing the interests of national politics and those of the Church, presupposed diplomatic competence, and included responsibility for the Luxembourg colony in Rome. The honors that Müller received are an indication of how much the Grand Duchy appreciated his role. In 1977, like his compatriot Gredt before him, he was made an officer of the Grand Duchy's Order of the Oaken Crown.

Fr. Jean Gribomont (1920–1986)

One could also rely on Fr. Johannes Müller's word. He fulfilled his monastic obligations conscientiously. But despite his cordiality and politeness, on a human level he was difficult to approach. According to his confrere Jean Gribomont,[96] he was limited by "his stoicism which prevented him even to think of complaining and consequently of ever permitting himself to do so." Thus, he showed no reaction when the doctor gave him the news that he was incurably ill. He bore this illness with quiet courage until the end, dying on November 2, 1979, in Clervaux, his monastery of profession.

[96] Fr. Jean Gribomont of Clervaux was born on November 17, 1920, at Bas-Oha in Belgium. He was professed at Clervaux on September 2, 1930, and ordained priest on July 9, 1944. He pursued his studies at the Catholic University at Louvain, completing them in 1953 with a dissertation on a topic which was to occupy him all his life, "Histoire du texte des asétiques de St. Basile," for which he obtained the degree, Dr. sc. orient. From 1951 he cooperated on the production of the edition of the Vulgate at the Abbey of St. Jerome in Rome, becoming academic director of the project in 1958. At the same time he was prior of the monastery. He began to teach at Sant'Anselmo in the academic year 1958–1959 with a seminar on ecclesiology and asceticism in Basil. For ten years he confined his academic activity at Sant'Anselmo to conducting seminars. In the academic year 1969–1970 he taught his first course, "De imagine Dei apud Patres graecos." From 1970 he taught Oriental patrology, becoming an extraordinary professor in 1972, and in 1978 being appointed to the chair of monastic studies and director of the "monastic specialization" within the faculty of theology at Sant'Anselmo. His main concern was to introduce students to the monastic literature of the East, not merely of the Greek but also of the Coptic and Syrian fathers. From 1973 he taught as invited professor at the Patristics Institute, the "Augustinianum" in Rome. He died suddenly on March 21, 1986. Cf. articles by H. de Sainte-Marie, G. I. Gargano, A. de Bernardino, V. Grossi, G. Rocca, and P.-R. Tragan, *L'Osservatore Romano*, December 20, 1986, p. 3.

Chapter 5

Difficult New Directions for Sant'Anselmo after the Council

1. The College after the Council

In 1966, Fr. Augustin Mayer, rector of Sant'Anselmo, invited Dr. Frederick Sontag, an American Protestant and professor at Pomona College in Claremont, California, to lecture during a sabbatical year in the faculty of philosophy at Sant'Anselmo. The theme of the lectures was "Problems of Atheism."[1] As Sontag himself said, "If an American Protestant comes to teach philosophy at S. Anselmo, what else is he qualified to teach but 'atheism'?" Sontag, a member of the Congregationalist United Church of Christ, lived with his family in Rome for the academic year 1966–1967. He was not only a well-loved teacher in that year but also—important itself in our context—a keen observer of the changes in the student scene in the Roman colleges, which he got to know one by one. By the middle of the year he came to the conclusion, "My conversations with the students lead me to believe that every imaginable idea is examined and tested. If the system of instruction is not changed to meet this wave of ferment, the situation could become explosive. But it also has the potential to become the most creative period in the history of Catholicism. My Protestantism is not a danger for the faith of any person in Sant'Anselmo because, as I remarked to the dean of theology, the students are more radical than I am."[2]

[1] AAt, Professori anziani [Former professors] I-Z. Here, there is also a letter from sixteen students to the rector dated June 28, 1967, in which they thank him for inviting Sontag to Sant'Anselmo and praise his teaching.

[2] APr, Ateneo IV, Pubblicazioni. The quotation is in the Anselmian student newspaper, *News and Views,* no. 2 (February–March 1967). This newspaper lasted for only two issues.

These remarks from an outsider give some idea of how restless Sant'Anselmo had become by the middle of the 1960s. The college hummed like a disturbed swarm of bees. Traditional methods of teaching, the content of the philosophical and theological lectures, and not least the forms of monastic life were cast into doubt and rejected by many students. Unrest and the desire for experimentation, however, ruled also outside of Sant'Anselmo and in many abbeys of the Order. The unavoidable tensions arising from this came to the surface when a new Congress of Abbots was opened in the autumn of 1966.

Today, the sober Latin minutes of the congress do not permit the reader to sense the liveliness that possessed the Order.[3] In the first place, there were endless debates on the monastic Liturgy of the Hours, its language and structure, which soon led one to see that the few weeks available to the congress could produce no result. Among the many other topics that arose was that of the form and future of Sant'Anselmo. The subversive abbot of Scheyern, Johannes M. Hoeck, pleaded for the separation of the offices of prior and rector, as had the Bavarian abbots in 1925. This suggestion, so old in itself and with nothing new to argue in its favor, was applauded by those who saw salvation in structural change and believed in the benefits of commissions and secretariats.[4]

On September 26, Rector Augustin Mayer reported on the situation in the university.[5] Following the model he had used so often, the rector began with a fitting expression of appreciation of all that was good and everything in Sant'Anselmo that was praised by the other Roman universities and by the Congregation for Studies. In the second part of his report, however, he mentioned "Difficulties and Defects." In this he distinguished between those that were more or less common to all Roman universities and those that concerned Sant'Anselmo alone. In general, according to the rector, there was a wish among students in the Roman colleges to have fewer lectures. Instead, independent acquisition of material to be learned was highly popular, in which process students were anxious to avail themselves of the services of a professor or tutor. There was a widespread desire for other, more flexible, forms of examination. Many wished to replace the hitherto obligatory course in the theology of the Eastern Church with an introduction to Protestant theology. In philosophy, the natural-scientific disciplines should be replaced

[3] *Acta Congressus Abbatum ac Priorum Conventualium Congregationum Confoederatarum OSB. In aedibus S. Anselmi de Urbe a die 18 Septembris ad diem 4 Octobris 1966,* Norcia.

[4] APr, Congr. Abb. 1966, Protocollum a Secretariis scriptum, Sessio XV, allegatum 3.

[5] Ibid. De statu Athenaei S. Anselmi.

with "anthropological" disciplines. Finally, students wished that more courses and academic exercises be taught or held in modern languages.

Mayer reported that the Congregation for Studies had already begun to respond to the kind of suggestions referred to above. The first steps away for the currently normative schedule of studies of Pius XI had been taken and others were to follow. But Mayer revealed that the rectors of the Roman academies had their own desiderata. Above all, they complained about the unsatisfactory linguistic preparation of many students, both in classical and in modern languages.

Apart from the critical situation in the faculty of philosophy, among the main worries of Sant'Anselmo the rector mentioned above all was the growing difficulty of obtaining new professors from the Order. It was true that the Abbot Primate, in accordance with article 134 of the *Lex Propria*, had the right to demand at least one monk from every monastery, but for understandable reasons he was unwilling to employ this final remedy. Then there was the continued pressing need for a new *aula magna*.

Before and during the congress radical voices had called for the abolition of the faculty of philosophy. On the late afternoon of September 26 the dean, Fr. Johannes Müller, responded to these.[6] First, he gave an unvarnished report about the situation of the faculty. In the previous years it was attracting ever-fewer students. If in 1961–1962 there had still been thirty students and in 1962–1963 twenty-three, the figure for 1965–1966 had sunk to thirteen. For the coming academic year 1966–1967, Müller reckoned with only five or six students. Thus the continued existence of the faculty was a question of the utmost seriousness. For this reason, Müller made an earnest appeal to the congress for a binding declaration on the matter. He himself appealed for the continuance of the faculty of philosophy. He could indeed understand that abbots were unwilling to send juniors who had just come out of the novitiate to Rome. At the same time, there were many monks and abbots who had clearly not been damaged by an early sojourn in Rome, and this objection was in no way valid when it concerned the *cursus superior* of the third year of philosophy. To the objection "But the language of instruction is Latin!" Müller asked if one should not avail oneself of the opportunity not only to learn philosophy but also to learn how to speak and write Latin. Both from a philosophical and theological point of view, everything suggested that the faculty of philosophy should be retained. The vote on the matter on October 1 resulted in an overwhelming majority for

[6] Ibid. De Facultate Philosophica Pont. Athenaei S. Anselmi.

retention of the faculty—142 placet (yes), 6 placet iuxta modum (yes, with reservations), 5 non placet (no), and 1 abstention.[7]

If the faculty of philosophy was suffering from emaciation, this was made good by the upsurge in the young liturgical institute, the report on which was delivered by its president, Fr. Salvatore Marsili.[8] From thirty-three students in the year of its foundation, the number had risen to 172. The professorial body had been expanded by the employment of qualified diocesan and regular, i.e., non-Benedictine, priests, and indeed by lay professors. The chronic lack of space in Sant'Anselmo was an annoyance, along with a lack of specialized literature in the house library.

At the last plenary assembly on October 9, 1966, the congress decided by a large majority to meet for a second period in the autumn of the following year. Some important decisions had, however, already been taken. The congress had decided to retain the faculty of philosophy and it asked for the separation of university and the Benedictine college. The latter should be placed under a prior, "The Abbot Primate should not have any direct role in the leadership of the college" (*Abbas Primas immediatum regimen Colegii S. Anselmi ne exerceat*). Finally, the congress expressed approval of a significant shortening of the common choral office to be celebrated at Sant'Anselmo.

Abbot Primate Benno Gut closed the congress on October 9 with a few bitter words. Above all, he saw destruction in the decisions that had been taken and forced on him. These were *contra Legem Propriam, contra Collegium S. Anselmi et contra ipsum Abbatem Primatem*—against the *Lex Propria*, against the College of Sant'Anselmo, and against the Abbot Primate himself.[9]

The decisions of the congress already had a strong effect for change during the academic year 1966–1967. The daily timetable was relaxed. Vigils, except on Sundays and feast days, were left to private recitation. Despite the decisions of the abbots, the basic course in philosophy could be maintained only by the attendance of external students. There was

[7] Ibid. De Facultate Philosophica Pont. Athenaei S. Anselmi.

[8] *Acta Congressus*, no. 45.

[9] "Tandem Abbas Primas declarat, se nullatenus sermonem conclusivam velle proferre, sed Domino tantum gratias agere, etiamsi Congressus, pro dolor, conclusiones magis negativas quam positivas dederit, et quidem contra Legem Propriam, contra Collegium S. Anselmi et contra ipsum Abbatem Primatem." *Acta Congressus*, no. 52. On p. 59 of the second edition of the *Acta Congressus*, which also contains the minutes of the second session of 1967, the phrase, from *et quidem* to *Abbatem Primatem* is missing!

not a single student for the *cursus superior*. The number of Benedictine students, in decline for some years, continued to fall.

Then, a new situation was created by two rapid changes at the top in Sant'Anselmo. On November 3, Rector Augustin Mayer was elected abbot of Metten. Since the separation of university and college had not yet been completed, in the same month the Abbot Primate appointed Fr. Johannes Müller as pro-rector.[10] In a letter some months later, on June 29, 1967, Gut informed the abbot of his creation as a cardinal, a promotion that would make necessary the election of a new Abbot Primate. For the last time the departing Primate reminded the abbots of the need to send students to Sant'Anselmo. Thus, Rector Augustin Mayer and Primate Benno Gut laid down their responsibilities for Sant'Anselmo at a time when the latter had landed in the greatest crisis to date in its seventy-year history.

2. The Years of Upheaval

It had been decided during the congress of 1966 to establish a *Commissio Anselmiana*, which was to concern itself with changes at Sant' Anselmo that were necessary or considered necessary. On September 19, 1967, Sebastian Bovo, abbot of Parma, former professor of Old Testament at Sant'Anselmo, and at this time one of the spokesmen of the "progressives," delivered to the assembled abbots a lengthy declaration of principles on behalf of the commission. This outlined, down to the last organizational detail, how the separation of university and college was to be effected.[11] With this, the role of the college was reduced to that of a house of studies.

There was no further talk about monastic life. The one slight sentence in this lengthy exposé, in which the writer emphasized the primacy of the liturgy among the tasks of the college, was a foreign body in the essay as a whole, a lip service that had already been contradicted in practice.[12] What followed from the master of clerics, Fr. Anselm Gendebien of Maredsous, in office for one year, strengthened the impression that Sant'Anselmo was rapidly drifting from its inherited traditions. Gendebien spoke much about a new "dynamic" community life, of

[10] Gut, circular letter dated *Dominica Pentecostes*, 1967.

[11] *Acta Congressus Abbatum . . . Sessio III, a die 18 Septembris ad diem 30 eiusdem mensis 1967*, Norcia.

[12] APr, Congr. Abb. 1967. S. Bovo, De regimine Collegii et Athenaei S. Anselmi, "Affirmatur pincipium primatus Operis Dei inter omnia munera et obligaitones vitae monasticae collegii," p. 5.

Cardinal Benno Gut

the need for greater openness to the outside world, of the desirability of a new discipline "which must be free from all cold and inflexible legalism." These were all demands that one could read as so many accusations against the old Sant'Anselmo.[13]

The then-pro-rector, Fr. Johannes Müller, described the changes that had already been made in the program of studies at Sant'Anselmo.[14] He did not avoid the pressing question of whether or not personnel could be found to run the planned "specializations." It would be necessary to create new professorial posts. Were the abbots prepared to make the necessary sacrifices? Would students come in sufficient numbers? Twenty years earlier, he added, students in the faculty of philosophy were divided into those who followed a two-year course that led to theology and a higher course that led to the doctorate in philosophy. "But there are no students." In the previous two years it had not been possible to run the higher course. In the last year there had only been thirteen students in the basic course. Müller emphasized that there could, of course, be no question of abolishing the faculty. This abolition could only be effected by the body that established the faculty, namely, the Holy See. "But there is a danger that it [the faculty] will pass away. I doubt however, if it will then rest in peace. In any case, it will not have an honorable grave."[15]

Two professors from the liturgical institute, Fr. Salvatore Marsili of Finalpia and Fr. Adrien Nocent of Maredsous, produced their own plan for the future shape of the university which was worthy of discussion. Since Sant'Anselmo was attracting ever-fewer Benedictine students, it should be transformed from a seminary for young monks into a university for the Church, albeit a university led by Benedictines. This would, however, require specialization, which both professors envisaged as being possible in the promotion of patristic and liturgical disciplines. For obtaining suitable future professors, always a problem for Sant'Anselmo, they suggested the conscious promotion of capable candidates already during their time as students as well as the signing

[13] APr, Congr. Abb. 1967. A. Gendebien, Schema relationis circa disciplinam Sancti Anselmi, "Nova legislatio disciplinaris deberet immunis esse a quocumque frigido et immobili legalismo," p. 4.

[14] APr, Congr. Abb. 1967. De statu Athenaei S. Anselmi.

[15] Ibid. "Certe non potest esse sermo de abolenda Facultate philosophica. Solus potest abolere his qui eam erexit, i.e., Sancta Sedes. Sed periculum minatur, ut obdormiat, licet dubitem num requiescat in pace. Sine ullo dubio, sepulchrum eius non erit gloriosum," p. 2.

of contracts of employment, each time of eight years' duration, with home monasteries.[16]

Other voices at the congress were much more radical. They were all answered on September 23, 1967, by Augustin Mayer, now abbot of Metten, with a corrective that even today has not lost its relevance.[17] Mayer rejected the use of the term "seminary" for Sant'Anselmo. This designation was neither juridically nor factually accurate. It was juridically inaccurate because the university was established by the Holy See, possessed several faculties, and was able to confer all academic degrees. Sant'Anselmo was also not a seminary since it enjoyed an international reputation thanks to its three series of scholarly publications and the activities of several of its professors. Some people, Mayer continued, would like to turn Sant'Anselmo into a "center for higher studies," would like to make it a training center for those who had already completed their philosophical and theological studies and wished to acquire specialized knowledge in patristics, monastic studies, or liturgy. If one

Abbot Primate Rembert Weakland in conversation with Pope Paul VI on the occasion of the beatification of Sr. Fortunata Viti on October 8, 1967

[16] APr, Congr. Abb. 1967. S.Marsili/A. Nocent, De renovanda ratione studiorum in Pont. Athenaeo Anselmiano propositiones quaedam.

[17] APr, Congr. Abb. 1967. Documenta varia, adnexum XLV. Cf. appendix 9 below.

were to bow to this wish, a blossoming faculty of theology would be destroyed and the liturgical institute would be robbed of its best reason for existing. Further, he doubted that a sufficient number of Benedictine students and professors could be found for such specializations.

Again, there were others, according to the speaker, who wanted to reform the faculty of theology. There were, it is true, two types of theological faculty, the "Louvain" type and the "Central European and Roman" type. In the first model, basic theological training was acquired in a seminary, and this was followed by a three- or four-year course at a faculty with a view to obtaining a university degree. This objective was achieved by courses that were more usually monographic in character and by means of seminars. By contrast, in the "Central European and Roman" model, basic theological training and possible academic specializations were available at one and the same faculty. Mayer conceded that this second aspect, i.e., specialization, required more attention. Both "formulae" had their advantages and disadvantages. Were the Louvain model now to be adopted, the consequences should be carefully considered. Furthermore, one could see that Sant'Anselmo had always, in practice, operated a *forma mixta.*

Fr. Ambroise Watelet (1912–2007) as President of the Congregation of the Annunciation

But these warnings fell on deaf ears. In the following years, Sant'Anselmo, above all under the urging of Fr. Cipriano Vagaggini, who was certain of support in the Congregation for Studies, adopted that dangerous "Louvain Model," the dangers of which for Sant'Anselmo had first been recognized by Mayer. It was only too clear that the driving forces behind the push for change at Sant'Anselmo were coming above all from the United States and from England, two countries with systems of education different from that on the Continent. With the election of an American Abbot Primate on September 29, 1967, the scene was set for the journey into a new but uncertain future.[18]

Rembert Weakland, since 1963 coadjutor abbot of the great American Abbey of St. Vincent, was forty years old when he became Primate. As a stu-

[18] *Acta Congressus Abbatum . . . duplici sessione celebrati 1966–1967*, nos. 106–9. In the final ballot, the fourth, the results were as follows: R. Weakland 142, A. Mayer 52, spoiled votes 1. For an American view on this Congress, cf. T. A. Doyle, "The Congress of Abbots," *ABenR* 18 (1967): 456–64.

dent, he had been to Sant'Anselmo, spoke several languages fluently, was very musical, and above all full of optimism concerning the many possibilities that seemed to present themselves in the Church and the Order following the Second Vatican Council. And so he immediately began energetically to pursue the implementation of the decisions of the Congress of Abbots regarding the new order in Sant'Anselmo. He appointed Fr. Ambroise Watelet of Maredsous as prior of the college. The appointment of a new rector took some time. Finally, in a circular letter on March 21, 1967, Weakland announced the appointment of Fr. Basil Studer of Engelberg. In 1964, Studer had taken over the chair of patristics from Fr. Basilius Steidle of Beuron. Fr. Salvatore Marsili became the new vice rector. The members of the faculty of theology elected Fr. Magnus Löhrer of Einsiedeln, since 1963 the successor of Fr. Cipriano Vagaggini in the chair of dogmatics, as their dean. The faculty of philosophy elected as dean Fr. Zeno Bucher of Sankt Ottilien, a specialist in natural philosophy.[19]

In the summer of 1968 two greatly esteemed professors of outstanding merit ended their long service as teachers in Sant'Anselmo and returned to their home monasteries. These were Fr. Edmund Beck of Metten and Fr. Basilius Steidle of Beuron. Beck's chair of Oriental languages, which was to disappear in the restructuring of the early 1970s, was taken over for a short time by Fr. Winfrid Cramer of Gerleve.

Fr. Basilius Steidle during a lecture

Steidle's departure seemed also to confirm the end of the monastic institute. In the academic year 1968–1969 there was only one single course in the area of monasticism. This was given by the Camadolese Benedetto Calati on topics from medieval monastic spirituality. It was only in 1970 that Fr. Adalbert de Vogüé of La Pierre-qui-vire began his lectures on the Rule of Benedict, which he continued until 1975. Fr. Basilius Steidle had worked

[19] Fr. Zeno Bucher, born on December 26, 1907, in Wollhausen, Lucerne, was professed at Sankt Ottilien on October 11, 1930, and ordained priest on October 11, 1934. From 1948 to 1960 he taught philosophy at the philosophical academy in Sankt Ottilien, was professor of natural philosophy at Sant'Anselmo from 1961 to 1971, and from 1971 until 1978 held the chair of Christian metaphysics and natural philosophy in the philosophical institute of the theological faculty at the University of Salzburg. He died on August 23, 1984.

in Rome for sixteen years.[20] Born on March 6, 1903, one of many children of a family of teachers at Heuberg, today in the district of Tuttlingen, Augustin Steidle was eleven years old when he made his acquaintance with Benedictine life. In September 1914 he went to the Beuronese oblates' school at the Abbey of Emmaus in Prague where he remained until this school was closed in 1918. Following the completion of his high school diploma in Ravensburg, he entered the Archabbey of Beuron in the spring of 1923. In the autumn of 1924, Archabbot Raphael Walzer sent the young newly professed to study philosophy and theology at Sant'Anselmo. Fr. Basilius Steidle completed these studies in the summer of 1930 with a doctorate in theology. His unpublished dissertation examined Origen's teaching on angels. In the autumn of the same year he began to lecture at the theological academy in Beuron, at first on dogmatics, then from 1933 on the Church Fathers. These lectures resulted in the publication in 1937 of a handbook for students titled *Patrologia seu Historia antiquae litteraturae ecclesiaticae*. In 1939 he issued a German abridgement of this under the title *Die Kirchenväter, ihr Leben und ihr Werk*. There also appeared in the 1930s some of his translations of short texts from the fathers.

This first phase of Steidle's work, during which he attempted to gain a comprehensive view of the patristic tradition, ended in January 1940, when the National Socialist Reich Literary Bureau forbade Steidle, because of his lack of political reliability, to engage in any literary activity. After the war, when lectures began once more at Beuron and with them Steidle's publications, the latter showed that in the interim he had chosen a limited area of patrology. This field, research into early monasticism and the Rule of Benedict, was a field that he could manage and one to which he remained faithful in the years that followed. In 1952, when Steidle accepted his appointment to the chair of patrology at Sant'Anselmo, he had just finished his commentary on the Rule of Benedict, *Die Regel St. Benedikts, eingeleitet, übersetzt und aus dem alten Mönchtum erklärt* (The Rule of St. Benedict, introduced, translated, and explained in the light of early monasticism). This was published at Beuron in 1952. The heated discussion on the relationship between the Rule of the Master and the Rule of Benedict that was just beginning and that ended in the victory of the protagonists of the priority of the Rule of

[20] ArchBeuron, Necrology P. Basilius Steidle. Obituaries by U. Engelmann, *EuA* 58 (1982): 149–51; A. Olivar, *StMon* 24 (1982): 415ff.; A. de Vogüé, *RegBenSt*, vols. 10–11 (1981–1982 = 1984): 1–10. This latter also contains bibliographical information. Further, B. Steidle, *Beiträge zum alten Mönchtum und zu Benediktusregel. Mit einem Vorwort und einer Einführung*, ed. U. Engelmann (Sigmaringen, 1986).

the Master meant that Steidle's commentary, he being convinced of the opposite, was soon forgotten. But Steidle's opus had the merit that his commentary was the first to have explained the whole Rule systematically in the light of biblical-monastic tradition, or as he liked to say, on the basis of its "topsoil." Unfortunately, in later years Steidle, although he often played with the idea, could not bring himself to produce another edition of this commentary, revised in the light of altered scholarly perspectives. Instead, his research was reflected in many individual articles on the Rule of Benedict and on early monasticism. The reason for this limitation lay perhaps deeper than the demands made on him as a teacher of patrology, as head of the newly established monastic institute, and as editor of three important joint works on early monasticism in the series *Studia Anselmiana*. Adalbert de Vogüé, Steidle's successor in Rome, is believed to have observed "une certaine faiblesse critique" (a certain critical weakness) and accused him of following the scholarly opinions of others too easily. In fact, Steidle, sensitive to criticism—although this is part of the scholars' trade—did tend as a researcher to hide behind the views of others. In later years this was particularly so with regard to the views of his former pupil, Eugène Manning, OCSO, whose disputable theses on the origins of the Rule of Benedict Steidle adopted in the later editions of his Latin-German version of that Rule. These reservations, however, should not cause Steidle's great contribution to be overlooked as the one who was decisive in promoting research on the Rule of Benedict in German-speaking countries. Further, his studies on the life of Benedict, which particularly fascinated him in his later years, will long continue to be used because of their circumspect and knowledgeable assessment of the sources.

Fr. Zeno Bucher (1907–1984)

Behind such a decadeslong preoccupation with the Rule and with the figure of Benedict lay a burning existential fascination with the message of early monasticism. The question of what in the Rule of Benedict was "conditioned by the times" and what remained "timelessly valid" always gave Steidle cause for murmuring. His was not a simple, uncomplicated character. He was a person of strong emotions that gave him much to cope with. He could be overflowingly jolly but also reach the depths of pessimism and be full of violent aversions. The rapid changes in Sant'Anselmo after the council increasingly overshadowed his last years in Rome and this led him to yearn to return

Fr. Benedetto Calati (1914–2000)

to his home monastery at Beuron. He died there, following a difficult illness, on February 19, 1982, in his seventy-ninth year.

By 1968 energetic planning was taking place at Sant'Anselmo for the restructuring of studies, a restructuring that was also demanded by the Roman Congregation for Studies.[21]

When the academic year 1968–1969 opened, the rector, Fr. Basil Studer, was in a position to present some of these plans. Three cycles were proposed: on the basis of a five-year fundamental course, a first specialization, lasting two years, was to follow, leading to the license. A third cycle, also lasting two years, would lead to the doctorate. Altogether this would mean that it would take nine years to obtain the doctorate in theology! In addition to the specialization in liturgical sciences, three further specializations were originally foreseen for Sant'Anselmo in the dogmatic-ecumenical, dogmatic-patristic, and patristic-monastic fields. In 1972 a specialization in sacramental theology was added, the latter possibly because such a specialization was not available at any other Roman academy. This was a time of trial and error and not all plans could be realized. Even in later years several desirable projects could not be pursued because of the lack of students, professors, or the necessary finance. Finally, in addition to liturgy, only two specializations in theology remained, i.e., sacramental theology and monastic studies. In the field of patristics, which ought in fact to have been a Benedictine strength, the "Augustinianum," under the direction of the Augustinian Order, opened in Rome in 1969, becoming a center of excellence with a rapidly expanding specialist library. A missed opportunity for Sant'Anselmo!

At the Synod of Abbots President held at Douai in England in 1969, the possibility of admitting female students to Sant'Anselmo was broached for the first time. Since hitherto Sant'Anselmo had been largely a monastic college, a training center for young monks, this matter was approached

[21] For what follows, the most important source for the academic years 1968–1969 to 1974–1975 is the *Liber annualis*, published at the initiative of Rector Fr. Basilius Studer, which provided a regular chronicle of the *actuositas Athenaei*. Unfortunately, this publication was not continued after 1975. See, too, the regulations of the Congregation for Studies issued in 1968, *Normae quaedam ad constitutionem apostolicam 'Deus scientiarum Dominus' de studiis academicis ecclesiaticis recognoscendam*, in Seminarium, 1968, pp. 765–87.

Christmas celebration 1969 with musical presentations from various linguistic groups

with great caution. Before the 1970 Congress of Abbots, the presidents consulted the abbots of their Congregations. At the congress itself, the superiors voted in favor of admitting women students at Sant'Anselmo with the proviso that the separation of college and university —and with this monastic enclosure—be preserved.[22] Whoever had feared or hoped for a rush of female students to Sant'Anselmo had the sobering experience that very few women, and these mostly religious sisters, found their way as students to the Aventine.

The year 1971 was particularly difficult. No fewer than eight Benedictine professors left Sant'Anselmo, among them the dean of the faculty of philosophy, Fr. Zeno Bucher, and both professors of dogmatics, Fr. Magnus Löhrer and Fr. Raphael Schulte. It was only with the greatest difficulty that it was possible for Rector Basil Studer to find replacements and maintain teaching activity.

Ash Wednesday 1971—
procession from Sant'Anselmo to the neighboring Dominican church of Santa Sabina

[22] *Acta Congressus Abbatum ac Priorum conventualium Congregationum confoederatarum OSB . . . 1970,* no. 72. The result of the vote was 137 in favor, 20 against. At the same Congress, the abbots voted in favor of using the funds that had been collected for the construction of an *aula magna* for the renovation of the house instead.

The academic year 1971–1972 brought a further diminution in student numbers. In all, there were 219 enrollments, of which 59 were Benedictine, most of the latter studying in the faculty of theology.[23] Italians, 116 in number, formed the largest language group. Only twenty-six came from German- or English-speaking countries. Latin as a language of instruction, which demanded much effort from all, professors and students alike, regardless of national origin, and as an international language favored no one, was increasingly abandoned. In the faculty of philosophy, most courses were taught in Italian. For a time, Latin dominated in the faculty of theology, while the liturgical institute had already moved completely to Italian. This change to Italian in no way removed the language barrier in an international university. If anything, it raised the bar a few notches higher, while containing within it the danger of a provincialism that became even greater to the degree to which Sant'Anselmo was unable to attract more non-Italians. In the coming years the number of students sank even further.[24] There were 171 students matriculating at Sant'Anselmo for the academic year 1974–1975, of whom thirty-three were still Benedictines.[25] In this serious situation in which Sant'Anselmo found itself, Fr. Cipriano Vagaggini, in the meantime back in Rome, reluctantly and despite his age, assumed the office of rector in 1974.

A happy aspect of these years was the uninterrupted academic influence of the university. This was evidenced by the many symposia held in the house on liturgy and ecumenical and monastic topics, and which were attended by outside experts of the first rank. It was also gratifying and surprising how many other theological institutes expressed an interest in affiliation with Sant'Anselmo. The oldest example of such an association is the Salzburg Philosophical Institute, part of the faculty of theology of the University of Salzburg. Since 1955, by a decree of the Roman Congregation for Studies, this institute had been

[23] In the academic year 1965–1966, in contrast, there were still 387 students enrolled at Sant'Anselmo, of which 183 were in the faculty of theology, not counting the monastic institute, and 172 in the liturgical institute. Statistics from Gut, circular letter dated festo Ss. Cordis Jesu, 1966.

[24] Fr. B. Neunheuser wrote a too-optimistic account of the years 1972–1973 to 1977–1978. Cf. *EuA* 49 (1973): 321–25; *EuA* 51 (1975): 393–96; *EuA* 52 (1976): 475–78; *EuA* 53 (1977): 477–80; *EuA* 55 (1979): 63–66.

[25] The last Dr. Phil. to be approved was in the academic year 1973–1974 for Fr. Notker Wolf of Sankt Ottilien. His dissertation was titled "Das zyklische Weltmodell der Stoa. Ein Beitrag zur Geschichte von der Ewigen Wiederkehr des Gleichen" [The cyclical world model of the Stoa: A contribution to the history of the eternal return of the same]. A nice irony of history!

affiliated with Sant'Anselmo.[26] This connection, on the basis of which the Salzburg institute could confer academic degrees in philosophy in the name of the faculty of philosophy at Sant'Anselmo, ended in 1978 when the Pontifical Philosophical Institute in Salzburg received a new legal structure.[27]

In the 1970s, the development of the college, now separated from the university, gave cause for concern. Benedictine students occupied barely half of the available accommodation. A whole set of reasons had led to this rapid change. The first was the frightening drop in religious vocations. In 1965 there were still 601 novices, in 1970 only 277. This decline meant the death of the theologates and house of studies of many Congregations. This, in turn, made less attractive the acquisition of academic degrees for teaching purposes.[28] But another, no less important, factor in these years was a strong "anti-Roman" feeling among younger monks that made study in Rome—not only in Sant'Anselmo—less attractive.

Naturally, a half-empty house caused new financial problems. Sant'Anselmo had never been free of such problems. These were now compounded by the impossibility of replacing the elderly lay brothers, most of whom had served Sant'Anselmo loyally and selflessly for decades, and were now increasingly unfit for further work. There simply were no lay brothers, either in the Beuronese Congregation or elsewhere. For a time, the old Beuronese brothers were replaced by brothers from Einsiedeln and the Congregation of Sankt Ottilen, but this too came to an end.[29] More and more the manual work in house and garden, as well as service at receptions, had to be entrusted to lay employees. This was

[26] Decree of the Congregation for Studies dated October 28, 1955, "Philosophiae Institutum in Theologica Salisburgensi Facultate canonice erigitur atque ad Philosophicam Facultatem Pontificii Athenaei Sancti Anselmi de Urbe aggregatur," *AAS* 47 (1955): 859f.

[27] Decree of the Sacred Congregation for Catholic Instruction dated May 14, 1978, *AAS* 70 (1978): 314ff.

[28] AAt, lecture by Fr. Basil Studer at the "Salzburg Abbots' Conference," held at Würzburg in 1970.

[29] The last of the old "Beuronese" brothers, Br. Andreas Avellin Stengel, lived at Sant'Anselmo until his death on November 1, 1984. For generations of Anselmians he was a legend. Born in Bisingen on January 9, 1891, he was professed at Maria Laach on January 25, 1912. In 1938 he came to Sant'Anselmo where he was employed in many different departments. Above all, he was a tailor and porter, but also, for a time, a cook. Later he became responsible for the organization of weddings in the abbey church as well as for the preparatory conversations with the couples. This was a task he particularly enjoyed. The last brothers to live in the college were Br. Wilhelm Lang of Sankt Ottilien, from 1954 to 1992, and Br. Heimrad Seibel of Münsterschwarzach, who was at Sant'Anselmo from 1959 until 1988.

Celebration for Br. Avelin Stengel (1891–1984), porter for many years

Br. Wilhelm Lang (1918–2006)

an expensive transition and not a real replacement for the brothers.

Discipline in the house had also changed. Little remained of the traditional observance of Sant'Anselmo.[30] The Benedictine students, supported by some professors and even by the Abbot Primate himself, preferred liturgical celebrations in small groups. Latin was despised as the language of a world and era that had been overtaken. Added to this came the increased average age of students, of whom half were already priests when they came to Sant'Anselmo. In previous decades, it was an exception for Benedictine students to study at other Roman institutes—an exception that met with scant approval. This now became simply a matter of course. Was Sant'Anselmo now to become a mere house of studies, like many others in Rome, without the burden of a full university?

Br. Heimrad Seibel (1910–1992)

[30] There is no mention any more in the statutes of 1970 of the "vita monastic" but, rather, of the "vita regularis" or the "vita communis." The College of Sant'Anselmo is defined as a "domus religiosa." The reduced choral office is no longer based on the Benedictine vocation to praise God, but on the demands of the "vita communis." Cf. *Statuta*, 1970, nos. 4–5, 51–52.

Many suspected and others hoped that this is what Abbot Primate Rembert Weakland had in mind when he was reelected at the Congress of Abbots in 1973.

At a symposium on monastic studies with representatives of the various Benedictine Congregations, the Primate sought to clarify what might be the future tasks of Sant'Anselmo for the Order and the Church.[31] He must have been disappointed by the results. It proved once more the different views concerning Sant'Anselmo present within the Order. While the German-speaking monasteries were anxious to retain basic philosophical and theological training at Sant'Anselmo and showed little enthusiasm for specialization, the English-speaking Congregations wanted the exact opposite. The Congregation of Solesmes, as ever, maintained a lofty distance from Sant'Anselmo. Neither one nor the other option was acceptable. Under these circumstances, Abbot Primate Weakland could hardly see a way out of the dilemma. He did not want the old Beueronese-monastic Sant'Anselmo, but he was unable to erect a substitute. Thus, it was no wonder that at the Congress of Abbots of 1977, dangerous talk that the University of Sant'Anselmo should be abolished surfaced—dangerous because it was all too appealing to the indifferent and antagonistic.[32] Thus, Weakland must have felt it as a rescue from a duty that increasingly felt like a burden when, in September 1977, during the Congress of Abbots, Pope Paul VI appointed him archbishop of Milwaukee. The abbots elected as his successor the archabbot of Sankt Ottilien, Viktor Dammertz.[33] Under his leadership, with a new rector, Fr. Magnus Löhrer, and finally with a new prior, Fr. Gerhard Békés,[34] it was possible to steer the ship into calmer waters.

Fr. Gerhard Békés (1915–1999)

[31] APr, Weakland, circular letter dated March 20, 1975, with appendix 4: "In many respects the Symposion was not a great success." Cf. Ph. Rouillard, "Theologische Studien und monastisches Leben. Ein Symposium zu St. Anselm/Rom," *EuA* 50 (1974): 480ff.

[32] *Acta Congressus Abbatum ac Priorum conventualium Congregationum Confoederatarum O.S.B.* . . . 1977, no. 24.

[33] Ibid., no. 57.

[34] Fr. Gerhard Békés was born on January 3, 1915, was professed on September 12, 1933, at Pannonhalma, and was ordained priest on September 11, 1938. In 1988 he

3. In Retrospect

The Sant'Anselmo, the birth and development of which has been described here, is gone forever. Its end was the result of profound and far-reaching changes over the last decades in the world, in the Church, and in the Order. The Benedictine students who occupy the college today—to speak only of these—are culturally, monastically, and liturgically of another stamp than previous generations. A part of a tradition—and also of a monastic way of life—has been interrupted. It is not the historian's task to make recommendations for the future, but it is his task to identify continuities and breaks in the history of an institution.

A painfully constant factor in the one hundred years of Sant'Anselmo has been caused by the markedly federalist constitution of the Benedictine Order. Monasteries are extremely unwilling to undertake common projects. That the superiors of the college, the Abbot Primate, and the rector have always had to beg for competent professors, more students, and more money—and often for all three at the same time—provides a depressing *cantus firmus* throughout Anselmian history. Was this a built-in fault in the plan of the founder himself? What Pope Leo XIII intended with the refoundation of Sant'Anselmo is crystal clear. He expressed this on several occasions, most succinctly in a papal brief to the Austrian Benedictine abbots on December 30, 1888.[35] Leo XIII did not intend to establish a new pontifical university. Rome did not need

---

was the longest-serving professor at Sant'Anselmo. Since 1946–1947 he had taught dogmatic theology in the *cursus seminaristicus* in Sant'Anselmo. From 1961–1962 on he also gave occasional lectures for the main academic course. During the Second Vatican Council he discovered his real life's work, the "ecumenical question"—this was the title of his first specialist course in 1964–1965. From the academic year 1976–1977 he was dean of the faculty of theology and from 1978 to 1983, prior of Sant'Anselmo. Cf. StAns, vol. 92 (Rome, 1985), 9–12. Cf. p. 244 below.

[35] "Nostris scilicet, dilecti filii, restitutum a Nobis in Urbe fuisse antiquum S. Anselmi collegium, ubi Ordinis vestri alumni sincerum haurirent Sancti Parentis sui spiritum, et prope hanc veritatis Cathedram sacras disciplinas docerentur. Proinde hoc opus non modo eo spectabat ut solidae doctrinae laus, qua vester Ordo ab exordiis suis iure gloriatur, eidem illibata maneret, sed eo praecipuae ut alumni perciperent penitus atque incorruptam servare assuescerent eam vitae disciplinam quae ab immortali Ordinis conditore tradita est. Iam vero ut hoc opus finem suum attingat, necesse est parem, imo eamdem in Monasteriis omnibus vigere disciplinam, ita ut nihil in iis differat, nihil intersit. Secus alumni, quos istinc etiam missum iri confidimus, quum ad suos erunt redituri, diversum nacti spiritum vitaeque genus non se in suas recipi familias autumabunt, sed advenarum instar versari inter alienissimos." Cf. *Gratulationis unanimis*, Leonis XIII P. M. Acta 8 (Rome, 1889), 412–16, here on 413.

another of these. At that time, the Eternal City already had the Gregorian University, with no fewer than 708 students, at which academic degrees in theology, philosophy, and canon law could be obtained. There was also the Pontifical Roman Seminary, later the Lateran University, itself with three faculties and the right to confer academic degrees. Further, there was the Apostolic Urban College of Propaganda Fide where, in addition to theology and philosophy, Oriental languages were especially promoted. Then there was the College of St. Thomas Aquinas, later the "Angelicum," that was intended primarily for Dominican students who could pursue academic studies in philosophy and theology there. The Franciscan Friars Minor had the College of St. Bonaventure, a nonacademic institute.[36]

Sant'Anselmo in morning light

[36] Cf. *La Gerarchia Cattolica* (Rome, 1888), 678–83. For studies in Rome in the 1880s, see, M. Kinter, "Die kirchlichen Studien in Rom unter dem Pontificate Leo XIII," *StudMitt* 10 (1889): 324f. Further, G. van Caloen, "Les études à Rome," *RBén* 8 (1891): 164–75. Naturally, the student numbers cannot be compared to those of the modern mass universities. In 1870, the University of Basle, when Friedrich Nietzsche taught there and Jacob Burckhardt was a colleague on the faculty, counted in all four faculties together only 116 students, the majority of these in theology. Even highly esteemed teachers could find themselves unable to teach certain courses for lack of students. Cf. C. P. Janz, *Friedrich Nietzsche, Biographie*, vol. 1 (Munich-Vienna, 1978), 284.

Of all these institutions, Sant'Anselmo most resembled the Dominican college. The conferring of degrees, however, the alpha and omega of a university, was not conceded to the new Sant'Anselmo from the beginning. In fact, Leo XIII had in mind a seminary for Benedictines from all over the world, even if this was to be a seminary with a high academic niveau. Here in Rome, young Benedictines from all countries were to get to know one another, study together, and at the same time grow into a unified and exemplary observance that would then be transplanted to all monasteries of the Order. Already at the time of the foundation of Sant'Anselmo—a foundation that took them by surprise—Benedictines were slow to accept this latter objective when, indeed, they did not actually reject it. This indicates that the pope either did not fully understand or underestimated the vow of monastic stability, as well as the Benedictines' sense of local traditions, supported by the autonomy of individual monasteries. This dissonance might, perhaps, have become clearer earlier on if the Beuronese Congregation, then in full expansion, had not taken up the pope's idea and formed Sant'Anselmo for generations, both in the areas of discipline and scholarship. Certainly "Beuron" had not grabbed Sant'Anselmo nor, indeed, seen it as a basis for further monastic "conquests." The Beuronese only stepped in when other Congregations, even if they had wished to do so, could not help because of lack of personnel. It is not purely coincidental that Sant'Anselmo experienced a deep crisis precisely at a time when the Beuronese Congregation was in decline monastically and intellectually.

Often over the past hundred years the Order must have felt that Sant'Anselmo was a Greek gift from Leo XIII. It would not be correct, however, looking back, to see Sant'Anselmo only as a burden heaped on the Order. Undoubtedly in the past the college has done much all over the world to breathe life into an Order that had been dispersed and made powerless by division. There were periods when almost all the abbots of the Order were Old Anselmians who knew one another from their time as students together and were formed by the same Anselmian observance, even when they continued to cling to the special traditions of their monasteries. This history of the influence of Sant'Anselmo has not yet been written. Here it suffices to cite one witness to the appreciation of Sant'Anselmo in the Order which is all the more significant since it was written in 1919 by a very influential critic of Beueronese monasticism, Abbot Cuthbert Butler of Downside:

> That the picked young monks of the various abbeys should be put through a good course of higher theological studies together was a good thing; that they should be subjected to the educative forces of

> a residence in Rome, with the opportunities the journeys afforded of seeing the artistic treasures and historical monuments of Italy, was also good; but best of all was it that these young men of all congregations and nationalities should live together, should come to know and appreciate one another and form friendships that outlived the years at S.Anselmo. For thus the barriers of national isolation were broken down, and the young monks carried back to their own abbeys not only a better theological formation but also a widened outlook and perhaps vistas of ideas they would not have perceived at home.[37]

The periods in which Sant'Anselmo flourished, above all in the 1930s and 1950s, were at the same time monastic and scholarly high points. This followed almost automatically from the seemingly inseparable unity of the Benedictine college, the primatial abbey, and the university. But it was precisely the exigencies of the university that made this unique symbiosis increasingly difficult. Already in 1931, the more stringent regulations governing studies contained in the constitution *Deus scientiarum Dominus* had been implemented only with difficulty in Sant'Anselmo and integrated with the concept of the foundation to date. The developments following the Second Vatican Council then led to the definitive break with Pope Leo XIII's idea, the consequences of which cannot yet be foreseen.

[37] C. Butler, *Benedictine Monachism. Studies in Benedictine Life and Rule* (London, 1924), 271.

Epilogue

1. Sant'Anselmo in Recent Decades

The Benedictine College and University of Sant'Anselmo have survived the profound changes described in the last chapter. This survival could be explained by a dogged holding fast to Benedictine *stabilitas* by the core Anselmian team in stormy times. Certainly, however, a factor in this survival was the desire of the Benedictine Confederation not to permit the inheritance of the papal founder of Sant'Anselmo to perish, despite all the defeatist voices inside the Order itself. If Sant'Anselmo did not want to die of exhaustion, it had to adjust as a college and university amid the as yet far from completed societal, demographic, cultural, and, of course, religious convulsions, with measures that would enable it to go into the future. It had to adjust without losing what was special to itself.

From many points of view, the imposing and solidly built complex on the Aventine Hill, one of the most beautiful locations in Rome, was, after more than a hundred years, in need of renovation. Above all, the roofs were in pressing need of renewal. The cost of such an operation always exceeded Sant'Anselmo's income. Many of the urgently needed repairs could not have been done without the generosity of benefactors. Right from the beginning of his period in office, it was Abbot Primate Notker Wolf, more than his predecessors, who made this project his own. Through his widespread network of personal contacts he was able to gather funds for Sant'Anselmo both inside and outside the Benedictine Confederation. Further, two foundations, one in the United States and another in Lucerne, Switzerland, helped Sant'Anselmo in recent years. It is primarily thanks to the Swiss foundation, "Foundation Benedict"—which was able, thanks to the energies of Fr. Markus Muff of Engelberg, to attract sponsors from Switzerland—that it has gradually been possible to undertake the necessary renovations. Much remains to be done.

The church at Sant'Anselmo has always been the apple of the college's eye. With the creation of Archbishop Augustin Mayer, rector

The newly elected Abbot Primate Viktor Dammertz at the general audience of Benedictines with Pope Paul VI on September 23, 1977

of Sant'Anselmo for many years, as cardinal deacon in June 1985, the church was raised to the dignity of a basilica and a titular church for cardinals deacon.[1] The present titular is Cardinal Fortunato Baldelli. The five-aisled crypt under the church was originally used for the celebration of the private Masses of the many priests in the house. Since 1987, when it was suitably adapted, it has served as the library for the university. But however imposing the building on the summit of the Aventine may be, it is simply a house for the real purpose of Sant'Anselmo —to be a Benedictine college and at the same time a university with the right to confer doctoral degrees. The college and university are a tension-filled duo, but both are inseparably linked. Not a few Benedictines observe with anxiety that for years, college and Athenaeum have been drifting apart.

[1] Paul Augustin Cardinal Mayer died in Rome on April 30, 2010, shortly before completing his ninety-ninth year. His life has been described by Stephan Haering, "In Memoriam. Kardinal Augustinus Mayer OSB," *SMGB* 122 (2011): 508–11. Reminiscences by various writers can be found in the publication *Alt und Jung Metten* 77 (2010/2011): 162–89, with a contribution from Pius Engelbert, "Augustin Mayer und Sant'Anselmo," pp. 168–72.

2. The College

The college, which as we described at the beginning of this book, was the original cell of the organism that is Sant'Anselmo. College and university are linked in the person of the Abbot Primate, he being not only chancellor of the Athenaeum of Sant'Anselmo but also abbot of the Primatial Abbey of Sant'Anselmo. From 1977 until September 1992, when he did not stand for election at the Congress of Abbots, Victor Dammertz, formerly archabbot of Sankt Ottilien, was Abbot Primate. Unexpectedly, he was appointed bishop of Augsburg on December 24 of the same year. He retired in January 2004. His successor as seventh Abbot Primate was the American Jerome Theisen, abbot of Saint John's, Collegeville. Abbot Primate Jerome died suddenly of a heart attack on September 11, 1995, and was buried at Saint John's. In accordance with the *Lex Propria* of the Order, the functions of Primate were assumed by the Abbot Primate's vicar, Francis Rossiter, abbot of Ealing in London, until the next Congress of Abbots in 1996.

Abbot Primate Jerome Theisen (1930–1995)

On September 18, 1996, the eighth Abbot Primate was elected in the person of Marcel Rooney, abbot of Conception, Missouri. Before his election as abbot of this large American monastery, Rooney had taught for several years at the Pontifical Liturgical Institute. Thus he knew Sant'Anselmo. For reasons that will not be entered into here, however, he resigned after only four years at the next Congress of Abbots in the year 2000. He was replaced by another archabbot of Sankt Ottilien, Notker Wolf, who was confirmed in this office by the Congress of Abbots in 2008.

As abbot of Sant'Anselmo, the Abbot Primate of the time is entrusted with the welfare of the college, a college which is aptly described as a "collegium monasteriale." These two words are intended to express the fact that Sant'Anselmo, as a Benedictine college, resembles a monastery and is not merely a house of studies. Nor is it a seminary, of which there are many. It is, rather, an international community of professors, officials, and students who follow a monastic rhythm of life to the extent that this is reconcilable with the main objective of the house, which is studies.

Since the 1960s the day-to-day administration of the college has been the responsibility of the prior who is appointed by the Abbot Primate. It has never been easy to find a suitable candidate for this post. Whoever has previously known Sant'Anselmo, be it as a student or

The newly elected Abbot Primate Marcel Rooney at the Congress of Abbots in 1996 with Archabbot Notker Wolf, later his successor

professor, has an initial advantage. But with most of the priors, this has not been the case. The last such person to become prior was Fr. Gerard Békés of Pannonhalma who, after many years as a professor, combined these two charges. He was in charge of the house from 1978 to 1983, a task he fulfilled in the gentle Austro-Hungarian tradition.[2] He was followed by priors who succeeded one another, often with some rapidity, and returned to their home monasteries. Not all of these were equal to the difficult task demanded of them, though all did their best to serve Sant'Anselmo. It was always a matter of reconciling the demands of a monastic college with those of the university while at the same time promoting community life in the house. Two priors in the period under examination, Fr. Mark Sheridan and Fr. Edmund Power, rose to higher things. The first was an American from St. Anselm's Abbey in Washington, DC. In 1983 he was appointed by Abbot Primate Dammertz and remained prior until 1992. Already in 1986 he began to hold seminars in the monastic institute. He was coordinator of the monastic institute from 1990 to 1998, then dean of the faculty of theology, finally being elected rector of the Athenaeum. Fr. Edmund Power, a monk of Douai Abbey in England, was appointed prior by Abbot Primate Rooney in 1997, an

[2] Cf. supra p. 237, n34. He died on July 29, 1999, in his eighty-fifth year. In the festschrift dedicated to him, *Unum omnes in Christo in unitatis servitio*, ed. A. Smorjai (Pannonhalma, 1995), see the short biography by R. Cleary, "Insights into the Man and Monk, Gerard J. Békés," pp. 11–23.

office he held until October 1, 2004. By then he had been simultaneously prior administrator of St. Paul's Outside the Walls for some time. On April 9, 2005, he was elected abbot of St. Paul's and confirmed by Pope Benedict XVI on May 7 of the same year.

A constant concern of the priors—and one that required much vigilance—was the proper constitution of the community at Sant'Anselmo. Benedictines were always welcome as residents. Today, resident members from Benedictine "branch orders" such as the Trappists are welcomed. In order to maintain the monastic character of the house, the policy is to ensure that the majority of the roughly one hundred available rooms are occupied by Benedictines. Unoccupied rooms are made available to members of other orders, students from the Oriental Churches, and diocesan priests, particularly when these are studying at Sant'Anselmo.

The monastic character of the college is shown in certain communal exercises, above all in the choral celebration of the Divine Office.[3] In contrast with other religious houses in Rome, there are servers at the common meals at midday and in the evening, the residents taking turns to perform this service. On five days of the week, supper (cena) takes place without conversation, there being either reading or recorded music during the meal. During the academic year, self-service meals take place regularly only on Sunday evenings and Wednesday evenings. What about the current daily timetable?

Abbot Primate Notker Wolf. Primate since 2000

At 6:20 a.m., Lauds and Mass are celebrated. Despite frequently expressed objections, these are still celebrated in different language groups. An important reason for this is the high number of concelebrants, which makes the reception of Communion at a common Mass unnecessarily long. This prolongation is not possible because many students have to leave the house early in order to arrive on time at other academic institutions, such as the Biblical Institute, the Oriental Institute, the Alphonsianum, and others. Naturally, the possibility of choosing in the morning between several liturgical groups caters to the wish of many for a celebration of the liturgy, along with its language tailored to their needs. In 2011, there were, along with a large group that celebrated

[3] See the unpublished "Regolamento del Collegio di S. Anselmo," September 2011.

An increasingly varied picture. The Congress of Abbots of 2000

the liturgy in the basilica in Italian, both English and Latin "chapels." The short Midday Office is celebrated by all in the chapter room. This office consists in a Latin hymn, one or two psalms sung in Latin, a short reading in Italian, followed by a concluding prayer in Latin. Lunch in the refectory follows immediately at 1:00 p.m., during which there is usually talking, which gives the members of the community who come from about forty nations the chance to get to know one another. Vespers is sung in Latin at 7:15 p.m. by all in the church, as is Compline at 8:30 p.m. On Sundays and major feasts the group Masses are replaced by sung Lauds at 6:50 a.m. in the church. Conventual Mass follows at 9:00 a.m. in Italian with the proper and ordinary sung in Gregorian chant. It should be noted here that the structure of the liturgy at Sant'Anselmo, which in the intervening period has proved itself successful, was devised by Marcel Rooney, then professor at the liturgical institute and approved by Abbot Primate Jerome Theisen in 1993.

3. The University

Let us now attempt to provide an overview of the university, the Athenaeum of Sant'Anselmo. At the head of the Athenaeum is the rector—the *Rector Magnificus*, to give him his full title. Unlike the prior, the rector is not appointed by the Abbot Primate but elected by all teachers who belong to one of the faculties, along with seven student representatives. The Abbot Primate in his capacity as grand chancellor presides over the election. The rector, who must be a monk of the Benedictine Confederation, is elected for four years and this election must be confirmed by the Congregation for Catholic Education. The statutes do not foresee the election of a woman, for example, a Benedictine nun or sister.

There have been six rectors since 1978. These are:

Fr. Magnus Löhrer from Einsiedeln, 1978–1986;

Fr. Anscar Chupungo of Manila, 1986–1990. Fr. Anscar was the first rector from Asia;

Fr. Pius-Ramon Tragan from Montserrat, 1990–1997;

Fr. Albert Schmidt of Beuron, 1997–2005. He was not a professor at Sant'Anselmo but was suggested to the electors by Abbot Primate Rooney as a kind of university president;

Fr. Mark Sheridan of St. Anselm's Abbey, Washington, DC, 2005–2009. In 2011 he transferred his stability to Dormition Abbey in Jerusalem; and

Fr. Juan Javier Flores Arcas from Silos, since 2009.

The university is divided into three faculties, those of philosophy, theology, and liturgy, the latter being identical with the Pontifical Liturgical Institute. The faculty of canon law, which existed in the early days of Sant'Anselmo, was suspended in 1928 and not revived since then. Like all similar Catholic institutions, the university is subject to the norms of the apostolic constitution *Sapientia Christiana* of April 15, 1979, supplemented for Sant'Anselmo by proper statutes, last revised in 2006, and detailed ordinances, updated in 2008.[4] To these have to be added adjustments made in the light of the so-called Bologna Process, which aims at mutual recognition of academic degrees and comparability of university teaching in the European area. Despite the partial increase in material to be examined, the exigencies of the Bologna Process caused far fewer problems in Sant'Anselmo than, for example, in German universities. Studies at Sant'Anselmo, as also in the other Roman universities are, in comparison with the German system, organized very much as in a school. Every faculty has three cycles. A basic cycle in the faculty of philosophy and faculty of theology leads to a bachelor's degree. A second, two-year cycle, leads to the license (the equivalent of a master's degree), with a third cycle leading to the doctorate. In contrast with earlier regulations, *Sapientia Christiana* requires specialization in the second and third cycles. This requirement does not pose any great difficulties for larger institutions such as the Lateran or Gregorian universities, since they have both a sufficiently large number of teachers as well as of students. The situation is different for a small university such as Sant'Anselmo, which can compete only if it offers something not available in the others.

Fr. Maternus Hoegen (1927–2009)

Of itself, the subject with which the Pontifical Liturgical Institute deals provides it with its uniqueness. Such is less easily found in the philosophical or theological faculties. Already a problem child before the Second Vatican Council, since the 1970s the faculty of philosophy has been limited to teaching the foundation course. It has constantly been in danger of collapse, a danger that has not yet been overcome. For eleven years,

[4] Constitutio Apostolica *Sapientia Christiana* dated April 15, 1979, *AAs,* vol. 71 (1979): 469–99; cf. also the *Ordinationes* of the Sacred Congregation for Catholic Education, ibid., 500–21.

the pro-dean was Fr. Maternus Hoegen from Maria Laach. Much loved by students because of his winning personality, he was, however, academically unproductive.[5] When his period in charge ended in 1988, Fr. Elmar Salmann courageously took on the task of rousing the faculty of philosophy from its long slumber. Following a suggestion from Abbot Primate Jerome Theisen and after much reflection, a second and third cycle were introduced under the title "Philosophy and Mysticism," which was first offered in the academic year 1999–2000. Later the course was called "the philosophy of religion" since under this title it was academically easier to "sell." This change of name did not mean any loss of interest in pursuing, through lectures and in seminars, the exciting combination of religious experience and philosophical thought.

Since 1952, the faculty of theology possessed an institute that fulfilled all the requirements of a specialization and which remains to this day capable of development. This is the monastic institute, which, along with the liturgical institute, is unique among the possibilities for study offered in Rome.[6] For years the lectures of Fr. Adalbert de Vogüé were undoubtedly a great attraction. In 1989, following a long pause, de Vogüé resumed his teaching at the monastic institute. Until 1999, he went to Rome every year for the first semester to hold an obligatory course. In addition to this program of monastic history and spirituality, at present the faculty offers two further specializations, one in sacra-

[5] Fr. Maternus Hoegen was born in Düsseldorf on February 26, 1927. As a sailor in the German navy, he was a prisoner-of-war in the United States for seven months. Back in Germany, he completed his secondary education and in 1947 began to study at the technical university in Karlsruhe. In May 1949, he entered Maria Laach where he made simple profession on September 10, 1950. He began his philosophical and theological studies at Maria Laach and, from 1952, continued these in Sant'Anselmo. Ordained priest in 1956, he obtained the doctorate in philosophy with a dissertation titled "Zum Problem des Bezugs von Sein und Mensch bei Martin Heidegger" [On the problem of the relationship of Being and the person in the thought of Martin Heidegger]. His moderator was Fr. Beda Thum. On his return to Maria Laach he had several tasks, among them holding the office of subprior. In 1971 he was invited to Sant'Anselmo as a guest lecturer in philosophy. Following higher doctoral studies in Salzburg, he became a full member of the teaching body at the faculty of philosophy at Sant'Anselmo in 1978. In 1998 he left Sant'Anselmo to become spiritual director at the College of St. Benedict at Salzburg. From September 2001, he was an assistant priest at the pilgrimage shrine of Maria Plain near Salzburg until in November 2006 a serious illness made all further work impossible. He died in the infirmary of his home monastery on September 9, 2009. Cf. Necrology of Fr. Maternus Wilfried Hoegen, Maria Laach, 2009.

[6] See M. Bielawski and A. Schmidt, eds., *Schola Christi. 50 anni dell'Istituto Monastico di Sant'Anselmo. Studi emblematici*, StAns, vol. 134 (Rome, 2002).

mental theology, "specializzazione dogmatico-sacramentaria," and since 2002–2003 one in the history of theology, the latter in the so-called Mabillon institute. The first of these two specializations was originally suggested by Cipriano Vagaggini. It proposes to analyze the sacraments of the Church from an ontological perspective. Vagaggini was the first coordinator of this specialization, first offered in the academic year 1972–1973. From the first, it was opposed by Salvatore Marsili, who saw in it a threat to his sacrosanct liturgical institute.[7]

Fr. Adalbert de Vogüé (1924–2011)

It is striking that over the decades there has been a constant desire on the part of academic institutions all over the world to establish some kind of legal affiliation with the faculty of theology at Sant'Anselmo. This can be seen as sign of the esteem in which Sant'Anselmo is held. At present, there are ten such affiliations supervised by the faculty of theology, which entails significant extra work for the already small number of permanent professors on the Aventine.[8]

[7] See S. Marsili, "Liturgia e teologia," *RivLi* 59 (1972): 445–73.

[8] In 1965, what proved to be a very fruitful cooperation with the Philosophical-Theological Institute of the Divine Word Missionaries at St. Augustin near Bonn in Germany was agreed. This association came to an end in 1999 when, for university-political reasons, St. Augustin wanted to become an autonomous faculty. The following are the institutes that are now legally affiliated with Sant'Anselmo: (1) Istituto di Liturgia Pastorale (The Institute of Pastoral Liturgy) at the Abbey of St. Giustina in Padua, Italy, which is incorporated in the faculty of theology; (2) Istituto Teologico S. Pietro (Theological Institute of St. Peter) at Viterbeo, Italy; (3) Instituto Teológico Mosteiro São Bento (The Theological Institute of the Monastery of St. Benedict) at Rio de Janeiro, Brazil; (4) Instituto Teológico São Paulo (Theological Institute of São Paulo) in São Paulo, Brazil; (5) Theologische Schule der Benediktinerabtei Einsiedeln (The Theological School of the Benedictine Abbey at Einsiedeln) in Switzerland; (6) Studium de l'Abbaye Notre Dame de Sept-Fons (Studium of the Abbey of Our Lady of Sept-Fons) in France; (7) Sapientia School of Theology of Religious Orders (Quadriennium Theologicum) at Budpest, Hungary; (8) Mount Angel Seminary (Quadriennium Theologicum) at St. Benedict, Oregon, USA; (9) Escola Teològica de Montserrat (Montserrat Theological School at Montserrat Abbey) in Catalonia; (10) Theologisches Studienjahr (Theological Study Year at Dormition Abbey) in Jerusalem, a division of the faculty of theology. In addition, there are two institutes which are loosely connected with Sant'Anselmo, the Studio Teologico per le Benedettine Italiane (Theological Studium for Italian Benedictine

The liturgical institute—to speak of this last—has never had to complain of a lack of students. At worst, it has to deplore the lack of preparation of candidates, for example, those that lack competence in Greek and Latin. The carefully mooted question of whether or not the pontifical institute should once more be incorporated into the faculty of theology as it had been from 1961 until 1973 should not be immediately rebuffed. Internationally, a doctorate in theology with a specialization in liturgy has a completely different weight from a doctorate in liturgical science—quite apart from the enrichment of the latter by genuine theolgico-speculative or pastoral investigation in teaching and research.[9]

Sant'Anselmo was never able to reach the student numbers of the large Roman institutes. Just to mention some statistics, numbers swung between 291 in 1988 and 383 in 2010. The statistics for the year 2006–2007 will give some idea of the distribution of students among the three faculties. In that year, without considering guests and participants attending propaedeutic courses in the required classical languages, there were altogether 360 students matriculating at Sant'Anselmo. Of these, twenty-nine were in the faculty of philosophy, 117 in the faculty of theology, and 214 in the liturgical institute. Benedictines have long since been a minority in all three faculties. Finding sufficient students is a constant worry in the two faculties of philosophy and theology. It is probably only with the help of scholarships for students, particularly from developing countries, that the number of students can be significantly increased. But Sant'Anselmo lacks the funds for such subventions.[10] On the other hand, Sant'Anselmo can hardly accommodate more students than at present because it lacks the necessary lecture theaters and other spaces. Additional building on the Aventine is not possible because of the care with which the Roman civic authorities safeguard Sant'Anselmo's architectural heritage. Further, potential archaeological discoveries are a barrier to new building operations.

The university's most pressing task today is the attraction of qualified and, if possible, Benedictine, experts in the various disciplines. Such people should not simply be invited guests who come from outside for a few

---

Women) and the Corso di formazione monastica dell'Ordine Cistercense (the Course in Monastic Formation of the Cistercian Order).

[9] Today, the faculty of liturgy offers, in addition to its core program, a nonacademic diploma in "liturgical studies," as well as a two-year course *Architettura e Arte per la Liturgia* (Architecture and Art for the Liturgy), which also ends in a diploma.

[10] Here, it should be noted with gratitude that for decades, Swiss monasteries have been supporting the academic work of Sant'Anselmo by means of the so-called *Fondo Accademico*, which is administered by the Abbey of Engelberg.

weeks, but stable professors who can be available on the spot to students for the whole academic year or at least for a whole semester, available with their teaching, advice, and activities. This is lacking at this time, first, because monasteries have fewer suitable vocations than was the case in earlier times, and second, because there are not sufficient funds for the proper endowment of academic chairs. Thus, for the future the motto must be: fewer teachers for short-term courses, more holders of permanent chairs. A university is attractive for students not only because of its physical location—in this Sant'Anselmo is admirably placed—but also by the program it offers. Students are attracted by professors who are internationally known and who in their own inimitable way incarnate the discipline entrusted to them. The reputation of a faculty stands or falls on the quality of its teachers. In the past, Sant'Anselmo always had such masters. They are still the pride of the university and their memory should be preserved. For this reason, I end this chapter with biographies of some of the deceased Benedictines who taught at Sant'Anselmo in recent decades.

4. Final Biographical Sketches of Professors

Fr. Kassius Hallinger (1911–1991)[11]

Following years of debilitating illness that made scholarly work impossible, Fr. Kassius Josef Hallinger died in the medical missionary clinic in Würzburg, Germany, on October 24, 1991. Two days later he was buried in the cemetery at Münsterschwarzach, his monastery of profession. Joseph Hallinger was born on August 8, 1911, at Gernsheim, in the district of Groß-Gerau in Hesse, Germany. His father was a master butcher and innkeeper. At the age of thirteen, having attended the local elementary and vocational school, he transferred on the recommendation of his parish priest to the seminary of the missionary

[11] This sketch is an abridgement of my article "Kassius Hallinger (1911–1991) und die Erforschung des hochmittelalterlichen Mönchtums" [Kassius Hallinger (1911–1991) and Research in the Monasticism of the High Middle Ages], *ZSRG. K* 79 (1993): 278–94. For Hallinger's bibliography, see *Consuetudines Monasticae. Eine Festgabe für Kassius Hallinger aus Anlass seines 70. Geburtstages*, ed. J. F. Angerer and J. Lenzenweger, StAns, vol. 85 (Rome, 1982), 20ff. There is a more complete bibliography in "Bibliographie der deutschsprachigen Benediktiner 1880–1980," in *SMGB*, Supplementary Volume 29/2 (St. Ottilien, 1987), 791–94. This is to be supplemented by entries in *CCM*, vol. 7/1 (Siegburg, 1984), p. 25, and *CCM*, vol. 7/1–3 (Sieburg, 1983–1984).

Benedictines at St. Ludwig near Würzburg. From 1926 until 1930, he attended the New Classical Grammar School in Würzburg, staying in Münsterschwarzach's college in that city. In March 1930, having completed his secondary education, he entered Münsterschwarzach Abbey, where he was admitted to the novitiate on May 13, receiving the name Cassius, a name which he later insisted on spelling with a "K," like many other names such as Cluny/Kluny. The Abbey of St. Felicity at Münsterschwarzach, which had been founded in Carolingian times and lasted until the secularization in 1803, had been revived by the missionary Benedictines of Sankt Ottilien in Bavaria in 1914. Under its first abbot, Plazidus Vogel, the monastery developed rapidly. Work had already begun on the new monumental abbey church. An indication of the tremendous growth of the monastery at that period is the fact that in 1930, apart from the monks on the missions, there were well over two hundred choir monks and lay brothers between Münsterschwarzach, St. Ludwig, and the college in Würzburg. In the following years the number increased even further.

Having studied philosophy at Sankt Ottilien from 1931 to 1933, Hallinger studied theology at the University of Würzburg from 1933 to 1936, being ordained priest on March 1, 1936. Abbot Plazidus sent the young priest for one year, 1936–1937, to the Benedictine academy at Maria Laach, which had been founded by Abbot Ildefons Herwegen. Hallinger always claimed that his experience of the then-blossoming monastery in the Eifel, his encounters with the fascinating Abbot Herwegen (who gave him essential insights into monasticism), and his first introduction to research into the history of the liturgy were among the strongest and most formative impressions of his life. From 1937 until 1940 he was

Fr. Kassius Hallinger (right) in conversation with confreres from Münsterschwarzach, Fr. Wunibald Keller (left) and Fr. Thomas Rücket (center), for many years cellarer of the College

entrusted with various tasks in his home monastery, finally working in the archives. Then the Second World War came, during which Fr. Kassius served as a medical orderly on different fronts. After the war, Abbot Burkhard Utz freed him once again for studies at the University of Würzburg, this time as a student of history in the faculty of philosophy. On September 25, 1948, he received the D.Phil. for a dissertation on a theme he had suggested himself, "Gorze-Kluny. Studien zu den monastischen Lebensformen und Gegensätzen im Hochmittelalter" (Gorze-Cluny: Studies on the forms and contrasts in monastic life in the High Middles Ages). His moderator was Michael Seidlmayer (1902–1961), but so different were the interests of both that this moderation was probably a matter of form.

Around this time, Fr. Matthäus Rothenhäusler (1874–1958) became aware of the young historian from Münsterschwarzach. As the reader will remember, Rothenhäusler was professor of ecclesiastical history at Sant'Anselmo and also at the time dean of the faculty of theology. It is thanks to him that by 1949, Hallinger was invited to Rome and that he was able to publish his extensive doctoral dissertation there in the series *Studia Anselmiana*, vols. 22 and 23, in 1950 and 1951.[12] Such a publication would hardly have been possible in the impoverished post-war Germany. Speaking in Latin, a language of instruction unusual for him, Hallinger began his lectures at Sant'Anselmo in the academic year 1949–1950 with the main lecture, "Historia Ecclesiae temporis antiqui" (Ancient church history). Incidentally, at the beginning, Rothenhäusler generously made his own manuscript available to Hallinger. For a few years Fr. Kassius lectured on all of church history as successor to Rothenhäusler himself and to the French Benedictine Charles Poulet. From 1955, however, he lectured only on medieval and modern history and finally, from 1961, his teaching was confined to the Middle Ages. From 1953 he held the chair of church history at Sant'Anselmo. Hallinger was popular as an academic teacher. His lecturing style was lively and his formulations, conditioned by Latin, the language of instruction, were clear and memorable. In his lectures, as in his publications, Hallinger loved sharp comparisons and glaring contrasts. This facilitated learning, indeed, but did not automatically lead to an understanding of the complexities of historical phenomena. Ending his teaching activity in the academic year 1977–1978, from then on Hallinger dedicated himself completely to his life's work, the publication of the *Corpus*

[12] This was reprinted without changes but with an introduction by H. Schmidinger, at Graz, Akadmischen Druck- und Verlagsanstalt, 1971.

Fr. Kassius Hallinger accompanied by Rector Augustin Mayer presents the first two volumes of the "Corpus Consuetudinum" to Pope Paul VI on February 11, 1964

Consuetudinum Monasticarum. He lived quietly and in retirement in Rome until 1986, not in Sant'Anselmo, but in order to have more freedom for research at the Generalate of the Premonstratensians close to the ancient basilica of St. Saba on the Little Aventine. Failing health meant that he had to return to Germany where he was graciously welcomed for a year at the Sankt Ottilien College in Munich. A stroke suffered during a visit in Austria forced him to return to his home monastery where he spent his last years in the infirmary.

Very early on, Kassius Hallinger discovered the theme of his academic life. Filled with zeal for research, the young historian was already stamped by that independence of judgment and purpose that characterized him in later life. The idea of tracing the relations between the medieval centers of monastic reform, Gorze and Cluny, however, did not come from him but from his Schwarzacher confrere Carl Wolff (1893–1965). Wolff was a very knowledgeable historian of the Order with an extraordinary feeling for new directions in medieval research. But he was disorganized and increasingly incapable of communicating his insights and discoveries. As early as 1930 Wolff spoke about "a work in progress on the full history of the observance of Gorze." This work came to nothing, or, better, Hallinger's *Gorze-Kluny* fulfilled Wolff's promise.

Hallinger's first work was universally received with enthusiastic approval, above all among German postwar medievalists. Critical voices tended toward restraint. With time, however, the chorus of those with doubts became louder. This not only was because of the undeniable weaknesses of Hallinger's work but also was a sign of the many impulses that this work had provided in the meantime for individual research. Hallinger based his work on two methodological pillars: on the "liturgical principle of consuetudo [usage]" and on the "principle of necrology." Both methods were to provide the two parts of a tongs with which he tried to grasp the contrasts between the reforms of Gorze and Cluny. There can be no doubt that in this, Hallinger hoped to glean much more from an analysis of the evidence from necrological material than from the consuetudines (customs). It must have been a particular blow to Hallinger that in the coming years, the harshest criticism of his work concentrated on his use of necrological sources. In fairness, one must say that it was he who managed to enable this long-neglected group of sources to speak again. He did this in a fascinating manner and with editions of texts that we know today to be unsatisfactory. Without Hallinger's pioneering work, the evaluation of medieval necrologies, which is pursued above all at the University of Münster in Westphalia, would not have developed so dramatically and, subsequently, with impressive results. Very early on, electronic data processing was used in this work. This may be one of the reasons why Hallinger, to whom at an impoverished Sant'Anselmo such technical support was not available, withdrew early from necrological research. This led him all the more to devote himself, from the middle of the 1950s, with a sure instinct for the necessary and for him, possible, second pillar of *Gorze-Kluny*, i.e., the research and publication of medieval monastic customaries. When in 1956 at the fourth "Settimana di Spoleto" (Spoleto Week), Hallinger presented his project of a *Corpus Consuetudinum Monasticarum* (Corpus of Monastic Customaries) to a wider scholarly public, there had already, since 1954, been intensive reflections and discussions at Sant'Anselmo, which ended in the winter semester of 1955–1956 with the decision, "The Most Reverend Abbot Primate [Benno Gut] has commissioned me to establish and direct the free working group of the *Corpus Consuetudinum Monasticarum*, whose task will be, over a reasonable period, to edit in a proper scholarly manner the most important foundation documents and main types of Benedictine customary. The financing of this project will be supported by Sant'Anselmo to the extent that it will cover the printing costs of completed manuscripts. Everything else will be based on voluntary participation."[13]

Fr. Kassius in conversation with the German Federal Chancellor Kurt Georg Kissinger

Sant'Anselmo's financial support ended with the publication of the first volume in 1963. Had the German Research Board, based in Bad Godesberg, not come quickly to its aid, the whole project would have been shipwrecked shortly after its launch. In contrast, the principle of "voluntary participation"—which means unpaid scholarly work—has been maintained to this day, with Hallinger himself leading by example. He lived modestly, even frugally, in his room with the Premonstratensians on the Little Aventine, totally devoted to his self-chosen task, now and then discreetly supported by benefactors. Following the appearance of the first volume of *CCM*, it was increasingly this great project of research into and editing of the customaries that gained Hallinger the respect and esteem of the scholarly world. The honors he received were an expression of that esteem. In 1973 he received the Cross of the Order of Merit, First Class, of the Federal German Republic; in 1974 he received the even-more prestigious (in his estimation) Cross of Honor for Science and Art, First Class, of the Austrian Republic; and

[13] K. Hallinger, "Neue Fragen der reformgeschichtlichen Forschung," in *Archiv für mittelrheinischen Kirchengeschichte* 9 (1957): 14f.

finally, in 1977, he received an honorary doctorate in theology from the Johannes Gutenberg University in Mainz.

Between 1963 and 1987, Hallinger, supported in later years by Sr. Candida Elvert, OSB, of Fulda, oversaw the production of twelve volumes of *CCM*—these in sixteen individual books. This was an unusual editorial achievement and one which was justifiably admired by the academic experts—all the more so when one takes into account the limited financial resources that prevented Hallinger as general editor from founding even a modest institute to take charge of the editing and publishing of *CCM*.[14]

Hallinger seldom abandoned his own narrower area of research—monastic reform in the High Middle Ages—continuing to publish his lively and source-based investigations in monastic history while continuing his activity as general editor of *CCM*. One example of such an investigation is his seminal study *Papst Gregor der Große und der hl. Benedikt*.[15] This caused a considerable stir, particularly among Benedictines. Up to then, Pope Gregory the Great, the biographer of St. Benedict, was considered without dispute to have been a Benedictine and in the liturgical books of the Order his name was followed by the letters ON (*Ordinis Nostri*—of Our Order). By patiently comparing the individual elements of Gregory's understanding of the monastic life, particularly as reflected in his letters, with the life reflected in the *Regula Benedicti*, Hallinger was able to demonstrate persuasively that in decisive points Gregory's observance did not follow that of the Rule of Monte Cassino. Consequently, according to Hallinger, Gregory "belongs to an intellectual world which still drew on the complete spectrum of monastic tradition." Statements such as this are completely familiar to every student of Benedictine history. It was Hallinger, however, who formulated these so succinctly and in doing so overturned centuries-old views of Gregory as "the greatest of the sons of St. Benedict."

The complete picture of Hallinger's personality and the influence of his research would be incomplete if one were to fail to mention the scholarly controversies in which he was involved from the beginning to the end of his career. Here, it suffices to mention his disputes with the East German medievalist Ernst Werner, with his colleague at Sant'Anselmo Jean Leclercq, and with Joachim Wollasch, the historian from Münster.

[14] Between 1999 and 2010 five further individual volumes appeared which Hallinger had not been able to oversee. These were, vol. 13, M. Albert, Ceremoniae Bursfeldensis; vol. 14, 1–2, P. Maier, Consuetudines Castellenses; vol. 15, 1–2, P. Engelbert, Constitutiones Hirsaugiensis.

[15] StAns, vol. 42 (Rome, 1957), 231–319.

His increasing isolation in Rome—chosen, indeed, by himself—led to the creation of imagined enemies who did not exist in reality. Further, he came to see irreconcilable differences where perhaps there were only complementary views of the same object. Those who knew him more intimately were aware that deep down he was a person with a good heart, exceedingly grateful for the smallest kindness and recognition. But did his opponents, whom he treated with *furor teutonicus*, know this? The storm is now over. Contemporary scholarship has reduced irreconcilable principles of reform to differences in reform decisions. Kassius Hallinger's contribution to international medieval scholarship is long since recognized. Sant'Anselmo, however, can look back at him as its greatest ecclesiastical historian.

Dom Adrien Nocent (1913–1996)

In the early hours of December 9, 1996, Dom Adrien Nocent died of a heart attack, alone in his cell at Sant'Anselmo. He was the last survivor of the three founders of Sant'Anselmo's liturgical institute.[16] Some days previously, on December 4, in the church at Sant'Anselmo, he had pronounced the *Laudatio* at the conferring of an honorary doctorate in liturgy. He was eighty-three years old and had been a Benedictine for sixty years and a priest for fifty-eight. Born on February 2, 1913, at Marcinelle in the mining region of Belgium to a family of industrialists—his father was the director of a large steel works—one might have foreseen a career for the young Maurice as an engineer or an economist. But he was more interested in Latin, Greek, and music. By the age of six he was learning the piano and at nine began to learn the violin, an instrument he continued to play into old age. He attended the Jesuit school at Charleroi. The Jesuits would have liked to have had him, but Maurice

Dom Adrien Nocent (1913–1996)

[16] In 1988, Nocent received a festschrift from Sant'Anselmo titled *Traditio et Progressio. Studi liturgici in onore del Prof. Adrien Nocent, OSB*, ed. Giustino Farnedi, StAns, vol. 95 (Rome, 1988). The sketch given here draws, with thanks, on I. Scicolone's essay "La liturgia è vita: Adrien Maurice Nocent," in *Traditio et Progressio*, 25–33. Obituaries by, among others, A. J. Chupungo, *Ecclesia Orans* 14 (1997): 3–13; *Notitiae* 34 (1997): 269f. For a bibliography, see Farnedi, *Traditio et Progressio*, 12–23, and B. Rizzi, *Ecclesia Orans*, vol. 14 (1997): 439, 442–49.

had already discovered the monastic life, the Abbey of Maredsous, situated only thirty-five kilometers from Charleroi.

At the age of nineteen he entered the community at Maredsous, which at that time was large and widely esteemed for its scholarship. Following the novitiate year under Fr. Idesbald Ryelandt, he made simple profession on January 15, 1933. His superiors were thinking of having him trained as a teacher of classical languages and as a teacher for the abbey school at Maredsous. First, however, he was sent for theological studies to Mont-César in Louvain where he came to know eminent experts such as Dom Odon Lottin, Dom Bernard Capelle, and Dom Bernard Botte. It was Capelle and Botte who awakened the young monk's enthusiasm for the study of liturgy. After an interruption for military service, he resumed his theological studies and was ordained priest on July 31, 1938. Once again his plans were interrupted by military service, and during the Second World War he served first in a military hospital and then as a military chaplain. Once back in Maredsous, his dreams of continuing his studies at Louvain came to an end. Abbot Celestin Golenvaux appointed him teacher of Latin, Greek, French, and religion in the abbey school. This charge lasted for nine years. In 1959 a new abbot appointed him prior of Maredsous, which at the time had well over one hundred monks. As well as the school and a very active guesthouse that offered retreats, the monks produced two prestigious reviews, the *Revue Bénédictine* and the *Revue liturgique et monastique*.

Dom Adrien Nocent at his desk

Because of illness, by 1950 Nocent had to relinquish the office of prior. The removal of this burden, however, gave the forty-three-year-old the chance to resume his beloved study of liturgy, this time in Paris. There he was one of the first students of the newly established Institut supérieur de liturgie, the director of which was no less a person than Dom Bernard Botte, whom he knew from Louvain. At the same time Nocent registered for lectures at the École pratique des Hautes Études. He completed his diploma studies at these two institutes by writing theses based on the evaluation of medieval manuscripts. A short visit to Maria Laach brought him into contact with Fr. Burkhard Neunheuser, one of the most significant experts in the field of liturgical scholarship. By coincidence he also met there Fr. Salvatore Marsili, who was at Maria Laach to work on the theology of Odo Casel. When in the following year Marsili became professor of liturgy at Sant'Anselmo, it was at who invited Nocent there for a special course. As is well known, Marsili, Nocent, and Vagaggini became the fathers of the new liturgical institute at Sant'Anselmo.

Already forty-seven years old, Nocent's transfer to Sant'Anselmo—all new to him—was not easy. For one thing, Latin was still the language of instruction. Like Marsili, he was a fighter by nature, irascible by temperament, and full of ideas, not all of which were practical. From the beginning, however, he shared Vagaggini's and Marsili's ideas without reservation so that there were no ideological tensions among them. Unlike his colleagues, Nocent was not a deep theological thinker, but he possessed other qualities. In Paris, he not only had received a thorough training in liturgical scholarship but also felt the need to communicate the riches of the liturgy to priests and laity in pastoral praxis. During his time at Sant'Anselmo, he did this in countless conferences and study sessions not only in Europe—in Italy alone he held lectures in over thirty dioceses—but also in French-speaking Africa and even in the United States, where, he proudly reported, his translator in the Trappist Abbey of Gethsemani was Thomas Merton. In Rome, Nocent was asked to be part of two study groups whose task it was to prepare postconciliar liturgical renewal. He belonged to Coetus XI for the lectionary for Mass and Coetus XVII for special rites such as the blessing of abbots and abbesses. In addition, he found time to publish widely in the

Dom Jordi Pinell i Pons (1921–1997)

service of liturgical renewal. Following his retirement, he remained at Sant'Anselmo. When the liturgical institute established *Ecclesia Orans* as its scholarly journal in 1988, Nocent, despite the fact that he was seventy years old, was invited to be its first editor. "I promise to be a good wet nurse to this little child," he promised when he was appointed. Up to his death, assisted by Dr. Ferdinando Canicci, he was tireless in his efforts on behalf of what in the meantime had become a strong child.[17]

Fr. Cipriano Vagaggini (1909–1999)

The name of Fr. Cipriano Vagaggini has already been mentioned several times in earlier chapters of this book. Here a summary of his life and work will be presented.

Born on October 3, 1909, in the village of Piancastagnaio not far from the Abbey of Monte Amiata near Sienna in Tuscany, famous in the early Middle Ages, Leonello Vagaggini came at

Fr. Cipriano Vagaggini (1909–1999)

[17] Just one month after the death of A. Nocent on January 8, 1997, at Sant'Anselmo, Dom Jordi Pinell i Pons, who had taught at the liturgical institute from 1963 until 1991, died at his home monastery of Montserrat, following a long illness. Born in Barcelona in 1921, Jordi Pinell i Pons was first interested in Catalan literature and theater. In 1945 he entered Montserrat where he was ordained priest in 1953. His already strong interest in liturgical research received a strong impulse from visits to Louvain, Maredsous, Saint-André, and not least to Maria Laach. His main interest was already focused on the old Spanish—i.e., the Mozarabic—liturgy. In 1963, the head of the Pontifical Liturgical Institute, Salvatore Marsili, invited him to Sant'Anselmo. He did not, however, have a recognized academic degree. In 1966 he defended his doctoral thesis at Sant'Anselmo, which he had written under the moderatorship of Burkhard Neunheuser and titled "Las horas vigiliares del Oficio monacal hispánico. Estudio e edición crítica" [The Vigil hours of the Spanish monastic Office: A study and critical edition]. In addition to his teaching activity at Sant'Anselmo, in the following years he published valuable studies on the non-Roman West European liturgies. In 1982, Cardinal Marcelo González, archbishop of Toledo, appointed him head of the commission for the reform of the Mozarabic Rite. He lived to see the publication of the two resulting volumes of the *Missale hispanico-mozarabicum*, Toledo, 1991/1994. Apart from his liturgical publications, Pinell also had a high profile as an expert on Catalan literature and even as a poet and author in his beloved mother tongue. In 1992, Sant'Anselmo offered him a festschrift, *Psallendum. Miscellanea di studi in onore del Prof. Jordi Pinell i Pons, OSB*, ed. I. Scicolone, StAns, vol. 105 (Rome, 1992).

the age of eleven to the secondary school of the Benedictines at Saint-André/Zevenkerken near Bruges in Flanders. It was his uncle, his father's brother and a monk of Saint-André, named Fr. Johannes, who took his nephew to Belgium in 1920. Against the wishes of his father, the young Vagaggini entered the monastery immediately after the completion of his secondary education and was simply professed on October 5, 1928. He was sent to Sant'Anselmo for his philosophical and theological studies and remained there until 1935. During this period he obtained the doctorate in philosophy in 1931 and, following a two-year sojourn at Louvain, the doctorate in theology in 1938. His supervisor for the doctorate was Fr. Anselm Stolz and his dissertation, "Maria in den Werken des Origenes" (Mary in the Work of Origen), was the first book he published.[18] In the meantime he had been ordained priest on July 30, 1934. He then went on to study at the Pontifical Oriental Institute where, in 1940, he obtained a further doctorate in *Scientiarum Ecclesiasticarum Orientalium* (Oriental Ecclesiastical Sciences).[19] The fact that from 1936 until 1942, the young academic was vice rector of the Greek college can be seen as a sign of the particular trust of his superiors. He began his academic teaching at Sant'Anselmo in 1940 with lectures on Oriental theology, which in those days meant Byzantine theology. He continued to give these lectures until 1956. Following the unexpected death of Anselm Stolz in 1942, however, he had to assume the latter's lectures in dogmatic theology. In these, as Stolz's pupil, he became the one to fulfill the intentions which the latter had no longer been able to realize. A first fruit of his new perspective of theological method, which aimed at the development of a sapientally stamped synthesis of theology based on the example of the fathers, was the book *Il senso teologico della liturgia. Saggio di liturgia teologica generale* (The theological sense of the liturgy: An essay in general liturgical theology). Published in Rome in 1957, it quickly became famous, lifted liturgical scholarship out of the trap of positivism, and was translated into other languages.[20] But the

[18] *Maria nelle opere di Origene*, Orientalia Christiana Analecta, vol. 131 (Rome, 1942).

[19] Published under the title, *I patriarchi orientali cattolici e dispense matrimoniali* [Oriental Catholic Patriarch and Matrimonial Dispensations], Orientalia Christiana Analecta, vol. 154 (Rome, 1959).

[20] Published in the United States as *Theological Dimensions of the Liturgy: A General Treatise on the Theology of the Liturgy*, trans. from the 4th Italian ed. (rev. and augmented by the author), by Leonard J. Doyle and W. A. Jurgens (Collegeville, MN, 1976). Three articles written for the *Nuovo Dizionario di Teologia*, ed. G. Barbaglio and S. Dianich (Cinisello Balsamo, 1977), are important for Vagaggini's later theological

book addressed another and ongoing purpose of Vagaggini: the link between liturgy and personal piety. Some have noted with a certain reserve his nomination of St. Gertrude of Helfta and her writings as a great example of this link. Veneration of St. Gertrude was, however, an inheritance from Solesmes and Beuron to which Vagaggini's monastery of profession, Saint-André, felt committed.

From 1952 until 1963 Vagaggini was dean of the faculty of theology and vice rector. It was in this period, in 1961, that the Pontifical Liturgical Institute was established, Vagaggini playing a determining role in this.[21] The confusion at Sant'Anselmo following the council prompted Vagaggini to leave Rome for a few years. From 1963 until 1967 he worked intensively in theological research at the Center for Religious Sciences in Bologna. He also lobbied for the establishment of a theological faculty at the Catholic University of Milan, a project that foundered on the objections of the Italian Bishops' Conference. As a result of this failure, Vagaggini, along with the archbishop of Milan, Giovanni Colombo, became one of the founders of the Inter-Regional Theological Faculty, later renamed the North Italian Theological Faculty. Here, from 1967 until 1971, Vagaggini taught dogmatic theology.[22] In 1969 he became a member of the International Theological Commission, remaining on until 1980. He returned to the faculty of theology at Sant'Anselmo in 1971. It was high time, because the American Abbot Primate Rembert Weakland was pursuing not only an irresponsible personnel policy but also was openly pressing for the abolition of the university. Vagaggini's personality played an essential role in ensuring that these plans were not realized.

Despite his age, he assumed the office of rector of the Athenaeum from 1974 to 1978. For a long time his reputation had already spread far beyond Sant'Anselmo. During the Second Vatican Council he was one of the experts, *periti*, responsible for the Constitution on the Liturgy. After the council, Paul VI appointed him to the committee entrusted with the reform of the liturgy, the *Consilium ad exequendam Constitutionem de Sacra Liturgia*. As a member of this committee he was responsible among other things for the preparation of a new Mass lectionary, but, above all, for the formulation of new eucharistic prayers. In the summer of

---

development. These are titled *Pluralismo teologico* [Theological Pluralism], *Storia della salvezza* [Salvation History], and *Teologia*.

[21] Cf. supra pp. 175ff.

[22] See the report of one of the students at the time, L. Crippa, "Ricordi 'milandesi' del P. Cipriano Vagaggini, OSB ['Milanese' reminiscences of Fr. Cipriano Vagaggini, OSB]," in *Benedictina* 46 (1999): 225–27.

Fr. Cipriano Vagaggini lecturing

1966, he buried himself for three months in the library at Mont-César in Louvain and there prepared two schemas for eucharistic prayers that he presented in Orselina, Switzerland, at the autumn meeting of Coetus X of the Consilium responsible for the Mass.[23] Fruit of this research was his book that appeared in the same year, *The Canon of the Mass and Liturgical Reform. Problems and Suggestions.*[24] It is clear from this that today's Eucharistic Prayer III is essentially Vagaggini's work, while Eucharistic Prayer IV, with its fixed Preface, bears less resemblance to what he had suggested.[25] Throughout the 1970s Vagaggini was closely connected

[23] S. Bugnini, "Lettera all'editore [Letter to the editor]," in *Lex orandi, lex credendi. Miscellanea in onore di P. Cipriano Vagaggini*, ed. G. J. Békés and G. Farnedi, StAns, vol. 79 (Rome, 1980), 13f.

[24] C. Vagaggini, *Il Canone della Messa e la riforma liturgica. Problemi e progetti*, Quaderni di Rivista liturgica, vol. 4 (Turin, 1966), 100–7, 110–21. Published in English as *The Canon of the Mass and Liturgical Reform*, trans. Peter Coughlan (London/Dublin/Melbourne, 1967).

[25] E. Mazza, "Il ruolo di Cipriano Vagaggini nella composizione delle Preghiere eucaristiche del Messale di Paolo VI [The Role of Cipriano Vagaggini in the composition of the eucharistic prayers in the Missal of Paul VI]," *Vita monastica* 65 (2011): 126–59.

with the work of the Vatican Congregations, being among other things a consultor for the Congregation of Catholic Education and Seminaries from 1974 to 1979. In addition, he found time and energy to continue to publish in the fields of dogmatics and spirituality. He left Sant'Anselmo definitively in 1978, withdrawing to the solitude of Camaldoli, near Arezzo, and also transferred his stability to the Camaldolese Congregation. In the meantime, as a result of political pressures, Saint-André had become a Flemish community in which the French language, which Vagaggini spoke fluently, was scorned. This may have been a factor in his decision to transfer his stability.

As a theologian he became ever more silent in his final decades. He often quoted the saying from the Apophthegmata Patrum, *Arseni, tace et Fuge* (Arsenius, keep silent and flee). One who accompanied him with understanding in his later years describes him as a person who created the impression of one coming from a distance and who held himself apart from the philosophical and theological currents of the postconciliar period.[26] Despite this, he remained an acute observer of the intellectual scene in theology. From the very beginning he was au fait with Oriental theology, deeply rooted as this is in monasticism and the liturgy. He was aware of Protestant research, but this was less of an interest. His final work remained unfinished and unpublished. It was intended to be a great—too wide-ranging, in fact—theological synthesis under the title "Teologia come sapienza" (Theology as Wisdom). In the quietness of Camaldoli he read his preferred authors, above all the Greek and Latin fathers, in the original languages, of course. In January 1982, he went to Sant'Anselmo to deliver some lectures on the hermeneutic of the magisterium. After that, to my knowledge, he went only once more to Sant'Anselmo when, in 1985, he acted as censor at the defense of a doctoral dissertation—the latter, incidentally, unsuccessful. He died at Camaldoli on January 18, 1999, in his ninetieth year.[27] He is remembered at Sant'Anselmo by the occasional Lectiones Vagagginianae, which renowned philosophers and theologians are invited to deliver.

[26] A. Barban, "Cipriano Vagaggini: figura insigne del '900 teologico [Cipriano Vagaggini, a prime figure of twentieth-century theology]," *Vita monastica* 54 (2000): 87–94, here, 93; see also ibid., 85–86, for an account of Vagaggini's life.

[27] Obituaries by A. Grillo, "Cipriano Vagaggini," *RivLi* 86 (1999): 423–26; A. M. Triacca, "Dom Cipriano Vagaggini OSBCam (1909–1999). In Memoriam," *EL* 113 (1999): 449–65. Finally, E. Massimi, "Profilo bio-bibliografico di dom Cipriano Vagaggini osb cam," *Vita monastica* 65 (2011): 9–38.

Fr. Magnus Löhrer (1928–1999)

Fr. Magnus Löhrer died in the late evening of May 29, 1999, in the railway station of Zug in central Switzerland. Traveling by train from Zurich, where he went three times a week from Einsiedeln for dialysis, he wanted to change trains at the station in Zug. Crossing the track, he was knocked over by an oncoming train. Although uninjured by this, his body had already been so weakened by constant dialysis that he died on the spot. He was buried at Einsiedeln Abbey on June 5. Sant'Anselmo was represented at the funeral by, among others, the rector, Albert Schmidt.[28]

Fr. Magnus was born on April 6, 1928, in Gossau, in the Canton of St. Gallen. Two days later he was baptized Paul Jakob. In 1939, he entered the first class of the abbey school at Einsiedeln. The delight in music which he discovered there remained with him all his life. Finishing his secondary education in 1947, he entered the novitiate at Einsiedeln some weeks later. He made simple profession on September 8, 1948. In October 1949, after a year of philosophy at the monastery's school of theology, he was sent for further studies to Sant'Anselmo by Abbot Benno Gut. At Sant'Anselmo he, like so many other students at the time, was fascinated by the lectures of Fr. Cipriano Vagaggini. He had no idea that one day he would be Vagaggini's successor in the chair of dogmatics. On July 17, 1952, during a Low Mass, he was ordained priest by the bishop of St. Gallen, Josephus Meile. The preacher at his first Mass on July 20 was Fr. Cunibert Mohlberg from Maria Laach, one of the professors at Sant'Anselmo. He completed his theological studies at Sant'Anselmo in November 1954 with a doctoral dissertation, "Der Glaubensbegriff des hl. Augustinus in seinen Schriften bis zu den Confessiones" (St. Augustine's concept of faith in his writings up to the *Confessions*), which he had written under the supervision of Cipriano Vagaggini. As assigned, on October 1 of that year, he began to lecture on dogmatic theology at the house school of theology at Einsiedeln. He also taught religion in the monastery school from 1958 to 1960, heard confessions in the abbey church, and was active as a supply priest in surrounding parishes.

[28] Thanks are due to Fr. Dr. Odo Lang of Einsiedeln for help in gathering biographical data. In addition to the death notice, there is an obituary which Fr. Joachim Salzgeber wrote for the journal *Maria Einsiedeln* 104 (1999): 242–44. See also, Chr. Schmitt, *Löhrer, Magnus*, in BBKL, vol. 18, Ergänzungen [Supplements] 5 (Herzberg, 2001), 838–42, with a bibliography on pp. 840ff.

Fr. Magnus Löhrer in June 1971

The year 1958 was one of the most important in Fr. Magnus's life. On July 3, Oscar Bettschart, director of the Benziger Publishing House, invited some theologians who were friendly with the firm to a meeting to discuss a plan for the production of an "Introduction to Theology." Even if at this stage much remained open, a beginning had been made.[29] Two systematic theologians were entrusted with the production of the work in several volumes, Johannes Feiner (1909–1985) from Chur and Magnus Löhrer. In contrast to a backward-looking neoscholastic dogmatics, the insights of the theological awakening of the 1950s and 1960s were to be taken into account. Hans Küng, at the time curate at the court chapel in Lucerne, provided important impulses, promoting the salvation-history direction of the planned work. Even more important was the new theological approach of Karl Rahner. His *A Scheme for a Treatise of Dogmatic Theology*, published in 1954, was a pointer for the Swiss work under construction. In 1959, the title *Mysterium Salutis* was chosen for the latter.[30] The first volume appeared in the autumn of 1965, shortly before the end of the council, the final volumes reaching well into the postconciliar period. The original list of theologians who had agreed to participate or who had been invited to do so, contained fifty-five names. When the project was completed, it amounted to seven comprehensive volumes with articles by seventy theologians, among them famous names such as Hans Urs von Balthasar and Karl Rahner. In fact, *Mysterium Salutis* was to become the most important compendium of Catholic dogmatic

[29] M. Löhrer describes the genesis of the project in *Mysterium Salutis. Ergänzungsband, Arbeitsheften und Weiterführungen* [Mysterium Salutis. Supplementary volume, Working Notebooks and Continuations], ed. M. Löhrer, Chr. Schütz, D. Wiederkehr (Zurich-Einsiedeln-Cologne, 1981), 13–37. There is an important article by M. Delgado, "*Mysterium Salutis* als innovativer systematischer Ansatz im Anschluss an das Zweite Vatikanische Konzil" [*Mysterium Salutis* as an innovative systematic initiative following the Second Vatican Council], in G. Bedouelle and M. Delgado, eds., *La réception du Concile Vatican II par les théologiens suisses = Die Rezeption des II. Vaticanums durch Schwiezer Theologen* [The reception of the Second Vatican Council by Swiss theologians] (Fribourg, 2011), 167–78.

[30] K. Rahner, Über den Versuch eines Aufrisses einer Dogmatik, in Rahner, *Schriften zur Teologie*, vol. 1 (Einsiedeln-Zurich-Cologne, 1954), 9–47. Published in English as *Theological Investigations, Vol. 1*, trans. with an introduction by Cornelius Ernst (Baltimore, MD/London, 1961), 19–38.

theology of the postconciliar era and was soon translated into several other languages. The amount of organization involved for Löhrer can only be guessed at, given that in 1963 he had succeeded his teacher Cipriano Vagaggini in the chair of dogmatics at Sant'Anselmo. In 1968 and again in 1977 he became dean of the faculty of theology. During this time he not only pressed on with the overdue reforms of the study regulations but also met Karl Barth, who encouraged and inspired the ecumenism in which he had always been interested. From the beginning, Barth's monumental *Church Dogmatics* had always been in the background as a model for *Mysterium Salutis*. Later, Löhrer's thinking was enriched by his meeting with the work and personality of Gerhard Ebeling, the Protestant theologian from Zurich. In contrast to his teacher, Vagaggini, Löhrer was always open to impulses from Protestant theology. It is also thanks to him that the faculty of theology at Sant'Anselmo established contacts with the only faculty of Protestant theology in Italy, the Waldensian faculty in Rome. From 1969, Valdo Vinay lectured on Protestant sacramental teaching. In 1983, Vinay was replaced by his colleague at the Waldensian faculty Paolo Ricca, who continues this activity to this day.

Fr. Magnus Löhrer with students, Fr. Alvin Downey of St. Vincent and Fr. Benedikt Köhler of Gerleve, in 1970

From 1971 to 1976 Löhrer's residence in Rome was interrupted when he was director of the Paulusakademie in Zurich. Here, he gained first-hand experience of the Church's problems in Switzerland and of the pastoral needs of the people, experience that benefitted his teaching. At the same time he lectured in dogmatics at the theological academy in Chur, lectures which he continued in later years. When he returned to Rome in 1976, he undertook to teach at the Lateran University as a guest lecturer. From 1978 until 1986 he assumed the burden of the rectorate of the university at Sant'Anselmo. This brought with it many administrative tasks with which he coped calmly but with a definite goal in mind. One of these tasks was the preparation of new statutes for the Athenaeum. Fr. Magnus wrote these himself in Latin; he never had a secretary. Whatever he wrote, he wrote with a small, Swiss typewriter. Students liked him because of the clarity of his teaching, his humanity, and his humor. His lecture in dogmatics was always timetabled for the first period, at 8:30 a.m. His listeners will never forget his capacity, always at 9:00 a.m., to reawaken their interest by the use of a "barzelletta," a little joke. How much he was loved in Sant'Anselmo both by professors and students is revealed by the contributions to an academic session held in the college on February 16, 1993, a year after he had been forced to leave Sant'Anselmo because of serious kidney disease.[31] When he had been able to recover somewhat in Switzerland, he resumed his teaching in the theological school at Einsiedeln and became prefect of studies. It is a cause of satisfaction to the writer of these lines that, in 1996, as dean of the faculty of theology at Sant'Anselmo, he was able to assist the school of theology at Einsiedeln to acquire a basis for future stability through affiliation with Sant'Anselmo. In 1997, on his seventieth birthday, Löhrer, along with Rector Fr. Pius-Ramon Tragan of Montserrat, who was also celebrating his seventieth birthday, was honored with a comprehensive festschrift, which gave an idea of Löhrer's broad theological interests and reflected the wide span of his publications.[32] One would be neglecting an essential element if one were to remain silent about his love for music, and in particular his love for the music of Mozart. In this, Karl Barth and Magnus Löhrer were also agreed. At the above-mentioned academic session in 1993, he addressed the question of his theological thought in a manner that must have deeply moved all who were present. The main points were as follows, in English translation:

> I have always understood myself to be a teacher, as an interpreter, not as a composer. I have never claimed to be original but wanted only to

[31] *Pontificio Ateneo S. Anselmo, Atto accademico in onore del Prof. Magnus Löhrer*, Rome, February 16, 1993, pp. 23f.

[32] *Patrimonium fidei. Traditionsgeschichtliches Verstehen am Ende? Festschrift für Magnus Löhrer und Pius-Ramon Tragan*, ed. M. Perroni and E. Salmann, StAns, vol. 124 (Rome, 1997).

Presentation of the festschrift for Professors Löhrer and Tragan in 1997. Front row, from left to right: Abbot Benno Malfèr of Muri-Gries, Cardinal Augustin Mayer, Fr. Magnus Löhrer, Fr. Pius-Ramon Tragan, guest, Abbot Bernardo d'Onorio, Rector Albert Schmidt

fulfill my task reliably. I have also tried to go beyond a mere passing on of certain material. It never seemed right to me to understand teaching as indoctrination. Instead, I wanted to lead to the *status quaestionis* and open up the connections, but also the tensions, between the historical and systematic aspect of a question. Further, I was and am convinced that theology must insert itself into a living context, in an experience of faith. It is not purely coincidental that the two theologians to whom I feel most deeply indebted are Karl Rahner and Gerhard Ebeling.

Were I to sum up all that I have wanted to say over all these years, I could find no better model than the answer that Eberhard Jüngel, undoubtedly on a higher level, outlined in an article in which he too responded to the question concerning his theology. Jüngel developed his reflections on the basis of the following points: "I believe, therefore I speak; I believe, therefore I listen; I believe, therefore I marvel; I believe, therefore I think; I believe, therefore I distinguish; I believe, therefore I hope; I believe, therefore I act; I believe, therefore I am; I believe, therefore I suffer." I am happy with this model, even if I am conscious that I have realized it only very imperfectly. For this reason, permit me at least to say what I wanted to be and do. For me, to be a theologian means, above all, to speak from a state of faith to a state of faith, to reflect about an existence based on faith, on a faith that is challenged, in a community of faith. Teaching theology for me is the beautiful and difficult attempt to communicate to students what I have learned myself, tested and reflected on within the limits of my capabilities and with the means that were at my disposal. Others could have said this differently and better. But at a particular point all our means are insufficient in the face of the mystery with which we must concern ourselves. With all respect for the really significant theologians and persons of great theological learning, I do not feel unhappy about the fact that my rather modest publications have their place in the works of the *theologi minores*. I only hope that at least some of what I wanted to say influenced the life of one or other student, male or female. The greatest satisfaction for a theologian is when, if only as a beginning, St. Paul's words come true: You are my letter.

Fr. Basil Studer (1925–2008)

Basil Studer wrote several reports on the different stages of his life. Seldom in these reports did he mention personal feelings or express himself on his religious life or on his undoubted love of Christ. His accounts nearly always confined themselves to his academic development and activities connected with this. I am grateful to the archivist of Engelberg, Herr De Kegel, for a copy of the report which Studer wrote on September 23 and 26, 2006, under the title "A Short Autobiography: Important Points for an Obituary." Strangely, he starts by speaking of himself in the third person but then changes to the first person when he recounts only significant individual details about his life. The autobiographical sketch, "On leaving Rome," also from 2006, is more precise in describing his academic development but says nothing about his childhood and youth. As early as 1992, however, he had given a partial account in an introduction to a collection of his own articles from the years 1972 to 1990.[33]

[33] The autobiographical sketch, *Zum Abschied von Rom* [On leaving Rome], can be found in his collection, *Durch Geschichte zum Glauben. Zur Exegese and zur Trinitätslehre der Kirchenväter* [Via history to faith. On exegesis and the doctrine of the Trinity in the fathers of the Church], StAns, vol. 141 (Rome, 2006), 15–25. Further, the introduction to a collection of his articles, *Dominus Salvator. Studien zur Christologie und Exegese der Kirchenväter* [The Savior Lord. Studies on the Christology and exegesis of the fathers of the Church], StAns, vol. 107 (Rome, 1992), 9–18. There is some autobiographical information in his "Discorso all'inaugurazione dell'anno accademico di S. Anselmo [Discourse at the Inauguration of the Academic Year at Sant'Anselmo]," on October 12, 1998, in B. Studer, *Mysterium caritatis. Studien zur Exegese und zur*

Fr. Basil Studer
as a teacher at the seminary in Otélé

Franz Xaver Studer was born on May 15, 1925, in Blasthal in the Canton of Solothurn, Switzerland. He had two stepbrothers from the first marriage of his father, Leo Studer, and seven siblings from the latter's second marriage with Maria von Burg from Balsthal. His father had opened a flower- and landscape-gardening establishment in which Xaver worked while attending elementary school. In the autumn of 1937, on the advice of the local chaplain for young people, he entered the abbey school at Engelberg, where after the usual eight-year course, he completed his secondary education in 1945. For reasons of health he was not able immediately to enter the novitiate at Engelberg as he wished. Instead, he began to study theology at the diocesan seminary in Lucerne. After two semesters, however, he entered Engelberg Abbey in September 1946 with four other students. There, he received the monastic name of Basil. As a novice he had to learn to play the organ, practice in the ice-cold church, and, as he himself recounts, in fear and trembling accompany first Compline and then also Vespers. But he played the piano sufficiently well that at a later stage he taught this instrument in the abbey school. On October 3, 1950, he made solemn profession along with three other confreres and on May 25, 1951, was ordained priest. Initially his theological training took place in the house theologate at Engelberg, but in October 1951, he began further studies at Sant'Anselmo. He completed these in 1954 with a doctorate in theology under the supervision of Cipriano Vagaggini. For the dissertation, "Die theologische Arbeitsweise des Johannes von Damaskus" (The theological method of John of Damascus) he only received the grade cum laude, a fact that caused critical comment in Engelberg.[34]

Trinitätslehre in der Alten Kirche [The mystery of charity. Studies on the exegesis and doctrine of the Trinity in the early Church], StAns, vol. 127 (Rome, 1999), 23–33. Also, B. Müller, "Erinnerungen an Basil Studer [Memories of Basil Studer]," *Titlisgrüße* 94 (2008): 3–7; and J. Driscoll in *Titlisgrüße* 94 (2008): 8–11. Finally, there is an obituary with bibliography by G. Rexin, *Studer, Basil*, in BBKL, vol. 32, Ergänzungen 19 [Supplements 19] (Nordhausen, 2011), coll. 1379–1390. Studer himself provided a list of his publications in the above-mentioned collections of articles.

[34] The work appeared as issue no. 2 of the *Studia Patristica et Byzantina* in the Ettaler Kunsverlag, 1956.

Back in Engelberg, he taught dogmatic theology in the house theological school and made every effort, as the house chronicler reports, more or less successfully, to teach religion, Italian, and the piano to the boys in the monastery school. In 1957 his life changed. In the Cameroons, the Abbey of Engelberg had assumed the direction of an interdiocesan seminary at Otélé. For a time, eighteen Benedictines worked there. In the summer of 1957, Studer was in Paris to learn French and in October began to lecture at Otélé on dogmatic theology and the exegesis of St. Paul. Following the declaration of independence by the Cameroons, anti-Swiss feeling began to arise among the seminarians which led, finally, to the cessation of Benedictine teaching activity. This also meant the end of Basil Studer's involvement with Africa.

In 1962, Abbot Leonhard Bösch allowed him to study in Paris, an opportunity that Studer, looking back, regarded as the high point of his theological training. The sixties were a brilliant period for French theology, above all in the area of patristics. Studer attended lectures at the Institut Catholique, at the Sorbonne, and above all, at the École pratique des Hautes Études. Among his teachers were Henri-Irénée Marrou, at that time the greatest expert on Augustine; Jacques Fontaine, who was to become best known for his works on the *Vita Martini* of Sulpicius Severus and on Isidore of Seville; and Jean Daniélou, later a cardinal, an outstanding authority on the early Church. There were several other such teachers. Professor Pierre Nautin accepted Studer's already existing introduction to patristic soteriology as an exercise for the diploma and so he became an "Élève diplômé de l'École pratique des Hautes Études" (graduate school of applied higher studies).

Fr. Basil Studer with students, Br. Jacques Damestoy of Belloc and Br. Fulbert Dufour of Saint-Benoît-sur-Loire, in 1970

In 1963 the way was already open for Studer's teaching activity at Sant'Anselmo, which began in the following year. In 1967 he was appointed to the chair of history of the early Church and patristics. In addition to the obligatory lectures connected with this appointment, at a later stage he also began to offer courses on dogmatico-historical questions concerning the doctrine of the Trinity and on Christology. He spoke in the monastic institute on the Church Fathers and monasticism and in the liturgical institute on the Church Fathers and the liturgy. His semester examinations were feared by the students at Sant'Anselmo. Similarly, when he believed himself to be in the right academically, his refutations in matters of theological controversy could be impulsive and ruthless. Starting in the summer semester of 1972, he also taught at the patristic institute, the Augustinianum, and from 1974–1975 in both semesters. In addition to Sant'Anselmo and the Augustinianum he occasionally held courses at other academic institutions, such as the Institute of Pastoral Liturgy at Padua, the Lateran University, the diocesan seminary in Roldoc in the Netherlands, and the theological study year at Dormition Abbey in Jerusalem—and there every year from 1974 to 1995. He also taught twice at the theological school of the Benedictine abbey in Rio de Janeiro and three times at the seminary at Mount Angel in the United States—and these are only some of his activities. For a time, from 1968 to 1974, he was also rector of Sant'Anselmo. His publications sprang from his lectures and flowed uninterrupted until 2006; books, encyclopedia entries, articles of various kinds which then appeared in anthologies. Studer was unsurpassed in his knowledge of the theology of the early church up to about the year 400. Although he also held the chair of early church history, he actually had little interest in history as such. His research dealt exclusively with the speculative theology of the fathers of the Church. If at the beginning he was interested in matters of soteriology, with the years his focus shifted toward Christology and then, finally, his main preoccupation was with the doctrine of the Trinity, particularly that of St. Augustine. In fact, it was St. Augustine's theology that was the center of his interest and love. Whenever one spoke with him he came quickly to speak of Augustine without considering that others did not share either his knowledge or his interest. Fr. Jeremy Driscoll, OSB, from the Abbey of Mount Angel, a pupil and friend of Studer's, recounts, "I asked him once whether he ever spoke about or read about anything else. Surprised by this question, he looked at me and said, 'No!' And so I accepted this clearly delineated form of mutual relationship and was always prepared to speak about some patristic topic whenever we met. I came more and more to be grateful for this. We became closer.

When he came to Rome last year [2006] he called me and I went to his room. We shook hands and, offering me a chair, began at once, 'In the thirteenth book of the *De Trinitate*, Augustine says . . .' That was our last time together. I remember how he once said to me, in a really childlike way, 'Origen and Augustine—these are my friends.' "[35]

Fr. Basil wrote as a patrologist for those patrologists who had similar speculative interests. In this, however, he paid no attention to new questions that were discussed in the theology of recent decades, nor did the possible consequences of his research for the contemporary Church interest him—at least, he did not discuss them. He dealt only with the limited field of the history of the theology and dogmatics of the early Church which, he knew, was limited both in subject matter and in time. Thus, there is something monotonous and one-sided about his many writings that makes their reading a chore, not least because he lacked a sure feeling for literary style. Fr. Basil liked to write and he liked to travel. He gladly accepted invitations to participate in and lecture at academic congresses and enjoyed the attendant trips and excursions. In this way he went to the United States, Brazil, Chile and Argentina, Israel, Egypt, India, Turkey, Greece, Spain, England, Scotland, Belgium, Holland, Germany, Austria, Czechoslovakia, and Hungary, not to mention his countless visits and appearances all over Italy. The chronicler at Engelberg writes, "Many journeys to congresses and symposia were so embellished with visits to places of interest and social events that it is sometimes difficult to decide which was more important: the academic symposium or the associated travel!"[36] In 1999 he left Rome and returned to Engelberg, from which base he continued his activities as a "wandering monk." He had many contacts with friends and colleagues and he cultivated these. He was also very receptive for public recognition of his scholarly research. Thus, in 1997, he was happy to receive an honorary doctorate from the faculty of theology of Lucerne University, where he had begun his study of theology fifty years before. On his seventieth birthday, his colleagues at Sant'Anselmo offered him a festschrift, *Mysterium Christi. Symbolgegenwart und theologische Bedeutung* (The Mystery of Christ: Symbolic presence and theological significance).[37] His friendships with Popes Paul VI, John Paul II, and Benedict XVI were important to him and he spoke about several meetings with

[35] J. Dricsoll, *Titlisgrüße*, no. 94 (2008): 9–11.

[36] B. Müller, *Titlisgrüße* no. 94 (2008): 5–6.

[37] *Mysterium Christi. Symbolgegenwart und theologische Bedeutung. Festschrift für Basil Studer*, ed. M. Löhrer and E. Salmann, StAns, vol. 116 (Rome, 1995).

Fr. Basil Studer (1925–2008)

them. He was able personally to present Benedict XVI with a copy of his last book, an introduction to the *De Trinitate* of St. Augustine. "Nevertheless, he could not resist criticizing some points of the pope's teaching on the Trinity."

A virulent cancer snatched him from the making of plans which he had continued without a break. The chronicler at Engelberg reports, "When Pope Benedict XVI heard of his severe illness, he sent him a personal letter and his blessing, an act greatly appreciated by Fr. Basil."[38] He died on April 25, 2008, in the cantonal hospital at Sarnen. He was buried on April 30 at his home monastery of Engelberg, to which he always felt attached, even if from afar.

[38] B. Müller, cf. n445 supra, p. 5.

Untitled view of apse and campanile of Sant'Anselmo

Appendices

I. Bibliography of Fr. Anselm Stolz

Books

1) *Glaubensgnade und Glaubenslicht nach Thomas von Aquin*. StAns 1. Rome, 1933.
2) *Theologie der Mystik*. Regensburg, 1936. Also published in Italian, Spanish, and French.
3) *Anselm von Canterbury*. Gestalten des christlichen Abendlandes I. Munich, 1937.
4–9) *Manuale Theologiae dogmaticae*.

Fascicle I.	Introductio in sacram theologiam. Freiburg-im-Breisgau, 1941.
Fascicle II.	De Sanctissima Trinitate. Freiburg-im-Breisgau, 1939.
Fascicle III.	De natura Dei De creatione—De angelis. Freiburg-im-Breisgau, 1943.
Fascicle IV.	Anthropoligia. Freiburg-im-Breisgau, 1940.
Fascicle V.	De sacramentis. Freiburg-im-Breisgau, 1943.
Fascicle VI.	De ecclesia. Freiburg-im-Breisgau, 1939.

10) *L'ascesi cristiana*. Brescia, 1943. Also in French.

Articles and Contributions to Joint Works

11) "Zu den Wunderkapiteln im 22. Buch der Civitas Dei." *ThGl* 18 (1926): 843–55.
12) "Was definiert das vatikanische Konzil über den Glaubenszweifel?" *ThGl* 111 (1930): 519–60.
13) "Der Hl. Geist und die Heiligung der Christen." *BenM* 12 (1930): 189–97.
14) "Das kirchliche Lehramt und die Lehre vom naturlichen Verlangen nach der Anschauung Gottes." *BenM* 13 (1931): 24–32.
15) "Das Elend der Thomasinterpretation." *BenM* 13 (1931): 158–61.
16) "Zur Theologie Anselms im Proslogion." *Cath* 2 (1933): 1–24.
17) "Theologisches zu Dreifaltigkeitsbildern." *BenM* 15 (1933): 322–40.
18) "Das Problem der Kirche in den Schriften Erik Petersons." *Hochl* 31 (1933/1934): 458–65.
19) Introduction to and commentary on "Gottes Leben, sein Erkennen und Wollen." *DthA*. 2, Salzburg-Leipzig, 1934.

20) "Neue Dogmen?" *BenM* 16 (1934): 187–201.
21) "'Vere esse' im Proslogion des hl. Anslem." *Schol* 9 (1934): 400–9.
22) "Positive und spekulative Theologie." *DT* 12 (1934): 327–43.
23) "Neue Literatur zur Lehre von der Kirche." *DT* 12 (1934): 350–58.
24) "Theologie der Sprache." *BenM* 17, 1(1935): 121–35. French, cf. no. 36 below.
25) "'Nouveaux' dogmes." *Iren* 12 (1935): 129–50.
26) "Gottes Leben, sein Erkennen und Wollen." *KathGed* 8 (1935): 80–84.
27) "Matthias Josef Scheeben und das Mysterium der Kirche." *KathGed* 8 (1935): 116–24.
28) "Maria und die Glaubensentscheidungen." *KathGed* 8 (1935): 220–30.
29) "Das Proslogion des hl. Anselm." *Rbén* 47 (1935): 331–47.
30) "Mystik und christliches Lebensideal." *DT* 13 (1935): 427–36.
31) "Natur und Gnade." *KathGed* 9 (1936): 116–23.
32) "Probleme der Mystik." *KathGed* 9 (1936): 198–206.
33) "Herr, lehre uns zu beten." *BenM* 18 (1936): 354–61. English, cf. no 34 below.
34) "Lord, teach us to pray." *OF* 10 (1936/1937): 386–93.
35) "Extra Ecclesiam nulla salus." *KathGed* 19 (1937): 101–12.
36) "Théologie des langues." *Suppl. Vie spir.* 51 (1937): 86–107.
37) "Charismatische Theologie." *KathGed* 11 (1938): 187–96.
38) "Das Mysterium der Eucharistie." *KathGed* 11 (1938): 311–12.
39) "Christlicher Kult und Mystik Theologie der Zeit." In *Beih. z. Seels*, Pastoral Supplement (Vienna, 1938), 172–82.
40) "Vom Worte Gottes: Christ-sein." In *Werkbll. zur Vertiefung von Beruf u.* Leben 8 (Salzburg, 1938), 49–53.
41) "Matthias Josef Scheeben und die neue Theologie." Lecture for the Celebration of Scheeben by the Association of Catholic Academics of Cologne on July 20, 1938. Published as manuscript. Dülmen, 1938.
42) "Théologie de la mystique." *Rthom* 44 (1938): 638–41.
43) "Ich glaube an die eine heilige Kirche." *Korrespondenz des Priester-Gebetsvereines* 59 (Vienna, 1938), 6–10. English, cf. no. 46 below.
44) Introduction to and commentary on "Gott der Dreieinige." *DthA*, vol. 3 (Salzburg-Leipzig), 939.
45) "Sacrement et Sacremental." *QLP* 24 (1939): 60–78.
46) "I Believe in a Holy Church." *OF* 14 (1939/1940): 117–21.
47) "Der Theologe und seine Sprache." *Die Schildgenossen* 19 (1940): 32–39.
48) "Mistica e psicologia." *VCr* 12 (1940): 407–19.
49) "St. Thomas and Some Eucharistic Practices." *OF* 14 (1939/1940): 433–38.
50) "De 'Theologia kerygmatica.'" *Ang* 17 (1940): 337–51.
51) "The Sacraments as Medicine." *OF* 15 (1940/1941): 241–48.
52) "The Holy Trinity in Christian Life." *OF* 15 (1940/1941): 481–84, 546–50.
53) "Come leggo la Sacra Scrittura." *VC* 13 (1941): 289–306.
54) "Liturgia e devozione personale." *VC* 14 (1942): 273–98.
55) "Theology and Piety." *OF* 17 (1942/1943): 58–63.
56) "Mysticism as the Normal Flowering of the Sacramental Life." *OF* 17 (1942/1943): 393–97, 447–55.
57) "Die Mittlerin aller Gnaden." In *Katholische Marienkunde*. Edited by P. Sträter. Vol. 2 (Paderborn, 1947), 241–71.

Book Reviews

58) Review of *De gratia. Tractatus dogmaticus*, by H. Lange. *DT* 8 (1930): 435–41.
59) Reviews of *L'exemplarisme divin selon saint Bonaventura*, by J. M. Bissen, and *Le Saint-Esprit et ses dons selon saint Bonaventure*, by J. Bonnefoy. *DT* 9 (1931): 356–58.
60) Review of *Le Rôle de l'analogie en théologie dogmatique*, by M.T.-L. Penido. *DT* 10 (1932): 558–60.
61) Review of *Fides quaerens intellectum. Anselms Beweis der Existenz Gottes im Zusammenhang seines theologischen Programms*, by K. Barth. *DT* 10 (1932): 560f.
62) Review of *Die Lehre von Gott dem Einen und Dreieinigen*, by L. Kopler. *DT* 12 (1934): 348f.
63) Reviews of *De Sacramentis Ecclesiae, Tractatus dogmatici. I. De sacramentis in communi, de baptismo, de confirmatione, de ss. Eucharistia*, by Francis J. Connell, and *Das Buch von den Engeln. Stellung und Bedeutung der heiligen Engel im Kultus*, by E. Peterson. *DT* 13 (1935): 385f.
64) Reviews of *Le corps mystique du Christ. Sa nature et sa vie divine d'après saint Paul et la théologie*, by E. Mura, and *De corpore mystico doctrina Seraphici*, by D. Culhane. *DT* 13 (1935): 359f.
65) Review of *Anselm von Canterbury. Leben, Lehre, Werke*, by R. Allers. *ThRv* 36 (1937): 238–41.
66) Review of *Die Gotteserfahrung in der Summa Theologiae mysticae des Karmeliten Philippus a Ss. Trinitate*, by H. Kummet. *ThRv* 38 (1939): 234f.
67) Review of *Die Kirche als der mystische Leib Christi nach dem Apostel Paulus*, by A. Wikenhauser. *DT* 17 (1939): 480f.
68) Review of *Urkirche und Ostkirche*, by Friedrich Heiler. *DT* 17 (1939): 483–85.
69) Review of *Morale et corps mystique*, by Emile Mersch. *DT* 20 (1942): 99.
70) Review of *Altkirchliche Autonomie und päpstliche Zentralismus*, by Friedrich Heiler. *DT* 20 (1942): 185–90.

II. Bibliography of Fr. Matthäus Rothenhäusler

1) *Zur Aufnahmeordnung der Regula S. Benedicti*. BGAM Vol. 3, 2 (Münster, 1912).
2) Review of *S. Benedicti Regula Monachorum*. Editionem critic-practicam adornavit D. Cuthbertus Butler. *StudMitt* 33 (1912): 564ff.
3) "Zur ältesten cluniazenischen Abtswahl." *StudMitt* 33 (1912): 620–50.
4) "Gregor I. und die Stabilität des Mönchs." *ZSRG. K* 3 (1913): 141–59.
5) "Von der Regel des hl. Benedikt." *SBSt* 38 (1914): 129–32.
6) "Der große Freund des ersten Mönches." *SBSt* 38 (1914): 169–74.
7) "Aus der Schule des hl. Benedikt." *SBSt* 39 (1915): 88–92, 143–45, 185–87.
8) "Meerfahrten. Zum 29. Juni." *SBSt* 39 (1915): 224–27.
9) "Die Taufe asl Siegel." *SBSt* 39 (1915): 264–70.
10) Review of *Die Wirtschaftsverhältnisse des Klosters St. Gallen von der Grüundung bis zum Ende des 13. Jahrhunderts, Eine Studie*, by H. Bickel. *StudMitt* 36 (1915): 343–48.
11) Review of *Les elections abbatiales en France, I, Epoque franque*, by H. Lévy-Bruhl. *ZSRG. K* 5 (1915): 517–24.
12) "Kleine Bilder aus den Anfängen des Mönchtums." *SBSt* 40 (1916): 262–64, 301–3, 334–37, 384–88, 427–30; ibid. 41 (1917): 25–27, 100–3, 137–40, 202–6, 248–52, 285–89, 445–48.

13) "Über Anlage und Quellen der Regel des hl. Benedikt." *StudMitt* 38 (1917): 1–17.
14) "Die Anlage der Regel des hl. Benedikts." *StudMitt* 39 (1918): 167–70.
15) "Voraussetzungen zum Verständnis des hl. Benedikt." *BenM* 1 (1919): 209–15.
16) "Advent und Leiden." *BenM* 1 (1919): 370–72.
17) "Hieronymus als Mönch." *BenM* 2 (1920): 380–91.
18) "Ältestes Mönchtum und klösterliche Beständigkeit." *BenM* 3 (1921): 87–94, 223–37.
19) "Die Beständigkeit des Benediktiners." *BenM* 3 (1921): 345–57.
20) "Ein Charakterbild des hl. Benedikt von Nursia." *BenM* 3 (1921): 390–92.
21) "Die rechtlichen Wirkungen der benediktinischen Beständigkeit." *BenM* 3 (1921): 440–54.
22) "Die Anfänge der klösterlichen Profess." *BenM* 4 (1922): 21–28.
23) "Der hl. Basilius der Größe und die klösterlliche Profess." *BenM* 4 (1922): 280–89.
24) "Unter dem Geheimnis des Kreuzes. Die klösterliche Profess bei Kassian." *BenM* 5 (1922): 91–96.
25) With K. Beyerle, "Die Regel des hl. Benedikt, das Gesetz des Inselklosters und seine Verwirklichung." In *Die Kultur der Abtei Reichenau*. Edited by K. Beyerle. Half-volume 1 (Munich, 1925), 265–315.
26) "Wege zur benediktinischen Geschichte." *BenM* 11 (1929): 129–37.
27) "Conversatio morum." *BenM* 12 (1930): 145f.
28) "Der Vatername Christi." *StudMitt* 52 (1934): 178f.
29) "Freude und Dank ob der Gotteserkenntnis." *BenM* 18 (1936): 334–44.
30) "La doctrine de la 'Theologia' chez Diadoque de Photike." *Iren* 14 (1937): 536–53.
31) "Zur asketischen Lehrschrift des Diadochus von Photike." In *Heilige Überlieferung. Festschrift für I. Herwegen*. Edited by O. Casel (Münster, 1938), 86–95.
32) "Honestas morum. Eine Untersuchung zu cap. 73 der Regula S.Benedicti." In *Studia Benedictina in memoriam gloriosi ante saecula XIV transitus S. P. Benedicti, cura professorum Instituti Pontificii S. Anselmi de Urbe*. StAns. Vols. 18–19 (Rome, 1947), 127–56.
33) "Das innere Leben der Zönobiten nach Joh. Cassian und die Regel des hl. Benedikt." In *Vir Dei Benedictus, Festgabe zum 1400, Todestag des hl. Benedict*. Edited by R. Molitor (Münster, 1947), 276–92.
34) "Kirche und Kloster. Der Brief des hl. Clemens von Rom (um 90) und die Regel des hl. Benediktus (um 530)." *BenM* 25 (1949): 378–80.
35) "Apotaxis." *RAC* 1 (1950): 558–64.
36) "Conversio morum." *RAC* 3 (1957): 422–24.

III. Abbots of Sant'Anselmo Have the Right to Wear the Pectoral Cross Inside and Outside the College

12 July 1988
Apr, Coll I, II 12 F
Unpublished.

Beatissimo Padre,

Piacque alla Santità Vostra di concedere al sottoscritto Abate e Rettore del Collegio Sant'Anselmo la facoltà di portare la croce pettorale dentro e fuori del Collegio.

Or egli, prostrato ai piedi della Santità Vostra, supplica che questa facoltà sia come concessa anche agli Abati che gli succederanno nella Direzione del Collegio; e implora umilmente l'apostolica Benedizione.

Il 5 Luglio 1888 D. Gaetone Bernardi

Vaticano, 12 Luglio 1888.

Il S. Padre accogliendo benignamente la preghiera, si è degnato di accordare agli Abati di Sant'Anselmo *pro tempore* la facoltà implorato per l'uso della croce pettorale.

G. Boccali, Uditore di S.S.

IV. The First Statutes of Sant'Anselmo

Manuscript in APr, S. Anselmi Collegium II 12 B.
Printed as, Statuta Collegii S. Anselmi in Urbe 'ad Summi Pontificis mentem redacta.' Linz, 1889, Jos. Feichtinger & Sons for the Abbey of Seitenstetten. 29pp.

REGULA S. P. BENEDICTI CUM STATUTIS SERVANDIS
IN COLLEGIO S. ANSELMI IN URBE

Introductio.

Collegium S. Anselmi, anno 1687, constitutione 'Inscrutabili', a Sanctissimo Domino Innocentio Papa XI, ad promovenda studia ecclesiastica in Congregatione Cassinensi, fundatum, tempore collapsum, nunc tandem litteris Sanctissimi Dni nostri Leonis Papae XIII feliciter regnantis, datis die 4 Januarii 1887, restituendum curatur, ea scilicet ratione, ut in eo scientiis excolendis ecclesiasticis operam detur, non solum ab Congregationis Cassinensis, sed etiam ab alumnis omnium aliarum Congregationum benedictinarum nigri habitus.

Eo consilio incipiendum putavit Summus Pontifex praeclarum hoc opus, ut duplex attingatur scopus, scillicet: 'ad studia doctrinae provehenda' in Ordine S. Benedicti, et ut in eodem Ordine nostro constituatur major unio inter diversa monasteria hinc inde dispersa; nam, ut dicit Sanctissimus Pontifex: 'quoniam eorum vires plus valent qui apte cohaereant inter se, spes rerum in posterum tempus longe meliorum tunc firmior multo consisteret, si varia ejusdem Ordinis membra latissime sparsa, quasi in corpus unum coalescerent, unis iisdemque legibus, una eademque rectione.[1]

PROLOGUS

Ausculta, o fili, praecepta, etc.

DECLARATIO. 'Constituenda est ergo a nobis Dominici schola servitii.'

Regula S. P. Benedicti, quam S. Gregorius Magnus discretion praecipuam praedicat, quoad spiritum saltem adamussim servetur in Collegio S. Anselmi de Urbe. Declarationes autem hic adiunctae, quae vel explicant S.Regulam, vel legitime ei derogant, ut speciali scopo Collegii huius, scilicet studiorum presolvendorum, provideatur, vel bonae valetudini prospiciunt, nisi materiam votorum legesve S. Ecclesiae tangent, vel ex contempt, aut cum scandalo violantur.

[1] This first section, lines 3–20, is not contained in the printed version.

CAPUT II.[2]

Qualis debeat esse Abbas.

Abbas qui praeesse dignus est, etc.

DECLARATIO. 'Abbas qui praeesse dignus est.'

Collegium S. Anselmi, immediate subiectum S. Sedi, gubernatur ab Abbate et Priore a Sancta Sede nominatis et constitutis. Ipse vero Abbas plena et ordinaria (potestate) iurisdictione gaudet in omnibus monachis, sacer-[/ p. 4]dotes sint an clerici, et laicis, pro tempore in supradicto Collegio degentibus.

Abbatis est, ad mentem Smi. Patris nostri Benedicti, vigilantissimo et oculo et corde domum regere, omniaque in domo Domini sapientissime ordinare, moderari, disponere; nec solum rei familiaris curam gerere, sed etiam, quantum fieri potest, regularibus praeesse exercitiis, maxime vero animabus monachorum sibi commissorum ad qualecunque consilium, solatium, subsidium praesto esse.

Omnia in timore Dei peragat, cuius voluntatem, si fedelissime exsequitur, pro sua parte religiosum sanctae obedientiae votum persolvit. Iam si Deum ut filius dirigi, monachos sibi commissos amabit ut Pater, paterna immo matris cura eorum saluti invigilans, familiamque pacifice ac placide gubernans, Angeli instar Custodis.

Praeterea ipsius est S. Regulae vim ac spiritum recte docteque interpretari, et de eius praeceptis exsequendis cum sancta discretion concedere dispensationes.

CAPUT III.

De adhibendis ad consilium fratribus

Quoties aliqua praecipua, etc.

DECLARATIO. 'Seniorum tantum utatur consilio.'

Abbas singulis saltem mensibus convocet seniors, scilicet Priorem, Magistrum, Oeconomum, i.e. Cellerarium, et lectores omnes, et eorum consilium circa institutionem, disciplinam, et administrationem rerum temporalium, etc., Collegii, requirat. Adhibito huiusmodi consiliio potest Abbas staturere et deliberare, quae pro sua prudentia magis expedire iudicaverit. Sententiam exponant seniores cum omni humilitate et libertate.

CAPUT IV.

Quae sint instrumenta bonorum operum.

In primis Dominus, etc. [/ p.5]

CAPUT V.

De Obedientia.

Primus humilitatis gradus est obedientia sine mora, etc.

CAPUT VI.

De Taciturnitate.

Faciamus quod ait Propheta, etc.

DECLARATIO. 'Loquendi concedatur licentia.'

[2] No reference in text to a CAPUT I.

Quantum fieri potest, tempore diurno omnes relgiose silentium servare studeant, ut, secundum S. Patriarchae sententiam, peccatum effugiant, mentisque in semetipsis recollationem custodiant. Iam vero, ut revelentur suaviterque sibi iungantur animi, concedatur recreatio sive colloquium, tam post prandium per unam fere horam, quam post coenam per mediam circiter horam secundum prudentiam superioris, necnon et in deambulatione quotidiana extra Collegium, quae Romae, praecipue tempore studiorum, omnino necessaria videtur ad servandam valetudinem. Ad primum vero campanae sonum, qui recreationis finem indicat, omne colloquium illico abrumpatur. Nemo a recreatione nisi cum permissu se disgiungat, et qui sero venit, exclusationem exprimat pre signum aliquod.

Caveant praecipue fratres, ne inopportuni sint, pertinaces, obstinati, vel aculeatis verbis utentes, ita ut suavissimus familiae Spiritus servetur, sancta morum elegantia et Pax illa, quae hereditas est pii Patris nostri Benedicti et dulcissimum spectaculum Angelis et hominibus.

Caveant insuper, cum sint congregate ex diversis nationibus, congregationibus vel monasteriis, ne unquam dicatue aliquid, quod possit laedere susceptibilitatem alicuius fratris.

Nunquam fiat contentio vel comparatio, etiam iocando[3], de usibus, constitutionibus vel observantiis diversarum Congregationum, sed in his praecipue servetur caritas. [/ p. 6]

CAPUT VII.

De Humiliate.

Clamat nobis Scriptura, etc.

CAPUT VIII.

De officiis divinis in noctibus.

Hyemis tempore, etc.

DECLARATIO I. 'Octava hora noctis surgendum es.'

Octo horae saltem somno fratrum concedantur statuto horario prout in calce.

DECLARATIO II. 'Sic temperetur hora vigiliarum.'

Horae Primae et Completorii semper ab omnibus in oratorio persolvantur. Dominicis vero diebus et festivis, officium completum celebretur in choro ab omnibus.

DECLARATIO III. 'Quod vero restat post vigilias, meditationi inserviatur.'

Fratres quotidie per semihoram orationi mentali incumbant.

CAPITA IX, X, XI, XII, XIII.

(De Officio Divino.)

CAPUT XIV.

In natalitiis sanctorum qual iter Vigiliae agantur.

In Sanctorum vero festivitatibus, etc.

DECLARATIO. 'Omnibus solemnitatibus.'

Festa de praecepto ferianda, in quibus etiam vacant scholae, sunt omnes quae Romae sunt de praecepto, et insuper festa S. Patris Benedicti, S. Mauri, S. Placidi,

[3] In the printed text, "iocando" is rendered "cocando."

S. Scholasticae, Omnium Sanctorum O.N. et S. Anselmi, patroni Collegii, necnon Commemoratio omnium Monachorum defunctorum O.N. [/ p. 7]

CAPITA XV, XVI, XVII.
(De Officio Divino.)

CAPUT XVIII.
Quo ordine psalmi dicendi sunt.

In primis dicatur versus, etc.

DECLARATIO. 'Modulatione canatur.'

Diebus Dominicis et festivis Missa conventualis et Vesperae canantur, si possibile sit. Cantu Gregoriano tantum seu cantu firmo utantur.

CAPUT XIX.
De disciplina psallendi.

Ubique credimus, etc.

DECLARATIO. 'Psallite sapienter.'

Opus Dei, cum sit principale vitae monasticae officium ac praecipua via ad divinarum rerum contemplationem, fratres omnem ahibeant sollicitudinem, illud ut cum summa gravitate, dignitate, unctione ac simplicitate persolvant.

Propterea dilgientissime eis explorandus est Psalmorum, Orationum, Lectionumque sacrarum sensus.

Ad Missam vero conventualem quae quotidie in choro vel cantatur vel legitur, fratres cum profunda cordis collectione summaque mentis attentione assistant quotiamo sacrosanctum sacrificium est omnis religionis fons et centrum.

CAPUT XX.
De reverentia orationis.

Si cum hominibus, etc.

DECLARATIO. 'Ex affectu inspirationis divinae gratiae.'

Fratres suam sollicite conscientiam examinent, non tantum, ut mos fert sub finem diei, sed aliis quoque tem-[/ p. 8]poribus, ita ut rationem sibi reddant de virtutum progressu, ac de imminuta passione dominante.

Quolibet anno, antequam lectiones tradantur, fratres saltem per hebdomadam vacent spiritualibus excercitiis, a quibus nihil nisi gravis vel infirmitas, vel occupatio, approbante superior excusat. Qua quidem recollectione peracta fratres sancta renovabunt professionis vota. Insuper instituatur dies recollectionis mensualis, ultima domenica mensis usque ad meridiem, in quo alumni patri spirituali relationem faciant de statu animae. Commendantur etiam fratribus reliqua sanctitatis monasticaeque asceseos adminicula, scilicet ardentissimus amor erga sacrosanctum Eucharistiam, quam quotidie visitabunt, pietas in amantissimum Cor Jesu, tenerrimum obsequium erga immaculatam Virginem Mariam, cultus SS. Angelorum et Sanctorum, imprimis Sti. Patriarchae Joseph er B. Patris nostri Benedicti, atque Sa. Anselmi. Diligant etiam S. Rosarium, Viam Crucis, aliaque pietatis excercitia, quae S. Ecclesia indulgentiis ditavit.

CAPUT XXI.
De Decanis Monasteriis.

Si magis fuerit congregatio, etc.

CAPUT XXII.

Quomodo dormiant monachi.

DECLARATIO I. 'In uno loco dormiant.'

Ut liberius fratres orationi lectionique vacent, unusquisque, quantum fieri potest, inhabitat cellam sibi assignatam. Nulla licet, absque Abbatis vel Prioris permissu cellam alterius fratris ingredi, nedum absentis curiose prescrutari: licet vero, sine superioris permissione, fratrem cum fratre in portae limine loqui. Licet etiam alumnum ingredi cellam proprii professori et professorem cellam discipulorum suorum, ad tractandum de rebus ad scholam pertinenti bus. [/ p. 9]

DECLARATIO II. 'In eadem cella.'

Lucerna ardea in cellarum dormitorio. In ipsis vero cellis lumen cautissime custodiendum, praescripta cubitum eundi hora extinguatur.

DECLARATIO III. 'Cum omni tamen gravitate et modestia.'

Ad corporis habitum quod attinet, fratres studeant, ut vocationis dignitas ex omnibus quodammodo motibus membrisque effulgeat. Corpus igitur sic sit verecunde graviterque compositum, ut omnino Deum glorificet aedificetque proximum. Tam gestus quam incessus sit simplex, haud exquisitus, purus ab omni vel levitate ac negligentia, vel mollitie et affectatione, ita ut fratres Religionem sacramque vestem commendent, ubilibet speciam sanctae prae se ferentes modestiae.

CAPUT XXIII.

De excommunicatione culparum.

Si quis frater contumax, etc.

CAPUT XXIV.

Qualis esse debeat modus excommunicationis.

Secundum modum culpae, etc.

DECLARATIO. 'In levioribus culpis.'

Sapienti iudicio Abbatis vel superiois remittitur modus repressionis culparum et negligentiarum, in quibus forte fratres ex fragilitate cadere poterunt.

CAPUT XXV.

De gravioribus culpis.

Is autem frater, qui gravioris, etc.

DECLARATIO. 'Gravioris culpae.'

Si quis ex alumnis Collegii in grave inciderit crimen, aut pacem turbet, sive disciplinam regularem, bonisque [/ p. 10] moribus infestus sit, aut prorsus agnoscatur impos ad studia, non expellatur nisi post binam admonitionem, et ex sententia maioris partis Senioratus, id est Consilii.

CAPITA XXVI, XXVII, XXVIII, XXIX, XXX.

(Adhuc de excommunicatis, etc.)

CAPUT XXXI.

De Cellerario Monasterii.

Cellerarius monasterii, etc.

DECLARATIO I. 'Eligatur de Congregatione sapiens.'

Cellerarius ab Abbate in Collegio constitutus, temporalium curam gubernationemque suscipit. Eius est, tam coemptiones et cuiusvis generis expensas facere, quam Collegii administrare rem familiarem, stipendia annua et deposita alumnorum recipere et administrare. Quapropter providebit, up suppetant, quae ad usum vitae, ad victum, vel ad sustentanda aedificia pertinent, praecisa omni superfluitate.

DECLARATIO II. 'Sine iussione Abbatis nihil faciat.'

Cellerarius a Superioris arbitrio ita pendit, ut quaecunque hic iusserit, vel ordinaverit, exsequatur, quae vero improbaverit, non aggrediatur. Quapropter saepius cum eo de rebus sibi mandatis consilium confert, ne quid negligat, et indices tenet computorum generales et librum diurnum, cui omnia mandat sive nummis sive rebus accepta, vendita vel expensa, quorum quidem statum singulis mensibus superiori, tertio quoque mense etiam senioribus proponit; sub finem autem anni scolastici summarium rationem coram utrisque reddit tam expensi et accepti, quam creditae et debitae pecuniae. [/ p. 11]

CAPUT XXXII.

De ferramentis vel rebus monasterii.

Substantiae monasterii, etc.

DECLARATIO. 'Breve teneat.'

Cellerarius inventaria supellectilis omniumque quae sunt in Collegio rerum perscribenda curat. Sacrista sibimet consignat inventarium rerum ecclesiae et sacristiae. Bibliothecarius librorum quos bibliotheca complectitur catalogum conficit; quae biblioteca sit ad usum omnium tam alumnorum quam professorum: nemo tamen libros secum deferat in cellam, nisi registro ad hoc apposito nomen suum et titulum libri inscripserit; libri vero restituantur infra mensem. Numquam licet libros auferre vel commodare alicui extra Collegium.

CAPUT XXXIII.

Si quid debeant monachi proprium habere.

Praecipue hoc vitium radicitus amputandum est, etc.

DECLARATIO. 'Neque aliquid habere proprium.'

Omnes monachi in Collegio commorantes, professores sint an clerici, sicut etiam fratres laici, quae hic sancta dicta sunt paupertate ad verbum servabunt. Hinc privatum, sub quocumque praetextu, habere peculium nuli licet. Si quis librum, vestem, vel quodcunque aliud, in usum suum proprium, de consensu proprii superioris, emere voluerit, adeat Cellerarium Collegii, qui solvat pretium. Pro parvis vero expensis quotidianis, quae occurrere possunt, verbi gratia pro vehiculis, adsit apud ostiarium depositum quoddam, de quo accipere licet, quantum opus est, exeuntibus cum licentia superioris. Ostiarius vero de supradicto depositio quavis hebdomada rationem dabit cellerario. [/ p. 12]

CAPUT XXXIV.

Si omnes debeant aequaliter necessaria accipere.

Sicut scriptum est, etc.

DECLARATIO. 'Infirmitatum consideratio.'

Sicut Superior cum omni cura providet necessitati bus fratrum, ita fratres cum simplicitate et humilitate animum Patris advertant, si vel ipsi aliqua re indigent, vel alterius necessitas superiorem fugit. Officialis si quem plus indigentem arbitratur, necessarium tribuat, petita Superioris venia. Quam quidem licenciam prudens ac discretus Pater, ratione habita et rei et personae, vel generatim vel ad casum ita concedat, ut servato religionis spiritu, exceptio Regulam comprobet.

CAPUT XXXV.
De septimanariis coquinae.

Fratres sibi invicem serviant, etc.

DECLARATIO. 'Sibi invicem serviant.'

S. Ecclesia, cum monachos seu professos Chori ad sacerdotium provehat, unde divinis potissimum et ecclesiasticis officiis aliisque ingenii laboribus vacant, ministerium coquina laicis committitur fratribus. Ut tamen aliquot modo S. Regulae satisfiat, certe ad mensam alumni, opitulantibus fratribus laicis, ministrant ad discretionem superioris.

CAPUT XXXVI.
De infirmis fratribus.

Infirmorum cura ante omnia, etc.

DECLARATIO I. 'Ipsi infirmi.'

Aegrotus frater ad omnia sese accommodet diaetae praescripta, nulla in re propriam sequens voluntatem. Ut infirmitates suas cum humilitate, simplicitate ac sinceritate exposuit, totum se tradet sanctae obedientiae divinaeque curae. [/ p. 13]

DECLARATIO II. 'Servitor timens Deum.'

Superior unum e monachis infirmarium constituat, qui valetudinis in Collegio curam suscipit, et cui aegrotantes fratres obedire debent. Eius est visitationibus medici assistere eiusque mandata exsequi et praescripta medicamenta procurare.

Cui quidem officio ut alacriter satisfaciat, necessaria ei concedantur solatia. Praetera reliqui etiam fratres, quantum opus fuerit, ex animo parati sint omni modo aegrotantibus subvenire, sive vigiliae exigantur, sive alia caritatis pietatisque officia. Infirmos vero non visitent nisi cum licentia superioris vel infirmarii. In infirmo fratre magis Jesum Christum, cuius ille electus est membrum, omni gratia, studio, religione, complectentur.

CAPUT XXXVII.
De senioribus vel infantibus.

Licet ipsa natura, etc.

CAPUT XXXVIII.
De hebdomadario lectore.

Mensis fratrum edentium, etc.

DECLARATIO. 'Lectio desse non debet.'

In communi mensa perpetuum servetur silentium, nisi raro contingat a superiori dispensari; legatur ex Novo Testamento vel ex Veteri, deinde ex libro designato, ultimo ex Regula S. Benedicti cum Declarationibus ex Statutis Collegii S. Anselmi. Venia loquendi a superiore data, numquam omittatur lectio ex Novo Testamento, vel e Veteri sub initio, et ex S. Regula in fine. Quilibet alumnus classium theologicarum bis in anno, Superioris indicio, pronuntiet in publico refectorio sermonem super indicato themate, quem tamen ab eo compositum antea reviserit Magister alumnorum, vel Praefectus studiorum. [/ p. 14]

CAPUT XXXIX.
De mensura ciborum.

Sufficere credimus ad refectionem, etc.

DECLARATIO I. 'Addatur et tertium.'

In prandio fratribus apponantur praetor iusculum duo pulmentaria cocta cum solitis obsoniis, seu frigidis seu calidis, et si qui forte existant fructus. Ad coenam apponantur pulmentaria duo.

DECLARATIO II. 'Panis libra una.'

Mensura panis fratrum permittitur arbitrio, exceptis ieiunii diebus.

DECLARATIO III. 'Debiles.'

Consideratis aetatis nostrae debilitate necnon et scopo principali collegii S. Anselmi, scilicet formatione iuventutis in studiis ecclesiaticis, dispensatur in eo a ieiunio et ab abstinentia regulari, et servetur solummodo ieiunia et abstinentiae ecclesiasticae, sicut in hac Urbe observantur. Mane fratribus permittitur ex more recepto ientaculum sumere; item, circa horam vesperae, praebetur iuventuti studiosae quae dicitur 'Caritas,' in refectorio sub silentio sumenda. Praeter ea et regulares refectiones nihil omnino gustetur, nisi forte superior vel infirmaries permiserit. Quae omnia a fratribus etiam extra Collegium observantur, nisi excusat ratio vel difficultas. Sit porro omnibus eadem ciborum et qualitas et mensura, nisi ob valetudinem aliud utili indicatum sit.

Fratres laici simpliciores cibos accipiunt eosque mensura ampliori.

CAPUT XL.

De mensura potus.

Unusquisque proprium habet, etc.

DECLARATIO. 'Per singulos sufficere.'

Pro hemina fratribus conceditur ad singulas refectiones vini circiter dimidia pars litrae. [/ p. 15]

CAPUT XLI.

Quibus horis oporteat reficere fratres.

A Sancto Pascha usque ad, etc.

DECLARATIO. 'Reficiantur fratres.'

Hora prandii est meridiana, coenae vero vel collationis pro diversitate temporum.

CAPUT XLII.

Ut post Completorium nemo loquatur.

DECLARATIO I. 'Silentio debent studere.'

Silentium quod hic S. Regula praecipit post Completorium, rigorose servandum est post signum serotinae dormitionis, usque ad 'Pretiosa' diei sequentis; studiosissime sanctum servetur atque inviolatum. A quo si quando necessitas vel specialis licentia excusat, temperetur verbis quantum fieri potest. Interdiu servetur silentium in Oratorio, in capitulo, in refectorio ac dormitoriis; quibus in locis si quid ex necessitate dicendum est, fiat id breviter ac submissa voce. Licet eadem ratione loqi in biblioteca, in claustro, in scalis et in sacristia, ubi quidem de nihilo agatur, nisi de eo quod ad ecclesiae servitium pertinet.

DECLARATIO II. 'Legat unus collationes.'

Conferentia spiritualis cum vix quotidie in hoc Collegio propter studia dari queat, fiat saltem, a Superiore pro omnibus Dominicis et festivis diebus, a Magistro vero semel in hebdomada, die quo vacant scholae, hora competenti, pro iis qui sub eius cura versantur.

CAPUT XLIII.

De his qui ad opus Dei vel ad mensam tarde occurrunt.

Ad horam divini Officii, etc.

DECLARATIO I. 'Publica satisfactione.'

Si quis fratrum ad Matutinum venerit incepto Hymno, adoret primum, deinde genuflectat medio in choro, usque ad signum superioris; quo facto surgat suumque post debitas [/ p. 16] reverentias locum petat; expleto choro se excusat apud Superiorem. Si quis vero ad chorum venerit, expleto primo psalmo cuiusvis horae, adoret, genuflectat medio in choro, et locum suum petat, non dante signum superiore.

DECLARATIO II. 'Ad mensem autem.'

Qui in refectorium intraverit inchoata mensae benedictione iuxta ianuam subsistat. Qui autem venerit benedictione iam completa, genuflectat in medio, factoque signo se excuset apud Superiorem, vel eo absente apud digniorem. Sero venientes ad conferentiam spiritualem, ad commune exercitium, vel recreationem, sine genuflexione se excusent. Quod si cui necesse est ab exercitio communi discedere, capitis inclinatione petat abeundi copiam; sin rediturus non est, expressam sibi licentiam conciliet.

CAPUT XLIV.

De his qui excommunicantur, quomodo satisfaciant.

Qui pro gravioribus culpis, etc.

CAPUT XLV.

De his qui falluntur in Oratorio.

Si quis, dum pronuntiat, etc.

DECLARATIO. 'Fefellerit.'

Frater qui psallens vel cantans notabiliter errat, satisfaciat in loco suo. Sin autem tam graviter deliquerit, ut in errorem alios abduxerit, aut correctus fuerit, vel qui strepitum, fragoremve fecerit, illico, aut si cantat vel legit solus, ut primum finierit, in medio genuflexus satisfaciat usque ad signum superioris.

CAPUT XLVI.

De his qui in aliis qibuslibet rebus delinquent.

Si quis dum in labore, etc.

DECLARATIO I. 'Ante Abbatem vel Congregationem.' [/ p. 17]

Ex more monastico fratres transgressiones vel negligentias contra regularem disciplinam factas, publice fatentur in Capitulo culparum. Quod quidem fit post Primam bis in mense, diebus quibus vacant scholae, non autem Dominicis neque festivis.

Capitulo culparum omnes inersunt; fratres laici facta culpa egrediuntur; deinde alumni; tandem soli cum Abbate manent patres. Frater a Superiore evocatus medio in capitulo humiliter atque ingenue quae contra regularem observantiam commiserit confitetur. Quo facto genuflexus a Superiore et reprehensionem et poentitentiam accipit, ex animo sibi gratulans, quod in paternum adducitur iudicium, delictaque tam levi humiliationis mortificationisve poena, sive palam in refectorio, sive secus luenda est, expiare sibi licet. Fratres sese etiam in capitulo accusent de confracta re aliqua vel illato damno, rem manibus tenentes,[4] si aeque fieri potest, ac similiter in refectorio satisfaciant. De interioribus delictis in capitulo nulla fit accusatio.

DECLARATIO II. 'Abbati aut spiritualibus senioribus patefaciat.'

Sacerdotes plurimos collegii iurisdictione ornet Abbas et confessarios familiae constituat; advocentur etiam confessarii extranei ordinarii. Detur insuper omnibus facultas, saltem quater in anno, et quando Abbati utili visum fuerit, confitendi confessario extraordinario. Cuncti fratres, tam clerici quam laici, singulis hebdomadibus ad sacramentalem confessionem accedant, et Superior est sollicite vigilare, ut praescriptio[5] haec impleatur. Neque hic omittenda est perquam salutaris, quae S. Patriarcha magistro in monasteriis inveteravit consuetudo, interiorem animae statum Superiori manifestandi, utpote qui monachis constitutus sit spirituali set Medicus et Magister. Quare fratres magno simplicique animo et filiali fiducia suum aperiant cor, nihil reticentes unde sanctum benigni patris consilium redundare possit. Qui quidem coenobitarum mos, quam uberes sanctitatis fructus afferat ad mores convertendos feliciterque confrigendas daemonum impugnationes, plane mirum est [/ p. 18], cum e contra, qui se ipsum regere praesumpserit, in maximo salutis discrimine versatur.

CAPUT XLVII.
De significanda hora operis Dei.

Nuntianda hora operis Dei, etc.

DECLARATIO I. 'Nuntianda hora.'

De more antiquo horae canonicae signo campanae indicantur; designet autem ipse superior, attentis loci rationibus, quo modo hoc fiat.

DECLARATIO II. 'Horis competentibus.'

Cum in Collegio Anselmiano Officium divinum disponere oportet pro opportunitate studiorum, nihil de hac re stabiliendum videtur.

Disponat ipse Superior cum consilio seniorum.

DECLARATIO III. 'Ut aedificientur audientes.'

Qui publici aliquid cantare aut legere debet, id antea perlustret, ut convenienter persolvatur, neve ulla ex incuria perturbatio fiat.

CAPUT XLVIII.
De opere manuum quotidiano.

Otitositas inimica est animae, etc.

DECLARATIO I. 'Occupari debent fratres.'

Opus Dei atque opus laboris, en duplex Dominici servitii ratio. Iure igitur labor secundum opus Dei insigne putatur monsticae vitae elementum. In quo ut fratres vere Deum quaerant, cum fide laborent, cum simplicitate, dilgentia, constantia atque hilaritate, spiritu poenitentiae purissimaque ducti intentione soli Deo placendi divinumque amandi Sponsum. In omnibus denique onmino laboribus sanctam sequantur obedientiam. Ante latore Deum orant, tamque studiose sunt semper occupati, un ne momentum quidem temporis perdant. [/ p. 19]

DECLARATIO II. 'Certis horis in lectione.'

[4] In the printed text, "tenenetes" is rendered "tenentur."

[5] In the printed text, "praescriptio" is rendered "praescripto."

Quod ad genus attinet laboris, SS. Dominus Leo Papa XIII, statuit, ut monachi collegii S. Anselmi occuparentur in traditione er studio scientiarum ecclesiastica rum. Cursus igitur studio rum hic esto:

Philosophiae scolasticae, Scientiarum mathematicarum et physicarum, biennio; reliquis quatuor annis: Theologiae dogmatico-scholasicae, linguae hebraicae et graecae, Exegesis biblilcae, Patristicae, Theologiae moralis, Historiae ecclesiasticae, Iuris canonici, Liturgiae, Archaeologiae christianae, et Cantus Gregoriani.

Horis quatuor quotidie in scholis alumni utantur. Lectores professionem fidei emittant iuxta formulam Pii Quarti et additamenta Pii IX. Sanctae recordationis.

In omnibus his laboris scientificis, haec communis monachis observandi est conditio inviolabilis, ut cum vita claustrali ceterisque monastici ordinis fundamentis congruant, ita ut et propriam monachi sanctificationem et palmare opus Dei non solum non destruant, sed compleant atque aedificent.

DECLARATIO III. 'Surgentes a mensa pausent.'

Tempore aestatis meridiatio concedatur omnibus qui ea indigent.

DECLARATIO IV. 'Tunc vere monachi sunt.'

Quamquam, ut nunc fert sacerdotalis monacorum ordo, officia servilia laicis iniungi solent, fratribus tamen opera manualis non plane cessat ad integritatem pertinere vitae monasticae.

Alumnorum nempe est, quid quid ab ipsis munditia cellae vestiumque exigit laboris, nisi excusaverit infirmitas, propria manu exsequi. Instituatur insuper interdum opus manuale commune pro omnibus monachis collegii. [/ p. 20]

CAPUT XLIX.

De Quadragesimae observatione.

Licet omni tempore vita, etc.

DECLARATIO. 'Quadragesimae observationem.'

Quoad ieunium et abstinentiam fratrum tempore Quadragesimae iam provi sum est in declaratione III. ad Caput XXXIX S. Regulae.

Fratres vero magni faciant diligantque disciplinam quadrigesimalem, quamvis reductam propter necessitatem, qua morum conversionem et caritatis martyrium absolvunt. Quod vero spectat ad castigationem illam, quae in Dominicae flagellationis fit memoriam, Feriis VIis additis etiam IVtis in Quadragesima, dicantur in commune post preces serotinas preces liturgicae ad disciplinam faciendam et postea se flagellant in cellis ii qui a patre spirituali licentiam obtinuerint.

CAPUT L.

De fratribus qui longe ab oratorio laborant, aut in via sunt.

Fratres qui omnino longe sunt, etc.

CAPUT LI.

De fratribus qui non longe satis proficiscuntur.

Fratres qui pro quovis, etc.

DECLARATIO. 'Foris manducare.'

Ad saecularium mensas Superior nec ipse accedat, nec fratribus concedat aditum, nisi ob rationabilem causam denegari nequeat. Quae licentia alumnis nunquam detur, nisi comitante eos patres quodam collegii. [/ p. 21]

CAPUT LII.

De Oratorio monasterii.

Oratoriuim hoc sit quod dicitur, etc.

DECLARATIO. 'Oratorium hoc sit.'

Sacristia plurimi faciat sanctum cui praepositus est muneris officium, sitque in sacris ritibus exercitatissimus. Curae habet omina ad ecclesiam pertinentia, cuius universam sacram supellectilem religiosissime tractet. Omnia suo tempore provideat, maximaque adhibita cura id agat, ut quaecunque ad divinum spectant cultum, sint omni modo munda ac dignitatis decorisque plena.

CAPUT LIII.

De hospitibus suscipiendis.

Omnes supervenientes ospites, etc.

DECLARATIO. 'Tamquam Christus.'

Si quis saecularium ad mensam monachorum invitatus fuerit, cum omni tractetur humilitate, reverentia, caritate atque humanitate. Caveatur autem, ne saeculares disciplinae regulari detrimentum afferant: imo ipsi recedant semper aedificati. Nemini fratrum nisi cui superior licentiam dederit, licet ospite vel saecularem aliquen in cellan suam introducere.

CAPUT LIV.

Si debeat monachus litteras vel aliquid accipere.

Nullatenus liceat monacho, etc.

DECLARATIO. 'Litteras accipere aut dare.'

Superior litteras qualescunque a monachis scriptas vel ad eos directas inspicere potest, nisi sunt directae ad superiorem proprium vel ab ipso proveniant; item Magister qoad alumnos et Instructor quoad conversos. [/ p. 22].

CAPUT LV.

De vestiariis et calceariis fratrum.

Vestimenta fratrum secundum, etc.

DECLARATIO I. 'Secundum locorum qualitatem.'

Unusquisque monachorum vestem et tonsuram portet secundum usum proprii sui monasterii, vel suae Congregationis. Quae quidem tonsura saepe renovanda est. Sacram vestem permagni fratres vestimento tamquam Signum vocationis a S. Ecclesia benedictum, quo quoad vivant moneantur de excelsa electione a divino Sponso ipsis benigne concessa.

DECLARATIO II. 'Lota ibi restituant.'

Amantissimi sint fratres, ut vestium ita corporis munditiae, quae purum mundumque prodit animum, et paupertatem nobilitat. Similiter munditiem ordinemque in suis servent cellis, quas semel, et pluries si necessitas postulaverit, per hebdomadam verrant, qoad cellas Lectorum hoc officium conversis committi potest.

DECLARATIO III. 'Dentur omnia.'

Qui linteorum curam habet, quamvis hebdomada quae necessaria sunt in cellas portat. Arrideat pauper et humilis cella supellex pauperrimo animarum Sponso. Sint in ea simplex lectulus, mensa, sedilia, modicum scrinium, librorum paulum, ac piarum imaginum sine ullo auri nitore, praeter piscinulam denique aquae benedictae simulacrum crucifixi, eaque omnia eiusmodi, ut et viventem monachum honorent, et morientem consolentur. Quidquid praeter necessitatem est, fratres ut vanum ac superfluum amputent neve sponte retineant.

CAPUT LVI.

De mensa Abbatis.

Mensa abbatis com hospitibus, etc.

DECLARATIO. 'Mensa abbatis.' [/ p. 23]

Superior habitet in communi dormitorio et clausura, refectoriumque sumat una cum fratribus in refectorio, nisi causa rationabilis excuset.

CAPUT LVII.

De artificibus monasterii.

Artifices si sunt in monasterio, etc.

DECLARATIO. 'Artifices si sunt.'

Ne desint manus in domo Dei quae officia servilia durioraque opera conficiant, inde ab undecimo saeculo in monasteriis separatum a monachis institutum conversorum, sive fratrum laicorum extat, Qui fratres, quamquam non poprie monachi, tamen veri religiosi sunt, constituuntque partem monasticae familiae. Praeficitur conversis instructor pius, qui in spiritu religionis eos intstruat et ecerceat. Conversi humillima ac filiali cum observantia colant monachos, qui rursus illos tamque fratres et carissima utilissimaque familiae membra paterno amore complectantur. Nec tamen monachis, exceptis competentibus officialibus, licet conversis proprio arbitrio quidquam praecipere.

Fratres laici in aliquo loco, post preces matutinas, meditationi student per quadrantem fere horae; postea, prouti labore iniuncti permittunt, divinum persolvant officium suum. Quod quidem officium cum recitant, pie se iungant ententionibis S. Ecclesiae, colentes mysteria quae in singulis celebrat et Festis et Horis canonicis. Sedulo dent operam conversi, ut capitulo culparum, diebus Dominicis et Festis etiam Missae solemni et Vesperis, praeterea sacramentali benedictioni, ceterisque ad totam familiam pertinentibus solemnitatibus ne desint. Exquisitissimo etiam in honore habeant munus ipsis proprie impositum serviendi ad SS. Altare.

Fratres laici regularem omnino teneant observantiam quoad ieiunium et abstinentiam, confessionem et communionem, Missam quotidianam et conventualem in festis. Iidem annuis intersint, quantum pro occupationibus licet [/ p. 24], exercitiis spiritualibus et communi certo semel per hebdomadam conferentiae spirituali.

CAPUT LVIII.

De disciplina suscipiendorum fratrum.

Noviter veniens quid ad, etc.

DECLARATIO I. 'Suscipiatur in congregatione.'

In Collegio S.Anselmi non suscipiantur novitii, nisi forte aliter in posterum S. Sedi visum fuerit.

DECLARATIO II. 'Annuatur ei ingressus.'

Monachi officiales et lectores Collegii S. Anselmi, necnon et alumni et fratres conversi, omnes sunt et manent filii proprii monsterii professionis; possunt revocari a superiore proprio, valetudinis vel alia gravi causa, praevia vero informatione superiori Collegii tempore congruo facta. Unumquodque monasterium pro quolibet alumno in vita communi alendo solvat collegio annuatim mille libellas. Insuper alumnus quisque in adventu deponat penes Rectorem Collegii summam quingentarum libellarum adhibendam pro extraordinariis circumstantiis. Ne quis ad Collegium admittatur alumnus, nisi habeat: a) epistolam proprii Abbatis; b) ludi litteraii confecti testimonium; c) fidei baptismatis, confimationis, et forte Ordinum receptorum. Primo mansionis anno alumnus quilibet iureiurando promittat coram Rectore, se rediturum praescripto tempore ad Monasterium et Congregationem, a quibus mittitur.

DECLARATIO III. 'Senior ei talis deputetur.'

Instituitur magister alumnorum, cuius sit cura paterna invigilare super alumnus, et formationem monasticam eorum novitiatis respectivis incoeptam complere, omnes secundum spiritum S. Regulae informando, singulosque in spiritu et amore Collegii S. Anselmì et Congregationis suae respective confirmando. Super omnia vero caveat ne dissensio vel discordia oriatur inter eos, ut in domo Dei regnet pax illa et Concordia quae ducit ad sanctitatem. [/ p. 25]

Instituitur etiam a Superiore Praefectus Studiorum e gremio seniorum sumendus, nisi ipse forte velit hoc officio fungi Superior; praefecti studiorum sit studia regere et ordinare, et in generali et speciali progressu in scientiis vigilare.

CAPUT LIX.

De filiis nobilium aut pauperem, qui offeruntur.

Si quis forte de nobilibus, etc.

CAPUT LX.

De sacerdotibus qui forte voluerint in monasterio habitare.

Si quis de ordine sacerdotum, etc.

DECLARATIO. 'Non citius assentiatur'

Alumni Collegii S. Anselmi e monasteriis suis respectivis quantum fieri potest mittantur immediate post novitatum, antequam coeperint studiis incumbere. Si quis eorum forte iam ordines susceperit, in omnibus tamen submittatur communi regulae alumnorum. Nemo unquam admittatur ut hospes ad facienda studia in alieno instituto.

CAPUT LXI.

De monachis peregrinis, qual iter suscipiantur.

Si quis monacus peregrinus, etc.

CAPUT LXII.

De sacerdotibus monasterii.

Si quis abbas sibi presbyterum, etc.

CAPUT LXIII.

De ordine congregationis.

Ordines suos in monasgterio, etc.

DECLARATIO I. ' Acedant ad Communionem,'

Intima ardentique pietate colant fratres SS. Eucharisiam; ardentiori in dies pii animi amore prosequantur [/ P. 26] coelestem illum in tabernaculo habitantem Emmanuelem, qui se ipsis tamquam dulcissimum praebet socium, convivium ac solatium. Qui non sacerdotes, sive clerici, sive fratres laici, singulis diebus Domenicis et Festis, vel etiam saepius, debitis permissionibus, sacra comminione se muniant.

DECLARATIO II. 'Qui prima hora diei venit.'

Principem in omnibus locum superior tenet; post eum prior et magister alumnorum locum accipiant, deinde alii patres, professores sint an officiales, secundum ordinem sacrae professionis. Alumni ordinentur etiam inter se secundum supradictum ordinem, sicut et fratres laici.

DECLARATIO III. 'Benedictionem petat.'

Haec quidem benediction etiam per solam capitis inclinationem peti potest.

CAPUT LXIV.

De ordinando abate.

In abbatis ordinatione, etc.

CAPUT LXV.

De praeposito monasterii.

Saepius quidem contingit, etc.

DECLARATIO. 'In abbatis pendere arbitrio ordinationem monasterii sui.'

Unusquisque officialium et professorum munus suum tamquam filius obediens a superiore suscipit et exsequitur, nihil omnino agens nisi quod et quamdiu voluerit ipse superior. Quamobrem ad superioris nutum possunt ab officio amoveri, si ita ipse iudicaverit.

CAPUT LXVI.

De ostiariis monasterii.

Ad portam monasterii, etc.

DECLARATIO I. 'Senex sapiens.' [/ p. 27]

Ostiarius, si non est senex aetate, sit certe morum maturitate. Quotidie post coenam ostium monasterii obserat clavesque deferì ad Superiorem, vel ad eum, qui is designaverit.

DECLARATIO II. 'Cum fervore caritatis.'

Ostiarius cum advenientibus omni utatur benignitate et officio. Si quis externus cum fratre colloqui vult, ostiarius superiorem adit, nec fratrem antea certiorem facit. Nemo igitur in auditorio vel ubicunque cum externis confabuletur, nisi cum superioris permissione. Qua data officiose omnino humaniterque se gerat, ospite tam caritate quam sancta verecundia ac modestia aedificans, diligenterque fugiens, quidquid spiritum obedientiae vel simplicitatis laedere aut mentem distrahere possit. Neque vero permittatur fratri, nisi gravem ob causam, colloquium cum externis tempore divini officii, regularium exercitiorum, nec tempore scholae.

Longe summa denique adhibetur cautio in conversatione cum mulieribus, quae nunquam fiat nisi in loco omnibus aperto.

DECLARATIO III. 'Regulam saepius volumus in congregatione legi.'

Fratres ut in litteram sensumque S. Regulae penitus se insinuent, perattente audient caput singulis diebus in refectorio ad prandium legendum.

CAPUT LXVII.

De fratribus in via directis.

Dirigendi fratres in via, etc.

DECLARATIO. 'Abbatis orationibus.'

Quicunque in obedientia extra Collegii septa prodire debet, prius flexis genibus benedictionem petat a Superiore, eandemque iterum petat reversus. Nullus egrediatur e conventu sine socio, nisi superior iusta de causa aliud indicaverit; alumni communiter deambulent, prout superior disposuerit. [/ p. 28]

CAPUT LXVIII.

Si fratri impossibilia iniunguntur.

Si cui fratri aliqua forte, etc.

CAPUT LXIX.

Ut in monasterio non presumat alter alterum defendere.

Praecavendum est ne quavis, etc.

DECLARATIO. 'Propinquitate iungantur.'

Vitium a beato Patriarcha hic reprehensum ut praecaveatur, studiosissime fratres privates fugiant amicitias. Hae enim perquam funestum animas damnum important, monasteriaque suvertunt, quae communi tantum amore omnium florere queant. Unde omnes solicite animi affectus observabunt, memoria simper repetentes, post dirupta carissima propinquitatis vincula sibi iam perfectionis via procedentibus summam a quavis creatura disiunctionem colendam esse.

CAPUT LXX.

Ut non praesumat quisquam alium caedere.

Vitetur in monasterio, etc.

DECLARATIO. 'Omnis praesumptionis occasion.'

Monemus hic ne quis fratrum audeat alterum vel reprehendere vel corrigere, nisi superior id mandaverit.

CAPUT LXXI.

Ut obedientes sibi sint invicem fratres.

Obedientiae bonum non solum, etc.

DECLARATIO. 'Obedientiae bonum.'

Fratres ut perfectae se liberent ab amore proprio, libenter praecepta a S. Patriarcha hic iniuncta exercitant, aliorum vota propriis ob mutuam caritatem studiose praeferentes. Quae de modo excipiendi vituperationem Legislator praecepit, ad eos tantum spectat, quos Superior vel Magister verbis castigat. Officialium vero admonitiones fratres profunda cum humiltate excipient. [/ p. 29]

CAPUT LXXII.

De zelo bono quem debent monachi habere.

Sicut est zelus amaritudinis, etc.

CAPUT LXXIII.

De eo quod non omnis iustitiae observatio in hac sit Regula constituta.

Regulam autem hanc descripsimus, etc.

DECLARATIO. 'Hanc minimam inchoationis regulam.'

Fratres quoties hunc Regulae exitum legunt, confirmatam in animis sentient summam existimationem, qua S. Patriarcha humilitatem prosecutus est, virtutem illam, cui amplissimum sacrae suae legis caput dedicavit.

Quod ad ipsam attinet sanctam Regulam, vix quidquam fratribus carius est debet maiorisque pretii. Nam si quis post S. Scripturam liber extat, quo religiosae perfectionis doctrina clare explicetur, profecto ille est codex vere benedictinus, quem tamquam Pii Patris testamentum accepimus. Quapropter aequum ac par est totam fratres vitam consumer in perdiscenda, gustanda atque exercenda hac sacra Regula. Quam si fideli ac dilatato corde expleverint, bono confidant animo, se una cum fulgentibus Sanctorum Ordinis nostri catervis beatifica dulcissimi Sponsi societate in aeternum esse perfruituros.

U.I.O.G.D.

Haec statuta cum originalibus concordant:

D. CAJETANUS BERNARDI
Abbas et rector Coll.

V. Pope Leo XIII Gives Sant'Anselmo the Right to Confer Academic Degrees in Theology

The original document is in the Archive of the Abbot Primate, Coll. S. Anselmi II 12 C. Unpublished.

Ex audientia Sanctissimi die XX Augusti 1891.

Sanctissimus Dominus Noster Leo Papa XIII referente subscripto Sacrae Studiorum Congregationis Eminentissimo Cardinali Praefecto, attentis peculiaribus circumstantiis, benigne annuit ut Moderatores Collegii S. Anselmi O.S.B. nuper in Urbe restituti, facultate conferendi gradus academicos servatis tamen servandis, in S. Theologia eiusdem Collegii alumnis ad triennium uti frui possint ac valeant.

Contrariis quibuscumque non obstantibus.

Fr. Thomas M. Card. Zigliara, Praef.
Augustus Guidi a Secretis

Accompanying letter to the above from Cardinal Zigliara. The original document is in the Archive of the Abbot Primate, Coll. S. Anselmi II 12 C. Unpublished.

A Sua Paternità Rma. D. Gaetano Bernardi O.S.B., Abate e Rettore del Collegio di S. Anselmo in Roma.

Roma, 20 Agosto 1891

Nel rimettere a Vostra Paternità il Rescritto della facoltà accordata ai moderatori del Collegio di S. Anselmo, mi pregio notificarle, per incarico ricevuto dal Santo Padre nell' udienza del 20 corrente, che il privilegio ora ristretto ad un triennio e per i soli gradi teologici facilmente potrà venire confermato in perpetuo ed esteso anche alla Filosofia, quando il Collegio avrà preso quell'incremento e quella stabilità che è nei desideri del Santo Padre. Nel frattempo ogni qualvolta vi fossero dei giovani ch giudicati meritevoli bramassero conseguire la laurea anche in Filosofia, potrà la P.V. far domanda a questa Sacra Congregazione per ottenerne le opportune facoltà.

Coi sensi di sincera osservanza
Della Paternità Vostra Rma
Affmo per servirla
Fr. Tommasso M. Card. Zigliara
Prefetto della C. Congr. degli Studi

VI. Sant'Anselmo Empowered to Confer Academic Degrees in Philosophy

The original document in APr, Coll. S. Anselmi II 12 C. Unpublished.

Sacra studiorum Congregatio utendo facultatibus a Sanctissimo Domino Nostro LeonePapa XIII tributis, attentis peculiaibus circumstantiis, Moderatoribus Collegii S. Anselmi O.S.B. nuper in Urbe restituti, facultatem ad triennium tribuit gradus academicos in Philosophia conferendi eiusdem Collegii alumnis, servatis tamen omnibus de iure servandis. Contrariis quibusqumque minime obstantibus.

Datum Roma die 25 Junii MDCCCX[C]IV.

C. Card. Mazzella Praef.
Joseph Magno a Secretis

VII. Communication from Abbot Primate Hildebrand de Hemptinne Stating That with Papal Permission, Ferial Matins May Be Prayed in Place of Sanctoral Matins at Sant'Anselmo during the Academic Year

APr, Collegio II 1893–1913, II 12 G. Unpublished.

Roma, Monte Aventino
Li 2 Marzo 1907

Ex audientia SSmi, habita mense Novembri 1893.

Sanctissimus Dominus Noster Leo Pp. XIII. fel. reg., quum infrascriptum primum admitteret, qua Abbatem Primatem O.S.B., ad audientiam privatam, benigne annuit ut, attentis studiis in Collegio S. Anselmi faciendis, per annum scholasticum loco Matutini Sancti occurentis diceretur Matutinum feriale, servato ab initio Laudum ordine consueto.

In quorum fidem idem infrasctiptus Abbas Primas has litteras expediri jussit propriisque signo ac sigillo munivit in Abbatia Primatiali S. Anselmi de Urbe, die et anno quibus supra.

† Hildebrandus, Abbas Primas O.S.B.
Rome, Aventine Hill
2 March 1907

VIII. Circular Letter from Rector Fr. Patrick Cummins, OSB, to the Abbots of the Order (undated but probably from 27 July 1925)

APr, Congr. Abbatum 1925, I 13/B3, 1a. Unpublished.

U.I.O.G.D.
DE RECTORE COLLEGII SANCTI ANSELMI

Abbatibus mense Octobri Romam conventuris, infrascriptus Rector Sancti Anselmi haec humillime exponit:

1. Breve Leonis XIII 'Summum semper' 12 Juli 1892 (A.S.S. T. 26, p. 371sq.) excludit Rectorem Sancti Anselmi ab iis, quae 'relationes Collegii com [*sic*] singulis congregationibus respiciunt', quas relationes, dicit, 'as Abbatem Sancti Anselmi velut Primatem omnium congregationum spectare.' Quoad ipsum collegium autem, 'quamvis de voluntate et consensus Abbatis,' ipse Rector est 'guberntationem et disciplinam ejusdem Collegii tenens.'

2. Collegium porro, quamvis non sit communitas proprie dicta Benedictina (cum non sit prioratus nec abbatia) vult tamen, natura sua, ratione monachorum ibi communiter degentium, gubernari inquantum fieri potest, ad modum communitatis sub Regula S.P.N. Benedicti.

3. Regula porro S. P. Benedicti abhorret ab omni auctoritate quae se extollat adversus supremam auctoritatem abbatis.

4. His perpensis, initio officii mei, pro mea persona statuebam Rectoris interim esse non tenere gubernationem et disciplinam Collegii, sed propter pacis caritatis custodiam totam gubernationem et disciplinam in manibus relinquere Abbatis Collegii, id est, Abbatis Primatis.

5. Juridice autem perdurat titulus Rectoris et officium. Accedente ergo conventu Abbatum, sentio mihi incumbere obligationem ipsos humiliter rogandi, ut opportunas petant a competente auctoritate determinationes.

6. Inter istas autem determinationes hae videntur praecipuae:

a) Cum Collegium Sancti Anselmi sit Universitas Pontificia Benedictina, ille qui ipsi praeest, quamvis debeat qoad jura aequiperari Abbati regiminis, vel Priori conventuali, debet etiam habere titulum Rectoris, quia est titulus proprius illius qui regit Universitatem.

b) Utrum melius retineatur necne titulus Abbatis Sancti Anselmi (cum non sit abbatia) meliori reliquo [*sic*] judicio. Sed si retineatur, detur Rectori.

c) Ut toto [*sic*] Ordini evidens sit jus ipsius et positio, eligatur Rector ab omnibus Abbatibus.

Rector statim post electionem nominet pro-Rectorem, qui pro casu vacationis officii (morte renuntiatione, etc.) habeat omnia jura Rectoris usque ad proximam electionem.

7. Rationes his expositae reales volunt esse, nullo modo personales. Valete

R. P. Patritius Cummins O.S.B.
Rector Sancti Anselmi

IX. Daily Timetable at Sant'Anselmo According to the Statutes of 1962

Statuta in Collegio Internationali Benedictinorum Sancti Anselmi de Urbe observanda, Romae, 14 Mensis Maji 1962, pp. 60–61.

ORDO DIEI

1: Tempora Hiemali

Diebus Ferialibus

Hora 4.55: Evigilantur Fratres (Feria V et diebus quibus schola vacat: hora 5.25).
5.15: Laudes, Prima, Tertia, Missae et Meditatio.
7.00: vel 7.30: Collatio.
8.30: Lectiones.
12.40: Sexta, Nona, Prandium, Vesperae. Post Vesperas recreatio usque ad Horam 15.00.
15.15: Lectiones.
18.45: Matutinum (18.30 quando erit officium XII Lectionum) deinde Coena et recreatio.
20.30: Completorium, Quies.

Diebus Dominicis et Festivis

Hora 5.25: Evigilantur Fratres.
5.45: Laudes, Prima, Missae et Meditatio.
7.30: Collatio.
9.30: Tertia, Missa Solemnis.
12.40: Sexta, Nona, Prandium, Recreatio.
15.00: Vesperae.

Feria III

Hora 18.15: Collatio spiritualis pro Alumnis et Fratribus Conversis.

Feria V

Hora 18.15: Capitulum culparum pro Alumnis.

Diebus Dominicis

Hora 12.00: Collatio spiritualis pro omnibus monachis.

2: Tempore aestivo

Omnia ut tempore hiemali praeter sequentia
Post Vesperas quies usque ad horam 15.
Hora 15.15: Lectiones.
19.00: Matutinum (18.45 quando erit officium XII Lectionum).

X. Augustin Mayer, Abbot of Metten, Defends the Course of Studies in Sant'Anselmo at the Abbots' Congress of 1967 (Session IX, 23 September 1967)

APr, Congressus Abbatum 1967, Documenta varia, adnexum XLV.
Unpublished.

Quaedam aequivicatio videtus adesse, quando plures Patres postulant, ut Athenaeum Anselmianum convertatur in domicilium '*studiorum superiorum*.' Ut praecaveatur talis confusio, sequentia prae oculis habere velitis:

1. Athenaeum non est 'Seminarium,' *neque iuridice* (utpote a S. Sede erectum ut Institutum academicum, variis Facultatibus praeditum, iure omnes gradus academicos conferendi instructum), *neque de facto*: potuistis videre, anno elapso, expositionem dissertationum publici iuris factarum inter quas plures in exemplar enitent; scitis Athenaeum edere tres collectiones scientificas ubique terrarum magni aestimatas; plures Athenaei Anselmiani magistri tum scriptis tum docendo optima forma gaudent.

2. Convesio illa a pluribus commendata:

a) secundum aliquorum mentem significaret, monachos maturioris, aetatis iam academicis gradibus instructos apud S. Anselmum studiis patristicis, monasticis atque liturgicis operam daturos esse.

Talis propositio accipi nequit:

—sic destrueretur Facultas theologica florens;

—sic privaretur etiam Institutum liturgicum suo optimo fundamento;

—vix invenirentur monachi O.S.B. numero sufficienti, qui pro huiusmodi studiis Romam convenirent;

—negatur tunc professores facilius inveniri posse.

b) secundum alios sifignificat potius quandam transformationem ipsius Facultatis theologicae. —Reapse existunt duo typi facultatis theologicae:

typus 'Lovaniensis': curriculo fundamentali theologico in Seminariis absoluto. per 3 vel 4 annos ipsa Facultas alumnus praeparat ad lauream (et magisterium) per cursos potius monographicos et maxime per exercitationes:

typus 'Europae Centralis' et 'romanus': in ipsa Facultate dantur tum institution academica indolis fundamentalis tum initialis quaedam specialisatio scientifica, cui—secundum legitima vota recentiora—maius in annos spatium et momentum tribuendum est.

Utraque 'formula' habet sua emolumenta et sua incommoda, quae a Commissione Conciliari accurate ponderata sunt. Si igitur postulatum 'conversionis ad studia superiora' intelligitur de introducenda 'formula Lovaniensi,' huismodi propositio meretur quae accurate consideratur. Attamen ne parvipendatur incommoda huius solu-tionis neve obliviscamur, iam ex pluribus annis in Athenaeo Anselmiano practice adhiberi aliquam 'formam mixtam': i.e. quaedam alumnorum pars a primo anno Facultatem Theologicam frequentat, alia vero pars alumnorum, quadriennio teologico alibi absoluto, ad nos accedit ut biennio supplementari ad Licentiam et postea ad Lauream conformentur. Insuper prae oculis habenda sunt ea quae a professoribus Facultatis theologicae eleborata sunt, up curriculum aptius dividatur in partem magis generalem vel institutionalem et in partem initialis specialisationis.

Abbreviations

AAS	*Acta Apostolicae Sedis*
AAt	Rome. St. Anselmo. Archives of the Athenaeum
Acta Fac. Theol.	Acta Concilii Academici Facultatis Theologicae Inst. Pont. S. Anselmi de Urbe, from the academic years 1933–1934 to 1957–1958
Libellus Actorum	Libellus Actorum Concilii Professorum Collegii S. Anselmi de Urbe from 1913/14 to 1939/40
ABenR	The American Benedictine Review
ALW	Archiv für Liturgiewissenschaft
Ang.	Angelicum
AOSB	Annales Ordinis Sancti Benedicti
APr	Rome. St. Anselmo, Archives of the Abbot Primate
Arch	Archive(s)
ASS	Acta Sanctae Sedis
ASV	Archivio Segreto Vaticano—Vatican Secret Archives
BBKL	Biographisch-Bibliographisches Kirchenlexicon, by F. W. Bautz (ed.), vols 1–14, Hamm, 1975–1999. Supplementary volumes 14ff., Hamm, 1999ff.
Ben.	Benedictina
BenM	Benediktinische Monatsschrift
BGAM	Beiträge zur Geschichte des alten Mönchtums und des Benediktinerordens
Cath	Catholica, Münster
CivCatt	La Civiltà cattolica
DT	Divus Thomas, Freiburg
DThA	Deutsche Thomas-Ausgabe [German edition of Thomas Aquinas]
DThC	Dictionnaire de théologie catholique
EL	Ephemerides liturgicae
EuA	Erbe und Auftrag
Hochl	Hochland
Irén	Irénikon

KathGed	Die katholische Gedanke
LThK	Lexikon für Theologie und Kirche
Molitor	R. Molitor, Aus der Rechtsgeschichte benediktinischer Verbände, Vol. 3, Unionsversuche im 19. Jahrhundert. Die Leonische Konföderation aller Kongregationen der Benediktiner, Münster, 1933.
OF	Orate Fratres
QLP	Questions liturgiques et paroissiales
RAC	Reallexikon für Antike und Christentum
RBén	Revue bénédictine
RegBenSt	Regulae Benedicti Studia
BegBenSt. Suppl	Regulae Benedicti Studia. Supplementa
Renner	F. Renner, Confoederatio Benedictina. Geschichte ihrer Konstituierung von Leo XIII. Bis zu Pius XII. *StudMitt* vol. 91 (1980): 232–90.
RHE	Revue d'historie ecclèsiastique
RivAC	Rivista di archeologia cristiana
RivLi	Rivista liturgica
RLM	Revue liturgique et monastique
RQ	Römische Quartalschrift
RThom	Revue thomiste
SBSt	Sankt-Benedikt-Stimmen
Schmitz	Ph. Schmitz, Geschichte des Benediktinerordens, 4 vols. Translated into German and published by R. Tschudy, Eineiedeln-Zurich, 1960.
Schol.	Scholastik. Freiburg
StAns	Studia Anselmiana
StMon	Studia Monastica
StudMitt	Studien und Mitteilungen aus dem Benedictiner- und Cistercienserorden/Studien un Mitteilungen zur Geschichte des Benediktinerordens und seiner Zweige.
Suppl.Vie spir	Supplément de la Vie spirituelle, ascétique et mystique
ThGl	Theologie und Glaube
ThQ	Theologische Quartalschrift, Tübingen
ThRv	Theologische Revue
TRE	Theologische Realenzyklopädie
VCr	Vita cristiana
ZSRG. K	Zeitschrift der Savigny-Stiftung für Rechtsgeschichte. Kanonistische Abteilung

Printed Sources and Literature[1]

Acta Congressus Abbatum ac Priorum Conventualium Congregationum Confoederatarum OSB. In aedibus S. Anselmi de Urbe a die 18 Septembris ad diem 4 Octobris 1966. Typis Officinae Millefiorini, Nursiae-Norcia.

Acta Congressus Abbatum ac Priorum Conventualium Congregationum Confoederatarum OSB. In aedibus S. Anselmi de Urbe duplici session celebrati 1966–1967. Typis Officinae Millefiorini, Vetustae Nursiae-Norcia.

Acta Congressus Abbatum ac Priorum Conventualium Congregationum Confoederatarum OSB. In aedibus S. Anselmi de Urbe celebrati a die 21 Septembris ad diem 1 Octobris 1970. Manuscripti instar. Secretaria Abbatis Primatis OSB, Abbatia S. Anselmi, Romae.

Acta Congressus Abbatum ac Priorum Conventualium Congregationum Confoederatarum OSB. In aedibus S. Anselmi de Urbe celebrati 1973 a die 19 Septembris ad diem 3 Octobris. Manuscripti instar. Secretaria Abbatis Primatis OSB, Abbatia S. Anselmi, Romae.

Acta Congressus Abbatum ac Priorum Conventualium Congregationum Confoederatarum OSB. In aedibus S. Anselmi de Urbe celebrati 1977 a die 14 ad diem 25 Septembris. Manuscripti instar. Secretaria Abbatis Primatis OSB, Abbatia S. Anselmi, Romae.

Acta Synodi Abbatum Praesidum Congregationum Confoederatarum OSB. In aedibus S. Anselmi de Urbe 1962. Typis O. Marzi, Romae.

Adlhoch, B., and M. Kinter. "Die Plenar-Versammlung der Benedictiner-Aebte zu Rom vom 16. April Bis zum 2. Mai 1893." *StudMitt* 14 (1893): 279–301.

Annales Ordinis Sancti Benedicti. 20 vols. 1893–1938, Subiaco, Typis Proto-Cenobii.

Békés, Gerard J., ed. *Sant'Anselmo. Saggi storici e di attualità*. StAns, Vol. 97. Rome, 1988.

Bernardi, Gaetano. *Circular Letters, 1888–1892.*

Calendarium Collegii S. Anselmi de Urbe pro anno scolastico 1899–1900.

Calendarium Collegii S. Anselmi de Urbe pro anno scolastico 1900–1901, Romae, E Schola. Typographica, vulgo 'Tata Giovanni,' 1902.

Comandini, Francesco. *L'abbazia di Sant'Anselmo in Roma*. Rome: Editrice Dedalo, 2009.

[1] Here, only those works that are quoted often or are in abbreviated form are indicated.

Della Marra, Luigi Taddeo. Il *Collegio Sant'Anselmo in Roma e il Cardinale Dusmet*, Catania, Stabil. Tipografica C. Galàtola, 1901.

Diaz i Carbonell, Romuald M. *Dom Bonaventura Urbach, L'home, el monjo, el biblista*. Próleg del Rvdm. Pare Dom Aureli M. Escarrè, Abat de Montserrat. Barcelona, 1962.

Eberle, Luke. "Abbot Primate Fidelis von Stotzingen." *ABenR* 4 (1953): 101–14.

Ghysens, Gisbert. "Dom Hildebrand de Hemptinne, architecte de Saint-Anselme, premier Abbé-Primat de l'Ordre bénédictin." *Lettre de Maredsous. Periodique trimestriel.* Maredsous Abbey. No. 1 (1979): 4–8; No. 2, 5–15; No. 3, 10–21.

Glogger, Placidus. *Monastischer Lenz, Monastischer Sommer. BenM* 16 (1934): 53–59, 131–43.

Gut, Benno. *Circular Letters 1959–1967.*

Hemptinne, Hildebrand de. *Oratio quam in Congressu Ordinis ad Consecrationem Ecclesiae S. Anselmi anno iubilari MCM Romae adunati habebat Illustrissimus et Reverendissimus Dominus Hildebrandus de Hemptinne, Primus Ordinis S. Benedicti, Abbas S. Anselmi de Urbe necnon S. Benedicti de Maredsous, die Festo Omnium Sanctorum OSB.* Romae, Typis Vaticanis MCM.

———. *Circular Letters 1893–1909.*

Houtin, Albert. *Dom Couturier, Abbé de Solesmes.* Angers, 1899.

Kälin, Bernhard. *Circular Letters 1948–1959.*

Kalendarium Lectionum Pontificii Instituti Academici Sancti Anselmi de Urbe OSB. Rome, 1936ff. From 1950 to 1969, titled *Pontificium Athenaeum Anselmianum. Kalendarium Lectionum.* From 1969, tilted *Ordo Anni Academici.* From 1980, titled *Calendario delle Lezioni.*

Leccisotti, Tommasso. *Il Cardinale Dusmet.* Catania, 1962.

———. "Gli inizi del rinnovato Collegio di S. Anselmo e della Confederazione benedettina. Note da alcune lettere dell'abate Bernardi." *Ben.* 23 (1976): 65–88.

Liber annualis: Pontificium Athenaeum Anselminanum. Liber annualis, Rome, 1968ff. 9 volumes.

Liber Usuum et Manuale Chori Abbatiae Primatialis et Collegii S. Anselmi de Urbe, Sublaci, excuderunt Monachi Typis Proto-Coenobii, 1909.

Locher, Gabriel. "Eröffnung und Konstituierung von Neu-St. Anselm." *BenM* 20 (1938): 216–23.

Molitor, Raphael. *Aus der Rechtsgeschichte benediktinischer Verbände. Untersuchungen und Skizzen.* Vol. 3, *Unionsversuche im 19. Jahrhundert.* Die Leonische Konföderation aller Kongregationen der Benediktiner. Münster, 1933.

Moreau, Hadelin de. *Dom Hildebrand de Hemptinne, Abbé de Maredsous, premier Primat de l'Ordre bénédectin (1849–1913).* Paris, 1930.

Neunheuser, Burkhard. "Abt Fidelis von Stotzingen, weiland Abt der Hl. Maria zu Laach, Abt-Primas der Konföderierten Kongregationen der Schwarzen Benediktinermönche." *Liturgie und Mönchtum.* Laacher Hefte 2 (1948): 57–63.

Ordo et Ratio Studiorum Collegii Internationalis S. Anselmi de Urbe. Published as manuscript. Subiaco, Typis Proto-Coenobii, 1920.

Ordo et Ratio Studiorum Collegii Internationalis S. Anselmi de Urbe. Published as manuscript. Subiaco, Typis Proto-Coenobii, 1928.

Protocollum seu Relatio de Sessionibus a Reverendissimis et Illustrissimis Praesidibus Congregationum OSB in aedibus S. Anselmi de Urbe mense Maio 1907 ab Illustrissimo et Reverendissimo D. Hildebrando de Hemptinne, Primate OSB, ad Synodum convocatis habitis. Romae, Typis Vaticanis, 1907.

Protocollum Synodi Revmorum et Illmorum Abbatum Praesidum Congregationum Confoederatarum OSB mense Maio anni 1920 in aedibus S. Anselmi de Urbe habitae. Published as manuscript. Rome, Typis Polyglottis Vaticanis, 1920.

Protocollum seu Relatio de Sessionibus quas R.mi et Illmi. Abbates Congregationum Confoederatarum OSB habuerunt in aedibus S. Anselmi mense Octobri 1925. Rome, Typographia Campielli, 1925.

Protocollum seu Relatio de Sessionibus quas Reverndissimi et Illustrissimi Abbates Praesides Congregationum Confoederatarum OSB habuerunt in aedibus S. Anselmi mense Majo 1931. Subiaco, Typis Proto-Coenobii, 1931.

Protocollum seu Relatio de Sessionibus qua Revmi et Illmi. Abbates Congregationum Confoederatarum OSB habuerunt in aedibus S. Anselmi 1937. Subiaco, Typis Proto-Coenobii, 1937.

Protocollum seu Relatio de Sessionibus quas Rmi et Illmi. Abbates Congregationum Confoedatatarum habuerunt in aedibus S. Anselmi de Urbe a die 9 Septembris usque ad 16 Septembris Anno Iubilaeo gloriosi Transitus S.P.N. Benedicti 1947. Nursiae Norcia, Typis Millefiorini.

Protocollum seu Relatio de Sessionibus quas Revmi et Illmi. Abbates Congregationum Confoederatarum OSB habuerunt in aedibus S. Anselmi 1953. Rome, Typis Sororum S. Benedicti ad Priscillam.

Protocollum seu Relatio de Sessionibus quas Rev.mi et Illmi. Abbates Congregationum Confoederatarum OSB habuerunt in aedibus S. Anselmi 1959. Rome, Typis Sororum S. Benedicti ad Priscillam.

Quaestiones et Desiderata Illistrussimis ac Reverendissimis Dominis Congregationum OSB capitibus Romae in aedibus S. Anselmi mense Maio anni a Christo nato MCMVII ad Synodum congregatis ab Illustrissimo ac Reverendissimo Domino D. Hildebrando de Hemptinne Primate Ordinis S. Benedicti necon Abbatge S. Anselmi de Urbe proponendo. Typis Vaticanis, 1907.

Quaestiones Congressui Rev. morum Abbatum proponendae. Rome, Typographia Campitelli, 1925.

Renner, Frumentius. "Confoederatio Benedictina. Geschichte ihrer Konstituierung von Leo XIII bis zu Pius XII." *StudMitt* 91 (1980): 232–90.

Somorjai, Ádám. "Leone XIII e la fondazione di S. Anselmo nell'Urbe." *Archivum Historiae Pontificiae* 47 (2009): 41–61.

Schmitz, Philibert. *Geschichte des Benediktinerordens*. Vol. 4. *Die Äußere Entwicklung des Ordens vom Konzil von Trient bis zur Mitte des 20. Jahrhunderts. Verfassungsgeschichte vom 12. bis zur Mitte des 20. Jahrhunderts*. German translation by Raimund Tschudy. Einsiedeln-Zurich, 1960. Original French edition, *Histoire de l'Ordre se Saint-Benoît*, vol. 4 (1948) of seven volumes. Maredsous, 1948–1956.

Statuta Collegii S. Anselmi in Urbe, 'Ad Summi Pontificis mentem redacta. Printed by Jos. Feichinger & Sons for the monastery of Seitenstetten. Linz, 1881.

Statuta in Collegio Sancti Anselmi de Urbe observanda. Printed as a manuscript. Subiaco, Typis Proto-Coenobii, 1919.

Pontificii Instituti Academici Sancti Anselmi de Urbe Statuta. Rome, Typographia "Madre di Dio," 1934.

Statuta in Collegio Internationali Benedictinorum Sancti Anselmi de Urbe observanda. Printed as a manuscript. Subiaco, Typis Proto-Coenobii, 1939.

Statuta in Collegio Internationali Benedictinorum Sancti Anselmi de Urbe observanda. Printed as a Manuscript. Rome, May 14, 1962.

Pontificii Collegii Internationalis Sancti Anselmi de Urbe Statuta, approbata a Congressu 1970 Abbatum O.S.B.

Stotzingen, Fidelis von. *Circular Letters, 1913–1946.*

Picture Credits

Drawing of the coat of arms of Sant'Anselmo on half title page by Dom Henry O'Shea of Glenstal Abbey, Ireland

Archives of the Abbot Primate, Sant'Anselmo, Rome—28, 46, 59, 72, 200

Archives of the Archabbey of Beuron—62, 70–71, 77, 120, 133, 145, 188

Archvies of the Monastery of Chevetogne—89, 182

Archives of Clervaux Abbey—178, 181, 215, 216

Archives of Douai Abbey—61

Archives of Einsiedeln Abbey—11, 18, 46, 73, 102, 117

Archives of Ettal Abbey—98, 120

Archives of Gerleve Abbey—146, 169, 180, 188, 201, 202

Archives of Göttweig Abbey—66, 69, 79

Archives of the Abbey of La-Pierre-qui-Vire—114, 251

Archives of Ligugé Abbey—61

Archives of Maredsous Abbey—36, 46, 52, 54, 57, 64, 68, 82, 84, 260

Archives of the Abbey of Maria Laach—73, 116, 121, 163, 211, 213, 227, 249

Archives of the Abbey of Maria Stein—274, 278

Archives of Metten Abbey—9, 46 , 118, 125, 172, 184

Archives of Montecassino Abbey—5

Archives of Münsterschwarzach Abbey—164, 235, 254, 258

Archives of Neuburg Abbey—183

Archives of the Archabbey of Pannonhalma—15, 37, 108, 174, 236

Archives of Seckau Abbey—65, 76

Archives of St. John's Abbey, Collegeville—167

Archives of the Abbey of St. Matthias, Trier—130, 143, 174, 181

Archives of St. Meinrad Archabbey—62, 192

Archives of the Archabbey of Sankt Ottilien—Title page, 190, 205, 223, 229, 235, 242, 243, 245, 246–47, 256

Archives of the Abbey of St. Paul Outside the Walls—76, 84

Archives of St. Stephen's Abbey, Augsburg—48, 75, 86

Archives of St. Vincent Archabbey, Latrobe—6, 19, 76

Archives of Uznach Abbey—244

Collection of the EOS-Publishing House—5, 8, 16, 43, 41, 44, 50, 51, 56, 59, 72, 80, 82, 156, 161, 178

Békés, Gerardo J., Farnedi, Giustino, Lex orandi—lex credendi, Miscellanea in onore di P. Cipriano Vagaggini, StAns, vol. 97, Rome, 1980—263

Calati, Benedetto, Sapinenza monastica. Saggi di storia, spiritualità e problemi monastici, StAns, vol 117, Rome, 1994—230

Engelbert, Pius, Geschichte des Benediktinerkollegs St. Anselm in Rome, StAns, vol 98, Rome, 1988—205

Farnedi, Giustino, Paschale Myserium. Studia in memoria dell'Abate Prof. Salvatore Marsili (1910–1983), StAns, vol 91, Rome, 1986—185

Il Collegio di Sant'Anselmo in Roma e il Cardinale Dusmet, Catania, 1901—32

Il servo di Dio Giuseppe Benedetto Dusmet: monaco—arcivescovo—cardinale, Montecassino, 1935—7

Private Collection Abbot President Albert Schmidt, Beuron—231, 232, 269, 270, 272, 275

Private Collection Abbot Emeritus Engelbert Baumeister, OSB, Scheyern—164, 165, 194, 198, 213

Private Collection Dr. Ferdinando Canicci—261

Private Collection Fr. Jacques Coté OSB, St-Benoît-du-Lac—Dust jacket, 238, 279

Private Collection Fr. Remigius Rudmann OSB, Sankt Ottilien—119, 176, 206, 266

Wunibaldiana Collection, Münsterschwarzach—43, 104, 155, 160, 165, 191, 226

Zur Erinnerung an das goldene Jubiläum der Gründung Beurons 1863–1913, Beuron, 1913—17, 75

Index